APOCALYPSE AND MILLENNIUM

D1336251

003461

Apocalypse and Millennium in English Romantic Poetry

MORTON D. PALEY

CLARENDON PRESS · OXFORD

*This book has been printed digitally and produced in a standard specification
in order to ensure its continuing availability*

OXFORD
UNIVERSITY PRESS

Great Clarendon Street, Oxford OX2 6DP
Oxford University Press is a department of the University of Oxford.
It furthers the University's objective of excellence in research, scholarship,
and education by publishing worldwide in
Oxford New York
Auckland   Cape Town Dar es Salaam   Hong Kong   Karachi
Kuala Lumpur Madrid Melbourne Mexico City   Nairobi
New Delhi Shanghai   Taipei Toronto
With offices in
Argentina Austria Brazil Chile Czech Republic France Greece
Guatemala Hungary Italy Japan South Korea Poland Portugal
Singapore Switzerland Thailand Turkey Ukraine Vietnam

Oxford is a registered trade mark of Oxford University Press
in the UK and in certain other countries
Published in the United States
by Oxford University Press Inc., New York

© Morton D. Paley 1999

The moral rights of the author have been asserted

Database right Oxford University Press (maker)

Reprinted 2009

ISBN 978-0-19-926217-5

In Memory of

MRS FANNY BRUNDAGE

Acknowledgements

IN WRITING this book I received invaluable criticism, suggestions, and encouragement from fellow scholars whose help it is my pleasure to acknowledge. Robert N. Essick, Tim Fulford, J. C. C. Mays, and Donald R. Reiman gave generously of their time and expertise; and I am also indebted to the knowledge of John Beer, David Bindman, Morris Eaves, Neil Freistat, Stephen Goldsmith, Peter J. Kitson, Celeste Langan, Jerome J. McGann, Anne K. Mellor, Joel Porte, Nicholas Roe, Joseph Viscomi, Jonathan Wordsworth, Carl Woodring, and David Worrall. Some other obligations are recorded in footnotes.

I am grateful to the editors and publishers of the following books and journals in which parts of my discussion appeared in earlier form: *Coleridge's Visionary Languages*, ed. Tom Fulford and Morton D. Paley (Cambridge: D. S. Brewer, 1993); *Revolution and English Romanticism* (ed. Keith Hanley and Raman Selden (Hemel Hempstead: Harvester Wheatsheaf, 1990); *A Companion to Romanticism*, ed. Ducan Wu (Oxford: Blackwell, 1998); *The Wordsworth Circle*; *European Romantic Review*; *Romanticism*; *Huntington Library Quarterly*; *Aligarh English Journal*; *Blake: An Illustrated Quarterly*. Drafts of parts of chapters were delivered as papers at the Wordsworth Summer Conference, the International Coleridge Conference, the British Association of Romantic Studies Conference, and the Romantic Circles Virtual Conference, and I thank the organizers of these gatherings for the stimulus they afforded.

My thanks to the librarians and staffs of the institutions at which my research was conducted: the Doe and Bancroft Libraries of the University of California at Berkeley, the Henry W. and Albert A. Berg Collection of the New York Public Library, the New York Public Library, the British Library, the Henry E. Huntington Library, the Butler Library of Columbia University, the Pierpont Morgan Library, the Dove Cottage Library, the Zentralbibliothek of Zürich, the English Seminar Library of the University of Zürich, and the Harry Ransom Humanities Center of the University of Texas. For support of travel and other research expenses, I appreciate the assistance I received from the Committee on Research and the Chancellor's Office of the

University of California at Berkeley. Once more, the confidence of Gunnel Tottie in my work-in-progress helped me more than I can say to complete it.

The dedicatee of this book is the teacher who introduced me in the ninth grade to the poetry of Coleridge.

M. D. Paley
Zürich, December 1998

Contents

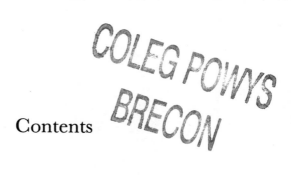

ILLUSTRATIONS

Abbreviations

Butlin
: *The Paintings and Drawings of William Blake* (2 vols., London and New Haven: Yale University Press, 1981)

BL
: S. T. Coleridge, *Biographia Literaria* (*CC* 7), ed. James Engell and W. Jackson Bate (2 vols., Princeton: Princeton University Press, 1983)

CC
: *The Collected Works of Samuel Taylor Coleridge* (16 vols., Princeton: Princeton University Press, 1969–)

CL
: *Collected Letters of Samuel Taylor Coleridge*, ed. Earl Leslie Griggs (6 vols., Oxford: Oxford University Press, 1956–71)

CN
: *The Notebooks of Samuel Taylor Coleridge*, ed. Kathleen Coburn *et al.* (5 vols., Princeton: Princeton University Press, 1957–)

CPW
: *The Complete Poetical Works of Samuel Taylor Coleridge*, ed. E. H. Coleridge (2 vols., Oxford: Oxford University Press, 1912)

E
: *The Complete Poetry and Prose of William Blake*, ed. David V. Erdman, rev. edn. (Berkeley and Los Angeles: University of California Press, 1982)

EOT
: S. T. Coleridge, *Essays on His Own Times* (*CC* 3), ed. David V. Erdman (3 vols., Princeton: Princeton University Press, 1978)

Lectures 1795
: S. T. Coleridge, *Lectures 1795 on Politics and Religion* (*CC* 1), ed. Lewis Patton and Peter Mann (Princeton: Princeton University Press, 1971)

Marginalia
: S. T. Coleridge, *Marginalia* (*CC* 12), ed. George Whalley and H. J. Jackson (3 vols., Princeton: Princeton University Press, 1980–92)

TT
: S. T. Coleridge, *Table Talk* (*CC* 14), ed. Carl Woodring (2 vols., Princeton: Princeton University Press, 1990)

Watchman
: S. T. Coleridge, *The Watchman* (*CC* 2), ed. Lewis Patton (Princeton: Princeton University Press, 1970)

Introduction

A major topos in English Romantic poetry is the imminence of an apocalypse that will be succeeded by a millennium. William Blake made this the central concern of the prophetic poems he wrote in the 1790s, and, after he recognized that this sequence could not be realized through the energy embodied in his revolutionary hero Orc, he established it in a very different way in the three long poems of his later career. In a series of poems written during the 1790s Samuel Taylor Coleridge also postulated a transformation of life through a revolution that would fulfil Old and New Testament prophecies. Coleridge too found himself prevented by historical events from supplying the millennial sequel to the apocalypse of revolution; but, unlike Blake, Coleridge ceased to make either component part of his poetry after the 1790s. William Wordsworth in *The Prelude* opened windows into various aspects of apocalypse and millennium, sometimes viewing each in isolation, but always with the plan of bringing them together in the end. Lord Byron artfully played upon his readers' familiarity with the prototype in order to tease, disappoint, frighten, and even antagonize his public by creating apocalypse without millennium. For Percy Bysshe Shelley the succession of apocalypse by millennium, in the broadest sense political, remained a crucial subject throughout his poetic career. John Keats's last attempt at epic narrative, incorporating a memorable scene of apocalypse, was left unfinished at the threshold of millennium. In all, despite some powerful attempts to create poetic narratives of apocalypse and millennium during the Romantic period, the issue remains problematic. This is only in part because no historical narrative, however mythologized, could successfully unite two historical moments that had refused to become a sequence. One way to escape this dilemma was to transfer the absent millennium to the natural world as Coleridge does in *France: An Ode*, but at the cost of an ablation of meaning that will be discussed in Chapter 2. Another recourse is the Wordsworthian process of internalization celebrated by M. H. Abrams as 'an act of unaided vision, in which the Lamb and the New Jerusalem are replaced by man's mind as the bridegroom and nature as the

Bride'.[1] Yet this too is problematic, for it results, in Wordsworth's memorable account of the ascent of Mount Snowdon, in a millennium in which there are no other human beings. Whether apocalypse and millennium are envisaged on the historical plane, in nature, or within the self, cracks and fissures develop in the seemingly continuous strata.[2] The shifting ratios of apocalypse and millennium in particular poems and the resulting lack of a sense of closure (no matter how firmly the poems may insist on it) is the subject of this study. As the Romantic poets characteristically wrote with a consciousness of the history of their subjects, that must be our starting-point, beginning with a definition of terms.

Sometimes in modern usage *apocalypse* is used to mean an enormous disaster, such as the burning of a skyscraper or the sinking of an ocean liner. While it is true that disaster is often associated with the apocalyptic mode, in religious or literary usage the emphasis is elsewhere. Northrop Frye remarks that 'The Greek word for revelation, *apocalypsis*, has the metaphorical sense of uncovering or taking a lid off',[3] and it is important to stress that the whole conception of apocalypse has to do with a revelation of ultimate truths. There may be colossal disasters without any revelation preceding or ensuing, but an apocalypse involves, as the *OED*'s primary definition states, uncovering or disclosure. Percy Bysshe Shelley, ever alert to etymologies, plays on this in *Prometheus Unbound*:

PANTHEA
What veiled form sits on that ebon throne?
ASIA
The veil has fallen! . . .[4]

The apocalyptic mode, both in the Bible and in secular literature, involves a seer who communicates his visions, and these apocalyptic

[1] M. H. Abrams, *Natural Supernaturalism: Tradition and Revolution in Romantic Literature* (New York and London: Norton, 1973), p. 56. As here and at some other points I take issue with Abrams's views, I must take this opportunity to record my admiration for this profoundly learned book.

[2] Although the analysis of biblical texts is beyond my scope, I should note that the Book of the Revelation itself has been characterized as 'a work that seems to offer total vision and structural wholeness but that actually dissolves into fragments in reading'. See Christopher Burdon, *The Apocalypse in England: Revelation Unravelling, 1700–1834* (Basingstoke: Macmillan, 1997), p. 29.

[3] Northrop Frye, *The Great Code: The Bible and Literature* (London: Routledge and Kegan Paul, 1982), p. 135.

[4] *Shelley's Poetry and Prose*, ed. Donald H. Reiman and Sharon B. Powers (New York and London: W. W. Norton, 1977), II. iv. 1–2. The Shelleyan irony that the verbal revelation that follows is partial and unsatisfying will be discussed in Ch. 5.

truths are conveyed not as a pure spiritual transmission, but through images and words.[5] A tormented version of this is expressed by Captain Ahab in *Moby Dick:*

All visible objects . . . are but as pasteboard masks. But in each event—in the living act, the undoubted deed—there, some unknown but still unreasoning thing puts the mouldings of its features from behind the unreasoning mask. If man will strike, strike through the mask![6]

Furthermore, as apocalyptic characteristically brings the reader to the end of time, it is often linked with eschatology, the knowledge of last things. In both Old and New Testament thought, however, there intervenes between the disasters that end the world as we know it a period of life in a regenerate society, known as the millennium. Although the word means a thousand years, as in the period that Jesus will rule with his resurrected martyrs in Revelation 20: 2–7, in the Old Testament and in post-biblical literature, the idea of the millennium is not confined to that. The means of getting from apocalypse to millennium has also been differently categorized and interpreted. Some Christian theologians and church historians distinguish between pre-millennialism and post-millennialism, according to whether Jesus was expected to appear to effect a 'radical discontinuity' at the beginning of the millennial period, or whether there would be a 'smooth, gradual and peaceable transition' through progress into a millennial world that would culminate with the Second Coming and the end of life on earth.[7] However, more useful for our discussion is the difference between millenarianism—the idea that the millennium will be dramatically inaugurated by the Second Coming of Christ—and millennialism—the belief 'that history, under divine guidance, will bring about the triumph of Christian principles, and that a holy utopia will come into being'.[8] Nor, as far as Romantic poetry is concerned, need Jesus be involved in the millennium at all—though he is for the later Blake and for Coleridge, he is not in the works of the earlier Blake, of Wordsworth, of Shelley, or of Keats (Byron, as we shall see, is a special case belonging to neither of these groups). Nor do the poets devote much attention to the subdivisions

    [5] On the apocalyptic mode in the Bible, see Burdon, *Apocalypse in England*, pp. 8–16.
    [6] Herman Melville, *Moby-Dick or, The Whale*, ed. Alfred Kazin (Boston: Houghton Mifflin, 1956), p. 139.
    [7] See W. H. Oliver, *Prophets and Millennialists: The Uses of Biblical Prophecy in England from the 1790s to the 1840s* (Auckland: Auckland University Press/ Oxford University Press, 1978), p. 21.
    [8] Ernest Lee Tuveson, *Redeemer Nation: The Idea of America's Millennial Role* (Chicago and London: University of Chicago Press, 1968), p. 34.

within the apocalyptic/millenarian scenario, to whether Satan or his equivalent will be loosed before or after the millennium, or whether the descent of the New Jerusalem or its equivalent completes the millennial world or does away with it. In this the poets' attitudes are similar to those of some millenarian believers. 'The absence of fine and delimiting distinctions between beliefs relating to the Second Coming', as one scholar put it, 'is in fact, a primary characteristic of apocalyptic millenarianism and is quite different from what may be found in academic millenarian speculation'.[9] What is important is that the narrative go from a revelation of the nature of human history, usually accompanied by great upheavals, to a society characterized by harmony and justice for a very long period of time, though not necessarily a thousand or any other fixed number of years. It is such a scenario that we find in poems such as 'Religious Musings', *America*, parts of *The Prelude*, *Prometheus Unbound*, and *The Fall of Hyperion*; while in Byron's 'Darkness' and his *Cain* we find its antithesis. Whether the poets' intention was to affirm or to deny apocalyptic expectation and millennial desire, these elements figured prominently in their works, and they were of course aware that behind the themes they presented lay a deep background of sacred writing, theological interpretation, and secular history.

The master prototype for the movement from apocalypse to millennium is of course the Book of Revelation. Beginning with John's description of the manifestation to him of 'one like unto the Son of man', and of being transported in the spirit through a door opened in heaven, this book made available a set of characters, objects, and situations familiar to all readers of literature: the four beasts full of eyes, the four and twenty elders, the book sealed with seven seals, the Lamb as it had been slain, the four riders on horses of different colours, the two witnesses slain and resurrected, the little book that is eaten, the great red dragon, the woman clothed with the sun and her child, the beast from the sea, the great winepress of the wrath of God, the whore that sitteth upon many waters and her scarlet-coloured beast. Also generally familiar is the division into 7s—the seven seals of the sealed book, the seven angels with seven trumpets that sound in sequence, the seven vials with the seven last plagues that are emptied in sequence. A sudden change occurs in chapter 19 with the rider on the white horse, clothed with a vesture dipped in blood. In chapter 20 Satan is chained in the

---

[9] Michael Fixler, *Milton and the Kingdoms of God* (Evanston, Ill.: Northwestern University Press, 1964), p. 32.

bottomless pit for a thousand years. Those who were beheaded for the sake of Jesus are resurrected to reign with him for a thousand years, after which Satan will break loose and, with the armies of Gog and Magog, suffer a final defeat by God. The second, general resurrection takes place, and the final Judgement. Chapter 21 begins with the announcement of a new heaven and a new earth, followed by the descent of the New Jerusalem from heaven and the marriage of Jerusalem and the Lamb. The rest of this chapter and the beginning of the final chapter, 22, are devoted to a description of the twelve-gated New Jerusalem, a city that needs neither temple nor sun nor moon because God and the Lamb are enthroned in it, with a river proceeding from their throne and on either side the tree of life bearing fruit perpetually. The book ends, as is common in apocalyptic literature, with a warning against altering the text and a blessing on its readers.

The poets of the Romantic period drew with great familiarity upon the situations, figures, and language of the Book of Revelation. However, far more important than any accumulation of details is their adaptations of the model underlying them, a model in which there is a transition from apocalypse to millennium. In appropriating, recasting, and radically revising material from the text of John of Patmos, the poets acted, as they must have known, very much after the example of its author, for Revelation is itself a recasting of Old Testament materials. In Revelation the description of the Temple ornaments in Kings, the vision of the Son of Man in Daniel 7, the structure of the Jewish liturgical calendar, and a myriad other details are assimilated in what Austen Farrer has aptly called a rebirth of images.[10] Furthermore, for the poetry of the Romantic period some of these primary texts, especially Isaiah and Daniel, were as important as texts unmediated by any other. In Isaiah 24–5, chapters cited near the beginning of Blake's *Marriage of Heaven and Hell*, there is a vision of the Day of the Lord: 'And all the host of heaven shall be dissolved, and the heavens shall be rolled together as a scroll: and all their host shall fall down, as the leaf falleth from the vine, and as a falling fig from the fig tree'.[11] This apocalypse is

[10] Austen Farrer, *A Rebirth of Images: The Making of St. John's Apocalypse* (Westminster: Dacre Press, 1949).

[11] It was recognized as early as St Jerome that there was more than one authorial hand in the Book of Isaiah and that chapters 24–7 had been written by someone other than the author of at least parts of the rest. By the later eighteenth century, the textual analysis of the Bible that was to become known as the Higher Criticism, was advancing. Coleridge was familiar with some of it, and Blake was probably aware of it as well. (See Jerome J. McGann, 'The Idea of an Indeterminate Text: Blake's Bible of Hell and Dr. Alexander Geddes', *Studies in*

followed by a millennium in which 'the desert shall rejoice, and blossom as the rose', and 'the parched ground shall become a pool, in the habitation of dragons, where each lay, shall be grass with reeds and rushes' (35. 7) This regenerate land will be the home of a regenerate community: 'the redeemed shall walk there. . . . And the ransomed of the LORD shall return, and come to Zion with songs and everlasting joy upon their heads: they shall obtain joy and gladness, and sorrow and sighing shall flee away' (9–10). Of course, the greatest Old Testament millennial vision is that of Isaiah's chapter 65, where God says: 'For, behold, I create new heavens and a new earth: and the former shall not be remembered, nor come into mind. But be ye glad and rejoice for ever in that which I create: for, behold, I create Jerusalem a rejoicing, and her people a joy' (17–18). Its concluding verse 25 became the source for countless poems and works of art: 'The wolf and the lamb shall feed together, and the lion shall eat straw like the bullock: and dust shall be the serpent's meat. They shall not hurt nor destroy in all my holy mountain, saith the LORD'.

Throughout the history of millenarian discourse, the book of Daniel holds a special place, especially its second and seventh chapters. Daniel 2 concerns the great image dreamt by Nebuchadnezzar and recounted by the prophet:

Thou, O king, sawest, and behold a great image. This great image, whose brightness was excellent, stood before thee; and the form thereof was terrible. This image's head was of fine gold, his breast and his arms of silver, his belly and his thighs of brass, His legs of iron, his feet part of iron and part of clay. Thou sawest till that a stone was cut out without hands, which smote the image upon his feet that were of iron and clay, and brake them to pieces. Then was the iron, the clay, the brass, the silver, and the gold, broken to pieces together, and became like the chaff of the summer threshingfloors; and the wind carried them away, that no place was found for them: and the stone that smote the image became a great mountain, and filled the whole earth. (31–5)

Daniel goes on to interpret the dream to Nebuchadnezzar. As the king of kings, 'Thou art this head of gold,' he tells him, and continues:

And after thee shall arise another kingdom inferior to thee, and another third kingdom of brass, which shall bear rule over all the earth. And the fourth kingdom shall be strong as iron: forasmuch as iron breaketh in pieces and

Romanticism, 25 (1986), 303–24; Elinor Shaffer, '*Kubla Khan' and the Fall of Jerusalem* (Cambridge: Cambridge University Press, 1972). The consciousness of multiple authorship of some books of the Bible may, indeed, have coloured some of their own works.

subdueth all things: and as iron that breaketh all these, shall it break in pieces and bruise. And whereas thou sawest the feet and toes, part of potters' clay, and part of iron, the kingdom shall be divided; but there shall be in it of the strength of the iron, forasmuch as thou sawest the iron mixed with miry clay. And as the toes of the feet were part of iron, and part of clay, so the kingdom shall be partly strong, and partly broken. And whereas thou sawest iron mixed with miry clay, they shall mingle themselves with the seed of men: but they shall not cleave one to another, even as iron is not mixed with clay. (39–43)

Daniel's prophecy concludes with a prediction of a fifth, millennial kingdom of a completely different order:

And in the days of these kings shall the God of heaven set up a kingdom, which shall never be destroyed: and the kingdom shall not be left to other people, but it shall break in pieces and consume all these kingdoms, and it shall stand for ever. Forasmuch as thou sawest that the stone was cut out of the mountain without hands, and that it brake in pieces the iron, the brass, the clay, the silver, and the gold; the great God hath made known to the king what shall come to pass hereafter: and the dream is certain, and the interpretation thereof sure. (44–5)

Daniel 7 concerns the prophet's vision of four beasts representing successive kingdoms, the Ancient of Days enthroned, and one who, 'like the Son of man', comes 'with the clouds of heaven'. The kingdoms are successively destroyed, and once more there is a fifth kingdom of an entirely different nature, ruled by the Son of man. 'And there was given him dominion, and glory, and a kingdom, that all people, nations, and languages, should serve him: his dominion is an everlasting dominion, which shall not pass away, and his kingdom that which shall not be destroyed' (14). These visions and their interpretation were important to millenarians in every age. Concerning the Middle Ages, Norman Cohn calls Daniel 2 and 7 'the central phantasy of revolutionary eschatology'.[12] In the seventeenth century, Thomas Burnet declared: 'both these Visions terminate upon the *Millennium*, or the Kingdom of Christ,' Daniel 2.4 introducing the fifth Monarchy, the kingdom of Christ, and Daniel 7.13 expressly declaring the reign of Christ.[13] In 1793, the first vision was the subject of a large 'hieroglyphical print' by the engraver Garnett Terry, which accompanied a pamphlet on the

[12] Norman Cohn, *The Pursuit of the Millennium*, rev. edn. (London: Temple Smith, 1970), p. 16.

[13] Thomas Burnet, *The Theory of the Earth, Containing an Account of the Original of the Earth, and of All the General Changes which it hath already undergone, or Is to Undergo Till the Consummation of all Things*, 3rd edn. (2 vols., London, 1697), 2: 110.

subject of 'the approaching Destruction of Antichrist, the Beast, the Whore, and the False Prophet; demonstrated from the Prophecies of Daniel, and confirmed by the Signs of the Times'.[14] Joseph Priestley in *The Present State of Europe Compared with Ancient Prophecies* (1794), saw the French Revolution as a fulfilment of Daniel's prophecies, pointing out that in Daniel 7: 18 'the administration of this kingdom of heaven is not said to be wholly confined to one person, but to be extended to many', and that in Daniel 2 'The little stone *smiting* the image, and *breaking it in pieces*, is far from giving the idea of a peaceable revolution, but one that will be effected with great violence, and in a short time'.[15] William Blake modified Daniel's great image in a passage of his *America*, Keats closed a sonnet denouncing the Prince Regent with a quotation from Daniel 2, and Shelley rewrote part of Daniel 7 in *The Triumph of Life*.[16]

There are of course many other Old and New Testament passages on apocalyptic and millennial themes, but as a background to the poetry of the Romantic period, only the best known and most frequently echoed need be mentioned here. Joel 2: 28–32, is one of these, combining as it does apocalypse and millennium in a brief space:

And it shall come to pass afterward, that I will pour out my spirit upon all flesh; and your sons and your daughters shall prophesy, your old men shall dream dreams, your young men shall see visions. . . . And I will shew wonders in the heavens and in the earth, blood, and fire, and pillars of smoke. The sun shall be turned into darkness, and the moon into blood, before the great and terrible day of the LORD come. And it shall come to pass, that whosoever shall call on the name of the LORD shall be delivered: for in mount Zion and in Jerusalem shall be deliverance, as the LORD hath said, and in the remnant whom the LORD shall call.

A similarly compressed conjunction of apocalypse and millennium appears in the New Testament in the so-called little apocalypse of Matthew 24: 29–30 (with parallels in Mark and Luke): 'Immediately after the tribulation of those days shall the sun be darkened, and the moon shall not give her light, and the stars shall fall from heaven, and

---

[14] See David Bindman, 'William Blake and Popular Religious Imagery', *Burlington Magazine*, 128 (1986): 717 and fig. 13; Jon Mee, *Dangerous Enthusiasm: William Blake and the Culture of Radicalism in the 1790s* (Oxford: Clarendon Press, 1992), pp. 49–55; E. P. Thompson, *Witness against the Beast* (New York: New Press, 1993), pp. 129–51.

[15] Joseph Priestley, *A Farewell Sermon: Letters to Members of the New Jerusalem Church 1791* and *The Present State of Europe Compared with Antient Prophecies 1794*, introduction by Jonathan Wordsworth (Oxford: Woodstock Books, 1989), p. 5.

[16] See Chs. 1 and 6 below, and Bryan Shelley, *Shelley and Scripture: The Interpreting Angel* (Oxford: Clarendon Press, 1994), pp. 161–5.

the powers of the heavens shall be shaken: And then shall appear the sign of the Son of man in heaven: and then shall all the tribes of the earth mourn, and they shall see the Son of man coming in the clouds of heaven with power and great glory'. Another frequently echoed passage is 2 Peter 3: 10–13. 'But the day of the Lord will come as a thief in the night; in the which the heavens shall pass away with a great noise, and the elements shall melt with fervent heat, the earth also and the works that are therein shall be burned up. . . . Nevertheless we, according to his promise, look for new heavens and a new earth, wherein dwelleth righteousness'.

The verbal influences of Isaiah, Daniel, Revelation, and other books of the Bible upon the Romantic texts to be discussed are manifold and important, but even more important is the conceptual structure that, up to a point, they share. Apocalypse, a revelation of the meaning of history typically accompanied by vast destruction, is succeeded by millennium, a period of social perfection upon an earth often pictured as regenerate in all its life. The meaning of each term can be defined only in relation to the other. As Thomas Burnet wrote of the Book of Revelation, 'And you may as well open a Lock without a Key, as interpret the *Apocalypse* without the *Millennium*.'[17] The importance of this doctrine was not limited to texts but was part of the living beliefs of early Christian communities, and the knowledge that this was so is also an important factor in shaping the ideas of poets who came long afterwards.

For the first two centuries of Christianity, there prevailed a literal belief in a world-week of 6,000 years to be followed by a millennium, 1,000 years in which the resurrected Just would feast on bread and wine in the New Jerusalem. This doctrine was affirmed by Church Fathers Justin Martyr, Irenaeus, and Lactantius, among others. The reader who could not study these in the original or find them in translation could learn about their doctrines in detail from Thomas Burnet's *Theory of the Earth*,[18] or, in summary form, from John Lawrence Mosheim's *Ecclesiastical History*.[19] Sir Isaac Newton wrote in his 'Observations upon the Apocalypse of St John', citing Justin Martyr:

He saith: 'But I, and as many as are Christians, in all things right in their opinions, believe both that there shall be a resurrection of the flesh, and a thousand years life at Jerusalem, built, adorned, and enlarged.' Which is as much as to

[17] Burnet, *Theory of the Earth*, 2: 111.   [18] Ibid. 2: 119–25.

[19] John Lawrence Mosheim, *An Ecclesiastical History*, trans. Archibald Maclaine, M.A. (2 vols., London, 1765), 1: 145–6.

say, that all true Christians in that early age received this prophecy: for in all ages, as many as believed the thousand years, received the Apocalypse as the foundation of their opinion: and I do not know one instance to the contrary.[20]

However, research on the history of this doctrine would hardly have been necessary, for an account was available in a book known to virtually every serious reader of the late eighteenth century—Edward Gibbon's *Decline and Fall of the Roman Empire*. In his celebrated fifteenth chapter about the beliefs and doctrines of the early Christians, Gibbon wrote:

The ancient and popular doctrine of the Millennium was intimately connected with the second coming of Christ. As the works of the creation had been finished in six days, their duration in their present state, according to a tradition which was attributed to the prophet Elijah, was fixed to six thousand years. By the same analogy it was inferred that this long period of labour and contention, which was now almost elapsed, would be succeeded by a joyful Sabbath of a thousand years; and that Christ, with the triumphant band of the saints and the elect who had escaped death, or who had been miraculously revived, would reign upon earth till the time appointed for the last and general resurrection.[21]

Gibbon, though himself no believer in such a millennium, which he dismissed as 'borrowed from a misrepresentation of Isaiah, Daniel, and the Apocalypse', nevertheless left no doubt that it had been 'the reigning sentiment of orthodox believers', and that this was accompanied by a parallel belief in the violent destruction of the mystic Babylon by 'pestilence and famine, comets and eclipses, earthquakes and inundations'.[22] These events were to be succeeded, according the early Christian belief, by a general conflagration—a belief that 'coincided with the tradition of the East, the philosophy of the Stoics, and the analogy of Nature'; Italy, 'chosen for the origin and principal scene of the conflagration, was the best adapted [country] for that purpose by natural and physical causes—by its deep caverns, beds of sulfur, and numerous volcanoes'.[23] The natural coincided with supernatural belief to prove a matrix for the apocalyptic.

After the Christian Church had abandoned its expectation of an

---

[20] Isaac Newton, *Opera Quae Exstant Omnia*, ed. Samuel Horsley (5 vols., London, 1785), 5: 446.
[21] Edward Gibbon, *The Decline and Fall of the Roman Empire*, ed. Oliphant Smeaton (3 vols., New York: Modern Library, n.d.), 1: 403. Gibbon cites Burnet's *Sacred Theory* as his authority for the tradition regarding Elijah.
[22] Gibbon, *Decline and Fall*, 1: 404–5.   [23] Ibid. 1: 405.

impending Second Coming to be followed by a millennium of feasting in Jerusalem, the Augustinian position that the millennium was a spiritual allegory of what had already taken place—the consequence of the Incarnation and the Crucifixion—became dogma. Nevertheless, there arose from time to time visionaries who proclaimed that a new order of being was imminent.[24] One of these was Joachim of Fiore, whom Dante placed in Paradise as 'the Calabrian abbot Joachim, endowed with prophetic spirit'.[25] Joachim envisioned history as divided into three epochs: that of the Father, that of the Son, and that of the Holy Spirit. The third *status* was about to arrive, and the laws of Church and State would no longer be necessary, for humanity would then pass into a condition of spiritual freedom. In a general study of millenarianism, Joachim of Fiore, whose thought strongly influenced the Spiritual Franciscans and, later, the revolutionaries known as Fratricelli, would bulk large; however, there is little evidence of direct knowledge of the writings of Joachim of Fiore in Britain during the later eighteenth and early nineteenth centuries.[26] Some scholars have tried to link the Romantic period, and especially William Blake, with Joachite thought through the intermediacy of seventeenth-century antinomian sects such as the Familists, the Ranters, and the Muggletonians.[27] There are no documented links, though it is possible to argue for correspondences between some of Blake's characteristic statements and the beliefs of these sects, including belief in the immediate availability of apocalyptic vision and the idea of a regenerate society to come in which all forms of law would be unnecessary. In support of such arguments, the term 'the everlasting gospel', which occurs in English as the equivalent of Joachim's *Evangelium Æternum* is sometimes introduced, but as all parties derived it from Revelation 14: 6, no conclusion can be drawn from this.

---

[24] See Marjorie Reeves, 'The Development of Apocalyptic Thought: Medieval Attitudes', in *The Apocalypse in English Renaissance Thought and Literature: Patterns, Antecedents, and Repercussions*, ed. C. A. Patrides and Joseph Wittreich (Ithaca, NY: Cornell University Press, 1984), pp. 40–72.

[25] Dante, *The Paradiso of Dante Alighieri*, trans. P. H. Wicksteed (London: J. M. Dent, 1958), p. 151.

[26] It should be noted, however, that Robert Southey's library included the following, with a MS note: 'VATICINIA, sive Prophetae Abbatis Joackim etc. 32 plates *Venet*, 1639.' According to the sale catalogue, 'This volume also contains the six prophetic Wheels, with their Explanations', as well as a MS note by Southey.—*Catalogue of the Valuable Library of the Late Robert Southey, Esq. L. L. D. Poet Laureate* (London: S. Leigh Sotheby & Co., 8–25 May 1844), p. 144, no. 2884.

[27] See esp. A. L. Morton, *The Everlasting Gospel* (London: Lawrence and Wishart, 1958). A more valuable account, emphasizing the antinomian tradition, is given by Thompson in *Witness against the Beast*.

It is difficult not to agree with those scholars who conclude that 'the medieval heresy of the *Evangelium Æternum* adds nothing to our appreciation of Blake and . . . could not have formed a significant part of his sources in the literature of the preceding two centuries'.[28] The same may be said of groups such as the Fifth Monarchy Men and the Diggers. However interesting these may be in their own right, with respect to the interlinked subjects of apocalypse and millennium in the Romantic period it seems more worthwhile to sketch the wealth of material that we know was part of the culture than to strain at verbal parallels.

How much the Romantic poets knew of the actual writings and doctrines of the political millenarians of the seventeenth century is for the most part a matter for speculation,[29] but there is no need to speculate about their knowledge of John Milton. 'Milton', it has been claimed, 'had been a radical millenarian long before an organized Fifth Monarchist movement existed.[30] Certainly in *Paradise Lost* Milton makes clear his belief in a millennium by having the Father tell the Son:

> The World shall burn, and from her ashes spring
> New Heav'n and Earth, wherein the just shall dwell
> And after all their tribulations long
> See golden days, fruitful of golden deeds,
> With Joy and Love triumphing, and fair Truth.[31]

This point is reiterated in Book XII, when Michael tells Adam that at the end of history the Son shall come:

> With glory and power to judge both quick and dead,
> To judge th' unfaithful dead, but to reward
> His faithful, and receive them into bliss,
> Whether in Heav'n or Earth, for then the Earth
> Shall all be Paradise, far happier place
> Than this of *Eden*, and far happier days.[32]

---

[28]   See Marjorie Reeves and Warwick Gould, *Joachim of Fiore and the Myth of the Eternal Evangel in the Nineteenth Century* (Oxford: Clarendon Press, 1987).

[29]   Of the six poets discussed in this book, Coleridge is the one with the most encompassing seventeenth-century interests, which will be discussed in Ch. 2.

[30]   Christopher Hill, *Milton and the Puritan Revolution* (Harmondsworth: Penguin, 1979), p. 283. Fixler, in *Milton and the Kingdoms of God*, argues that Milton was not a millenarian, but that 'he was close enough to his millenarian contemporaries to sound like them at times, and he certainly shared, though not at this late date [1651] with the same intensity, their apocalyptic longing and hope' (p. 170).

[31]   *Paradise Lost*, iii. 334–8; p. 266, in *Complete Poems and Major Prose*, ed. Merritt Y. Hughes (New York: Odyssey, 1957).

[32]   *Paradise Lost*, xii. 460–5; pp. 464–5.

Although the establishment of something like Paradise at the Second Coming might be regarded as a symmetry suggestive of a cyclical view of history,[33] Michael's discourse makes it clear that the millennial state is 'far happier', although but a prelude to the 'New Heav'ns, new Earth, Ages of endless date' after the final conflagration.[34] Whether, or the extent to which, Milton was a millenarian continues to be discussed by Milton scholars, but that he presented the doctrine of a millennium on earth in *Paradise Lost* is as evident as the fact that his was the most powerful single voice in the tradition underlying English Romantic poetry.

Close to the end of the seventeenth century, there appeared Thomas Burnet's *Theory of the Earth*, a rich source of information and theory concerning apocalypse and millennium and a great imaginative work, of which Gibbon wrote: 'He blends philosophy, Scripture, and tradition, into one magnificent system; in the description of which he displays a strength of fancy not inferior to that of Milton himself'.[35] Burnet's book almost certainly helped to shape Blake's cosmogony; Coleridge thought of translating Burnet's Latin original into blank verse; and Wordsworth, who was evidently familiar with some of Burnet's ideas by 1804–5, appended a long Latin quotation from Burnet's book to Book III of *The Excursion*.[36] Paralleling natural and political revolutions in a way anticipating Constantin de Volney a century later, Burnet writes: 'What subject can be more worthy the thoughts of any serious person, than to view and consider the Rise and Fall, and all the Revolutions, not of a Monarchy or an Empire . . . but of an intire World'.[37] After his imaginative reconstruction of the causes of the

---

[33] See Fixler, *Milton and the Kingdoms of God*, p. 227.

[34] See *Paradise Lost*, iii. 549, p. 466.

[35] *Decline and Fall*, p. 406 n. 70. John Wesley in 1770 found Burnet's writing on the general conflagration 'one of the noblest tracts which is extant in our language', and his account of the new heavens and the new earth 'highly probable'. See *The Journal of the Rev. John Wesley*, *M.A.*, ed. Nehemiah Curnock (8 vols., London: R. Culley, 1909–16), 5: 351–2.

[36] See John Livingston Lowes, *The Road to Xanadu: A Study in the Ways of the Imagination* (Princeton: Princeton University Press, 1986), pp. 16, 417 n. 41, 458 n. 28; Vincent A. De Luca, *Words of Eternity: Blake and the Poetics of the Sublime* (Princeton: Princeton University Press, 1991), pp. 154–5, 162–3; Morton D. Paley, 'Blake and Thomas Burnet's *Sacred Theory of the Earth*', *Blake: An Illustrated Quarterly*, 2 (1991): 75–8; *The Poetical Works of William Wordsworth*, ed. E. de Selincourt and Helen Darbishire (5 vols., Oxford: Clarendon Press, 1966), 5: 420–1); Duncan Wu, *Wordsworth's Reading 1800–1815* (Cambridge: Cambridge University Press, 1995), pp. 36–7.

[37] Burnet, *Theory of the Earth*, 1: 4.

Deluge and of its effects, Burnet proceeds to the Conflagration that will destroy the world as we know it:

The next Catastrophe is the CONFLAGRATION, to which a new face of Nature will accordingly succeed, *New Heavens* and a *New Earth, Paradise* renew'd, and so it is call'd the *Restitution* of things, or *Regeneration* of the World. And that Period of Nature and Providence being expir'd, then follows the *Consummation of all things*, or the General *Apotheosis*; *when Death and Hell shall be swallowed up in victory*; When the great Circle of Time and Fate is run; or according to the language of Scripture, *When the Heavens and the Earth shall pass away and Time shall be no more.*[38]

The amount of time involved in this transformation is derived from classical, Jewish, and Christian sources. At the end of the Magnus Annus, or Platonic Great Year, there will be 'a Restitution of the Heavens and the Earth to their former state; that is, to the state and posture they had at the beginning of the World'. This will occur by a rectifying of the axis of the earth, setting it 'parallel with the Axis of the Ecliptic', and the resulting 'Great Instauration' will bring back the Golden Age.[39] The Jewish belief that the world will last 6,000 years, a tradition from '*Elias* the *Rabbin*, or *Cabbalist*', accords with that of the Church Fathers, who 'supposed the great Sabbatism would succeed after the World had stood Six Thousand Years' (Irenaeus is cited to the effect that 'the consummation of all things will be in Six Thousand Years, and then the great Sabbatism to come on in the blessed reign of Christ'[40]). The final conflagration will involve earthquakes, which in Scripture are 'the highest expression of the Prophets concerning the *Day of the Lord*', and the eruption of volcanoes such as Vesuvius and Etna.[41] The result of all this will not, however, be the end of the world. From the chaos of the old earth a perfect new one will be reconstituted, a phenomenon for which Burnet uses the terms *Palingenesia* (citing (Matt. 19: 28, 29) and *Apocatastasis* (citing Acts 3: 21), translating both as 'Regeneration'.[42] The regenerate world will be inhabited by the resurrected Just, 'Heirs of the Millennium', who will reign with Christ for a thousand years.[43] This millennial state, says Burnet, will be characterized by '*Indolency*'. There will be no '*Indigency*'. There will be 'Plenty',

---

[38] Burnet, *Theory of the Earth*, 1: 223.   [39] Ibid. 2: 20–1.   [40] Ibid. 2: 21–4.
[41] Ibid. 2: 37–40, 46, 62. 'Earth-quakes are taken notice of in Scripture, as signs and fore-runners of the last day, as they usually are of all great changes and calamities' (2: 46).
[42] Ibid. 2: 185. The *OED*'s first example of *apocatastasis* is from Cudworth's *Intellectual System* (1678).
[43] Burnet, *Theory of the Earth*, 2: 100–2.

characterized by universal peace, righteousness, and the absence of diseases and other forms of pain and sorrow.[44] The activities of the 'Heirs of the Millennium' will be devotion and contemplation, and Burnet includes under the latter the extension of knowledge. One of the lessons there will be the *Theory of the Earth*. After the millennium, the empty earth will become a star.[45]

Burnet, like some other Christian writers on the subject, stressed the classical parallels to apocalypse and millennium, including the Stoics with their idea of cycles of history and periodic conflagrations, the 'one general fire' predicted in Lucan's *Pharsalia*, and Virgil's Fourth Eclogue.[46] Indeed, the Fourth Eclogue, celebrating the birthday of a son of Virgil's patron Pollio, had long been viewed as a parallel to messianic prophecy, proclaiming the renewal of the age of Saturn and the establishment of universal peace. Nature would be purified and renewed in terms very close to Isaiah's:

> The Serpents' Brood shall die: the sacred ground
> Shall Weeds and pois'nous Plants refuse to bear,
> Each common Bush shall *Syrian* Roses wear.
>
> . . . . . .
>
> Unlabour'd Harvests shall the Fields adorn,
> And cluster'd Grapes shall blush on every Thorn.
> The knotted Oaks shall show'rs of Honey weep,
> And through the Matted Grass the liquid Gold shall creep.[47]

The Fourth Eclogue, like biblical prophecy and apocalyptic, could be applied to the immediate future, a possibility that did not escape Edmund Burke when he sarcastically inverted its tenor, writing in 1791 of Mirabeau's speech concerning universal peace: 'Such is the approaching golden age which the Virgil of your Assembly has sung to his Pollios!'[48] As for the supposed Sibylline sources of the Fourth Eclogue, these too could be seen as vatic confirmations of millenarian doctrine. Such a view was also taken by Sir John Floyer, who made the so-called *Sibylline Oracles* available in English translation.[49] In his

---

[44] Ibid. 2: 125–33.   [45] Ibid. 2: 142, 152.   [46] Ibid. 2: 73–4, 102.

[47] 'The Fourth Pastoral, or, Pollio', in *The Works of Virgil in English*, in *The Works of John Dryden* (Berkeley and Los Angeles: University of California Press, 1987), 5: 95, lines 28–30, 33–6.

[48] Edmund Burke, *Letter to a Member of the National Assembly*, in *The Writings and Speeches of Edmund Burke*, vol. 8, ed. L. G. Mitchell (Oxford: Clarendon Press, 1989), p. 320.

[49] Sir John Floyer, *The Sibylline Oracles, Translated from the Best Greek Copies, and Compar'd with the Sacred Prophecies, Especially with Daniel and the Revelations* (London, 1713).

dedication, Floyer asserts that Revelation and the Oracles agree in the doctrine of 'Christ's Reign in the Millennium', and in his preface he reiterates that 'By the *Oracles* 'twill appear, that the *Millennium* is a description of the happy state of the Christian Church in this World'.[50] The translated *Oracles* say that there was a golden age after the Flood, a reign of Saturn characterized by great fertility, and that this will be restored after a judgement in which the wicked will be consigned to eternal torments. In the millennium that follows there will be world-wide peace, and the earth will yield 'infinite Fruits'. There will be no king or leader, and all things will be held in common. The alternation of the seasons and of day and night shall be no more, 'for there shall be a long Day'.[51] In an essay following his translations, Floyer argues that the narratives of Revelation and of the Oracles are basically the same, and he appends a collection of passages from the Church Fathers on the millennium. Like Burnet before him, Floyer states that the sense of the millennium changed in the later writings of St Augustine, and he attempts to rebut Augustine's allegorical interpretation, closing with comparisons between the millennial doctrines of the Old Testament prophets and the Sibyls.

Later in the eighteenth century, William Cowper unfolded near the end of *The Task* a vision of apocalypse and millennium. With the advent of 'the promis'd sabbath' will come an end to 'Six thousand years of sorrow', when God descends 'in his chariot pav'd with love'.[52] Cowper's imagery of the millennial world seems to combine Isaiah and Virgil:

> Rivers of gladness water all the earth,
> And clothe all climes with beauty; the reproach
> Of barrenness is past. The fruitful field
> Laughs with abundance . . . [53]

The 'eternal spring' of Milton is here, as is the child playing with the snake of Isaiah, and the singing of a song of the Lamb as in Revelation. Jerusalem is built again, and the nations come up to it in lines that make us see why Cowper was so much admired by Blake:

> Bright as a sun the sacred city shines;
> All kingdoms and all princes of the earth

---

[50] Sir John Floyer, *The Sibylline Oracles*, pp. xv–xvi.
[51] Ibid., pp. 14–15, 26–31, 80–1.
[52] *The Poetical Works of William Cowper*, ed. H. S. Milford, 3rd edn. (London: Oxford University Press, 1926), p. 235, lines 733–4, 744.
[53] Ibid., p. 236, lines 763–6.

Flock to that light; the glory of all lands
Flows into her; unbounded is her joy,
And endless her increase. . . .
        .   .   .   .
                Eastern Java there
Kneels with the native of the farthest west;
And Æthiopia spreads abroad the hand,
And worships. Her report has travell'd forth
Into all lands. From ev'ry clime they come
To see thy beauty and to share thy joy,
O Sion! an assembly such as earth
Saw never, such as heav'n stoops down to see.[54]

As interesting as what is in this long passage is what is not in it: no Satan to be chained and break loose, no vials of wrath to be emptied, no conflagration. Cowper's Calvinist evangelicalism did not colour a description of the millennium that foreshadows the last pages of Blake's *Jerusalem* and Act IV of Shelley's *Prometheus Unbound*.

As in the times of the early Christians, in the later eighteenth century a preoccupation with the subject of apocalypse and millennium was to be found not only in visionary texts but also among groups of believers who had as their goal the regeneration of the world. Perhaps the most notorious of these was the group known as the Illuminati. It was founded in 1776 by Adam Weishaupt, who was professor of canon law at the University of Ingolstadt, a fact which may have led Mary Shelley to send young Victor Frankenstein to that university to do his research in secret. Weishaupt conceived of a secret organization whose members assumed *noms de guerre* in communicating with one another—his own was Spartacus, after the leader of the Roman slave rebellion. In meetings patterned on the mysterious proceedings of Freemasonry, novices were introduced to truths that were to liberate them from prejudice and illusion and lead to the peaceful achievement of a new, egalitarian world. As J. M. Roberts puts it, 'The Order was both an agency for the transmission of the commonplaces of Enlightenment ideas and attitudes and a quasi-religious sect, meeting the needs of men dissatisfied with the traditional sources of faith and contemplating an ultimate utopian regeneration of society'.[55] In 1785 the Illuminati were condemned by the Bavarian authorities, but Weishaupt had already fled,

---

[54] Ibid., pp. 236–7, lines 800–4, 810–17.
[55] See J. M. Roberts, *The Mythology of the Secret Societies* (New York: Charles Scribner's Sons, 1972), p. 122.

and he published his *Apologie der Illuminaten* in 1786. Edmund Burke refers to two books attributed to Illuminati in support of his statement that 'Many parts of Europe are in open disorder. In many others there is a hollow murmuring under ground; a confused movement is felt, that threatens a general earthquake in the political world'.[56] Coleridge owned and annotated Weishaupt's *Apologie des Misvergnügens und Uebels* (Frankfurt and Leipzig, 1790), now in the British Library, and he and Robert Southey used *illuminize* as a verb in political controversy. 'You illuminize I perceive in all your paragraphs,' Southey wrote of Coleridge's leading articles for the *Morning Chronicle*, and Coleridge replied: 'You say, I illuminize—I think, that Property will some time or other be modified by the predominance of Intellect, even as Rank & Superstition are now modified by & subordinated to Property. That much is to be hoped of the Future. . . . Therefore if to act on the belief that . . . inapplicable Truths are moral Falsehoods, be to illuminize— why then I illuminize!'[57] However, although some of the letters of Spartacus were translated into English by the conspiracy theorist John Robison,[58] Weishaupt's writings were for the most part known first hand in the Anglophone world only by the few who could obtain and read hard-to-get German books printed in black letter. This explains Percy Bysshe Shelley's keen interest in the Abbé Augustin Barruel's *Memoirs Illustrating the History of Jacobinism*.[59] 'Altho it is half filled with the vilest and most unsupported falsehoods,' the poet wrote in 1812, 'it is a book worth reading'.[60] Percy Shelley first read Barruel's *Memoirs* while a

---

[56] Edmund Burke, *Reflections on the Revolution in France*, ed. Conor Cruise O'Brien (Harmondsworth: Penguin, 1984), p. 265. Burke supports this contention in a footnote referring to two of Weishaupt's books: *Einige Originalschriften des Illuminatenordens* and *System und Folgen des Illuminatenordens* (Munich, 1787).

[57] Southey to Coleridge, letter dated 16 Jan. 1800, in *New Letters of Robert Southey*, ed. Kenneth Curry (2 vols., New York and London: Columbia University Press, 1965), 1: 215; Coleridge to Southey, letter dated 25 Jan. 1800; *CL* 1: 563–4.

[58] John Robison, *Proofs of a Conspiracy against all the Religions and Governments of Europe, Carried on in the Secret Meetings of Free Masons, Illuminati, and Reading Societies* (London, 1797).

[59] Augustine de Barruel, *Memoirs Illustrating the History of Jacobinism* (4 vols., London, 1797–8). In a note in *Notes and Queries* for 10 Feb. 1917, John H. Sandham Griffith claimed possession of Shelley's set. Walter Edwin Peck, who says vol. 2 bears the poet's autograph and the date 1810, hypothesizes that Shelley left these volumes at Horsham after his expulsion from Oxford and later acquired Barruel's work again. (See Peck, 'Shelley and the Abbé Barruel', *PMLA* 36 (1921): 347–53.) In the Berg Collection of the New York Public Library is a copy of vol. 1 of the *Memoirs*, 2nd edn., rev. and corr., with the signature on the upper right of the title-page: 'Percy B. Shelley/1810—.' There are no annotations.

[60] Letter to Elizabeth Hitchener, 27 Feb. 1812, in *Letters of Percy Bysshe Shelley*, ed. F. J. Jones (2 vols., Oxford: Clarendon Press, 1964), 1: 264.

student at Oxford, and again in 1814–15.[61] The book was vile to Shelley because of its reactionary politics, but from the first it gained his attention. One can imagine his feelings upon reading the first sentence of the book: 'At an early period of the French Revolution, there appeared a sect calling itself the JACOBINS, and teaching that all men were equal and free!'[62] On 2 March 1811 Shelley wrote to Leigh Hunt of 'the very great influence, which some years since was gained by *Illuminism*', suggesting that 'a society of equal extent might establish *rational liberty* on as firm a basis as that which would have supported the visionary schemes of a completely-equalized community', and indications of Shelley's reading about the Illuminati have been found in his *Proposals for an Association of Philanthropists* (1812).[63] Shelley's interest in the subject was well known enough for his friend Thomas Love Peacock to include it in the comedy of his Shelley-figure Scythrop in *Nightmare Abbey*: 'He built many castles in the air, and peopled them with secret tribunals, and bands of illuminati, who were always the imaginary instruments of his projected regeneration of the human species'.[64] As we shall see in Chapter 5, this interest in the illuminati was only one of the manifestations in Shelley's work of the millennial visions of the later eighteenth century.

Toward the end of the eighteenth century, the Unitarian divine Richard Price applied the idea of the millennium to events in contemporary history, specifically the American and then the French Revolution. In 1784 Price asserted that the American Revolution meant that 'the old prophecies be verified, that the last universal empire upon earth shall be the empire of reason and virtue, under which the gospel of peace (better understood) *shall have free course and be glorified*'.[65]

---

[61] See T. J. Hogg, *Life of Shelley*, in *The Life of Percy Bysshe Shelley*, ed. Humbert Wolf (London: J. M. Dent, 1933), and the reading list compiled by F. J. Jones from Mary Shelley's journals, *Letters* 2: 469.

[62] Barruel, *Memoirs*, 1: 1.

[63] Shelley, *Letters*, 1: 54; K. N. Cameron, *The Young Shelley: Genesis of a Radical* (New York: Collier, 1962 [1950]), p. 351. James Rieger suggests the influence of Barruel upon Shelley's *The Wandering Jew*. See *The Mutiny Within: The Heresies of Percy Bysshe Shelley* (New York: George Braziller, 1967), pp. 62–7.

[64] Thomas Love Peacock, *Nightmare Abbey* and *Crotchet Castle*, ed. with an introduction by Raymond Wright (Harmondsworth: Penguin, 1981), p. 47. After meeting Stella (Mary Wollstonecraft Godwin), 'Scythrop listened with delight to her repetitions of her favourite passages from Schiller and Goethe, and to her encomiums on the sublime Spartacus Weishaupt, the immortal founder of the Sect of the Illuminati' (p. 94).

[65] Richard Price, *Observations on the Importance of the American Revolution* (London, 1784), pp. 6–7. See Jack Fruchtman, *The Apocalyptic Politics of Richard Price and Joseph Priestley*, *Transactions of the American Philosophical Society*, 73, part 4 (Philadelphia: APA, 1973). There had been a millennial strain in some American Protestant preaching in America during the

Three years later, at the Meeting-House in the Old Jewry, Price preached a sermon declaring that 'that kingdom of the Messiah which our Saviour came to establish' was the kingdom described in the prophecy of Daniel: 'which was *to be given to the Son of Man, and* to increase gradually *till it broke in pieces all other kingdoms, and filled the whole earth*'.[66] Praising the experiment now in the making by 'our brethren on the other side of the Atlantic', Price saw Isaiah's prophecy that 'The wolf will dwell with the lamb [*sic*]' in the process of being fulfilled, and 'the world outgrowing its evils, superstition giving way, antichrist falling, and the *Millennium* hastening'.[67] Quoting Condorcet on perfectibility as well as Revelation 11: 15 on the thousand-year reign of Christ, Price led up to a vision of a millennial dawn and a society in which 'a government of consummate order will be established; and all the faithful and worthy of all religions . . . gathered into it'.[68] The French Revolution added to Price's sense of an impending millennium. In *A Discourse on the Love of our Country*, addressed to the Revolution Society on 4 November 1789, Price contrasted the darkness of the old order with the light produced by the two revolutions, presenting the 'friends of freedom' with an apocalyptic image of their accomplishment: 'Behold, the light you have struck out, after setting AMERICA free, reflected to FRANCE, and there kindled into a blaze that lays despotism in ashes, and warms and illuminates EUROPE!'[69] Price's successor at the Gravel-Pit Meeting, Joseph Priestley, continued to present a view of the two revolutions as the fulfilment of prophecy and apocalyptic, and as concluding in a millennium. At first, Priestley, like his predecessor, stressed the millennial aspect. In his reply to Burke's *Reflections*, Priestley calls the American and French revolutions the beginning of a 'reign of peace' that had been 'distinctly and repeatedly foretold in many prophecies, delivered more than two thousand years ago'.[70] In *The Present State of Europe Compared with Antient Prophecies*, written in the darker time following the outbreak of war between England and France, the ascendancy of the Jacobins, and the Reign of

Revolution; see Melvin B. Endy, Jr., 'Just War, Holy War, and Millennialism in Revolutionary America', *William and Mary Quarterly*, 42 (1985): 3–25.

[66] Richard Price, *The Evidence for a Future Period of Improvement in the State of Mankind* (London, 1787), pp. 1–2.   [67] Ibid., pp. 22–5.

[68] Ibid., pp. 51–6.

[69] Richard Price, *A Discourse on the Love of Our Country* (London, 1789), p. 50. It was of course Price's *Discourse* that prompted Burke's *Reflections on the Revolution in France*.

[70] Joseph Priestley, *Letters to the Right Honourable Edmund Burke* (London, 1791), p. 147.

Terror, Priestley stressed the apocalyptic, identifying the French Revolution with the earthquake of Revelation 11: 33 in which 'the tenth part of the city fell, and in the earthquake were slain of men seven thousand'.[71] An earthquake, Priestley wrote, could signify 'a great convulsion, and revolution, in states'; and he also called attention to other passages in Revelation involving great violence. The appearance in Revelation 19: 11 of the messianic rider on the white horse, for example, was to be followed by a 'great slaughter of men', but it would be a prelude to the millennium described in Revelation 20: 4.[72] After destruction and slaughter, apocalypse would be followed by millennium.

As W. H. Oliver remarks, 'The need to interpret the French Revolution . . . stimulated a boom in prophetical publishing', much of which 'was republication'.[73] The engraver Garnet Terry brought out a series of *Prophetical Extracts*, of which Number V is subtitled 'Relative to the Revolution in France, and the Decline of Papal Power in the World'.[74] The title-page bears an engraving, dated 1794, of the Beast from the Sea of Revelation 13 confronted by an angel with a shield and a flaming sword. Among the many other authors who related the French Revolution to the apocalyptic and the millennial was William Button. In his *Prophetic Conjectures on the French Revolution and Other Recent and Shortly Expected Events*, Button pointed out that the French Revolution produced little bloodshed before the interference of foreign powers, and he printed extracts from eleven sources ranging from 1551 to 1748, all of which 'on the authority of certain passages of scripture, predict a grand and important REVOLUTION IN FRANCE'.[75] Button himself relates the movement of the wheels in Ezekiel 10 to the idea of revolution: 'As if to inform us that the design and tendency of the wheels, is to effect REVOLUTIONS as well in nations and communities, as in the affairs of families and individuals. The world subsists by *revolutions*'; and Button foresees a millennial outcome to 'the present convulsions'—when they subside, '*the remnant shall give glory to the God of heaven—*'.[76] The Baptist

---

[71] Priestley, *Farewell Sermon*, pp. 25–6. A misprint in the original makes the allusion appear to be to Rev. 11: 3.

[72] Priestley, *Present State of Europe*, pp. 12–14.

[73] Oliver, *Prophets and Millennialists*, p. 43.

[74] The extracts are from 'Fleming, Usher, Jerieu, Goodwin, Gill, Love, Daut, Brown, Knox, Willison, More, Newton, Lacey, Owen, Marion, Cavalier, and Mary More.' On Terry, see Mee, *Dangerous Enthusiasm*, pp. 63–5; and Jon Mee, 'Is there an Antinomian in the House? William Blake and the After-Life of a Heresy', in *Historicizing Blake*, ed. Steve Clark and David Worrall (London: St Martin's Press, 1994), pp. 49–54.

[75] William Button, *Prophetic Conjectures* (London, 1793), p. 56.   [76] Ibid., pp. 61–3.

minister Joseph Bicheno, in his learned and allusive *Signs of the Times*, consistently identified Louis XIV as the Beast of Revelation and preached the literal fulfilment of 'new heavens and a new earth' with the return of the Jews of Jerusalem.[77] Not all writers on these topics were supporters of the Revolution. In 1794 Alexander Pirie identified the 'great earthquake' of Revelation 9: 13 as the Revolution, but denounced the Republic as 'the beast that ascendeth out of the bottomless pit' in Revelation 11: 7.[78] The physiognomist J. C. Lavater declared during the Terror that 'if the Gospel is true, the Antichrist is the greatest despot of all and he appears to me to be announcing himself by means of the French democrats'.[79] However, although the apocalyptic could be assumed by either side, in the 1790s the millennial was territory occupied by sympathizers with the Revolution.

Among those who thought in terms of an imminent millennium were some of the followers of the Swedish visionary Emanuel Swedenborg, who had died in London in 1772. Swedenborg's doctrine of correspondences in expounding the 'internal sense' of the Bible, his reports of conversation with angels, and his narratives of journeys to other worlds, all gave his works a powerful appeal to the imagination. This is no doubt why Samuel Taylor Coleridge wrote an ingenious, psychological interpretation of Swedenborg's visions in three pages of manuscript notes.[80] Coleridge presented three hypotheses concerning Swedenborg's visions and voices. The first was Swedenborg's own assertion of supernatural illumination. The second was 'That that great and excellent Man was led into this belief by becoming the Subject of a very rare but not (it is said) altogether *unique* conjunction of the somniative faculty (*by* which the products of the understanding, viz. words, Conceptions, &c. are rendered simultaneously into forms of Sense with the voluntary and other powers of the waking state'. In that case, Swedenborg would have 'thought and reasoned thro' the

---

[77] Joseph Bicheno, *The Signs of the Times* (London, 1799). This is one of a series of editions, the first of which was published in 1793. W. H. Oliver calls Bicheno 'the most interesting prophetical specialist to emerge from the English Dissenters'. See Oliver, *Prophets and Millennialists*, pp. 46–9; and Burdon, *Apocalypse in England*, pp. 95–9.

[78] Alexander Pirie, *The French Revolution Exhibited, in the Light of the Sacred Oracles: or, a Series of Lectures on the Prophecies now Fulfilling* (Perth, 1797).

[79] Letter dated 16 Jan. 1794, quoted by Auguste Viatte, *Les Sources occultes du romantisme, illuminisme—théosophie, 1770–1820* (2 vols., Paris: H. Champion, 1928), 1: 325 ('. . . si l'Évangile est vrai, l'Antéchrist est le plus grand despote de tous les despotes, et il me semble s'annoncer par les démocrates français').

[80] The notes are on the rear flyleaves of Samuel Noble's *Appeal in Behalf of the Views of the Eternal World and State* (London, 1826), British Library.

medium and instrumentality of a series of appropriate and symbolic visual and auditual [sic] Images spontaneously arising before him'. The third hypothesis was merely 'the modest suggestion, that the first and second may not be so incompatible as they appear—'. Coleridge's second hypothesis, to which he devotes by far the longest exposition and which clearly conveys his own conviction, is remarkably like his own account of how he composed 'Kubla Khan' in a state 'in which all the images rose up before him as *things*, with a parallel production of the correspondent expressions, without any sensation or consciousness of effort'.[81] Swedenborg's visions could be regarded as having poetic and symbolic truth, and this helps to explain his appeal to artists and intellectuals as well as to 'respectable tradesmen'.[82]

Nevertheless, Swedenborg was not, strictly speaking, a millenarian, for he believed the millennium had come as a result of the opening to him of a vision of the Last Judgement in 1757.[83] As the ex-radical and police informer William Hamilton Reid put it, 'With them [Swedenborgians] the day of judgement is more a *figure* than a *fact*: that it commenced about 1758 [sic], in the printing and publication of the judgement of Emmanuel [sic] Swedenborg to condemn, collectively all the doctrines of the *Old*, or Trinitarian church'.[84] Similarly, apocalypse should, for Swedenborgians, have been concluded with the last of Swedenborg's visions. However, there was an underlying antinomian spirit in Swedenborgianism that supplemented, if it did not contradict, the writings of the Messenger. As John Augustus Tulk, one of the signers of the Minute Book of the April 1789 Conference, remarked of one of the groups in which he had participated: 'The distinguishing characteristic of all the known members of the London Universalist Society seems to have been a millennial enthusiasm for the overt and universal manifestation of Swedenborg's New Church'.[85] Reid sensed

[81] See Coleridge, *Poems*, ed. John Beer, 3rd edn. (London: J. M. Dent, 1993), p. 203.
[82] See Robert Southey, *Letters From England by Don Manuel Alvarez Espriella*, 2nd edn. (London: Longman, Hurst, Rees, and Orme, 1808), 3: 113.
[83] See Emanuel Swedenborg, *A Treatise Concerning the Last Judgment and the Destruction of Babylon* (London: R. Hindmarsh, 1788), p. 86, no. 45.
[84] William Hamilton Reid, *The Rise and Dissolution of the Infidel Societies in this Metropolis* (London: J. Hatchard, 1800), p. 53. On Reid, see Iain McCalman, *Radical Underworld: Prophets, Revolutionaries, and Pornographers in London, 1795–1840* (Cambridge: Cambridge University Press, 1988), p. 1; and David Worrall, *Radical Culture: Discourse, Resistance, and Surveillance, 1790–1820* (Hemel Hempstead: Harvester Wheatsheaf, 1992), p. 90.
[85] John Augustus Tulk, *A Letter Containing a Few Plain Observations* (London, 1807), quoted by Raymond H. Deck, Jr., *'Blake and Swedenborg'* (Ph.D. diss., Brandeis University, 1978), p. 319.

this spirit when he equated the Swedenborgians' belief with that of the antinomian group known as the Muggletonians: 'The principal article of this self-called *New* church . . . is just as *Old* as Muggleton and Reeve . . . that the whole godhead is circumscribed in the person of Jesus Christ, still retaining the human form in heaven.'[86] After the founding of the New Jerusalem Church in 1789, the Swedenborgians went through schisms and separations that left the dominant group assertively loyalist, but this did not prevent a conspiracy theorist like the Abbé Barruel from attacking their New Jerusalem as 'a plea for those revolutions which, in order to recall ancient times, are, in the name of God and of his prophet, to overthrow all the altars and thrones existing under the present Jerusalem, that is to say, under the present churches and governments'.[87] To this, one of the leading non-sectarian Swedenborgians, the Revd John Clowes of Manchester, replied in 1799 with a letter 'Containing a full and complete Refutation of the Abbé Barruel's Calumny, by which he would stigmatize Baron Swedenborg as an enemy to social order and good government'.[88] While Clowes may have expressed the view of what was by 1799 the majority, early Swedenborgianism had also attracted millenarian radicals like two Swedes who attended the organizational conference of the New Jerusalem Church in London in April 1789, Augustus Nordenskjöld and Carl Bernhard Wadström. Nordenskjöld, who had endeavoured to produce gold by alchemical means for King Gustav III, and Wadström, who had published his *Observations on the Slave Trade*[89] after a trip to Africa in 1789, were involved in planning a community in Sierra Leone in which black and white people would live as equals.[90] Wadström and Nordenskjöld were among those who were expelled from the New Jerusalem Church in 1790 as a result of what became known as the 'concubinage dispute' (see Chapter 1). Other seekers passed through Swedenborgianism as a phase in their quests, and a brief glance at three of these will convey an idea of the apocalyptic expectation and millennial desire that pervaded the millenarian subculture of the time.

---

[86] Reid, *Rise and Dissolution*, p. 53. On the Muggletonians, founded by Ludowick Muggleton and John Reeve in the mid-seventeenth century, see Thompson, *Witness against the Beast*, pp. 65–105.   [87] Barruel, *Memoirs*, 4: 131–2.

[88] John Clowes, *Letters to a Member of Parliament on the Character and Writings of Baron Swedenborg* (London: H. C. Hodgson, 1822), Letter x.

[89] Carl Bernhard Wadström, *Observations on the Slave Trade* (London, 1789).

[90] See Morton D. Paley, ' "A New Heaven Is Begun": William Blake and Swedenborgianism', *Blake: An Illustrated Quarterly*, 13 (1979): 83–5.

Ralph Maher or Mather, who lived in Bolton, Lancashire, became a Methodist evangelist in the 1770s, and was evidently a charismatic preacher.[91] Early in 1774, John Wesley found Mather 'deep in grace' and wrote to his brother Charles: 'When I talk to Ralph Mather I am amazed and almost discouraged. What have I been doing for seventy years?'[92] However, just a few months later, Wesley was disappointed to find Mather fallen into 'Mysticism and Quakerism'.[93] Mather would not long remain a Methodist, but his seeking was not inclined toward quietism. In 1780 he published a pamphlet in defence of Bolton spinners accused of machine smashing, calling attention to the cycle of poverty that had been caused by the introduction of jennies and other machines some ten years before.[94] By 1785 Mather belonged to a Swedenborgian discussion group in London known as the Theosophical Society. After becoming Swedenborgians, Mather and his associate Joseph Salmon, true to their Methodist background, felt impelled, in the words of the early historian of the New Jerusalem Church, 'to promulgate the heavenly doctrines of the New Jerusalem by preaching and proclaiming them in the streets, highways, and market-places of the most considerable towns of England'.[95] He afterwards emigrated to America and became the first pastor of a New Jerusalem Congregation there, but returned to England in 1800. Mather then visited Paris, presumably during the Peace of Amiens, and participated in a Swedenborgian circle that may have been a remnant of the community known in England as the Prophets of Avignon.[96] He returned to America in 1802 and died in Norfolk, Virginia, in 1803. Two other English seekers

---

[91] See Peter James Lineham, 'The English Swedenborgians 1770–1840: A Study in the Social Dimensions of Religious Sectarianism' (Ph.D. dissertation, University of Sussex, 1978), pp. 130–3.

[92] Letter of 17 Jan. 1774, in *John Wesley's Letters*, ed. John Telford (8 vols., London: Epworth Press, 1931), 6: 67–8.

[93] Wesley, *Journal*, ed. Curnock, 6: 11.

[94] Ralph Mather, *An Impartial Representation of the Case of the Poor Cotton Spinners in Lancashire, &c.* (London, 1780).

[95] Robert Hindmarsh, *Rise and Progress of the New Jerusalem Church* (London: Hodson and Son, 1861), p. 64. Hindmarsh's book must be used with care because of his tendency to ignore whatever is unsuited to his conservative views, but it is nevertheless an invaluable resource. According to Hindmarsh, Salmon, who died in Norwich in 1826, came to regret 'the irregularity and disorder, into which he had been betrayed by the enthusiasm of his companion' (p. 66).

[96] See R. DeCharms, 'A Report on the Trine to the Central Committee and Other Documents for New-Church History', *New Churchman-Extra*, iv–xvi: 76–93; Clarke Garrett, 'Swedenborg and the Mystical Enlightenment in Late Eighteenth-Century England', *Journal of the History of Ideas*, 45 (1984): 67–81.

also became, at least for a time, Swedenborgians and also had contact with the Avignon group. John Wright, a carpenter in Leeds, was told by the Holy Spirit to go to London in 1788. 'I accordingly set off', he writes, '*and as I thought*, to find out a *sect* of people that belong to the *New Jerusalem Church*, to which *Salmon and Mather* belonged, who came to *Leeds* as Preachers, who cried it up for some great and wonderful *light*, such as never appeared before, and of which Baron Swedenburg was the forerunner, as *John* the *Baptist* was of CHRIST.'[97] Wright went to the New Jerusalem church in Eastcheap, but he found it adhered to the old forms of worship, 'although called by the blessed name of *New Jerusalem*, in which the old forms have neither part nor lot'.[98] A converted Jew named Samuel told Wright of William Bryan, a copperplate printer by trade and a man of whom Robert Southey later declared, 'his resemblance to the pictures of our Lord . . . was so striking as truly to astonish', and that he possessed 'natural and unaffected eloquence'.[99] In January 1789 Wright set off with Bryan for Avignon. It was in Avignon that Wright first heard of Richard Brothers, one of whose disciples he was to become. The brethren at Avignon told him 'that the prophecy of *Christopher Love* was true, and that such a person therin described would most certainly arise in *England*'.[100] As for Bryan, he had been born into the Established Church, gone seeking among the Dissenters, and become a Quaker, but this did not satisfy him, and subsequently he and John Wright lived with the Avignon community for seven months. (As they left on 23 January 1789, they must have been in France when the Bastille fell.) After returning to England, Bryan asserted at a meeting held at the Revd Mr Smith's, Fitzroy Street, Tottenham Court Road, on 9 December 1791, that Swedenborg had been divinely taught, but had introduced many of his own fantasies into his published works.[101] He also thought that Wright was mistaken to follow Richard Brothers, but when Bryan went to see Brothers in

---

[97] John Wright, *A Revealed Knowledge of Some Things That Will Speedily be Fulfilled in the World* (London, 1794), p. 3. [98] Ibid., p. 4.

[99] Southey, *Letters from England*, 3: 199.

[100] Wright, *Revealed Knowledge*, p. 23. Christopher Love was a seventeenth-century Presbyterian martyr. Iain McCalman points out that Richard Brothers's follower George Riebeau republished some of Love's prophecies, including *Extracts from the Prophecies Given to Christopher Love* (London, 1794), foretelling the appearance of a prophetic deliverer in 1795. See McCalman, 'New Jerusalems: Prophecy, Dissent and Radical Culture in England, 1786–1830', in *Enlightenment and Religion: Rational Dissent in Eighteenth-Century Britain*, ed. Knut Haakonsen (Cambridge: Cambridge University Press, 1996), pp. 323–4.

[101] See Clarke Garrett, *Respectable Folly: Millenarianism and the French Revolution in France and England* (Baltimore: Johns Hopkins University Press, 1975), p. 110.

December 1794, he remembered a dream in which he was in the New Jerusalem and Brothers was in the temple, bearing the sword of Gideon, and he consequently realized that Richard Brothers was the Elias whose coming Matthew prophesied.[102] Asserting the imminent restoration of the house of Israel to Zion, Bryan writes:

they will have a manifestation in this world, together with all the old prophets and the holy men spoken of in the scriptures, it being the time of the first resurrection, and the commencement of the period mentioned by St John in his Revelation, in which the Lord shall reign with his saints upon the earth, when Paradise shall be again revealed unto man, and evil shall disappear.— The serpent and dragon, being chained down in the abyss, shall have no longer a manifestation in man, but every man shall become a real manifestation of GOD, as he was in Paradise before the fall.[103]

Robert Southey, who relied upon Bryan for the account of the Prophets of Avignon in *Letters from England*, wrote of the Wright and Bryan pamphlets: 'These are two of the most curious Pamphlets in my possession. There is an account of them in Espriella's Letters, where what is said of Bryan is from my personal knowledge of him when he lived near Bristol in the winter of 1794–5. R. S.'[104]

The Avignon group visited by Wright and Bryan, known in France as 'les illuminés d'Avignon',[105] also had other contacts with England, such as Thomas Spence Duché, artist and pupil of Benjamin West, whose father, the Revd Jacob Duché, was host to the early meetings of the Theosophical Society.[106] The founder of the group was Dom Pernety, a Benedictine monk once attached to the abbey of St Germain-des-Prés, and he may have chosen Avignon because it was a centre of Freemasonry. Pernety had read with approval the works of Boehme and Swedenborg, and he translated into French Swedenborg's

---

[102] William Bryan, *A Testimony of the Spirit of Truth Concerning Richard Brothers* (London, 1795), pp. 3, 34.

[103] Ibid., p. 6. Bryan also denounces the Fast Day of 25 Feb. 1795 (p. i), and he warns Bristol that the traffic in slaves is 'innocent blood to be avenged' (p. 6).

[104] MS note in Bodleian copy, on inside flyleaf facing Bryan's title-page. At the time Southey knew him, Bryan was working in a hospital dispensary tending sick soldiers just landed from Ireland.

[105] See Joanny Bricaud, *Les Illuminés d'Avignon: Étude sur Dom Pernety et son groupe* (Paris: Libraire Critique Émile Nourry, 1927); M. L. Danilewicz, 'The King of the New Israel: Thaddeus Grabianka 1740–1807', *Oxford Slavonic Papers*, NS 1 (1968): 49–73; Garrett, *Respectable Folly*, pp. 97–120; M. Meillassoux-Le Cerf, *Dom Pernety et les Illuminés d'Avignon* (Milan: Arché, 1992).

[106] See Albert Frank Gegenheimer, 'Artist in Exile: The Story of Thomas Spence Duché', *Pennsylvania Magazine of History and Biography*, 79 (1955): 3–26.

Heaven and Hell (1782) and *Divine Love and Divine Wisdom* (1786). His chief co-worker, with whom he later fell out, was the Polish Count Grabianka, a pretender to the throne of Poland. Their doctrines appear to have been a combination of Freemasonry, illuminism, occultism, alchemy, Swedenborgianism, and the cult of the Virgin Mary. In 1786 Grabianka visited London, where he mingled with the Swedenborgians in an attempt to recruit them, and in the following year Robert Hindmarsh published a letter received from Grabianka and five others in Avignon which included the ringing millenarian declaration: 'For, my very dear Brethren, the Angel that stands before the Face of the Lamb, is already sent to sound his Trumpet on the Mountains of Babylon, and give notice to the Nations that the God of Heaven will soon come to the Gates of the Earth, to change the Face of the World, and to manifest his Power and Glory.'[107] A decisive break between the London Swedenborgians and the Avignon group was announced in the *New-Jerusalem Magazine* in 1790. Because it promulgated the worship of the Virgin Mary and the separation of the persons of the Trinity according to the Athanasian Creed, 'the Avignon Society may with great propriety be stiled the *Antipodes* of the New Church, erected on the very borders of Babylon'.[108] More important to the group's actual future were developments regarding Avignon itself. In 1791 the Illuminés had been ordered by the Roman Catholic authorities to disperse after a report by the Holy Office, but the effect of the Revolution was to nullify this command by incorporating what had been papal territory. However, with the Jacobin ascendancy in 1793, the police became interested in the group, and its numbers began to dwindle. This process was no doubt accelerated by Pernety's death in 1796, and by 1803 the group had practically disappeared. Robert Southey wrote: 'The Revolution broke out—those who had raised the storm could not direct it: they became its victims—and knavery reaped what dishonesty had sown'.[109]

After returning to England, John Wright and then William Bryan became disciples of Richard Brothers, who styled himself 'Prince of the Hebrews' and 'Nephew of the Almighty', and who attracted a considerable following in the mid-1790s.[110] Had Brothers been merely a

[107] *Copy of a Letter from a Society in France, To the Society for Promoting the Heavenly Doctrine of the New Jerusalem Church in London* (London, 1787), n.p.
[108] Anon., 'Annals of the New Church', *New-Jerusalem Magazine*, 1 (1790): 175.
[109] Southey, *Letters from England*, 3: 221.
[110] See M. D. Paley, 'William Blake, the Prince of the Hebrews, and the Woman Clothed with the Sun', in *William Blake: Essays in Honour of Sir Geoffrey Keynes* (Oxford: Clarendon Press,

would-be Messiah, he might have had no difficulties with the government. His teachings, however, as expressed in two volumes entitled *A Revealed Knowledge of the Prophecies and Times*, however, included strong statements affirming the innocence of the radicals on trial for their lives in the State Trials of 1794, denouncing the war against France as 'many men fighting against the Spirit of God' and declaring that because of British colonial conquest God 'will break the Empire in pieces'.[111] Brothers was arrested on 4 March 1795, charged with 'fond and fantastical prophesies', examined by the Privy Council, and subsequently found insane. William Hamilton Reid sardonically remarked: 'Prophecies, relative to the destruction of almost every kingdom and empire in the world, teemed from the British press, some of them in weekly numbers, till government, perfectly aware of these inflammatory means, prudently transferred the prince of prophets to a madhouse'.[112] Confined to a private lunatic asylum, Brothers continued to write and publish, as did some of his supporters.[113] These included political radicals as well as religious enthusiasts, and some who were both.[114] William Sharp, one of the leading engravers of his time, was an important enough member of the Society for Constitutional Information to be considered for prosecution in the State Trials of 1794, and in 1795 he engraved a portrait of Brothers with the legend 'Fully believing this to be the Man whom GOD has appointed:—I engrave his likeness.

1973), pp. 260–93; J. C. F. Harrison, *The Second Coming: Popular Millenarianism 1780–1850* (New Brunswick, NJ: Rutgers University Press, 1979), pp. 57–85; and John Barrell, 'Imagining the King's Death: The Arrest of Richard Brothers', *History Workshop*, no. 37 (Spring 1994): 1–32.

[111] Richard Brothers, *A Revealed Knowledge of the Prophecies and Times* (2 vols., London, 1794–5), 2: 8, 16.   [112] Reid, *Rise and Dissolution*, p. 2.

[113] One of these, the Sanskrit scholar and MP Nathaniel Brassey Halhed, published in 1795 *A Calculation on the Commencement of the Millennium* that ingeniously manipulated the calendar so as to schedule the millennium later that very year. Before presenting his calculation, Halhed summarizes the Christian tenets concerning the millennium in the middle of the fourth century, including the rebuilding of Jerusalem, the fall of Antichrist, and Christ's descent to reign with his servants for a period during which 'the saints . . . shall enjoy all the delights of a terrestrial paradise' (pp. 5–6). Taking as his point of departure 2 Peter 3: 8, 'that one day is with the Lord as a thousand years, and a thousand years as one day', Halhed interprets the Mosaic account of the Creation as signifying 'six thousand years under the yoke of labour and tribulation' to be followed by 'one thousand years of Christ's Kingdom' (p. 10). There follows the calculation itself, in which, faced with the inconvenient possibility that in the year 1794 eighty-seven years would remain until the end of the sixth day, Halhed postulates a year of 360 days, which enables him to conclude that the millennium would begin on 16 November 1795 at dawn in the latitude of Jerusalem. A more characteristic millenarian attitude, however, was that although the event was imminent, its precise date was unknown.

[114] On the overlap between Painites and followers of Brothers, see McCalman, 'New Jerusalems', 324–5.

WILLIAM SHARP'. Conversing with Thomas Holcroft about Richard Brothers *c*.1799, Sharp declared, according to Holcroft, 'that Egypt, which meant "the tongue of Wisdom", was now subdued. Syria, Palestine, and all these countries are soon to be revolutionized; and those who do not take up arms against their fellow men, are to meet at the Grand Millennium.'[115]

Indeed, it is sometimes difficult to discriminate between the discourses of millenarianism and those of secular radicalism. Thomas Spence, for instance, is usually thought of as an example of the latter, but in the 'Songs' he published after moving from Newcastle to London in 1792, there is a strong millennial strain, as in the following:

A Receipt to Make a Millennium or happy World

To the tune of 'Sally in Our Alley':

Then let us all join Heart in Hand,
  Through Country, Town, and City,
Of Every Age and every Sex,
  Young Men and Maidens pretty;

To have this golden Age's Reign
  On every Hill and Valley,
Then Paradise shall greet our Eyes
  Through every Street and Alley.[116]

Despite the jingly quality of these verses, it's difficult not to think of Blake. Again, upon the publication of *Rights of Man* in the spring of 1791, one secular radical, Thomas Holcroft, wrote jauntily to another, William Godwin, about a third: 'Hey for the New Jerusalem! The millennium! And peace and beatitude be unto the soul of Thomas Paine.'[117] And just as there were numerous points of intersection between religious millenarianism and political dissent, so there were between the language and imagery of the 'lower' aspects of the print culture and that of the 'higher' literary culture to which we now turn.

---

[115] Thomas Holcroft, *The Life of Thomas Holcroft*, ed. E. Colby (2 vols., London: Constable, 1925): 2: 245–6.

[116] Undated broadside, 'second edition', in the British Library. In *The Politics of Language 1791–1819* (Oxford: Clarendon Press, 1984), pp. 98, 103, Olivia Smith comments on the 'millennial cast' of Spence's thinking. See also Mee, *Dangerous Enthusiasm*, pp. 5, 38, 74, 103, 224.

[117] See C. Kegan Paul, *William Godwin: His Friends and Contemporaries* (2 vols., London: Henry King, 1876), 1: 69.

In choosing the poems to be discussed in the following chapters, I have, necessarily, exercised a certain selectivity. For example, Blake's treatments of apocalypse and millennium are so extensive that a truly comprehensive account of them could not be given even in a very long chapter. However, my motive has been not comprehensiveness but the wish to present a focused literary discussion of some important and representative poems. Therefore for Blake I have chosen a group of interrelated works from the years immediately following the French Revolution and, as embodying his later view, *Milton*. For Coleridge I have taken a line of poems written in the 1790s, and although I am aware that some of Coleridge's other works may be interpreted as involving displacements of the apocalyptic and the millennial, I have found more than enough material in works which explicitly address those themes. In the case of Wordsworth my choice was clear, as his greatest long poem involves a series of shifting views of apocalypse and millennium and of the relationship between them. Byron, who alone among these poets made an explicit subject of the failure of millennium to follow apocalypse, is represented by three poems which take this as their theme. Shelley, like Blake, provides a superabundance of material; the poems considered here are the early millennial *Queen Mab*, the attempt in *The Mask of Anarchy* at an apocalyptic/millenarian poem with broad appeal, and the supremely ambitious *Prometheus Unbound* in one of its many aspects. Keats virtually defines the choice for us in his *Hyperion* poems, although some preliminary consideration will show that the apocalyptic is not as far from his concerns elsewhere as is sometimes assumed. Taking the poets in chronological order (with the exception of the Coleridge chapter, in which the poems considered were all written before the completion of the 1805–6 *Prelude*), I begin with Blake, who inaugurates the subject in 1790 with the return of Adam to Paradise.

I

Blake

a new heaven is begun

As a new heaven is begun, and it is now thirty-three years since its advent: the Eternal Hell revives. And lo! Swedenborg is the Angel sitting at the tomb; his writings are the linen clothes folded up. Now is the dominion of Edom, & the return of Adam into Paradise; see Isaiah xxxiv & xxxv Chap:[1]

With this remarkable statement, William Blake introduces the millennium, which in *The Marriage of Heaven and Hell* (and nowhere else in Blake's writings) is coeval with apocalypse. Blake displays his knowledge of millenarian tradition (and assumes his reader's knowledge of it) throughout: the flames of the Eternal Hell, in which the figure pictured at the head of plate 3 lies swathed, will be linked in the text of plate 14 with the apocalyptic destruction of the world at the end of the world-week. 'The ancient tradition that the world will be consumed in fire at the end of six thousand years is true. as I have heard from Hell' (E 39). This is immediately followed by the declaration that Eden will no longer be barred to humanity: 'For the cherub with his flaming sword is hereby commanded to leave his guard at the tree of life, and when he does, the whole creation will be consumed, and appear infinite. and holy whereas it now appears finite & corrupt'. The apocalyptic delivers the millennial in the here-and-now: 'This will come to pass by an improvement of sensual enjoyment.' The millennial announcement of plate 3 is reinforced by allusions to chapters 34 and 35 of Isaiah, in which destruction is immediately followed by the creation of an earthly paradise:

And all the host of heaven shall be dissolved, and the heavens shall be rolled together as a scroll: and all their host shall fall down, as the leaf falleth off from the vine, and as a falling fig from the fig tree. (Isa. 34: 4)

[1] William Blake, *The Marriage of Heaven and Hell*, plate 3, E 34.

The wilderness and the solitary place shall be glad for them; and the desert shall rejoice, and blossom as the rose.   (Isa. 35: 1)

Blake also draws on these chapters in 'The Argument' of *The Marriage* (plate 2), with its account of the temporal (and temporary) displacement of 'the just man' from an earthly paradise of roses and honey by 'the villain', who drives the just man to raging 'in the wilds / Where lions roam'. Framing 'The Argument', two repeated lines seem to promise an imminent apocalyptic event:

> Rintrah roars & shakes his fires in the burdend air;
> Hungry clouds swag on the deep.

Here is the first appearance of the figure who embodies wrath in Blake's mythology, Rintrah—presumably in this context the prophetic wrath of the just man. We would expect the villain, who as 'the sneaking serpent' (2: 17) apes humility, to defend his usurped territory, yet, as we have seen, no Armageddon follows. Instead, plate 3 begins with the confident, sardonic declaration of the narrator.

As has been widely recognized, the narrator dates his reference to the year 1790, a date Blake actually wrote in copy F (Pierpont Morgan Library) over the words 'new heaven' on plate 3.[2] The subtraction of 'thirty-three years' brings us back to 1757, the year in which, according to Emanuel Swedenborg, a Last Judgement took place in the spiritual realm.[3] The facts that Blake himself was born in 1757 and that 33 was the Christological age were not likely to have escaped the author, who had already shown himself capable of ironically mocking his own sense of self-importance in the figure of Quid the Cynic in *An Island in the Moon* (1784). However, the brunt of the irony is reserved for Swedenborg. He is presented as 'the Angel sitting at the tomb', in the sense of the New Testament episode in which the three women who come to the tomb of Jesus encounter 'a young man sitting on the right side, clothed in a long white garment', who tells them: 'Ye seek Jesus of Nazareth, which was crucified: he is risen; he is not here: behold the place where they laid him' (Mark 16: 6). Although in Blake's Gospel source there is nothing negative about the angel (or angels—there are two in Luke and in

---

[2] See William Blake, *The Early Illuminated Books*, ed. Morris Eaves, Robert N. Essick, and Joseph Viscomi (London: The Tate Gallery for the William Blake Trust, 1993), p. 145.

[3] This has been recognized since S. Foster Damon's pioneering work *William Blake: His Philosophy and Symbols* (Boston: Houghton, Mifflin, 1924), p. 316. Damon cites Swedenborg's *Last Judgment*, no. 45: 'This Last Judgement was commenced in the beginning of the year 1757, and was fully accomplished at the end of that year'.

John), Blake has given him the implication of one who lingers by the dead letter after its spiritual essence has escaped. This implication is continued in the meaning given here to the cloth that Joseph of Arimathea purchased for Jesus' cerements: 'his writings are the linen clothes folded up'.

And he [John] stooping down, and looking in, saw the linen clothes lying; yet went he not in. Then cometh Simon Peter following him, and went into the sepulchre, and seeth the linen clothes lie, And the napkin, that was about his head, not lying with the linen clothes, but wrapped together in a place by itself. (John 20: 5–7)

Swedenborg had written voluminously about the doctrines that were imparted to him in his visions, but Blake locates the reality of Christ elsewhere. The shock Blake intended to deliver to contemporary Swedenborgians can only be understood if we remember the extent to which their activities centred on printing, publishing, and distributing the writings of their Messenger. (William Hamilton Reid even called Swedenborgianism 'a sect, which literally originated in a printer's job!'[4]) In particular, Robert Hindmarsh, one of the key figures in British Swedenborgianism in 1790 and for a long time afterwards—he would gain control, in large part, of the movement and also write its history—was a printer by profession; he was rapidly becoming the chief printer of the English translations of Swedenborg's works, each volume of which was preceded by a list of those already produced. To denigrate the value of these activities by representing them as a heap of discarded grave-clothes was an insult calculated to make Swedenborg's followers turn 'almost blue', like the Angel of the Memorable Fancy in plate 23.

At this point it must be asked: why Swedenborg? The answer lies both in Swedenborg's own writings and in those who promoted them. Swedenborg himself was a visionary who brought messages from other worlds, who promulgated the idea of heaven as comprising a human form, and who elaborated a system of correspondences between the exterior and interior worlds. The natural world could be seen, as Charles Baudelaire later put it, as 'forests of symbols';[5] and the correspondences could be used to establish the 'internal sense' of biblical

---

[4] William Hamilton Reid, *The Rise and Dissolution of the Infidel Societies in this Metropolis* (London, 1800), p. 55.
[5] Charles Baudelaire, 'Des forêts de symboles', in 'Correspondances', in *Œuvres Complètes*, ed. Y.-G. Le Dantecrev and Claude Pichoise (Paris: Gallimard, 1961), p. 11.

texts. There were many further points with which Blake could feel and express enthusiastic agreement, as he did in annotating Swedenborg's *The Wisdom of Angels, concerning Divine Love and Divine Wisdom*, probably in 1790, having already read the *Treatise concerning Heaven and Hell*. For example, he found his own budding doctrine of contraries incipient in no. 68:

Man is only a Recipient of life. From this Cause it is, that Man, from his own hereditary Evil, reacts against God, but so far as he believes that all his Life is from God, and every Good of Life from the Action of God, and every Evil of Life from the Reaction of Man. Reaction thus becomes correspondent with action, and Man acts with God as from himself.

Blake bracketed this passage and, choosing to ignore 'from his own hereditary Evil'—so at variance with Blake's own view at this time— wrote: 'Good & Evil are here both Good & the two contraries Married' (E 604). He could also work Swedenborgian conceptions into *Songs of Innocence* like 'The Little Black Boy', where the mother's intuitive knowledge of God in the rising sun reflects Swedenborg's idea of the Most Ancient Church in the interior of Africa, and 'The Little Girl Lost' and 'The Little Girl Found', in which the beasts of prey that surround the sleeping Lyca correspond to her own instinctual life. Also prominent in Swedenborg's writings were statements that his followers could interpret as announcements of imminent apocalypse and millennium.

At the very beginning of his *Heaven and Hell* (no. 1) Swedenborg declared that the existing Christian institutions had become exhausted, applying the words of Matthew 24: 30 that (in the language of the Authorized Version) 'then shall appear the sign of the Son of man in heaven: and . . . they shall see the Son of man coming in the clouds of heaven with power and great glory'. A new church had begun, comprising not external institutions, but the interior beings of those who understood the internal sense of the Word. Nevertheless, Swedenborg is not literally to be considered a millenarian, for the Last Judgement that he affirmed had already taken place. As mentioned in the Introduction, it was some of the members of early Swedenborgian groups who created a sense of apocalyptic expectation and millennial desire. Even the usually prosaic Robert Hindmarsh, self-appointed historian of the New Jerusalem Church, was moved to describe the first General Conference, which he attended along with five dozen or more others, including William and Catherine Blake, in April 1789, in terms very like Blake's 'return of Adam into Paradise': 'The tree of life, whose roots are planted in the gardens and streets of the New Jerusalem, as well as on either bank of its river, spontaneously sprung up before our eyes, luxuriant in foliage, and laden with the sweetest fruits of paradise in endless variety and abundance.'[6] At the General Conference Blake would have met figures such as Ralph Mather,[7] the abolitionists Nordenskjöld and Wadström, and the composer F. H. Barthélemon.[8] There were also Swedenborgians who did not participate, such as Blake's friend the sculptor John Flaxman,[9] with whom Blake shared many interests. It must have seemed to Blake that in subscribing to the new movement by signing a declaration of belief at the end of the conference, he and his wife were becoming part of the germ of a new society.

What happened to alienate Blake from the Swedenborgian movement I have discussed elsewhere[10] and need only be summarized briefly here with a view to its probable impact on *The Marriage*. In 1790 there developed among members of the Great Eastcheap Society a rift that became known as 'the concubinage dispute'. Swedenborg had taught that under certain circumstances—such as disease, insanity, difference of faith, or adultery—a man who received the doctrines could abandon marital intercourse and engage in concubinage. This doctrine (which did not assert any parallel right for a woman) was, it must be stressed, not a prominent one in Swedenborgianism. It was promulgated in Swedenborg's *De Amore*, which was not to be published in English until 1794, when Hindmarsh issued it in a translation by John Clowes as *Conjugial Love*.[11] Nevertheless, concubinage became a

---

[6] Robert Hindmarsh, *Rise and Progress of the New Jerusalem Church in England, America, and Other Parts*, ed. Edward Madely (London: Hudson and Son, 1861), pp. 40–1. On Blake and the Swedenborgians, see my '"A New Heaven Has Begun": William Blake and Swedenborgianism', *Blake: An Illustrated Quarterly*, 13 (1979): 64–90; Jon Mee, *Dangerous Enthusiasm: William Blake and the Culture of Radicalism in the 1790s* (Oxford: Clarendon Press, 1992), pp. 49–55; E. P. Thompson, *Witness against the Beast* (New York: New Press, 1993), pp. 129–51.

[7] Mather was one of the signers of the Circular Letter issued in advance of the conference. See Hindmarsh, *Rise and Progress*, p. 78.

[8] For information concerning Barthélemon's attendance, I thank Marsha Keith Schuchard.

[9] Flaxman was in Italy at the time of the General Conference, but he was deeply interested in Swedenborg's doctrines and briefly participated in New Jerusalem Church activities after his return.   [10] See Paley, '"A New Heaven Is Begun" '.

[11] Not to be confused with an extract from Swedenborg's *Apocalypsis Explicata* published by J. Denew as *A Sketch of the Chaste Delights of Conjugal Love* in 1789. The first fifty-five paragraphs of *De Amore* were published in English in 1790, first in the *New Jerusalem Magazine*, then as a separate volume.

contested issue among the London Swedenborgians. We do not know the immediate occasion, as the entries for the period 4 May 1789 to 11 April 1790 were torn out of the Society's Minute Book,[12] and Hindmarsh fails to mention the episode in his *Rise and Progress*. The later testimony of other observers gives a broad outline of what occurred. Six members were expelled from the New Jerusalem Church for upholding the doctrine—Robert Hindmarsh, Henry Servanté, Charles Bernhard Wadström, Augustus Nordensjköld, George Robinson, and Alexander Wilderspin.[13] It is instructive that the group included both the radical abolitionists Wadström and Nordensjköld and the conservative Hindmarsh, who at the General Conference of 1791 would support a protest 'against all such principles of infidelity and democracy as were then circulating in this country'.[14] It seems likely that such a controversy would have arisen from a practical situation, and it is known that the marriage of one of the expelled members, Alexander Wilderspin, broke up some time afterward, but there are no further details.[15] There could be no evading the fact that the doctrine of concubinage was Swedenborg's; but the majority of the Great Eastcheap Meeting not only could not accept it, but also could not coexist with those who did. Blake's turning against Swedenborg was a result not of his doctrines in this instance, but of what his followers made of them. In one sense one could take Blake's 'Swedenborg' throughout not as a historical figure and author but as the beliefs and attitudes that had accumulated around his name, as in the case of Blake's 'Newton' or his 'Locke'. In this sense 'Swedenborg' could be seen as barring the way to the millennium by blocking the improvement of sensual enjoyment.

Because apocalypse and millennium are presented in *The Marriage* as conterminous, there is little sense of a narrative leading from the one to the other. Yet at times they are presented in contrast, as in the head and tail pieces of the unit comprising plates 21–4. This was, as Joseph

[12] See Thomas Robinson, *Remembrances of a Recorder* (Manchester and Boston, 1864), p. 94.

[13] See Manoah Sibley, *An Address to the Society of the New Church meeting in Friar Street, near Ludgate Hill* (London, 1834), pp. 3–4. In 1791 the expulsion was deplored in a pamphlet by the surgeon Benedict Chastanier, *Emanuel Swedenborg's New-Years Gift to His Readers for MDCCXCI*, but Chastanier gives no further information.

[14] Hindmarsh, *Rise and Progress*, p. 142.

[15] In their biography of Wilderspin's son, the educator (and Swedenborgian) Samuel Wilderspin, Phillip McCann and Francis A. Young suggest this possible connection, pointing out that Mrs Wilderspin was not a Swedenborgian. See *Samuel Wilderspin and the Infant School Movement* (London and Canberra: Croom Helm, 1982), pp. 1–7. Samuel Wilderspin was baptized in the Swedenborgian chapel in Great Eastcheap in April 1791, but by then Robert Hindmarsh, one of the expelled members, was in control of the chapel.

Viscomi persuasively argues, the kernel of the whole book.[16] The unit is framed by two half-page designs, one showing man being resurrected, the other the bestial Nebuchadnezzar. They correspond respectively to millennium and apocalypse, presented in inverted order as if to demonstrate Blake's indifference to temporal sequence here. The naked male figure about to rise is an icon of resurrection that Blake turned to again and again—in *There is No Natural Religion* b (plate 1, where it is Lazarus who is being raised), in *America* (plate 6), and in the great white-line etching *Death's Door*. In copy D (Library of Congress) of *The Marriage* Blake added another element of contrast by adding the pyramids of Egypt as a background. This new Adam finds a counterweight on plate 24 in the grotesque form of Nebuchadnezzar as described in Daniel 4: 33: 'The same hour was the thing fulfilled upon Nebuchadnezzar: and he was driven from men, and did eat grass as oxen, and his body was wet with the dew of heaven, till his hairs were grown like eagles' *feathers*, and his nails like birds' *claws*'. Drawing upon a rich iconographical tradition that extends from Cranach and Dürer to John Hamilton Mortimer,[17] Blake would revisit this subject as he would his resurrected man, re-presenting it in his powerful colour-printed drawings (Butlin nos. 300–4) of 1795 and in *Night Thoughts* water-colour 330. Crowned and bestial, the Nebuchadnezzar of *The Marriage* also foreshadows an image whose apocalyptic meaning is entirely explicit: the seven-headed beast of the 1809 water-colour *The Whore of Babylon* (British Museum).

Rich in historical allusion, *The Marriage* does not attempt a sustained historical narrative, although it does display narrative components that have historical reverberations. In the fourth 'Memorable Fancy' the manifestation of Leviathan is, as has been widely recognized, a vision of the French Revolution[18]—or, rather, two visions, an Angel's and the speaker's. Leviathan is described in mock-sublime terms: 'his

---

[16] Joseph Viscomi, 'The Evolution of *The Marriage of Heaven and Hell*', *Huntington Library Quarterly*, 58 (1997): 281–344; see esp. pp. 289–99.

[17] Kenneth Clark, *The Romantic Rebellion* (New York: Harper & Row, 1973), p. 168, proposes the original source as a German engraving (possibly of a werewolf) attributed to Lucas Cranach. Butlin suggests an iconographical connection between the colour-printed drawing and Dürer's *The Penance of St John Chrysostomus* (see Butlin, 1: 165). Mortimer presented the next moment in the story with *Nebuchadnezzar Recovering his Reason*, etched by Blyth in 1781 (see Geoffrey Grigson, 'Painters of the Abyss', *Architectural Review*, 108 (1950): 218.

[18] The direction of Leviathan 'to the east, distant about three degrees' (E 41) indicates the direction of Paris, as Martin K. Nurmi was the first to point out. See Blake's '*Marriage of Heaven and Hell*': A Critical Study, *Kent State University Bulletin*, Research Series, 3 (Kent, Oh., 1957), p. 51.

forehead was divided into streaks of green & purple like those on a tygers forehead.' Blake's Leviathan is as much an apocalyptic manifestation as Nebuchadnezzar, and he presents both in caricature because (to use Northrop Frye's words from a different context) they are jokes on their own existence. It is likely that this part of the episode parodies Swedenborg's vision of the destruction of Babylon in *A Treatise Concerning the Last Judgement and the Destruction of Babylon*. The relevant passage of Swedenborg concerns the 'Last Judgement [that] commenced in the Year 1757, and was fully accomplished at the end of that same year'. An earthquake is followed by 'an Ebullition from below, which overturned every Thing in the City . . . after the Ebullition there came a strong Wind from the East, which laid bare, shook, and overthrew every Thing from the very Foundations: then all who were in that Quarter were brought forth from every Part and hiding Place, and cast into a Sea of black Water, to the Amount of several Myriads'.[19] Whatever Swedenborg may have intended, it is easy to see how this could have been read in 1790 as a prophecy of revolution. The vision continues:

Afterwards there arose a Smoke from that whole Region, as from a great Fire, and at last a thick dust, which was conveyed by the eastern wind to the sea, and covered it all over. . . . At length there was seen as it were Something black flying over the whole Tract, which had the appearance of a Dragon; a sign that the Whole of that great City, and the Whole of that Tract, was made a Desert . . . because by Dragons are signified the Falses of that Religion, and by the Place of their abode is signified a Desert.

Blake's terrified Angel retreats, but his speaker remains steadfast and finds himself in a tiny pattern of the millennial world, 'sitting on a pleasant bank beside a river by moon light hearing a harper who sung to his harp'. Apocalypse and millennium turn out to be the same, only differently perceived according to the spiritual condition of the beholder.

The Marriage, as Blake published it, concludes with an epic in miniature modelled after the Song of Deborah of Judges 5. 'A Song of Liberty'[20] celebrates the defeat of a tyrant, a 'jealous king' who prefigures Albion's Angel in *America*, just as 'the new born terror' who opposes him prefigures Orc. As has been widely recognized, the actors in this

[19] Swedenborg, *Treatise Concerning the Last Judgment and the Destruction of Babylon* (London: R. Hindmarsh, 1788), no. 45, pp. 86–7, 129–30. See Joseph Viscomi, 'Lessons of Swedenborg: or the Origin of Blake's *Marriage of Heaven and Hell*', in *Lessons of Romanticism*, ed. Robert Gleckner and Thomas Pfau (Durham, NC: Duke University Press, 1998), p. 206 n. 15.

[20] See Viscomi, 'Evolution of *The Marriage of Heaven and Hell*', for the argument that this too was originally intended as a separate pamphlet.

scenario are those of Revelation 12—mother, divine child, and threatening monster—with the establishment of a millennial kingdom as the outcome.[21] This separates, for the first time in *The Marriage*, the components of apocalypse and millennium into a story with a beginning, a middle, and an end. It indicates the direction in which Blake would go during the next few years, in what Detlef Dörrbecker has aptly termed the 'Continental Prophecies'.[22] First, however, Blake would attempt to present apocalypse in history in a different form—a narrative poem without designs, printed in letterpress.

this great starry harvest of six thousand years

As is well known, *The French Revolution* exists only in a single copy, printed for Joseph Johnson in 1791. The title-page announces it a 'A POEM, / IN SEVEN BOOKS', priced at one shilling, but although it is announced that 'The remaining Books of this Poem are finished, and will be published in their Order' (E 286), only the first is known to have been printed. Even Book the First is a set of proofs and not a published copy,[23] so it is doubtful whether any part of Blake's *French Revolution* ever reached the public. Various reasons have been suggested for this, including pusillanimity on Johnson's part or on Blake's,[24] though both must have known that the content of the poem was hardly actionable. Whatever the reason for its non-publication, the fact that Blake kept the proofs throughout his life before giving them to John Linnell should tell us something about the value he placed on this work.[25] The reason for its non-completion may emerge from a discussion of the poem itself.

Before going further, something must be said about another book. *The French Revolution* and the succeeding *Continental Prophecies* are as much replies to Edmund Burke's *Reflections on the Revolution in France* (1790) as are Mary Wollstonecraft's *Vindication of the Rights of Men* or

[21] See, e.g., Lawrence Lipking, *The Life of the Poet: Beginning and Ending Poetic Careers* (Chicago and London: University of Chicago Press, 1981), p. 45.

[22] William Blake, *The Continental Prophecies*, ed. Detlef W. Dörrbecker (London: William Blake Trust / Tate Gallery, 1995). References to this edition will be abbreviated in the text as *Continental Prophecies* followed by page number(s).

[23] The reasons for this conclusion, including defective register, uneven inking, and misprints, are presented in *The Poetical Works of William Blake*, ed. John Sampson (London: Oxford University Press, 1925), pp. xxxi–xxxii, li.

[24] See David V. Erdman, *Blake: Prophet against Empire: A Poet's Interpretation of the History of his own Times*, rev. edn. (Princeton: Princeton University Press, 1969), p. 152 n. 2.

[25] See G. E. Bentley, Jr., *Blake Records Supplement* (Oxford: Clarendon Press, 1988), p. 85.

Paine's *Rights of Man*. One commentator goes so far as to call *The French Revolution* 'a poetic dialogue in which Blake challenges the underlying assumptions of Burke's counterrevolutionary text'.[26] This is especially true with respect to their respective presentations of the apocalyptic and the millennial. As is well known, Burke's *Reflections* had its origin as a letter to a young French legislator but evolved in a very different direction as a result of Burke's furious reaction to Richard Price's *Discourse on the Love of Our Country*, delivered as a sermon in the Presbyterian meeting-house of the Old Jewry on 4 November 1789. Price's audience was the London Revolution Society, a body that met annually on the birth date of William III to commemorate the 'Glorious Revolution' of 1688.[27] In his sermon, Price viewed events in France as leading to a millennium in which the nations of the earth 'would beat (as Isaiah prophesies) *Their swords into plowshares, and their spears into pruning-hooks*'.[28] Like many other early supporters, Price viewed France's Revolution as parallel to England's. One of Burke's tactics is to try to sever that connection and instead to link recent events in France with the previous English Revolution, that of 1649–50 and its aftermath, connecting Price and his audience with the regicides of that era. Among the main points of his attack are the interrelated ideas of prophecy, oracles, and the millennium. Price is made out to be a false prophet who misleads his listeners with the aid of intoxicants.[29] The Society dined after the sermon at the London Tavern, so Burke presents the audience as 'reeking from the effects of the sermon' (p. 93).[30] Price's toast expressing the hope that Parliament would become a National Assembly is later troped to the apocalyptic image of the Whore of Babylon: 'Those amongst us who have wished to pledge the societies of Paris in the cup of their abominations have been disappointed' (p. 204; cf. Rev. 17: 4). In the tavern 'the same Dr Price, in whom the fumes of his oracular tripod were not entirely evaporated, moved and carried the resolution, or address of congratulation, transmitted by Lord Stanhope to the National Assembly

---

[26] See William Richey, '*The French Revolution*: Blake's Epic Dialogue with Edmund Burke', *ELH* 59 (1992): 817–37.

[27] See Albert Goodwin, *The Friends of Liberty: The English Democratic Movement in the Age of the French Revolution* (Cambridge, Mass.: Harvard University Press, 1979), pp. 85–7, 106–10.

[28] Richard Price, *A Discourse on the Love of Our Country* (London, 1789), p. 30.

[29] See J. T. Boulton, *The Language of Politics in the Age of Wilkes and Burke* (London: Routledge and Kegan Paul, 1963), pp. 116–17.

[30] Edmund Burke, *Reflections on the Revolution in France*, ed. Conor Cruise O'Brien (Harmondsworth: Penguin, 1984), p. 93. Subsequent references to this edition are by page number in parentheses in the text.

of France' (p. 159). This false prophet is the minion of unnamed intriguers, who 'set him up as a sort of oracle; because, with the best intentions in the world, he naturally *philippizes*, and chaunts his prophetic song in exact unison with their designs' (pp. 93–4).[31] In contrast, the acts of the Glorious Revolution of 1688 and its aftermath were 'unerring, unambiguous oracles' (p. 101) and Sir Edward Coke, 'that great oracle of our law' (p. 117). Furthermore, this idea of false prophecy is inexorably linked with millennial promise: 'I allow this prophet [Price] to break forth into hymns of joy and thanksgiving on an event which appears like the precursor of the Millennium, and the projected fifth monarchy, in the destruction of all church establishments' (p. 166).

Burke's strategy is to yoke Price and other supporters of the French Revolution with the millenarian hopes and civil conflicts of the mid-seventeenth century, with references to 'our solemn league and covenant' (p. 94), 'noble *Seekers*' (p. 95), and 'new *Mess-Johns*' (p. 96), whom he imagines preaching to regiments of soldiers.[32] A special place in this part of Burke's discourse is given to the Independent minister Hugh Peters, chaplain of the Parliamentary army, who was executed in 1660 on a charge of concerting the King's death. Burke wants to link Price with Peters as another would-be regicide preacher. 'That sermon is in a strain which I believe has not been heard in this kingdom . . . since the year 1648, when a predecessor of Dr. Price, the Reverend Hugh Peters, made the vault of the king's own chapel at St. James's ring with the honour and privilege of the Saints, who with the "high praises of God in their mouths, and a *two*-edged sword in their hands, were to execute judgement on the heathen, and punishments upon the *people*; to bind their *kings* with chains and their *nobles* with fetters of *iron*" ' (p. 94).[33] Price is further identified with Peters in what has become known as the *nunc dimittis* passage of the *Reflections* (pp. 157–9), beginning with a quotation from Price's *Discourse* in which the Song of Simeon, the words of the Jew who took the infant Jesus in his arms and praised God, is quoted: '*Lord, now lettest thy servant depart in peace, for mine eyes have seen thy salvation*' (Luke 2: 29–30; slightly different in the AV). The occasion for this, in Price's words, is the spectacle of 'Their King led in triumph, and

---

[31] O'Brien, p. 379 n.7, observes that Demosthenes said that the Delphic Oracle *philippized*—serving the political interests of Philip of Macedon.

[32] Ibid., p. 380 n. 12, identifies a *Mess-John* as a familiar name for a Presbyterian minister.

[33] Ibid., p. 94. Burke footnotes 'Psalm cxlix' (verses 6–8, slightly different in AV).

an arbitrary monarch surrendering himself to his subjects', which Burke seizes on as alluding to the events of 6 October 1789, when the king and queen were forced by the Paris mob to move from Versailles to virtual imprisonment in the Tuileries.[34] He again draws a parallel with Hugh Peters, calling him Price's 'precursor' (p. 158), who quoted the same text on the day Charles I was brought to London for trial: 'This sally of the preacher of the Old Jewry ... differs only in place and time, but agrees perfectly with the spirit and letter of the rapture of 1648' (p. 158). Ironizing the terms 'precursor' (which, as the *OED* notes, is especially 'applied to John the Baptist') and 'rapture' in the sense of religious ecstasy, Burke makes Price out to be a sectarian fanatic and would-be regicide, and intimates for him the fate of his predecessor.

In alluding to Price as 'the preacher of the Old Jewry', Burke seems at first to identify his target in a neutral sense. The Old Jewry had, of course, not been a Jewish quarter since the expulsion of the Jews from England some five centuries earlier, and at first Burke's references to the Old Jewry appear merely locative. However, these develop into anti-Semitic insinuations pointing the way to an attack upon another figure associated with millenarianism and pro-French politics. Burke goes from 'the sermons of Old Jewry' (p. 117) to 'Jew brokers contending with each other' (over profits to be made from issuing paper money, p. 136) to 'the Jews in Change Alley [who] have not yet dared to hint their hopes on a mortgage on the revenues belonging to the see of Canterbury' (p. 204). These slurs are linked to an attack upon Lord George Gordon, a figure of whom Blake had some previous knowledge, for Blake had witnessed the Gordon No-Popery riots of 1780. Blake's early biographer Alexander Gilchrist portrayed him as having been swept away by 'a great surging mob' to witness the burning of Newgate Prison, but later scholars have been more sceptical about whether the 23-year-old Blake was entirely uninterested in the liberation of the prisoners.[35] In 1790 Gordon, who had converted to Judaism in 1788, was himself confined to Newgate (where he would die in 1793) for traducing Queen Marie Antoinette. 'We have rebuilt Newgate', Burke

---

[34] In a note to the 4th edn. of his *Discourse*, published on 24 Nov. 1790, Price asserted that his statement referred to the fall of the Bastille and the subsequent return of the King to Paris (July 14 and 17, 1789). See D. O. Thomas, *The Honest Mind: The Thought and Work of Richard Price* (Oxford: Clarendon Press, 1977), p. 339.

[35] See Alexander Gilchrist, *Life of William Blake*, ed. Ruthven Todd, rev. edn. (London: J. M. Dent, 1945), p. 30; Erdman, *Blake: Prophet against Empire*, p. 9. Gilchrist's biography, first published in 1863, was in its account of the riots much influenced by Dickens's *Barnaby Rudge*.

boasted, 'and tenanted the mansion' (p. 179).[36] Gordon's friend Robert Watson, in a sympathetic memoir, stressed Gordon's Republican, pro-French Revolutionary sympathies, his hatred of slavery, and his millenarian tendencies, suggesting that Gordon may have hoped to realize a prophecy he had often quoted, that the Lord would lead the seed of Israel 'out of the *North Country*' back to their fathers' land.[37] Watson's description of the reaction in Newgate to the news of the fall of the Bastille is almost worthy of Beethoven's *Fidelio*: 'The prisoners were freed from their shackles, and the day of human redemption seemed to be at hand. . . . Even the solitary tenants in Newgate seemed to forget their misfortunes, and anticipated in imagination the approaching millennium.'[38] Evidently this millenarianism had links with contemporary radicalism: the shoemaker Thomas Hardy, one of the founders of the London Corresponding Society to be prosecuted in the State Trials of 1794, has been described as 'a disciple of Lord George Gordon';[39] and Daniel Isaac Eaton was co-publisher of Watson's memoir. Burke therefore has a political motive when he ironically suggests that the French could ransom Gordon 'to please your new Hebrew brethren' (pp. 179–80). 'He may then be enabled to purchase, with the hoards of the synagogue, and a very small poundage, on the long compound interest of the thirty pieces of silver the lands which are lately discovered to have been usurped by the Gallican church'. This Judas could put to work Price's well-known research on the economics of life insurance and annuities: 'Dr. Price has shewn us what miracles compound interest will perform in 1790 years' (p. 180). As ever, millennium is to Burke a product of the wish-fulfilment fantasies of religious fanatics and political revolutionaries, and the French Revolution a false apocalypse.

In producing his own interpretation of the French Revolution, from the meeting of the Estates in May 1789 through the removal of the King's troops from Versailles in mid-July,[40] Blake did not try to provide a verse narrative of the course of events. Rather, influenced in some

[36] This vaunt seems an odd lapse on Burke's part. It left him open to Paine's riposte: 'It is difficult not to believe that Mr. Burke is sorry, extremely sorry, that arbitrary power, the power of the Pope, and the Bastille, are pulled down' (Thomas Paine, *Rights of Man*, ed. Eric Foner (Harmondsworth: Penguin, 1985), p. 51).

[37] Robert Watson, M.D., *The Life of Lord George Gordon: with a Philosophical Review of his Political Conduct* (London, 1795), p. 79.   [38] Ibid., p. 91.

[39] Conor Cruise O'Brien, *The Great Melody: A Thematic Biography and Commented Anthology of Edmund Burke* (Chicago: University of Chicago Press, 1992), p. 396.

[40] On dates and events, see Erdman, *Blake: Prophet Against Empire*, pp. 162–4.

ways by the treatment of the American Revolution in the American poet Joel Barlow's *Vision of Columbus* (1787), Blake composed an account in which chronicle is subordinate to poetic vision.[41] Blake dealt with history freely, like Shakespeare in his history plays or Sergei Eisenstein in his epic films, compressing time, rearranging locations, and inventing characters to suit his poetic and ideological purposes. (Even when characters in *The French Revolution* had historical existence, they are entirely fictitious constructions.) Narrative is subordinated to a succession of speeches, something that would become characteristic of Blake's longer poems. As one would expect, the apocalyptic and the millennial figure prominently in Blake's treatment of the French Revolution, but these are no longer concurrent as they were in *The Marriage*. Adam had not yet returned to Paradise, though, with some of his contemporaries, Blake lived in anticipation of the event. He begins by demonstrating the necessity of apocalypse.

What dominates the first pages of the poem is a description of the structure and occupants of an imaginary Bastille (lines 18–53). Blake follows the popular mythology of the French prison, but also has in mind England and something like Burke's 'prisons almost as strong as the Bastille, for those who dare to libel the queens of France'. Blake's prison comprises seven towers, perhaps because of the frequency of septenaries in the Book of Revelation, and each is described in terms combining Graveyard poetry (ever an interest of Blake's) and what Steven Bidlake aptly identifies as 'Gothic sublimity'.[42] These seven towers and their prisoners provide the microcosm of a world crying out to be delivered. First, 'In the den nam'd Horror' is a Blake-surrogate 'Chain'd hand and foot', a man whose crime was 'a writing prophetic'—perhaps the very poem that we are reading. In the second, a version of a well-known legendary figure is horribly 'Pinion'd down to the stone floor' of the tower named Darkness: 'a mask of iron on his face hid the lineaments / Of ancient Kings'. Here Blake has been shown to reflect the popular belief that the skeleton of the Man in the Iron Mask had been discovered in the Bastille shortly after its fall, although Blake depicts his character as still alive.[43] The third tower,

[41] On the relationship between Blake's *America* and Barlow's work, see David. V. Erdman, 'William Blake's Debt to Joel Barlow', *American Literature*, 26 (1954): 94–8.

[42] Steven Bidlake, 'Blake, the Sacred, and the French Revolution: 18th-Century Ideology and the Problem of Violence', *European Romantic Review*, 3 (1992): 9.

[43] See David Chandler, 'Blake's Man in the Iron Mask', *Notes and Queries*, NS 44 (1997): 321–2. Chandler points out that two engravings of the subject were published soon

Bloody, holds the chained skeleton of a prisoner of conscience who 'refus'd to sign papers of abhorrence'. In 'the den nam'd Religion' lies a bound 'loathsome sick woman' who is a forerunner of Puccini's Tosca: 'She refus'd to be whore to the Minister, and with a knife smote him'. The tower named Order holds a figure well known in his time although non-existent: 'an old man, whose white beard cover'd the stone floor like weeds / On margin of the sea'. He is Blake's version of the Comte de Lorges, a folk hero described as 'an old man whose beard descended to his waist, made venerable by his sufferings and the length of his captivity'.[44] Blake's contribution to the myth is to make the Count's crime something analogous to the sermons of Price and Priestley: 'he, by conscience urg'd, in the city of Paris rais'd a pulpit, / And taught wonders to darken'd souls'. Next, a Samson-like figure, a strong man blinded and chained to the wall, provides an exemplary tale: 'He was friend to the favourite'. Last, in the Tower of God, is a man who was confined for a letter of advice to the King and who has gone insane pining for liberty, 'with chains loose, which he dragg'd up and down'. The prominence of chains in these descriptions, though to be expected in a treatment of the subject, inescapably bears associations with the first sentence of the first chapter of the most famous single treatise of the eighteenth century: 'Man is born free, and everywhere he is in chains',[45] linking Blake with other Romantic poets who use the imagery of chains in a similarly charged way. At the same time, the emphasis on death, decay, and charnel-house imagery prepares us for an apocalypse to be followed by a resurrection of the dead. This is the burden of the immediately following vision of the counsellors of ancient kings, which derives from what happens in Revelation after the opening of the sixth seal:

> Crying: Hide from the living! Our b[a]nds and our prisoners shout
>   in the open field,
> Hide in the nether earth! Hide in the bones! Sit obscured in the
>   hollow scull.

afterwards, and that in London a play about the Man in the Iron Mask, *The Island of St. Marguerite* by John St John, was produced in Nov. 1789.

[44] See David Bindman, *The Shadow of the Guillotine: Britain and the French Revolution* (London: British Museum Publications, 1989), pp. 39–41. Bindman, who suggests this connection, points out that the Comte de Lorges is identifiable in James Gillray's engraving after James Northcote, *Le Triomphe de la Liberté en l'élargissement de la Bastille*, dated 12 July 1790.

[45] J.-J. Rousseau, *The Social Contract*, trans. Gerard Hopkins, in *Social Contract*, ed. Sir Ernest Barker (New York: Oxford University Press, 1962), p. 169.

Our flesh is corrupted, and we [wear] away. We are not numbered
    among the living. Let us hide
In stones, among roots of trees. The prisoners have burst their dens,
Let us hide; let us hide in the dust; and plague and wrath and
    tempest shall cease.

(74–8)

In Revelation 6, after the stars of heaven have fallen to earth, 'the kings
of the earth, and the great men, and the rich men, and the chief captains, and the mighty men, and every bondman, and every free man,
hid themselves in the dens and in the rocks of the mountains; And said
to the mountains and rocks, Fall on us, and hide us from the face of him
that sitteth on the throne, and from the wrath of the Lamb' (15–16).[46]
Early in *The French Revolution* apocalypse appears imminent.

The apocalyptic is further represented by the fictitious Duke of
Burgundy, whom Blake has created for this purpose because of his
association with grapes and wine: 'red as wines / From his mountains,
an odor of war, like a ripe vineyard, rose from his garments' (83–4).
Here is an early appearance of imagery that would in Blake's later
works become associated with the winepress of the wrath of God in
Revelation 14: 19 and 19: 15. He also bears with him imagery of the
associated theme of the apocalyptic harvest that will occupy much of
the last Night of *Vala* and the end of *Milton* as well, while the babes in his
burning robe make him, as Northrop Frye aptly points out, 'a ghastly
parody of the Sistine Madonna':

> Cloth'd in flames of crimson, as a ripe vineyard stretches over
>   sheaves of corn,
> The fierce Duke hung over the council; around him croud,
>   weeping in his burning robe,
> A bright cloud of infant souls; his words fall like purple autumn
>   on the sheaves.

(86–8)[47]

---

[46] This allusion is noted by W. S. Stevenson in his Longman Annotated English Poets
edition, *Blake: The Complete Poems*, 2nd edn. (London and New York: Longman, 1989), p. 130 n.
Some other allusions to Revelation in the poem are discussed by William F. Halloran, '*The
French Revolution*: Revelation's New Form', in *Blake's Visionary Forms Dramatic*, ed. David V.
Erdman and John E. Grant (Princeton: Princeton University Press, 1970), pp. 30–56. See also
David G. Halliburton, 'Blake's *French Revolution*: The *Figura* and Yesterday's News', *Studies in
Romanticism*, 5 (1966): 158–68.

[47] See Northrop Frye, *Fearful Symmetry: A Study of William Blake* (Princeton: Princeton University Press, 1947), p. 203.

Burgundy's rhetoric matches Burke's in its extensive use of rhetorical questions:

> Shall this marble built heaven become a clay cottage, this earth an oak
>   stool, and these mowers
> From the Atlantic mountains, mow down all this great starry harvest of six
>   thousand years?
> And shall Necker, the hind of Geneva, stretch out his crook'd sickle o'er
>   fertile France,
> Till our purple and crimson is faded to russet, and the kingdoms of earth
>   bound in sheaves,
> And the ancient forests of chivalry hewn, and the joys of the combat burnt
>   for fuel;
> Till the power and dominion is rent from the pole, sword and scepter from
>   sun and moon,
> The law and gospel from fire and air, and eternal reason and science
> From the deep and the solid, and man lay his faded head down on the rock
> Of eternity, where the eternal lion and eagle remain to devour?
>
> (89–97)

Is our monarchy to be annihilated [Burke wrote] with all the laws, all the tribunals, and all the antient corporations of the kingdom? Is every land-mark of the country to be done away with in favour of a geometrical and arithmetical constitution? Is the house of lords to be voted useless? Is episcopacy to be abolished? Are the church lands to be sold to Jews and jobbers; or given to bribe new-invented municipal republics into a participation in sacrilege? Are all the taxes to be voted grievances, and the revenue reduced to a patriotic contribution, or patriotic presents? Are silver shoe-buckles to be substituted in place of the land tax and the malt tax, for the support of the naval strength of this kingdom? Are all orders, ranks, and distinctions to be confounded, that out of universal anarchy, joined to national bankruptcy, three or four thousand democracies should be formed into eighty-three, and that they may all, by some sort of unknown attractive power, be organized into one?

(Reflections, p. 144)

Key words like 'ancient' and 'chivalry' in Burgundy's speech reinforce Burgundy's connection with Burke. 'The ancient forests of chivalry hewn' (93) and 'the ancient forests of Europe' (101) contain two of the fourteen instances of 'ancient' in the poem—a considerable number for a work of 306 lines. 'Chivalry' of course recalls the celebrated 'the age of chivalry is gone' passage on Marie Antoinette in the *Reflections*:

I thought ten thousand swords must have leaped from their scabbards to avenge even a look that threatened her with insult.—But the age of chivalry is gone.—That of sophisters, oeconomists, and calculators, has succeeded; and the glory of Europe is extinguished for ever.   (p. 170)

Two sentences later, Burke declares that the system of values that he is praising 'had its origin in the antient chivalry' (p. 170). *Ancient*, charged with positive meaning, is also a keyword elsewhere in the *Reflections*. 'The Revolution [of 1688–9] was made to preserve our *antient* laws and liberties, and that *antient* constitution of government which is our only security for law and liberty' (p. 117). These ancient liberties preserved by the Glorious Revolution contrast with the modern liberties invented by the French. All the great men of law from Coke to Blackstone 'endeavor to prove, that the antient charter, the Magna Carta of King John' and another granted by Henry I 'were nothing more than a re-affirmation of the still more ancient standing law of the kingdom' (p. 118). As Blake's 'London' demonstrates, Blake saw charters much as did Thomas Paine, who wrote that 'Every chartered town is an aristocratical monopoly in itself, and the qualification of electors proceeds out of these chartered monopolies'.[48] Just a few paragraphs later, Paine says: 'Conquest and tyranny transplanted themselves with William the Conqueror from Normandy into England, and the country is yet disfigured with the marks'; and surely these are related to the 'Marks of weakness, marks of woe' that Blake discerned in every face he met in 'each charter'd street' of London.[49] One can only imagine Blake as cheering the explosive metaphor that Burke applied to the followers of Price and Priestley: 'They have wrought under-ground a mine that will blow up at one grand explosion all examples of antiquity, all precedents, charters, and acts of parliament' (p. 148). In *The French Revolution* Blake's use of 'ancient' and related words has, in opposition to Burke's, a negative resonance, as in 'with slime / Of ancient horrors cover'd' (41), 'terrors of ancient Kings' (59), and 'blood ran down the ancient pillars' (246). The one apparent exception is lines 7–8: 'the ancient dawn calls us / To awake from slumbers of five thousand years'. However, the speaker here is 'the kingly mourner', and his 'five thousand years' applies not to the world-week of history ('six thousand years', as in line 90), but to the mythical extent of the reign of kings, for the only other instance of that number in all Blake's works is the beginning of the King's speech a little later on: 'The nerves of five thousand years

[48] Paine, *Rights of Man*, p. 75. On this subject, see E. P. Thompson, 'London', in *Interpreting Blake*, ed. Michael Phillips (Cambridge: Cambridge University Press, 1978), pp. 5–31.
[49] Paine, *Rights of Man*, p. 75; 'London', E 26–7.

tremble' (70). 'The ancient dawn' is not the millennial dawn but a royal illusion that apocalypse must burn away.

Burgundy's speech continues with imagery glorifying war in terms that recall another work of Burke's, one that Blake asserted that he read 'with Contempt and Abhorrence'[50] when very young: *A Philosophical Enquiry into the Origin of Our Ideas of the Sublime and Beautiful*:

> Thy Nobles have gather'd thy starry hosts round this
>   rebellious city,
> To rouze up the ancient forests of Europe, with clarions of cloud
>   breathing war;
> To hear the horse neigh to the drum and trumpet, and the trumpet
>   and war shout reply;
> Stretch the hand that beckons the eagles of heaven; they cry
>   over Paris, and wait
> Till Fayette point his finger to Versailles; the eagles of heaven
>   must have their prey.

(100–4)

The Burkean sublime, predicated upon identification with power, finds one of its examples in a passage from Job 39. 'The horse in the light of a useful beast', writes Burke, '. . . has nothing of the sublime; but is it thus that we are affected with him, *whose neck is cloathed with thunder, the glory of whose nostrils is terrible, who swalloweth the ground with fierceness and rage, neither believeth that it is the sound of the trumpet?* In this description the useful character of the horse entirely disappears, and the terrible and the sublime blaze out together'.[51] Blake characteristically dismisses such physical power as a source of the sublime, and sets against it a different, human-centred sublime based upon his artistic training, the sublime of Winckelmann, of the Raphael of the Cartoons and the Stanze, and the precepts and examples of international neo-classicism.

With its imagery of wine and harvest, Burgundy's speech is a chief source of the apocalyptic in *The French Revolution*. The millennial is present at several other points, beginning with 'the loud voice of France calls to the morning, the morning prophecies to its clouds' (15), which has been compared to the 'great voice out of heaven' that announces the advent of the New Jerusalem in Revelation 21: 3.[52] The millennial

[50] Annotations to *The Works of Sir Joshua Reynolds*, E 660.
[51] Edmund Burke, *A Philosophical Enquiry into the origin of our Ideas of the Sublime and Beautiful*, ed. J. T. Boulton (Notre Dame, Ind.: University of Notre Dame Press, 1968), pp. 65–6. Boulton notes that the passage is misquoted from Job 39: 19–24.
[52] See Erdman, *Blake: Prophet Against Empire*, p. 165.

'dawn of our peaceful morning' is awaited in line 216, and near the end of Book the First there occurs a seeming Last Judgement and resurrection:

> And the bottoms of the world were open'd, and the graves of arch-angels unseal'd;
> The enormous dead, lift up their pale fires and look over the rocky cliffs.

> (301–2)

Yet who these 'enormous dead' may be is uncertain; they sound more like the pre-Adamites of William Beckford's *Vathek* than anything either Scriptural or historical. Whatever Blake may have envisaged for the succeeding six books, the end of Book the First is not a millennium, though it bears an uneasy relation to the millennial. The apocalyptic and millennial features of the poem, no longer united, as in *The Marriage of Heaven and Hell*, have only a loose relationship to each other. Perhaps it was Blake's intention to carry through the events of the Revolution to a point where a regained Paradise would be achieved. If so, it may have been the sheer recalcitrance of history that explains the lack of any serial advancement from the apocalyptic to the millennial in *The French Revolution* as we have it—as well as Blake's apparent decision not to continue the poem.

The morning comes, the night decays

In his next historical work, Blake moved even further from the confines of historical narrative. The American Revolution had engaged his imagination from its beginning, as he wrote in the verse account of 'my lot in the Heavens' already cited from a letter to John Flaxman:

> . . . terrors appeard in the Heavens above
> And in Hell beneath & a mighty & awful change threatend the Earth
> The American War began   All its dark horrors passed before my face
> Across the Atlantic to France.

> (E 707–8)

Writing retrospectively about it in 1793, Blake could project the American Revolution as opening with an apocalyptic war and as promising a millennial society, without incurring the risk of unknown vagaries. However, knowing how things had come out incurred, as we shall see, its own liabilities.

At the beginning of the main part of *America*, subtitled 'A Prophecy', a group of 'warlike men' rise to confront the power of 'Albions fiery Prince' (3: 1–5), represented as the great red dragon of Revelation 12: 2–9, 'a dragon form clashing his scales' (15). The human antagonists in this apocalyptic encounter, seven in number, are divided between three famous as soldiers, three as civilians, and one as both. Washington was of course inevitable, as was Franklin. Gates had commanded the victorious Continental troops at Saratoga, one of the very few American victories before the stark winter of 1776–7 at Valley Forge ('All its dark horrors passed before my face',) and Greene was later in charge of preventing George III from keeping the half loaf of the southern colonies. Hancock had famously signed the Declaration of Independence in letters large enough for the King to read without his spectacles. Warren, by profession a doctor, was killed at Bunker Hill. He was eulogized in Barlow's *Vision of Columbus* as 'Dearest of chiefs', and was portrayed in John Trumbull's *Death of General Warren*, painted in London in 1785–6, as a dying Christ being bayoneted by an English soldier.[53] (In contrast to these, no historical figures appear on the British side, adding to its spectral quality.) When in 14.2 Allen and Lee replace Greene and Hancock, the balance is kept, assuming that Lee is Richard Henry Lee (1732–94) of Virginia,[54] who moved the Declaration of Independence with the stirring resolution 'That these United Colonies are, and of right ought to be, free and independent States'.[55] His military counterpart Ethan Allen was the general who brought cannon across the back roads of Vermont and western Massachusetts to Washington on Cambridge Common and who captured Fort Ticonderoga. In two other contexts the seven are distilled to three: 'Washington / And Paine and Warren with their foreheads reard toward the east' (9: 10–11; see also

[53] Joel Barlow, *The Vision of Columbus*, in *The Works of Joel Barlow*, with an introduction by William K. Bottorff and Arthur L. Ford (2 vols., Gainesville, Fla.: Scholars' Facsimiles and Reprints, 1970), 2: 267. Dörrbecker observes that Warren wrote for the *Boston Gazette* under the name 'True Patriot' (*Continental Prophecies*, p. 129). Benjamin West called Trumbull's *Death of Warren* 'the best picture of a modern battle that has been painted': Irma B. Jaffe, *John Trumbull: Patriot-Artist of the American Revolution* (Boston: New York Graphic Art Society, 1975), pp. 84–90. See also Ronald Paulson, 'John Trumbull and the Representation of the American Revolution', *Studies in Romanticism*, 21 (1982): 341–56.

[54] Lee was author of an *Address to the Inhabitants of Great Britain*, in which he warned the British: 'Your liberty will be the price of your victory'. (The less likely alternative would be the cavalry commander Henry Lee (1756–1818), known as 'Lighthorse Harry' Lee.) See Lillian B. Miller *et al.*, *'The Dye Is Now Cast': The Road to American Independence 1774–1776* (Washington: Smithsonian University Press for the National Portrait Gallery, 1975), pp. 256–8; and Dörrbecker, in Blake, *Continental Prophecies*, p. 133.

[55] See Miller *et al.*, *'The Dye Is Now Cast'*, pp. 257–8.

12. 7). A further word should be said about the prominence given here to the one member of the group of 'fierce Americans' (15: 12) whom Blake had actually known.

Despite the highly questionable nature of the anecdotes told by Blake's early biographers, there can be little doubt that Blake and Thomas Paine were acquainted, probably having met in the circle of the publisher Joseph Johnson.[56] It is also significant that Paine was first and foremost a writer, and that it was as a writer that he had changed the world. A few years later, Blake would daringly compare Paine's *Common Sense* to one of Jesus' miracles: 'Is it a greater miracle to feed five thousand men with five loaves than to overthrow all the armies of Europe with a small pamphlet?', he wrote in his copy of Bishop Richard Watson's attack on Paine, *An Apology for the Bible* (1798, E 617). And even more daringly, Blake asserted that 'the Holy Ghost . . . in Paine strives with Christendom as in Christ he strove with the Jews' (E 614). Having given powerful voice to the American Revolution, Paine heartened the supporters of the French Revolution in the early 1790s by finding, in *The Rights of Man*, an answerable style with which to oppose Burke's *Reflections*.[57] The enormous circulation of the two successive volumes of this book, abetted by Paine's waiving of copyright to encourage cheap editions, made Paine a revolutionary force in Europe as he had been in America. Though denying supernatural agency in history, Paine, who from the first had expected the American Revolution to spread to Europe and beyond it to Africa and Asia, had a millenarian streak that was expressed in statements like: 'We see [in the preface to the Declaration of Rights] a scene so new, and so transcendently unequalled by anything in the European world, that the name of a Revolution is diminutive of its character, and it rises into a Regeneration of man'.[58] We can visualize the regenerate man of *America* 6 as rising, metaphorically, from this sentence. Both historically and retrospectively, Paine had earned his place with Washington and Warren among the 'warlike men' whom Blake saw meeting 'on the coast glowing with blood from Albion's fiery Prince' (3: 5).

---

[56] On this subject, see Robert N. Essick, 'William Blake, Thomas Paine, and Biblical Revolution', *Studies in Romanticism*, 30 (1991): 189–212.

[57] On the salient characteristics of Paine's style, see Boulton, *Language of Politics*, pp. 134–48; and Olivia Smith, *The Politics of Language 1791–1819* (Oxford: Clarendon Press, 1984), pp. 43–90.

[58] Paine, *Rights of Man*, p. 114. On this aspect of Paine, see Jack Fruchtman, Jr., 'The Revolutionary Millennialism of Thomas Paine', *Studies in Eighteenth-Century Culture*, 13 (1984): 65–77; and J. F. C. Harrison, 'Thomas Paine and Millenarian Radicalism', in *Citizen of the World: Essays on Thomas Paine*, ed. Ian Dyck (London: Christopher Helm, 1987), pp. 73–85.

At this point occurs the fiery manifestation of Orc, whose getting free is the subject of the 'Preludium' preceding 'A Prophecy'. There Orc, bound in 'tenfold chains' (1: 12) recalls Erasmus Darwin's poetic representation of France on the eve of Revolution as a Gulliver tied down by Lilliputians:

> Long had the Giant-form on GALLIA's plains
> Inglorious slept, unconscious of his chains;
> Round his large limbs were wound a thousand strings
> By the weak hands of Confessors and Kings;
> O'er his closed eyes a triple veil was bound,
> And steely rivets lock'd him to the ground;
> While stern Bastile with iron cage inthralls
> His folded limbs, and hems in marble walls.
> —Touch'd by the patriot-flame, he rent amazd
> The flimsy bonds, and round and round him gazed;
> Starts up from earth, above the admiring throng
> Lifts his Colossal form.[59]

Orc's captivity is assigned a time period of 'fourteen suns' (1: 2)— according, as Leslie Tannenbaum suggests, with the calculation of epochs in Matthew 1: 17—fourteen generations from Abraham until David, fourteen from David to the Babylonian exile, and fourteen from the Babylonian exile to Christ; the American Revolution, as has been further suggested, would then be fourteen generations from Christ.[60] Darwin's giant form 'rent amazed / The flimsy bonds' after being 'Touch'd by the patriot-flame' (385–6); Orc, when he appears in 'A Prophecy', brings with him the fires of Energy seen in *The Marriage of Heaven and Hell*:

> And in the red clouds rose a Wonder o'er the Atlantic sea;
> Intense! naked! a Human fire fierce glowing, as the wedge
> Of iron heated in the furnace; his terrible limbs were fire

(4: 7–9)

[59] Erasmus Darwin, *The Botanic Garden* (1791), Part I: *The Economy of Vegetation* (London: J. Johnson, 1791), p. 92, ll. 377–88). It is the Goddess of Botany who speaks. These lines and the prose note accompanying them, a description of a descent into the dungeons of the Bastille from Helen Maria Williams's *Letters from France*, have been suggested as a source for some lines in *The French Revolution*. See Desmond King-Hele, *Erasmus Darwin and the Romantic Poets* (Basingstoke: Macmillan, 1986), pp. 41–2; and David Worrall, 'William Blake and Erasmus Darwin's *Botanic Garden*', *Bulletin of the New York Public Library*, 78 (1975): 406. Coleridge would draw on the same passage in 1794 (see Ch. 2), and Blake would later appropriate Darwin's term 'Giant form' Albion in *Milton* 15: 38 (E 109).

[60] See Leslie Tannenbaum, *Biblical Tradition in Blake's Early Prophecies: The Great Code of Art* (Princeton: Princeton University Press, 1982), p. 142; and E. S. Shaffer, '"Secular Apocalypse":

On a natural level, volcanic activity as described by Erasmus Darwin is behind this imagery.[61] The volcano as a trope for revolutionary upheaval would also be a feature of Shelley's poetry, as seen in the approach to the cave of Demogorgon in *Prometheus Unbound*:

> . . . the mighty portal,
> Like a volcano's meteor-breathing chasm,
> Whence the oracular vapour is hurled up[62]

Beyond the natural, Orc appears to be parallel to the Christ of the Parousia: 'For as the lightning cometh out of the east, and shineth even unto the west; so shall also the coming of the Son of Man be' (Matt. 24: 27). Yet 'heat but not light went thro' the murky atmosphere' is disquieting, for in the thought of Jakob Boehme, whom Blake had long admired, this characterizes the principle of Wrath separated from that of Love,[63] and in *Paradise Lost* it is a feature of the flames of hell: 'Yet from those flames / No light, but rather darkness visible'.[64] This is but one significant detail undermining Orc's status as an apocalyptic saviour who will lead humanity from apocalypse to millennium, though it may be temporarily forgotten in the great burst of poetry of the succeeding plate.

At the top of plate 5 reappears in amplified form the resurrected man of *The Marriage of Heaven and Hell*, looking toward the sky as in the text below Orc announces the millennial dawn:

> The morning comes, the night decays, the watchmen leave their stations;
> The grave is burst, the spices shed, the linen wrapped up;
> The bones of death, the cov'ring clay, the sinews shrunk & dry'd.
> Reviving shake, inspiring move, breathing! awakening!

$$(6: 1-4)$$

The imagery of resurrection, carried over from *The Marriage of Heaven and Hell*, is now applied to all of humanity, as in Ezekiel's vision of the valley of dry bones. 'And when I beheld, lo, the sinews and the flesh

---

Prophets and Apocalyptics at the End of the Eighteenth Century', in *Apocalypse Theory and the Ends of the World*, ed. Malcolm Bull (Oxford: Blackwell, 1995), pp. 137–58.

[61] See Dörrbecker, in Blake, *Continental Prophecies*, p. 32 n.

[62] *Prometheus Unbound*, II. iii. 2–4, in *Shelley's Poetry and Prose*, pp. 168–9. See G. M. Matthews, 'A Volcano's Voice in Shelley', in *Shelley: Modern Judgements*, ed. R. B. Woodings (London: Macmillan, 1968), pp. 162–95.

[63] See my *Energy and the Imagination: A Study of the Development of Blake's Thought* (Oxford: Clarendon Press, 1970), pp. 42–4.

[64] I. 62–3, as first suggested by S. Foster Damon, *William Blake: His Philosophy and Symbols* (Boston: Houghton Mifflin, 1924), p. 335.

came upon them, and the skin covered them above: but there was no breath in them. . . . So I prophesied as he commanded me, . . . and they lived' (37: 8–10). Orc is more than oracular, for unlike Ezekiel, he needs no commanding voice other than his own. What follows appears to be a performative or kerygmatic utterance,[65] freeing by *fiat* the slave and the prisoner:

> Let the slave grinding at the mill, run out into the field:
> Let him look up into the heavens & laugh in the bright air;
> Let the inchained soul shut up in darkness and in sighing,
> Whose face has never seen a smile in thirty weary years;
> Rise and look out, his chains are loose, his dungeon doors are open.

> (6: 6–10)

Returning refugees are imagined as singing a song derived from Revelation and from Blake's own *Song of Liberty*:

> The Sun has left his blackness, & has found a fresher morning
> And the fair Moon rejoices in the clear & cloudless night;
> For Empire is no more, and now the Lion & Wolf shall cease.

> (6: 13–15)

After the opening of the sixth seal in Revelation, 'lo, there was a great earthquake; and the sun became black as sackcloth of hair, and the moon became as blood' (12). Now this blackness is imagined as being dissipated by a millennial dawn, and the exuberantly optimistic declaration of the end of Empire is reiterated.

At this point, less than half-way through *America*, it appears as if a straightforward scenario going from apocalypse to millennium is being played out. However, this shortly turns out not to be so, and there is in Orc's speech itself one disquieting indication that Orc's grand declaration is yet to be fulfilled. When *America* was produced, the slave was still grinding at the mill, or harvesting cotton and sugar, in America. Thomas Paine had called upon Americans to 'discontinue and renounce' slavery in 1775, and he had also linked Britain's traffic in human flesh with the idea that 'the Almighty will finally separate America from Britain'.[66] Paine's expectation had not been fulfilled.

---

[65] On this subject, see Robert N. Essick, *William Blake and the Language of Adam* (Oxford: Clarendon Press, 1989), pp. 25–7.

[66] Thomas Paine, 'African Slavery in America', in *The Thomas Paine Reader*, ed. Michael Foot and Isaac Kramnick (Harmondsworth: Penguin Books, 1987), p. 55; *idem*, 'A Serious Thought', in *The Complete Writings of Thomas Paine*, ed. Philip Foner (2 vols., New York: Citadel, 1945), 2: 20. Richard Price had told the Americans that until they abolished slavery,

Instead, as Blake well knew, slavery had become embedded in the Constitution of the United States. Orc's great speech could be read in 1794 not as a performative act but only as an expression of unfulfilled desire, and Orc's very nature as a millennial saviour is consequently called into question.

Another case in point is plates 7–9, where Albions Angel first hurls at Orc resounding questions that reverberate like Edmund Burke's:

> Art thou not Orc, who serpent-form'd
> Stands at the gate of Enitharmon to devour her children;
> Blasphemous Demon, Antichrist, hater of Dignities;
> Lover of wild rebellion, and transgresser of God's Law;
> Why dost thou come to Angels eyes in this terrific form?
>
> (7: 3–7)

Previously, Albion's Angel was himself shown to be the great red dragon of Revelation. Now he tries to reverse this identification with a reference to Revelation 12: 4: 'And the dragon stood before the woman which was ready to be delivered, for to devour her child as soon as it was born'. As is widely recognized, the design on this page undermines him. A boy and a girl sleep with a ram, birds of paradise perch on a gracefully arching birch-tree, and grape leaves sprout in an early version of what Blake would later call Beulah, that sweet and pleasant rest from the labours of Eternity. (Yet these children, clearly approaching pubescence, had better not sleep too long: in two copies Blake brushed in a multi-coloured dawn as if to wake them.) This situation appears very similar to the two different perceptions of Leviathan in *The Marriage* 18–19, and if *America* were a serial narrative leading from apocalypse to millennium, Orc should in response affirm his human form as an antitype of Jesus. Yet, though his reply partly corrects the accusation, it does not entirely contradict it: 'I am Orc, wreath'd round the accursed tree' (8: 1). Orc is not the great red dragon, but he *is* the serpent of Genesis 3 mediated by pictorial renditions such as the

'it will not appear that they deserve the liberty for which they have been contending' (*Observations on the Importance of the American Revolution* (London: 1784), p. 83). In 1785 Price wrote to Thomas Jefferson about the continuation of slavery in Virginia: 'Should such a disposition prevail in the other united states, I shall have reason to fear that I have made myself ridiculous by speaking of the American Revolution in the manner I have done; it will appear that the people who have been struggling so earnestly to save *themselves* from slavery are very ready to enslave *others*: the friends of liberty and humanity in Europe will be mortify'd, and an event which has raised their hopes will prove only an introduction to a new scene of aristocratic tyranny and human debasement', quoted by Thomas, *Honest Mind*, pp. 272–3.

famous one executed by Raphael's pupils in the Vatican *Logge*. Orc's serpent form is prefigured earlier, in a trope in plate 5: 'the terror like a comet' (2), which links him to Milton's simile for Satan in *Paradise Lost*:

> *Satan* stood
> Unterrifi'd, and like a Comet burned,
> That fires the length of *Ophiucus* huge
> In th' Arctic Sky, and from his horrid hair
> Shakes Pestilence and War.
>
> (ii. 708–12)

Ophiucus, the serpent-holder, is a constellation next to Serpens, and so we have close by each other in the night sky Orc's alternative forms, expressive of his complex ambiguity.

Each of Orc's forms, human and serpent, is imbued with its own double meaning. As serpent, Orc can embody the cycle of historical recurrence, which Albions Angel emphasizes when he says 'Eternal Viper, self-renew'd . . . now the times are return'd upon thee' (9: 15–19). Yet, although Albion's Angel sees only the cycle of history, the serpent can also represent the possibility of millennial regeneration, suggested by the snake's annual casting of its slough. Shelley, in the final Chorus of *Hellas*, would seize on this as a figure:

> The world's great age begins anew,
> The golden years return,
> The earth doth like a snake renew
> Her winter weeds outworn.[67]

In addition, Orc's serpent form has explicitly revolutionary dimensions. For the masthead of the Patriot newspaper *The Massachusetts Spy* Paul Revere engraved the design *Join, or Die*, showing the undulating American serpent confronting the griffin of the British Empire.[68] Ethan Allen's Green Mountain Boys had on their flag a similar snake, with the legend 'Don't Tread on Me'. The American serpent crossed the Atlantic to appear with the inscription 'UNITE OR DIE' at the bottom of a broadsheet (British Museum, Department of Prints and Drawings) dedicated to the Society for Constitutional Information in 1782.[69] Designed by Blake's friend Thomas Stothard and engraved by

---

[67] *Shelley's Poetry and Prose*, pp. 438–9.

[68] See Miller *et al.*, '*The Dye Is Now Cast*', p. 59, fig. 34; S. Foster Damon, *A Blake Dictionary* (Providence, RI: Brown University Press, 1965), p. 145.

[69] Reproduced in David Bindman, *William Blake As an Artist* (Oxford: Phaidon, 1977), fig. 16.

William Sharp, this *Declaration of Rights* features an additional serpent, one with its tail in its mouth, designated as 'An emblem of eternity'. Anti-Revolutionary cartoons also fastened on the coiling snake to represent America, as in James Gillray's *The American Rattlesnake* (1782) and the anonymous *The American Rattlesnake presenting Monsieur his Ally a Dish of Frogs* (1782).[70] Blake's own pictorial version is seen in *America* 11, where three naked children ride the coils of a jolly-looking, bridled snake in what may be a visual reference to Isaiah's millennial prophecy: 'And the sucking child shall play on the hole of the asp' (11: 8).[71]

If Orc's serpent form is ambiguous, so is his human form. On plate 10 we see him as in one sense a version of the resurrected man of plate 6, but with head turned round toward his right and arms raised. Yet his expression is anguished, his palms are turned downward in a repressive gesture, and he is posed so as to be a mirror image of his adversary Urizen as pictured in plate 8.[72] Nevertheless, in Blake's work the naked human form is always a potentially millennial figure, and that possibility is projected in Orc's rendition of a favourite millenarian text, Daniel 2: 32–3, in which Daniel first renders, then interprets, the dream of Nebuchadnezzar: 'This image's head was of fine gold, his breast and his arms of silver, his belly and his thighs of brass, His legs of iron, his feet part of iron and part of clay'. Significantly, Blake rings a change on this, making it a progressive sequence: 'his [man's] feet become like brass, / His knees and thighs like silver, & his breast and head like gold' (8: 16–17). In addition to implying progress towards the millennium, Blake, relying on his reader's knowledge of the Bible, implies the completion of the dream, the destruction of the great image by a stone that then 'became a great mountain, and filled the whole earth', and the prophet's interpretation of it as signifying the destruction of successive kingdoms and the establishment by God of 'a kingdom, which shall never be destroyed' (2: 35, 44). In Daniel's interpretation of the dream, apocalypse is confidently placed as the prelude to millennium, but in *America* the relationship between the two is profoundly disjunctive, to an extent that may reflect Blake's uncertainty about the fulfilment of Daniel's prophecy by means of the revolutions of his own time.

---

[70] Both are reproduced in Blake, *Continental Prophecies*, p. 251, figs. 2 and 3.

[71] See H. M. Margoliouth, *William Blake* (London: Oxford University Press, 1951), p. 86; Dörrbecker, in Blake, *Continental Prophecies*, p. 64.

[72] See Janet A. Warner, *Blake and the Language of Art* (Kingston and Montreal: McGill–Queen's University Press, 1984), pp. 92–4.

The latter part of *America* is dominated by interrelated images of fertility and sterility, health and disease, all bearing apocalyptic overtones. From the early part of his career Blake had been virtually obsessed with the themes of famine and plague, along with war and fire, as in the now untraced water-colour exhibited at the Royal Academy in 1784, *War Unchained by an Angel, Fire Pestilence, and Famine Following* (Butlin 187). He continued to link these themes in the *History of England* series he projected in 1793 (E 672), and later in four powerful watercolours of 1805 (Butlin 193–6). It is almost as if Blake had had a precognition of Malthus:

> The vices of mankind are active and able ministers of depopulation. . . . But should they fail in this war of extermination, sickly seasons, epidemics, and plague, advance in terrific array, and sweep off their thousands and ten thousands. Should success be still incomplete, gigantic inevitable famine stalks in the rear, and with one mighty blow, levels the population with the food of the world.[73]

Malthus's first *Essay on the Principle of Population* was not published until 1798, but Blake was expressing similar anxieties in curiously similar personifications. We have already had Fire and War in *America*, but with the defeat of the British troops in 13: 6–9, we might have expected the subject to shift to the fulfilment of Orc's millennial vision. Instead, famine and then plague become increasingly important. Orc has from the first been associated in the designs (as, for example, in plate 2) with grape-vines and ears of wheat, seeming to promise a millennial Eucharist and a 'Great Harvest & Vintage of the Nations' as in the last line of verse in *Milton* (43[50]: 1, E 144). In contrast, Albions Angel laments in *America* 9: 5 that his minions 'cannot smite the wheat, nor quench the fatness of the earth'. Such contrasts were also typical of the political discourse of the 1790s, in which radical authors frequently used the imagery of planting and harvesting as tropes in the service of their cause. Price, for example, wrote that Liberty in his time had been prepared by philosophers and scholars who had 'sowed a seed which has since taken root, and is now growing up to a glorious harvest', and that every country was either 'a fruitful field or a frightful waste, according as it possesses or wants this blessing'.[74] Yet the design on plate 9 is disquieting, for we cannot be sure of whether the baby

---

[73] Thomas Robert Malthus, *Population: The First Essay*, with a foreword by Kenneth E. Boulding (Ann Arbor: University of Michigan Press, 1959), p. 49.

[74] Price, *Discourse on the Love of our Country*, pp. 14, 19.

lying in a sea of wheat is dead or alive.[75] Such apparent indeterminacy may be part of Blake's strategy of rousing the reader/viewer's faculties to act; yet the baby does appear stiff, like the indisputably dead infants in the 'Holy Thursday' of *Songs of Experience* and plate 6 of *Europe*. Later, the plagues unleashed upon the Americans by Albions Angel are troped to 'a blight [that] cuts the tender corn when it begins to appear' (14: 6). 'Arm'd with diseases of the earth' (13: 5), the Angels of Albion are at least parodically like the 'seven angels having the seven last plagues' seen by John of Patmos (Rev. 15: 1) and identified by him as bearing the wrath of God. In Revelation 16 these plagues, poured out of seven vials, scourge the entire earth; in *America* 14: 20 'the plagues recoil'd', and plates 15 and 16 describe their effects upon Britain. In so doing, they demonstrate the futility of Edmund Burke's advice. Addressing the French legislator to whom the *Reflections* were originally directed, Burke wrote that the English must 'keep at a distance, your panacea, or your plague', and continued: 'If it be a panacea, we do not want it. We know the consequences of unnecessary physic. If it be a plague, it is such a plague, that the precautions of the most severe quarantine ought to be established against it.'[76] Blake's revolutionary plagues in conjunction with Orc's fires have the power to destroy the repressive institutions of society and their representatives, while leaving the women of Britain 'naked and glowing' (15: 22). Their health is represented by a metaphor of fertility:

> They feel the nerves of youth renew, and desires of ancient times,
> Over their pale limbs as a vine when the tender grape appears
>
> (15: 25–6)

Echoing but with a contrary meaning 'as a blight cuts the tender corn when it begins to appear', these lines are a reminder that war, fire, plague, and even famine have the potentiality of preparing the way for millennium. However, in *America* such a transition does not take place.

In the last plate of *America*, the tutelary power behind Albions Angel, the 'leprous' sky-god Urizen, intervenes, temporarily deep-freezing the energies of revolution with the 'stored snows' of 'his icy magazines'. France, Spain, and Italy—significantly, the benighted nations that figure

---

[75] Erdman, e.g., sees the infant as protected by the wheat, while Dörrbecker argues that the baby is dead (Blake, *Continental Prophecies*, p. 61). See David V. Erdman, *The Illuminated Blake* (Garden City, NY: Anchor Press / Doubleday, 1974), p. 147.

[76] Burke, *Reflections*, p. 185.

in *A Song of Liberty* 3–5—attempt to carry out a Burkean quarantine by shutting 'the five gates of their law-built heaven' (16: 19). However, they have already been infected by 'mildews' and 'fierce disease' (20–1), so their attempt to seal the gates of the five senses is doomed:

> But the five gates were consum'd, & their bolts and hinges melted
> And the fierce flames burnt round the heavens, & round the abodes of men.
>
> (22–3)

In imagery reminiscent of *The Marriage of Heaven and Hell*, Blake holds out the possibility of a millennium yet to come. Even the time span is given:

> Till Angels & weak men twelve years should govern o'er the strong:
> And then their end should come, when France reciev'd the Demons light.
>
> (14–15)

The transmission of the revolutionary spirit from America to other nations in terms of light or flame was also a feature of radical discourse. 'From a small spark kindled in America', wrote Paine, 'a flame has arisen, not to be extinguished. Without consuming, like the *ultima Ratio Regum*, it winds its progress from nation to nation and conquers by a silent operation.'[77] The period of twelve years may be, as has been suggested, 1781–93, from the British surrender at Yorktown to the execution of Louis XVI.[78] It is thus implied that the prophecies of Orc may yet be realized although the millennium has, retrospectively, been deferred. Yet there is something paradoxical in the nature of a millennium deferred, especially when its promulgation has been asserted as dramatically as it has in *America*. Had the view projected been a millennialist one like Godwin's, envisaging the progression of human perfectibility over a very long period of time according to the laws of Necessity, a hiatus of a mere twelve years would present no problem. But Orc's millennial assertions have been so imbued with millenarian urgency that their unfulfilment opens a deep gap between apocalypse and millennium, a gap that widens further in Blake's next prophetic work, published in 1794, *Europe*.

---

[77] Paine, *Rights of Man*, part 2, p. 210. Cf. Price's words, previously quoted in the Introduction: 'Behold, the light you have struck out, after setting AMERICA free, reflected to FRANCE, and there kindled into a blaze that lays despotism in ashes, and warms and illuminates EUROPE!' (*Discourse on the Love of Our Country*, p. 50).

[78] See Erdman, *Blake: Prophet Against Empire*, p. 208.

In the vineyards of red France

Like *America, Europe* is divided into a 'Preludium' and 'A Prophecy'. In the Preludium, two views of time are projected. One is cyclical: the 'nameless shadowy female' gives birth to a succession of 'howling terrors, all devouring fiery kings' who, 'Devouring & devourd' (2: 4–5), promise nothing but endless repetition within history. Yet an antithetical vision is given her of the Incarnation of Jesus:

> And who shall bind the infinite with an eternal band?
> To compass it with swaddling bands? And who shall cherish it
> With milk and honey?

> (2: 14–16)

In Luke 2: 12 the angel tells the shepherds, 'Ye shall find the babe wrapped in swaddling clothes', and Milton mentions the 'swaddling bands' of the infant Jesus in *On the Morning of Christ's Nativity*.[79] Yet what seems innocuous, as so often in Blake, may have negative adumbrations. Do these bands imply constraints like those experienced by the speaker of 'Infant Sorrow', 'Striving against my swadling bands' (E 28)? The ambiguity is carried further as the first lines of 'A Prophecy' imitate the beginning of Milton's ode:

> The deep of winter came;
> What time the secret child,
> Descended thro' the orient gates of the eternal day:
> It was the Winter wild,
> While the Heav'n-born child,
> All meanly wrapt in the rude manger lies;[80]

It seems as if a millennial era is about to begin: 'War ceas'd, & all the troops like shadows fled to their abodes' (3: 4). Yet this visionary moment collapses, to be followed by the announcement that 'Urizen unloos'd from chains / Glows like a meteor in the distant north' (3: 11–12). This parallels the moment that *ends* the millennium in Revelation, where the resurrected martyrs reign with Jesus for a thousand years.

---

[79] Line 227. On links with Milton's ode see Michael J. Tolley, '*Europe*: "to those ychain'd in sleep"', in *Blake's Visionary Forms Dramatic*, ed. David V. Erdman and John E. Grant (Princeton: Princeton University Press, 1970), pp. 115–45.

[80] Blake, *Europe*, 3: 1–3; Milton, *On the Morning of Christ's Nativity*, 1–3. See Damon, *William Blake*, p. 343; Tolley, '*Europe*', p. 120; Stevenson (ed.), *Blake*, p. 228 n.; Dörrbecker, in Blake, *Continental Prophecies*, p. 268.

'And when the thousand years are expired, Satan shall be loosed out of his prison' (20: 7).

This failure of the millennial is underscored by the reiteration of the apocalyptic as Orc in all his terrible ambiguity. His mother Enitharmon, evidently not having read *America*, mistakenly thinks that he is still 'bound', and she summons him up as if he were a Dionysiac reveller to be crowned 'with garlands of the ruddy vine', not realizing that these are actually grapes of wrath from the vineyards of red France.[81] However, Orc immediately manifests himself as 'the Demon red' of *America* 15: 13:

> The horrent Demon rose, surrounded with red stars of fire,
> Whirling about in furious circles round the immortal fiend.
>
> (4: 15–16)

'Horrent', to be repeated of Orc in 14: 27, is given as 'Chiefly *poet.*', by the *OED*, with one of its primary meanings 'Bristling, standing up as bristles; rough with bristling points or projections'. We are reminded of Orc's being a 'hairy youth' in the Preludium of *America* (1: 11) and of the 'horrent hair' of the comet in Milton's trope for Satan. (One of the *OED*'s examples, from Addison's *Pleasures of the Imagination*, 2: 699, is 'Horrent hair'.) Orc's masculinity can be erotically alluring or Satanically domineering, and this is another aspect of his ambiguity. Enitharmon thinks she is toying with the first aspect, when in reality she invites the second. At the same time, the possibility of a human form divine for Orc is raised in the design on this same plate.

The lower half of plate 4 depicts a naked woman on a cloud lifting a cloth to reveal a figure below. Although the possibility that she might be covering him has been raised,[82] it is apparent from the body language and dramatic emphasis of the design that this is an unveiling, a revelation, literally *apokalupsis*. What is revealed is the prone, naked body of a

---

[81] 4: 9, 12; E 62. The identity of the speaker of these lines 10–14 has been disputed. Sir Geoffrey Keynes (*The Complete Writings of William Blake*, rev. edn. (Oxford: Oxford University Press, 1966), p. 239) adds quotation marks to make these lines part of a longer passage spoken by Los, while Erdman (E 803) and Stevenson (*Poems*, p. 229) argue that lines 10–14 belong to Enitharmon, and Dörrbecker (in Blake, *Continental Prophecies*, p. 269) that they belong to Los. Although Blake used no quotation marks here, it is Enitharmon who on the following plate calls upon each of her children by name, and it is therefore very likely that this sequence begins at 4: 10.

[82] See David Worrall, 'The Immortal Tent', *Bulletin of Research in the Humanities*, 84 (1981): 287. The two possibilities are discussed by Dörrbecker, in Blake, *Continental Prophecies*, pp. 183–4, who concludes that she is lifting the veil.

sleeping youth, whose thick, curly hair is crowned by a fiery halo. This design has been aptly compared with Raphael's depiction of the Madonna drawing a veil away from the baby Jesus.[83] This rich-haired youth has the power to renew the world, but that power will not be realized in *Europe*. Instead, Enitharmon sleeps for 1800 years, and in that sleep all of history from the time of Jesus to the present of Europe takes place, climaxing in a link with the end of *America*, as 'Albions Angel smitten with his own plagues fled with his bands' (9: 9). The moment when revolution would leap the firebreak from America to Europe, the moment prophesied by Price, by Paine, and by Blake, has indeed come, but it has come in a terrible form that they had not anticipated: the coiling Orc serpent, portrayed on the title-page of *Europe*, mounts up the side of plate 10 in seven folds. An ironical link with Orc's human form is the serpent's fiery halo. This image, derived from the Comte de Caylus's *receuil d'Antiquité Egyptiennes, Etrusques, Greques, et Romaines*,[84] and also alluding to the 'rising folds' of Milton's serpent in *Paradise Lost* (9: 498) parodies Jesus, just as the serpent temple described in the text, in being an 'image of infinite / Shut up in finite revolutions' (10: 22–3), parodies the New Jerusalem. The coils of the Orc serpent are revolutions in both senses of the word, representing a historical process that continually promises millennium but never achieves it.[85] The serpent temple itself is made 'of massy stones, uncut / With tool' (10: 7–8), seemingly in keeping with God's injunction to Moses, 'And if thou wilt make me an altar of stone, thou shalt not build it of hewn stone: for if thou lift up thy tool upon it, thou hast polluted it' (Exod. 20: 25); and the 'colours twelve' (10: 9) of the stones are related to the twelve precious stones of the foundations of the wall of the New Jerusalem in Revelation 21: 19–20. Blake's source for the serpent temple, the antiquarian William Stukeley, believed that Stonehenge and Avebury had been built by Druids, that they reflected features of the temple of Solomon,

[83] John Beer has shown that the source of this image of unveiling is the Raphael painting known as the *Madonna di Loreto*, probably transmitted via an engraving by G. Ghisi. See John Beer, *Blake's Visionary Universe* (Manchester: Manchester University Press, 1969), figs. 53 and 54.

[84] Paris, 152–7, 5: plate 23, no. v. See my '"Wonderful Originals": Blake and Ancient Sculpture', in *Blake in his Time*, ed. Robert N. Essick and Donald Pearce (Bloomington, Ind., and London: Indiana University Press, 1978), p. 177.

[85] As James E. Swearingen puts it, 'Whereas in the earlier *America* (1793) events move forward toward apocalyptic renewal in a linear system of wordly events, in *Europe* (1794) the image of linear time becomes problematic as the time of natural cycles appears to subordinate and deploy linearity within the pattern of repetition' ('Time and History in Blake's *Europe*', *Clio* 20 (1991): 111).

and that the supposed serpent form of Avebury symbolized the divine.[86] The serpent could, Blake knew, be a symbol of eternity or a symbol of cyclical recurrence.[87] (In *Prometheus Unbound*, Shelley would distinguish between these two meanings by assigning one to the amphisbaenic snake, the other to the ourobouros.) Both the serpent and the serpent temple are in this context deeply ambiguous images.

Attention has been called to the synecdochic relationship of plate 10 to the whole of Europe, and to Blake's other works of this period as well.[88] Indeed, with this plate we reach a crucial point in Blake's view of history. If Orc's only form is the upward-spiralling serpent—his human form will not reappear in the Lambeth books—then history cannot culminate in a millennium. At best, the serpent might cast its slough in a temporary regeneration that would only result in the nightmare of historical recurrence. This leads to the nightmarish theme, also to be featured in Byron's 'Darkness' and in Mary Shelley's *The Last Man*, of apocalypse without millennium. The imminence of apocalypse becomes even greater than in Blake's preceding works. 'For Urizen unclaspd his book' (12: 4) is a parody of the Lamb's opening of the first seal of 'the book written within and on the backside' in Revelation (5: 1 and 6: 1). Similarly, the unsuccessful attempts of Albions Angel to blow 'the Trump of the last doom' followed by the blowing of 'the enormous blast' by the 'mighty spirit' Newton parody the blowing of the seventh trumpet in Revelation 11: 15: 'And the seventh angel sounded; and there were great voices in heaven, saying, The kingdoms of this world are become the kingdoms of our Lord, and of his Christ; and he shall reign for ever and ever'. Blake would jubilantly adapt these words in a letter to John Flaxman after the news of the Peace of Amiens in 1801, but in *Europe* what follows is anything but peace. First comes a grotesque transformation of the Last Judgement, rendered in a Miltonic simile:

---

[86] William Stukeley, *Stonehenge: A Temple Restor'd to the British Druids* (London, 1740); *idem, Abury—A Temple of the British Druids* (London, 1743). See my 'The Fourth Face of Man: Blake and Architecture', in *Articulate Images: The Sister Arts from Hogarth to Tennyson*, ed. Richard Wendorf (Minneapolis: University of Minnesota Press, 1983), pp. 192–5.

[87] In an important discussion of plate 10 of *Europe*, Hazard Adams refers to the Gnostic interpretation according to which the serpent can be a figure of Christ (cf. John 3: 14, interpreting Num. 21: 4–9), but can also be a dragon 'containing the fallen form of creation identified with Leviathan' ('Synecdoche and Method', in *Critical Paths: Blake and the Argument of Method*, ed. Dan Miller *et al.* (Durham, NC: Duke University Press, 1987), p. 55).

[88] Ibid., p. 68.

Yellow as leaves of Autumn the myriads of Angelic hosts,
Fell through the wintry skies seeking their graves;
Rattling their howling bones in howling and lamentation.

(13: 6–8)

As one writer puts it, this is a 'reverse millennium'.[89] Newton is chosen because his influence upon Western thought encapsulated in Blake's view a body of error that cast its long shadow through the eighteenth century, and perhaps also with a wry reference to Newton's own considerable interest in the Book of Revelation.[90] His act precipitates not a resurrection of the dead but a fall of the Angelic host and with it an end to the old order. At one time Blake meant to place the moment of the blowing of the trumpet at the end of plate 14 and the beginning of plate 15, with:

Till morning ope'd the eastern gate, and the angel trumpet blew.

Then every one fled to his station, & Enitharmon wept.

But terrible Orc, when he beheld the morning in the east,
Shot from the heights of Enitharmon, before the trumpet blew:
And in the vineyards of red France appear'd the light of his fury.[91]

Presumably the present plate 13 was created after the present 14 and 15, and the two latter were changed in order to accommodate the relocation of the blowing of the trumpet. This is an indication of how unimportant the temporal becomes when the relationship between apocalypse and millennium is abandoned. By the end of *Europe* it isn't significant whether Orc shot from the heights of Enitharmon before the last trump or after it, or whether the apocalypse is a result of the blowing of the trumpet or is precipitated by it. All that is left is a seemingly endless apocalypse:

Then Los arose his head he reard in snaky thunders clad:
And with a cry that shook all nature to the utmost pole,
Call'd all his sons to the strife of blood.

FINIS[92]

[89] See Barton R. Friedman, *Fabricating History: English Writers on the French Revolution* (Princeton: Princeton University Press, 1988), pp. 64–5.

[90] See Newton's *Observation upon the Apocalypse of St John*, in *Opera Quae Exstant Omnia*, ed. Samuel Horsley (5 vols., London, 1785), vol. 5, part 2.

[91] See E 803, and Blake, *Continental Prophecies*, additional plates 16 and 17 reproducing from copy *a* the first states of plates 14 and 15 (= *Continental Prophecies*, 16[17] and 17[18]), and p. 279. Copy *a* (British Museum), is discussed by A. E. Popham, 'Early Proofs of William Blake's *Europe*', *British Museum Quarterly*, 11 (1937): 184–5; and by A. W. J. Lincoln, 'Blake's *Europe*: An Early Version?', *Notes and Queries*, NS 25 (1978): 213.

[92] 15: 9–12, E 66.

Europe ends with the image of a family fleeing the flames of war behind them, the father carrying the mother on his back while he draws a child by the arm. The broken column towards which he strides suggests a ravaged city. This culminating design is one of a group depicting war, famine, plague, and fire, themes that, as we have seen, Blake engaged early in his artistic career, and that are even more prominent in *Europe* than in *America*. War is shown as a crowned figure with a sword, wearing scaly armour and flanked by angels.[93] A hand other than Blake's has written 'War' at the top of this plate in copy D, and if that hand, which provided a number of annotations in that copy, belonged to someone close to Blake, we may see here a reference to William Pitt, for the inscription reads: 'O war! thou Son of Hell, / Whom angry heavens do make their minister!'[94] Famine appears as a full-page design on the next plate of the copy B sequence (used in *The Continental Prophecies*), where two women in anguished postures are apparently preparing to cook a dead child, supine as in *America* 11, in a cauldron over a roaring fire.[95] Plague is the subject of full-page design 19 13(10), with a Bellman in traditional black costume towering over three afflicted figures against the wall inscription 'LORD / [H]AVE MERC[Y] / ON US/†'. This scene, like Blake's *Pestilence* drawings, is associated with the Great Plague of 1665, of which Blake no doubt had knowledge through Defoe's great narrative *A Journal of the Plague Year*, still regarded by many in the late eighteenth century as a true account rather than a novel.[96] Earlier, two naked trumpeters in a rococo swirl pour out, as the annotator writes, 'Mildews blighting ears of Corn', in

[93] *Europe*, plate 7(8) in *Continental Prophecies*, corresponding to plate 5 in Erdman's foliation. As the immediate discussion concerns only designs, and as Erdman does not include full-page designs in his foliation, only the *Continental Prophecies* numbers will be given here. The parenthetical numbers given by Dörrbecker refer to Bentley's *Blake Books* (Oxford: Clarendon Press, 1977).

[94] These glosses have been ascribed on the basis of handwriting to Blake's friend George Cumberland, although copy D belonged to the painter Ozias Humphry and Cumberland owned copy C. Bentley (*Blake Books*, pp. 158–9) hypothesizes that Cumberland borrowed Humphry's copy for the purpose. For further discussion and a full transcription, see Dörrbecker, in Blake, *Continental Prophecies*, pp. 207–10.

[95] The writer of the glosses inscribed here lines from Dryden's *Indian Emperor*, beginning 'Famine so fierce' (*Continental Prophecies*, p. 209). This plate has generated considerable commentary: see especially Stephen C. Behrendt, '*Europe* 6: Plundering the Treasury', *Blake: An Illustrated Quarterly*, 21 (1987–8): 85–94.

[96] For this point I am indebted to George Starr. On the *Pestilence* designs, see Butlin, 1: 70–5, and Joseph Viscomi, 'A Breach in the City the Morning After the Battle: Lost or Found?', *Blake: An Illustrated Quarterly*, 28 (1994): 44–61. 'The Plague' was one of the subjects Blake intended for his 'History of England' series in 1793; see E 672.

contrast to the situation in *America* 8: 5, where Albions Angel laments
that his punishing Demons 'cannot smite the wheat, nor quench the
fatness of the earth'.[97] Now the fertility once associated with Revolution
has failed before the onslaught of what Blake in *The Four Zoas* would call
'Endless Destruction never to be repelld'.[98] These terrible forces parallel (though not in number) the plagues of Egypt in Exodus 7–12, about
which Blake had intended to make a series of designs;[99] and they also
parallel the 'four sore judgements' of Ezekiel 14: 21,[100] the four riders of
Revelation 6 popularly known as the the four horsemen of Apocalypse,
and the seven angels pouring from their vials the seven last plagues
in Revelation 15 and 16. The difference between these biblical precedents and Blake's rendering in *Europe* is that the biblical plagues are
conceived as leading to something else—the freeing of the Hebrews
from their Egyptian bondage, the cleansing and regeneration of the
house of Israel, the establishment of the New Jerusalem. This is
not true of the end of Blake's *Europe*. When Orc appears 'in the
vineyards of red France', it may be to work 'the great winepress of
the wrath of God' (Rev. 14: 19), but this apocalypse will lead to no
millennium.

A year after *Europe*, Blake stopped producing new illuminated books
for a long period. However, he gave up neither on writing poetry nor
on the idea of building an ambitious poem on the theme of apocalypse
and millennium. After finishing the enormous project of illustrating
Edward Young's *Night Thoughts* in 1796, Blake began an epic poem that
he first called *Vala* and then *The Four Zoas*.[101] The date 1797 on the title-
page indicates that the work was at least under way by then. Blake took
the poem to Felpham with him when he moved there in 1799, and he
continued to work on it during his time in Sussex and after his return to
London in 1803. His plan was to pull together aspects of the myth he
had created in the Lambeth books, that would include the birth,

---

[97] Michael Tolley cites Exod. 9: 31: 'And the flax and the barley was smitten: for the
barley was in the ear, and the flax was bolled' (*'Europe*: "to those ychain'd in sleep"', p. 131;
and, for a parallel from Erasmus Darwin, Dörrbecker, in Blake, *Continental Prophecies*,
p. 193.

[98] Night the Eighth, 101 [2nd portion]: 31, E 374.

[99] See E 673. Its position in the notebook shows that the list was made close to the time of
that for the History of England series. Blake later executed *Pestilence: The Death of the First-born*
(Butlin 442) for Thomas Butts.

[100] As suggested by Dörrbecker, in Blake, *Continental Prophecies*, p. 204.

[101] See E 300, 818.

chaining, and breaking free of Orc and the conflict of Orc and Urizen. To these and other familiar elements he added the overarching myth of the fall of the Eternal Man, the battle within him of the forces constituting his mind and body, and his regaining of a unified identity, this intrapsychic drama paralleled by events in the socio-political world. The whole was always to end with the Last Judgement of Night the Ninth, in which an apocalyptic Last Judgement is accompanied by a millennial return to an earthly paradise.

Had Blake completed *Vala* according to what appears to have been his original plan, it is difficult to see what meaning the millennium, in the world of the Anglo–French wars, could have had, except as a narrative in the past tense whose meaning was yet to be realized in the present. This, however, is not what created the impasse that resulted in *The Four Zoas'* remaining a palimpsest manuscript. During his residence at Felpham and immediately afterwards, Blake had a series of visionary experiences that resulted in what can only be called a religious conversion.[102] He joined no church or other religious group, although his experience corresponded to the idea of a 'new birth' expressed in the sermons of the Methodists Whitefield and Wesley.[103] Blake incorporated his new spiritual views into *The Four Zoas* and his subsequent works as well. Among the new names and concepts that now appeared were the Council of God, the Seven Eyes of God, the doctrine of Individual and States, the Winepress of Los, and the descent of Jesus in Luvah's robes of blood.[104] The result is a combination of Christian and non-Christian elements that does not result in a synthesis. 'The Last Judgment simply starts off with a bang', as Frye puts it,[105] and the beautifully described feast of the Eternals (feasting in the New Jerusalem being a conspicuous feature of early Christian descriptions of the millennium) takes place in an atemporal zone made none the more convincing by the song of a former African slave. At some point, without necessarily ceasing to revise *The Four Zoas* immediately, Blake decided to make his conversionary experience the central subject of a new epic poem, one that he would continue working on in London

---

[102] On this subject see Jean H. Hagstrum, ' "The Wrath of the Lamb": A Study of William Blake's Conversions', in *From Sensibility to Romanticism: Essays Presented to Frederic A. Pottle*, ed. Frederick W. Hilles and Harold Bloom (London and New York: Oxford University Press, 1965), pp. 311–30, esp. pp. 321–6.
[103] See Paley, *Energy and the Imagination*, pp. 146–7.
[104] See ibid., pp. 142–70.   [105] Frye, *Fearful Symmetry*, p. 308.

and that would become his first new illuminated book after some fifteen years.

Milton, the Awakener

In the central action of Blake's *Milton*, the eponymous hero descends from heaven to enter William Blake, empowering him as poet and prophet. Consequently Blake has a vision of Los, 'the Spirit of Prophecy' in which he and Los become 'One Man',[106] and Los declares:

> I am that Shadowy Prophet who Six Thousand Years ago
> Fell from my station in the Eternal bosom.   Six Thousand Years
> Are finishd. I return! both Time & Space obey my will.

(22[24]: 15–17, E 117)

With the end of the sixth day of the world-week will presumably come the Sabbath, and indeed the millennium appears imminent. Although Los's sons Rintrah and Palamabron do not realize this, and also mistake Blake/Milton for the unregenerate Milton of history, they accurately describe the historical moment and its immediate background:

> Seeing the Churches at their Period in terror & despair:
> Rahab created Voltaire; Tirzah created Rousseau;
> Asserting the Self-righteousness against the Universal Saviour,
> Mocking the Confessors & Martyrs, claiming Self-righteousness;
> With cruel Virtue: making War upon the Lambs Redeemed;
> To perpetuate War & Glory, to perpetuate the Laws of Sin:
> They perverted Swedenborgs Visions in Beulah & in Ulro;
> To destroy Jerusalem as a Harlot & her Sons as Reprobates;
> To raise up Mystery the Virgin Harlot Mother of War,
> Babylon the Great, the Abomination of Desolation!
> O Swedenborg! strongest of men, the Samson shorn by the Churches!
> Shewing the Transgresors in Hell, the proud Warriors in Heaven:
> Heaven as a Punisher & Hell as One under Punishment:
> With Laws from Plato & his Greeks to renew the Trojan Gods,
> In Albion; & to deny the value of the Saviours blood.

(22[24]: 40–54, E 117–18)

---

[106] 25[27]: 71, E 121, 22[24]: 12, E 117. 'Spirit of Prophecy' is a quotation from Rev. 19: 10. The experience described is very similar to that in verses Blake sent to his friend Thomas Butts on 22 Nov. 1802, saying they were composed 'above a twelvemonth ago' (E 720–2).

As Frye remarks, 'Milton finds in the world he returns to a crisis in history with the Napoleonic wars, a crisis in religion with the collapse of Swedenborg and the failure of anyone to make a genuinely imaginative development out of the challenge of the Methodist movement'.[107] Voltaire and Rousseau, once seen as neutral if not positive signs of the times, are now viewed as idols set up by the interrelated Whore of Babylon and her converse, the virgin temptress.[108] In their separate aspects they preside over an age of Reason and Sensibility; together, their bodies having been ceremoniously enshrined in the Panthéon in enormous *fêtes*,[109] they are idols of a new form of state religion. Swedenborg, in contrast, is now viewed ambivalently—the 'strongest of men', but a shorn Samson. Here Blake may be recalling the opening of his own early prose poem 'Samson': 'Samson, the strongest of the children of men, I sing' (E 443). In *Poetical Sketches*, Blake had concluded before his hero's humiliation, stressing instead the Christ-like aspect of Samson by making the angel's words to Manoa similar to Mary's Magnificat: 'Hail, highly favoured! said he; for lo, thou shalt conceive, and bear a son, and Israel's strength shall be upon his shoulders, and he shall be called Israel's Deliverer!' (E 445). However, in two watercolours of *c*.1800–3, Blake gives equal weight to Samson's God-given strength and to his vulnerability to the Female Will.[110] In about 1804 he turned his rising Albion into a type of Samson, drawing upon Milton's *Samson Agonistes* for his two-line inscription to the plate.[111] This Blakean Samson thematizes the choice of sacrifice of Self over Sacrifice of enemies, while the shorn Samson Swedenborg is still regarded as having, in the words of *The Marriage*, 'written all the old falshoods' (E 43), and his separation of the Heavens with their inhabitants and the Hells with theirs repeats, in Blake's view, the old churches' bifurcation of all human experience into Good and Evil. Nevertheless, he is

---

[107] Frye, 'Notes for a Commentary on *Milton*', in *The Divine Vision*, ed. V. de Sola Pinto (London: Victor Gollancz, 1957), pp. 135–6.

[108] In *The French Revolution* (276–82, E 298), Voltaire and Rousseau are viewed as positive forces behind the Revolution; but in *The Song of Los* they are at best equivocal: 'Clouds roll heavy upon the Alps round Rousseau & Voltaire' (5: 17, E 68).

[109] See Emmet Kennedy, *A Cultural History of the French Revolution* (New Haven and London: Yale University Press, 1989), pp. 331–6; Simon Schama, *Citizens: A Chronicle of the French Revolution* (New York: Vintage, 1989), pp. 561–6.

[110] See Butlin, nos. 453 (pl. 529) and 455 (pl. 530).

[111] See Robert N. Essick, *William Blake, Printmaker* (Princeton: Princeton University Press, 1980), pp. 182–3, 186. As is widely recognized, the first line of Blake's inscription, 'Albion rose from where he labourd at the Mill with Slaves', subsumes line 41 of *Samson Agonistes*, 'Eyeless in *Gaza* at the Mill with Slaves'.

presented as one whose visions were genuine, but were 'perverted' by institutional forces, and this change of emphasis has some important implications.

One source of Blake's renewed interest in Swedenborg may have been his friendship with Charles Augustus Tulk, son of a founding member of the New Jerusalem Church and also a friend of John Flaxman and of Samuel Taylor Coleridge.[112] (It was Tulk's copy of Blake's *Songs* that Coleridge borrowed in February 1818, and it was probably information from Tulk that led Coleridge to write of Blake: 'He is a man of Genius—and I apprehend, a Swedenborgian'.[113] Tulk's daughter claimed that William and Catherine Blake 'became much impressed with the Spiritual Truths in Swedenborg's Writings', and that William 'made drawings from the Memorable Relations, one of them of a female Angel instructing a number of children in the spiritual world'.[114] Although we know nothing more of such a picture, we do know that in 1809 Blake exhibited *The spiritual Preceptor, an experiment Picture*, which he described as follows:

This subject is taken from the visions of Emanuel Swedenborg, Universal Theology, No. 623. The Learned, who strive to ascend into Heaven by means of learning, appear to Children like dead horses, when repelled by the celestial spheres. The works of this visionary are well worthy the attention of Painters and Poets; they are foundations for grand things. . . . O Artist! you may disbelieve all this, but it shall be at your own peril.[115]

This shows an attentive reading of part of a major work of Swedenborg's (*Universal Theology* is an alternative title for *True Christian Religion*) that had probably been known to Blake early on and that he revisited with enthusiasm at around the time he was completing *Milton*.[116] Blake took his own advice to painters and poets, as some important conceptions of Swedenborg's are to be found in *Milton*.

---

[112] On Tulk, see Geoffrey Keynes, 'Blake, Tulk, and Garth Wilkinson', *Library*, 4th ser., 26 (1945): 190–2; and Raymond H. Deck, Jr., 'New Light on C. A. Tulk, Blake's Nineteenth-Century Patron', *Studies in Romanticism*, 16 (1977): 217–36.

[113] Letter to H. F. Cary, 6 Feb. 1818; *CL* 4: 834.

[114] Bentley, *Blake Records*, p. 250.

[115] *A Descriptive Catalogue*, E 546. The location of this picture is unknown.

[116] The editors of the Blake Trust edition of *Milton a Poem* (London: William Blake Trust/ Tate Gallery, 1993), Robert N. Essick and Joseph Viscomi, show that *Milton* was still a work in progress in 1809 and that its initial printing took place in late 1810 or early 1811 (pp. 36–8). Blake opened his exhibition in 1809 and produced his *Descriptive Catalogue* for it, and although we do not know the date of *The spiritual Preceptor*, it is reasonable to assume that Blake's catalogue entry was written close to the time.

The ultimate purpose of Milton's redemptive descent to 'Eternal Death' is to awaken the sleeping body of Albion. Blake's notion of the Eternal Man is itself derived from Swedenborg, who conceived of three Heavens composing a Grand Man, with his various members and organs having corresponding celestial parts. (This doctrine was probably encountered by Blake when he read Swedenborg's *Heaven and Hell*, nos. 59–67, possibly in 1788, but it does not appear in his work before *The Four Zoas*.) In his great speech prior to descending into the lower world, Milton declares:

> I in my Selfhood am that Satan: I am that Evil One!
> He is my Spectre! in obedience to loose him from my Hells
> To claim the Hells, my Furnaces, I go to Eternal Death.

$$(14[15]: 30-2, E 108)$$

Swedenborg says in *True Christian Religion*, no. 115, that the Last Judgement of 1757 involved 'the subduing of the Hells, restoring the Heavens to Order, and establishing a new Church'; and elsewhere he asserts that 'the Lord was to come into the world, to accomplish a complete or final Judgement, and thereby subjugate the then prevailing power of the Hells, which was effected by Spiritual Combats, or temptations admitted to assault the Humanity derived from the Mother, and by continual victories then obtained'.[117] Blake's Milton likewise triumphs over temptations and assaults 'in conflict with those Female forms' who are his wives and daughters.[118] Some of the difficulties about gender that this indicates must be discussed in connection with the Virgin Ololon and the prelude to the Great Harvest & Vintage.

Even more important for the theme of a possible apocalypse leading to a possible millennium is the model of history shared by Swedenborg and Blake, according to which 'Churches' succeed one another, each in turn reaching its 'period',[119] and then giving way to its successor.

---

[117] Emanuel Swedenborg, *The Doctrine of the New Jerusalem Concerning the Lord* (London: R. Hindmarsh, 1791), no. 3.

[118] 17[19]: 7 E 110. The conception of the 'Maternal Humanity' that Blake derived from Swedenborg will appear in *Jerusalem*, where 'his [Christ's] Maternal Humanity must be put off Eternally' (90: 36, E 250); cf. Swedenborg: 'The Lord Successively put off the humanity from the Divinity in Himself, which is the Divine Humanity and the Son of God' (*New Jerusalem*, no. 35). The Maternal Humanity is identified with the purely material aspect of Christ's being that must be 'put off' so that he may 'put on' his spiritual body. Such bifurcation is very close to what happened when 'Milton drove' his emanations 'Down into Ulro' (21[23]: 16–17, E 115), as will be discussed below.

[119] S. Foster Damon was the first to suggest this connection, in *William Blake: His Philosophy and Symbols*, p. 427.

Swedenborg postulates five Churches, beginning with Adam and Eve. Second comes 'the Ancient Church', comprising Noah, his three sons, and their posterity. Heber, the eponymous founder of the Hebrew Church, instituted sacrificial worship. The Word was written under the Israelitish and Jewish Church, which is sometimes viewed as one with Heber. These four Churches of the Old Testament are represented in Daniel's description of Nebuchadnezzar's dream, with the Christian Church as the fifth Church. 'And it may be seen from the Word, that all these Churches in Process of Time declined, till there was an End of them, which is called the Consummation'.[120] The idea of a crisis in the modern Church leading to its 'Consummation' is also common to Blake and Swedenborg as evidenced by the passage from *Milton*, 22[24] quoted above and *Divine Providence*, no. 328, where Swedenborg writes: 'But the successive Vastation of the Christian Church in it's final Period, is described by the Lord in Matthew Chap. xxiv, in Mark, Chap. xiii, and in Luke, Chap. xxi; and the Consummation itself in the Apocalypse'. This theme was sounded at the opening of the General Conference of 1789, where an extract from *True Christian Religion* was read, asserting that 'the Christian Church, which is founded on the Word, and is now at it's Period, may again revive and derive Spirit through Heaven from the Lord'.[121] Both 'Period' and 'Consummation' (cf. 'the Great Consummation' (*Milton*, 20[22]: 23, E 114) are, furthermore, technical Swedenborgian terms appropriated by Blake.[122] However, for Blake the 'Period' of the Churches is the consolidation of state religion with the rationalistic systems that he calls Deism, a phenomenon that necessarily precedes the Last Judgement, and Blake conceives Swedenborg himself as a victim of the mindset of the institutional churches. Deliverance from the cycle of history must come from somewhere else.

In the passage under discussion, Blake takes George Whitefield and John Wesley as exemplars. Rintrah says:

> But then I rais'd up Whitefield, Palamabron raisd up Westley,
> And these are the cries of the Churches before the two Witnesses[']
> Faith in God the dear Saviour who took on the likeness of men:

[120] Emanuel Swedenborg, *Angelic Wisdom Concerning the Divine Providence* (London: R. Hindmarsh, 1790), no. 328.

[121] See James Speirs (ed.), *Minutes of the First Seven Sessions of the New Jerusalem Church Reprinted from the Original Editions* (London: James Speirs, 1885), p. 9.

[122] See also *Milton*, 25[27]: 37, E 120; 18[20]: 28, 29, E 111. 'Consummation' appears once in the Bible (Dan. 9: 27: 'even until the consummation'), 'period' not at all.

Becoming obedient to death, even the death of the Cross
The Witnesses lie dead in the Street of the Great City
No Faith is in all the Earth: the Book of God is trodden under Foot:
He sent his two Servants Whitefield & Westley; were they Prophets
Or were they Idiots or Madmen? shew us Miracles!
Can you have greater Miracles than these? Men who devote
Their lifes whole comfort to intire scorn & injury & death.[123]

Presumably Whitefield was raised up by Rintrah (Wrath) because he emphasized the Calvinist belief in the predestination of some to grace and others to damnation, while Palamabron (Pity) raised up the mild Arminian Wesley. The two founders of Methodism are equated with two witnesses of Revelation 11 who are killed by the beast from the bottomless pit, but who return to life after three and a half days. Although Whitefield and Wesley were not martyred literally, they frequently risked death in the course of their ministry. As Robert Southey reported in his biography of Wesley, Whitefield was nearly murdered in Dublin in 1743.[124] In their history of dissent first published in 1809, David Bogue and James Bennett wrote: 'On a tour to Birmingham and its neighborhood, Mr Wesley endured still more severe trials. . . . Here the rector and the neighboring gentry, set the mob upon them at every opportunity; so that many of the hearers were wounded, and the preaching house rased to the ground. As usual, however, the blood of the martyrs was the seed of the church'.[125] Blake takes the willingness of Whitefield and Wesley to risk their lives as a symbolic death. In another sense, they could say with Blake's Milton 'I go to Eternal Death!'[126]—the willing sacrifice of the Selfhood. The fact that Wesley was still active when Blake was an adult, furthermore, made his example available to Blake in a special way.[127]

At first, Whitefield and Wesley may seem unlikely candidates for Blakean heroes. Whitefield's Calvinist predestinarianism would certainly have been unacceptable to Blake, and although Wesley's Arminianism could have been more attractive to him, Blake can

---

[123] 22[24]: 55–62, 23[25]: 1–2, E 118.
[124] Robert Southey, *The Life of Wesley and the Rise and Progress of Methodism*, 2nd edn. (London: Longman, Hurst, Rees, Orme, and Brown, 1820), 2: 271.
[125] David Bogue and James Bennett, *The History of Dissenters, from the Revolution in 1688, to the Year 1808* (London, 1810), 3: 64.   [126] 14[15]: 14, E 108.
[127] Wesley took cold while preaching in Lambeth (while Blake was residing there) and died on 17 Oct. 1791. His body was viewed by large crowds of people during the following days.

hardly have been unaware of Wesley's having sided with the Crown in the American War and having defended John Wilkes's exclusion from Parliament.[128] Blake chooses to ignore at this point the schism between Calvinist and Arminian Methodists, just as, for example, he ignores whatever differences he may have had with Thomas Paine in annotating Bishop Richard Watson's *Apology for the Bible* in 1798. What is germane for Blake here is not theology but the ceaseless activity of Whitefield and Wesley on behalf of the regeneration of Albion. The theological question does, however, enter *Milton* in another way, when Los instructs his sons and helpers on how to bind the three classes of men in sheaves for the Last Judgement. As is generally recognized, the three classes are categorized as if in Calvinist terms, but with ironical inversions of meaning.

> The first, the Elect from before the foundation of the World:
> The second, the Redeem'd. The Third, The Reprobate & form'd
> To destruction from the mothers womb.

> (7: 1–3, E 100)

Blake's Elect, instead of being predestined for salvation, are in a Satanic state of error, accusing others of sin. 'They cannot believe in Eternal Life / Except by Miracle & a New Birth' (25[27]: 33–4, E 122). The Reprobate, rather than being predestined to damnation, are prophetic figures who 'never cease to Believe' (35). The Redeemd 'live in doubts & fears perpetually tormented by the Elect' (36); they have not completed the process of redemption but are in a perpetual state of taking part in it. These concepts and terms bring with them a rich aura of associations from Blake's time and the period immediately preceding it. For the purposes of illustration, one Wesley text, *Predestination Calmly Considered* (first published in 1752) will show the remarkable parallels between Wesley's treatment of the subject and Blake's.

Early in *Predestination Calmly Considered*, Wesley quotes Calvin's definitions of election and reprobation in *Institutes of the Christian Religion*:

All men are not created for the same end; but some are fore-ordained to eternal life, others to eternal damnation. So according as every man was created

---

[128] See Maldwyn Edward, *John Wesley and the Eighteenth Century* (London: Allen and Unwin, 1933). Edward points out, however, that Wesley preached against slavery and that many Methodists followed him in embracing abolitionism. On the theological relationship between Blake and Wesley, see Richard E. Brantley's important discussion in *Locke, Wesley, and the Method of English Romanticism* (Gainesville, Fla.: University of Florida Press, 1984), pp. 129–36.

for the one or the other, we say he was *elected*, i.e. predestinated to life, or *reprobated*, i.e. predestinated to damnation.[129]

Wesley then goes on to summarize the Calvinist view as follows:

Before the foundations of the world were laid, God of his own will and pleasure, fixt a decree concerning all the children of men who should be born unto the end of the world. This decree was unchangeable with regard to God, and irresistible with regard to man. And herein it was ordained, that one part of mankind should be saved from sin and hell, without help, and all the rest left to perish for ever and ever, without help, without hope.[130]

Wesley accuses those who hold such of view as saying in effect:

[Christ] Loved *thee*, thou reprobate! Gave himself for *thee*? Away, thou hast neither part nor lot herein. Thou believe in Christ thou accursed spirit! damned or ever thou wert born! . . . . And from the time thou wast born under the irrevocable curse of God, thou canst have no peace. For there is no peace to the wicked, and such thou art doomed to continue, even from thy mother's womb.[131]

The whole scheme, argues Wesley, amounts to irresistible grace for the elect with unconditional reprobation as its companion, and, controverting such a view, he argues: 'In disposing the eternal states of men . . . it is clear, that not sovereignty alone, but justice, mercy, and truth hold the reins'.[132] Esau, commonly regarded as a type of the reprobate, had his heart changed by God, and 'there is great reason to hope, that *Esau* as (as well as *Jacob*) is now in *Abraham's* bosom'.[133] Some of Blake's correspondences in phraseology are striking, to a point where his text and Wesley's may be read as glosses on each other. However, Blake goes beyond Wesley in two important respects.

According to Wesley, the reprobate can be saved because Christ 'willeth all men to be saved'.[134] However, for Blake the Elect and the Redeem'd must be saved by the Reprobate:

Then an Eternal rose
Saying. If the Guilty should be condemn'd, he must be an Eternal Death
And one must die for another throughout all Eternity.
Satan is fall'n from his station & never can be redeem'd
But must be new Created continually moment by moment

[129] John Wesley, *Predestination Calmly Considered*, 5th edn. (London: R. Hawes, 1776), pp. 5–6.   [130] Ibid., p. 9.
[131] Ibid., pp. 26, 32.   [132] Ibid., p. 41.   [133] Ibid., p. 42.   [134] Ibid., p. 69.

And therefore the Class of Satan shall be calld the Elect, & those
Of Rintrah. the Reprobate, & those of Palamabron the Redeem'd

(11[12]: 16–22, E 105)

Therefore Milton's Elect self must endure 'Eternal Death' by descending to earth to redeem his past errors, entering William Blake's
foot in the form of a falling star and investing the Reprobate Blake with
his own psychic energies. Mistakenly, the sons of Los identify Milton /
Blake as the historical Milton whose 'Religion is the cause' of endless
'destruction' in the contemporary world (22[24]: 39). Los, however,
recognizes this manifestation as a signal of impending apocalypse:

> But as to this Elected Form who is returned again
> He is the Signal that the Last Vintage now approaches
> Nor Vegetation may go on till all the Earth is reapd.

(24[26]: 41–3, E 120)

Blake continues to take both Milton and Wesley further than either
would wish to go. Although Milton has been claimed as a radical millenarian on the basis of some of his early prose (see Introduction, p. 12),
in *Paradise Lost* Michael's exposition to Adam puts no term to the historical period preceding the millennium:

> thy Saviour and thy Lord,
> Last in the Clouds from Heav'n to be reveal'd
> In glory of the Father, to dissolve
> *Satan* with his perverted World, then raise
> From the conflagrant mass, purg'd and refin'd,
> New Heav'ns, new Earth, Ages of endless date
> Founded in righteousness and peace and love,
> To bring forth fruits Joy and eternal Bliss.[135]

Wesley distanced himself from any form of millenarianism, but as the
example of Ralph Mather shows, Methodism attracted seekers who
would not be content with immanentism but who were imbued with
millennial desire. As E. P. Thompson remarks, 'There was, indeed, a
millenarial instability within the heart of Methodism itself. . . . Even if
literal belief in the millennium was discouraged, the apocalyptic manner of Methodist revival meetings inflamed the imagination and prepared the way for the acceptance of chiliastic prophets after 1790'.[136]

---

[135] *Paradise Lost*, xii. 544–51, p. 466.
[136] E. P. Thompson, *The Making of the English Working Class*, rev. edn. (Harmondsworth: Penguin, 1968), pp. 52–3.

It is this 'millenarian instability' that gives Blake an opportunity to enlist Methodism as well as Milton in his scenario of apocalypse and millennium.

The main confluence of these two elements manifests itself in the idea of 'Milton the Awakener' (21[23]: 33, E 116). Los cries to the Labourers of the Vintage:

The Awakener is come. Outstretchd over Europe! The Vision of God is fulfilld
The Ancient Man upon the Rock of Albion Awakes.

(25[27]: 22–3, E 122)

It was impossible to use such language without stirring associations of the Great Awakening of 1740–2 in America, in which Whitefield had personally participated, and the manner in which they stressed words associated with the verb *awake*. George Whitefield in his journals speaks of a clergyman who 'had lately been awakened' and tells of 'talking and giving advice to awakened souls'.[137] He writes of a sermon 'which under God began the awakening at London, Bristol, Gloucester, and Gloucestershire', and while in America he says: 'My dear and honoured friend, Mr Wesley, is left behind to confirm those who are awakened'.[138] One congregation, after hearing Whitefield preach, 'seemed like persons awakened by the last trump, and coming out of their graves to judgement'.[139] The term was also frequently used by Wesley, as when he wrote of 'that uncommon awakening' that Ralph Mather had occasioned among a group of schoolchildren.[140]

Although, ironically, Rintrah and Palamabron are ignorant of the true identity of Milton as the Awakener, in their long speech to Los they urge:

Awake thou sleeper on the Rock of Eternity Albion awake
The trumpet of Judgment hath twice sounded: all Nations are awake
But thou art still heavy and dull: Awake Albion awake![141]

Remaining 'unconvincd by Los's arguments' (24[26]: 45, E 120), they are also unaware of the fact that Albion's awakening, precipitated by Milton's descent and his entering Blake's left foot, has already begun. In 15[17]:

[137] *George Whitefield's Journals (1737–1741)*, a facsimile reproduction of the edition of William Wale in 1905 with an Introduction by William V. Davis (Gainesville, Fla.: Scholars' Facsimiles and Reprints, 1969), pp. 71, 77.
[138] Ibid., pp. 79, 186.   [139] Ibid., p. 424.
[140] *John Wesley's Journal*, 6: 11. On Maher, see Introduction, above.
[141] 23[25]: 3–5, E 118.

Milton saw Albion upon the Rock of Ages,
Deadly pale outstretchd and snowy cold, storm coverd;
A Giant form of perfect beauty outstretchd on the rock
In solemn death.

(36–9, E 109–10)

It is on this same plate (lines 47–9) that Milton invests Blake with poetic/prophetic power:

Then first I saw him in the Zenith as a falling star,
Descending perpendicular, swift as the swallow or swift;
And on my left foot falling on the tarsus, enterd there.

The situation parallels John's vision in Revelation 9: 1: 'And the fifth angel sounded, and I saw a star fall from heaven unto the earth: and to him was given the key of the bottomless pit'. At the same time, as is widely recognized, 'tarsus' involves a pun on Saul of Tarsus, and Saul's conversionary experience on the road to Damascus in Acts 9.[142] Although Milton's way is temporarily barred by Urizen, the principle of patriarchal repression that Blake regards as having dominated Saul, the historical figure Milton, and some aspects of himself, Milton overcomes his opponent by a form of non-violent combat, moulding 'the red clay of Succoth' and 'Creating new flesh on the Demon cold' (19[21]: 10, 13, E 112). It is this refusal to employ the methods of his adversary—'one giving life, the other giving death' (line 29), parallel to Prometheus's unsaying of his curse against Jupiter in *Prometheus Unbound*, that makes the regeneration of humanity begin:

Now Albions sleeping Humanity began to turn upon his Couch;
Feeling the electric flame of Miltons awful precipitate descent.

(20[22]: 25–6, E 114)

The use of the word 'electric' here demands special notice, as it illustrates a characteristic aspect of Blake's imagination: the tendency to combine the archetypal and the personal.

There are only three uses of the word 'electric' and its cognates in Blake's writings, and this is the only one in his poetical works. The other two are in letters alluding to a treatment for rheumatism

---

[142] See, e.g., Erdman, *Illuminated Blake*, p. 233. On the interplay of Blake and Paul throughout *Milton*, see David Riede, 'Blake's *Milton*: On Membership in the Church Paul', in *Re-membering Milton: Essays on the Texts and Traditions* (New York and London: Methuen, 1987), pp. 257–77.

undergone by Mrs Blake, and the conjunction of these forges an interesting link between the apocalyptic and the domestic. On 23 October 1804 Blake wrote to William Hayley:

My wife returns her heartfelt thanks for your kind inquiry concerning her health. She is surprisingly recovered. Electricity is the wonderful cause; the swelling of her knees is entirely reduced. She is very near as free from rheumatism as she was five years ago, and we have the greatest confidence in her perfect recovery. (E 756)

The electricity was supplied by a physician named Thomas Birch, whose 'Electrical Magic' Blake again praises in another letter to Hayley.[143] A mutual friend of the Blakes and of the Butts family, Birch evidently took four copies of the *Designs for a Series of Ballads written by William Hayley* (Chichester, 1802) with Blake's engravings), receiving three copies for Butts and keeping one himself.[144] He was the founder of an electrical department at St Thomas's Hospital, and it has been plausibly suggested that Blake intended a compliment to him in referring to that institution as 'one of the most amiable features of the Christian Church' in the second *Prospectus* to his *Canterbury Pilgrims* engraving.[145] The methods Birch used are described in his *Essay on the Mechanical Application of Electricity*.[146] His apparatus comprised 'a moderate-sized cylinder, conductor, and Leyden jar, with an insulating chain and electrometer; a glass-mounted director with a wooden handle, to the extremity of which a brass ball or wooden point are fitted, and a brass director mounted on wood'.[147] Treatments consisted of applying 'the fluid', friction (by sparks), and shock. Although Birch does not mention rheumatism, which is what Catherine Blake is supposed to have had, a number of his cases involved the swelling of joints, which was one of her symptoms. These Birch treated by the shock method, and this is likely to have been the 'electric flame' which Blake credited with restoring his wife, as well as beginning the awakening of Albion.

Blake had further reason to admire John Birch because of his

---

[143] Letter to Hayley, 18 Dec. 1804, E 759.

[144] See Letter to Thomas Butts dated 25 Apr. 1803, E 728; and Bentley, *Blake Records*, p. 116.

[145] E 569. See John Adlard, 'Blake and Electrical "Magic"', *Neophilologus*, 53 (1969): 422–3. Information about Birch from *DNB*, *s.v.*

[146] Thomas Birch, *Essay on the Mechanical Application of Electricity* (London, 1802). Birch notes that this is a revision of a former work written with George Adams.

[147] Ibid., pp. 1–2.

authorship (as indicated in the British Library Catalogue of Printed Books) of an anonymous pamphlet entitled *A Dressing for L**D T**R**W, Prepared by a Surgeon* (London, 1797). The author attacks Lord Thurlow (whom Blake is believed to have caricatured as 'the Guardian of the secret codes' in *Europe*[148]) for opposing higher standards for military surgeons. 'Mankind', the Surgeon writes, 'while they condemn your barbarity may admire the economy that produced it: for a *horse* is estimated at *twenty-eight* pounds, and a man only at *fifteen*'.[149] ('The Horse is of more value than the Man', sing the Cities in their war song in Night I of *The Four Zoas*.)[150] 'But perhaps', the author continues, 'it is the interest of government to sacrifice the lives of the wounded, rather than incur the expence of their maintenance'. Birch's courage in advocating the cause of wounded soldiers, as well as the personal benefit Catherine Blake felt she had derived from his treatments, gave him a place of honour in Albion's awakening. At the same time, the introduction of the electrical therapy that he gave Catherine Blake is a gateway to the millennial aspect of *Milton*. This may at first seem an odd statement; but, as we shall see again in discussing Coleridge's 'Reflections on Having Left a Place of Retirement', the rural cottage inhabited by a loving couple can be seen as a microcosm of the millennium. Apocalypse is almost everywhere in *Milton*; as Susan Fox remarks, 'All the actions of the poem occur in the last segment of the moment, the last fragment of time itself, the instant before the apocalypse puts an end to time'.[151] Millennium is present, in contrast, only in the Blakes' cottage at Felpham and in its garden, where the concluding actions of the work take place, a sequence initiated by the appearance of the Virgin Ololon and immediately preceded by the splendid evocation of the twenty-eight Larks who span all of history.

In *Milton* there are several references to the traditional world-week of 6,000 years. This structure should include the Seven Eyes of God and the twenty-seven heavens with their Churches, but a contradiction exists between the Churches of history and the idea of a millennial state at the end of history. The Churches go round from Adam to Luther:

> And these the names of the Twenty-seven Heavens & their Churches
> Adam, Seth, Enos, Cainan, Mahalaleel, Jared, Enoch,

---

[148] See *Europe*, 15: 20, E 64; Erdman, *Blake: Prophet against Empire*, pp. 216–18.
[149] John Birch, *A Dressing for L**DT**R**W* (London, 1797), p. 6.
[150] 15: 1, E 309.
[151] Susan Fox, *Poetic Form in Blake's Milton* (Princeton: Princeton University Press, 1976), p. 18.

> Methuselah, Lamech: these are Giants mighty Hermaphroditic
> Noah, Shem, Arphaxad, Cainan the second, Salah, Heber,
> Peleg, Reu, Serug, Nahor, Terah, these are the Female-Males
> A Male within a Female hid as in an Ark & Curtains,
> Abraham, Moses, Solomon, Paul, Constantine, Charlemaine
> Luther, these seven are the Male-Females, the Dragon Forms
> Religion hid in War, a Dragon red & hidden Harlot.

(37[41]: 35-43, E 138)

But because they are time-bound—'Remember how Calvin and
Luther in fury premature / Sow'd War and stern division between
Papists & Protestants' (23[25]: 47–8, E 119)—their number is the cube
of three, Blake's most negatively valorized numerical symbol.[152] 'The
millenarian tradition', as Edmund Leach has observed, 'is a theory
about temporal recapitulation'.[153] However, implicit in that theory is
an escape from temporal recapitulation. The conception of an exit
from the cycle is suggested in *Milton*, 15[17]: by the addition of a shadowy eighth to the Seven Eyes—an eighth day of the world-week, as it
were. Originally this Eighth was Jesus, who was 'driven away with the
Seven Starry Ones into the Ulro' (22[24]: 1, E 116), and whose surro-
gate is the form of Milton's sleeping body, 'Which now arose and
walk'd with them in Eden, as an Eighth / Image Divine tho' darken'd'
(15[17]: 5–6, E 109). However, as the apocalyptic climax of *Milton* nears
in 35[39] there are once more 'Eight / Immortal Starry-Ones' (29–30).
And as a parallel alternative to time-boundedness, Blake introduces an
important symbol: a twenty-eighth Lark added to the twenty-seven
that are dispatched through the Churches of Beulah.

> Just at the place to where the Lark mounts, is a Crystal Gate
> It is the enterance of the First Heaven named Luther: for
> The Lark is Los's Messenger thro the Twenty-seven Churches
> That the Seven Eyes of God who walk even to Satans Seat
> Thro all the Twenty-seven Heavens may not slumber nor sleep

(35[39]: 61–5, E 136)

---

[152] On the general subject of Blake's numerical symbolism, see G. M. Harper's valuable essay, 'The Divine Tetrad in Blake's *Jerusalem*', in *William Blake: Essays for S. Foster Damon*, ed. Alvin Rosenfeld (Providence, RI: Brown University Press, 1969), pp. 235–55.

[153] See Edmund Leach, 'Melchisedech and the Emperor: Icons of Subversion and Ortho-doxy', *Proceedings of the Royal Anthropological Institute of Great Britain and Ireland* (1972): 7. Blake would be an excellent example of Leach's characterization of millenarianism as presenting an 'icon of subversion' against an 'icon of orthodoxy'.

The lark is traditionally associated with the dawn, as in Shakespeare's 'Hark, hark! the lark at heaven's gate sings /And Phoebus 'gins to rise'.[154] Later, Blake would picture the lark of Milton's *L'Allegro* as a radiant angel rising into the dark sky, in illustration of Milton's lines:

> To hear the Lark begin his flight
> And singing startle the dull Night
> From his Watch Tower in the Skies
> Till the dappled Dawn does rise.[155]

The twenty-eighth Lark can also be associated with images of the millennial dawn in Blake's earlier works. The product of Blake's two most highly valorized numbers, 7 and 4, this Lark provides a way out of the cycle of history, both at the end of time for collective humanity and at any moment in the life of a given individual, and these two possibilities are momentarily brought together in Blake's garden.

The ascent of the Twenty-Eighth Lark, which could be compared to the arrival of the Spirit of the Hour in *Prometheus Unbound*, coincides with the descent of the Ololon:

> When on the highest lift of his light pinions he arrives
> At that bright Gate, another Lark meets him & back to back
> They touch their pinions tip tip: and each descend
> To their respective Earths & there all night consult with Angels
> Of Providence & with the Eyes of God all night in slumbers
> Inspired: & at the dawn of day send out another Lark
> Into another Heaven to carry news upon his wings
> Thus are the Messengers dispatchd till they reach the Earth again
> In the East Gate of Golgonooza, & the Twenty-eighth bright
> Lark. met the Female Ololon descending into my Garden

$$(36[40]: 1-10, E 136)$$

Blake deliberately made the design for this plate appear naïve: a two-dimensional, comic-book-like rendering of a thatched cottage with himself walking in the green garden before it and a larger-than-life-Ololon descending from the sky, her filmy garments swept by the air. When Blake addresses Ololon as a 'Daughter of Beulah', it is in a tone in keeping with the design. The keynote is domesticity, in keeping with the idea of the Cot as a potential microcosm of the millennial: 'Virgin of Providence fear not to enter into my Cottage' (36[40]: 28). This could be, considering the 'Mighty Hosts' that have clothed themselves

---

[154] *Cymbeline*, II. iii. 22–3.

[155] See Butlin, 1: 396 (no. 243) and 2: pl. 673. The lines are given as transcribed by Blake.

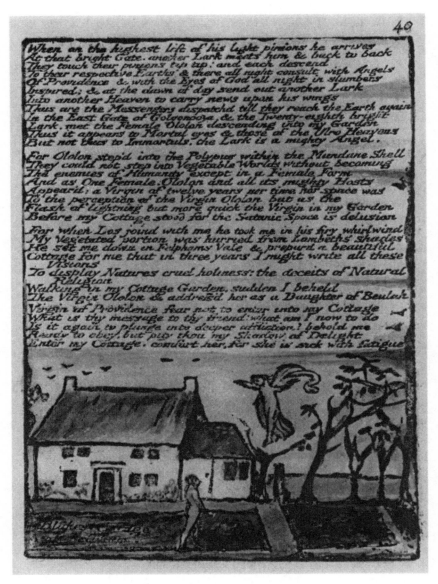

1. William Blake, *Milton*, plate 40 of copy D

'in a Female Form' (15–16), the visit of the gods in disguise to Deucalion and Pyrrha, or the 'three men' whom Abraham invited into his and Sarah's tent in the plains of Mamre (Gen. 18: 1–10). Divine beings descend to the realm of the pastoral in appropriate guise. However, as soon as Ololon asks for directions—'Knowest thou of Milton who descended / Driven from Eternity; him I seek!' (37[41]: 1–2), enormous forces break through the thin partitions of nature. One result is the manifestation in their true forms of Satan and Rahab Babylon, linked to Blake's paradigmatic text as 'A Dragon red & hidden Harlot which John in Patmos saw' (40[46]: 22, E 142). Once these excrementitious husks have been cast off, the culminating apocalypse(s) of the last two plates can take place.

> Then as a Moony Ark Ololon descended to Felphams Vale
> In clouds of blood, in streams of gore, with dreadful thunderings
> Into the Fires of Intellect that rejoic'd in Felphams Vale
> Around the Starry Eight: with one accord the Starry Eight became
> One Man Jesus the Saviour. wonderful! round his limbs
> The Clouds of Ololon folded as a Garment dipped in blood
> Written within & without in woven letters: & the Writing
> Is the Divine Revelation in the Litteral expression:
> A Garment of War, I heard it namd the Woof of Six Thousand Years.

$$(42[49]: 7–15, E 143)$$

The Garment dipped in blood refers to Jacob's prophecy in Genesis 49: 11: 'he washed his garments in wine, and his clothes in the blood of grapes', which is here identified with the vesture of Jesus for which the soldiers gambled after the Crucifixion; and in both senses it is here a figure of the body in which Jesus was incarnated. Lines 13–14 refer to the book seen in vision by John, 'written within and on the backside, sealed with seven seals' (Rev. 5: 1). This is the Book of Revelation itself, or rather, Blake's version of it, reinscribed in an engraver's mirror writing. As Nelson Hilton perceptively points out, the spelling 'litteral' was already an anachronism in Blake's time and so calls attention to itself as having a special meaning (one could compare 'Tyger'), in this instance emphasizing 'the letter that is its etymon . . . not an entity, but a process . . . a textual weaving'.[156] Ololon here is no longer the Virgin of twelve

---

[156] Nelson Hilton, *Literal Imagination: Blake's Vision of Words* (Berkeley: University of California Press, 1983), p. 7. David Riede remarks: 'Inevitably, Blake's poem does not end with a seamless vision, but with a woven garment of language that prevents, or defers, revelation' ('Blake's *Milton*', p. 275).

years but the multiple identity, too terrible for human sight, that had
veiled itself in her form.

What of the Virgin Ololon? A few lines before the passage quoted
above there was a separation into two components, Virgin and Ololon,
and the Virgin united, in a sense, with an aspect of Milton:

> . . . the Virgin divided Six-fold & with a shriek
> Dolorous that ran thro all Creation a Double Six-fold Wonder!
> Away from Ololon she divided & fled into the depths
> Of Miltons shadow as a Dove upon the stormy Sea.
>
> (3–6)

One could imagine a different scenario, one in which the millennial
would be the sexual union of Milton with his Emanation, along the
lines of 'an improvement of sensual enjoyment' as in *The Marriage*
(E 39). This is what Blake has deliberately made impossible in *Milton*.
The New Testament prototype here is the raising of the daughter of
Jairus, the ruler of the synagogue in Mark 5: 22–43 and Luke 8: 41–56.
Before Jesus can arrive at the house of Jairus, he is informed that the girl
is dead. 'And when he was come in, he saith unto them, Why make ye
this ado, and weep? the damsel is not dead, but sleepeth.' Whereupon
Jesus calls upon the girl to arise: 'And straightway the damsel arose, and
walked; for she was of the age of twelve years. And they were astonished
with a great astonishment.'[157] By making Ololon pre-pubescent, Blake
obviates any sexual interpretation of the figurative meaning of the
action. As Betsy Bolton remarks, 'gender and sexuality in particular
run through the fabric of this prophecy as a frayed and contradictory
strand'.[158] Whatever might be said about Blake's anticipating Freud's
notion of polymorphous perversity, there is nothing either polymorphous or perverse about the union, if that is what it is, of Milton
and the Virgin. It is *pre*sexual, and that is what it must be in the dynamic
of *Milton, a Poem*, as Ololon explains just before her/their division:

> Altho' our Human Power can sustain the severe contentions
> Of Friendship, our Sexual cannot: but flies into the Ulro.
> Hence arose all our terrors in Eternity!
>
> (41[48]: 32–4, E 143)

This leaves the millennial to be overwhelmed by the apocalyptic at the

---

[157] Mark 5: 39, 42. This parallel is observed by Hilton, *Literal Imagination*, p. 42.
[158] Betsy Bolton, '"A Garment dipped in blood": Ololon and Problems of Gender in
Blake's *Milton*', *Studies in Romanticism*, 36 (1997): 61.

end of *Milton, a Poem*. It is true that Blake's transformative visionary experience is brought back just a dozen or so lines from the end:

> I fell outstretchd upon the path
> A moment, & my Soul returnd into its mortal state
> To Resurrection & Judgment in the Vegetable Body
> And my sweet Shadow of Delight stood trembling by my side
>
> (42[49]: 25–8, E 143)

However, after such 'terrific'—to use a favourite Blakean word—manifestations of the apocalyptic, the millennial appears to have no space in which to exist. A faint historical trace appears when 'Los listens to the Cry of the Poor Man: his Cloud / Over London in volume terrific, low bended in anger' (34–5), yet this ethical element appears almost unrelated to the sporting of Lions and Tygers and the gathering of all Animals upon the earth in the poem's last line, 'To go forth to the Great Harvest & Vintage of the Nations' (43[50]: 1, E 144).

Milton, a Poem promises throughout to realize an apocalypse that will be succeeded by a millennium. Apocalypse occurs at several points—on an individual level in the form of William Blake's receiving Milton as a falling star and Blake's subsequently becoming one with Los, the Spirit of Prophecy, and on a communal level in the anticipation of the last Harvest and Vintage, realized at the end of the poem. Millennium is announced in the great chiliastic lyric of plate 1:

> I will not cease from mental Fight,
> Nor shall my Sword sleep in my hand:
> Till we have built Jerusalem
> In Englands green & pleasant Land.
>
> (E 95–6)

Yet this collective millennium is never achieved or even attempted in *Milton*. There are millennial traces in some magnificent visions of the natural world, and a potential microcosm of it in the lives of Blake and his 'sweet Shadow of Delight' at Felpham, but the broader millennial potential that might lie in the freeing of Orc by Milton is introduced only to be abandoned. Los tells Rintrah and Palamabron:

> I recollect an old Prophecy in Eden recorded in gold; and oft
> Sung to the harp: That Milton of the land of Albion.
> Should up ascend forward from Felphams Vale & break the Chain
> Of Jealousy from all its roots.
>
> (23[25]: 35–8, E 119)

This prophecy, remembered by Los in almost the same words in 20[22]: 56–61, is left unrealized, for reasons not difficult to imagine. The freeing of what Orc represents could now have no correlative in history. We glimpse the Orc of the Lambeth books—'Lo Orc arises on the Atlantic. Lo his blood and fire /Glow on Americas shore' (23[25]: 6–7, E 118), but without effect or aftermath. This virtual abandonment of the millennial redounds upon the apocalyptic, making not only Blake's account of his personal experience but also the Great Harvest and Vintage entirely immanent. Despite Blake's opening address to the 'Young Men of the New Age' (E 95), he appears to have sensed that something had gone awry, for he greatly scaled back his original plans for *Milton*. Originally subtitled 'a Poem in 12 Books', it was altered in the first two copies produced to 'a Poem in 2 Books'.[159] The two books are, in addition, greatly asymmetrical, the first comprising about twice as many plates as the second. Of course, Mathematical Proportion, to use Blake's terms, should be subdued to Living Proportion, but these terms do not help us to find artistic grounds for the compression or truncation of Book the Second. These difficulties suggest Blake's realization that in *Milton* he had promised apocalypse and millennium in history but had delivered them only within the self.

[159] The change was made not in the etched plate but in colouring the title-pages. See *Milton, a Poem*, ed. Essick and Viscomi, p. 111. All four copies consist of two books, and the single line of verse on the last plate of Book the Second is followed by 'Finis' (E 144), so the reason for Blake's not changing the title-page numeral in copies C and D remains conjectural.

2

Coleridge

Preternatural Agency

In the autumn of 1794 Coleridge wrote what was up to then his most ambitious poetic work. Not to be published under his own name until 1817, and then in the radically altered form of 'The Destiny of Nations', this long passage was contributed to Book II of Robert Southey's epic *Joan of Arc* (Bristol, 1796), where in the prose Argument it was designated 'Preternatural agency'. Although we cannot tell which of the poets made up the rubric, 'preternatural' is a good Coleridgean word. One of the two essays he intended to annex to *Christabel* was 'on the Praeternatural',[1] and it has been argued that *Christabel* should be understood as a poem of the preternatural— uncanny but not supernatural.[2] It is therefore as 'Preternatural Agency' that I shall refer to this work. It is virtually a poem complete in itself, one whose importance as such has not been generally recog- nized, even to the point of its being considered in some Coleridge criticism as over a hundred lines shorter than it is.[3]

[1] Letter to Thomas Poole, 16 Mar. 1801; *CL* 2: 707.
[2] See Arthur M. Nethercot, *The Road to Tryermaine* (Chicago: University of Chicago Press, 1939), pp. 199–205. Jerome Christensen suggests that Coleridge's use of the term may derive from David Hartley's. See Christensen, *Coleridge's Blessed Machine of Language* (Ithaca, NY: Cornell University Press, 1981), p. 172. Cf. David Hartley, *Observations on Man: His Frame, His Duty, and His Expectations*, ed. Rev. Herman Andrew Pistorius (London: Joseph Johnson, 1791): '. . . in mad persons the vibrations in the internal parts of the brain are preternaturally increased . . .' (1: 402).
[3] Ernest Hartley Coleridge (*CPW* 1: 131 n.) declared that 255 lines in book II of *Joan of Arc* were Coleridge's, a figure repeated by E. L. Griggs (*CL* 1: 172 n. 2); H. W. Piper, 250 lines (*The Active Universe* (London: Athlone Press, 1962), p. 37); Reeve Parker (*Coleridge's Meditative Art* (Ithaca, NY: Cornell University Press, 1975), p. 96); and James Engell and W. J. Bate (eds., *Biographia Literaria*, 1: 26 n. and 1: 123 n.). Carl Woodring, however, gives it as 365 lines (*Politics in the Poetry of Coleridge* (Madison: University of Wisconsin Press, 1961), p. 170. Woodring's tally would accord with Southey's own statement (preface to *Joan of Arc*, p. vi) that Coleridge wrote the first 450 lines of book II, with the exception of four passages, which he enumerates and which would give Coleridge approximately 361 lines ('approximately',

'Preternatural Agency' is, of course, important for reasons other than its length. It is the first of a group of poems written in the 1790s—among the others are 'Religious Musings', 'Ode on the Departing Year', 'Fire, Famine, and Slaughter', and 'France: an Ode'—in which Coleridge views the political events of his time as apocalyptic in nature. In 'Preternatural Agency' Coleridge pours apocalyptic wrath upon England's war against Revolutionary France and hints at a millennial future to follow what is regarded as the Revolution's inevitable victory. The subject of *Joan of Arc* is, as Southey warns the reader, 'the defeat of my country' (p. vii), and 'Preternatural Agency' projects that defeat in visionary terms. In Book I Southey implicitly sets his narrative against Shakespeare's patriotic myth of the fifteenth-century Anglo–French war, anticipating Hazlitt's view in *The Characters of Shakespeare's Plays* (1817). *Henry V* glorified the English invasion; *Henry VI, Part I* represented Joan as a liar and a strumpet; but Southey begins by describing English atrocities witnessed by Joan during and after the siege of Harfleur, giving the lie to Henry V's promise of mercy to the inhabitants after their surrender (Act III, scene iv), and he continues with the present disasters going on in Rouen. Joan, a mere spectator at first, changes after encountering the warrior Conrade, who represents a type of English Jacobin ideal, characterized by his look of 'fierce and terrible benevolence' (1. 375)—an expression that Charles Lamb singled out for praise.[4] Book I ends with Joan rescuing the wounded Dunois, the bastard son of Louis I, who would subsequently fight beside her. Although these incidents are hardly necessary to an understanding of 'Preternatural Agency', they do give an idea of the political assumptions that both poets expected would be shared by the reader.

Coleridge's purpose is to show how British aggression against France and its consequences are part of a divinely guided pattern building towards a historical apocalypse with a millennium to follow. For this reason he begins with a philosophical passage of some ninety lines that constitutes, as John Beer puts it, 'a very successful attempt to

because some of the four passages begin or end in the midst of lines). However, it is very likely that Coleridge's contribution ends not at line 450, but with the conclusion of Joan's prayer at line 452, because line 452 repeats line 442, already assigned to Coleridge, and line 453 takes up the narrative where it was left at the end of book I. This gives a figure of approximately 361 lines.

⁴ Letter to Coleridge dated 8–10 June 1796, in *The Letters of Charles and Mary Lamb*, ed. Charles W. Marrs, Jr. (Ithaca, NY: Cornell University Press, 1975), 1: 15; subsequent citations will be given in the text.

express in verse the processes of thought',[5] and that serves as a preamble to the mythical and visionary material to come. Coleridge begins with first principles: his 'deep preluding strain' is 'pour'd / To the Great Father, Only Rightful King' (2–3)—that 'Only' having unmistakable political reference in 1794. He then covers subjects as various as the poetry of liberty (the harp that hangs between the shields of Brutus and Leonidas, 9–12), the symbolic nature of sense perception ('one mighty alphabet / For infant minds' (20–1), our residence in Plato's cave (21–4), the busyness of God's 'component Monads' (47) in the natural world,[6] and the nature of Fancy, 'That first unsensualizes the dark mind' (81), as illustrated by a Lapp tale anticipatory of 'Frost at Midnight' (64–80). What do these divers elements have to do with what follows? In 'Preternatural Agency' Joan, a libertarian heroine under the direction of a divinely appointed Tutelary Spirit, will receive visions drawn from the imagery of the natural world through the mediation of Fancy, visions that reveal the intentions of the only Lawful King. The visionary parts of 'Preternatural Agency' are thus validated by the map of reality established in the preamble. The transition is not, however, directly from one to the other but through an intermediate mythological passage proleptic of the visions themselves.

The story of the Greenland Wizard that occupies lines 98–114, one of many indications of Coleridge's interest in the folk traditions of Northern peoples, is, as Coleridge's own note tells us, derived from David Crantz's *History of Greenland.*[7] As Mallet's *Northern Antiquities* served Blake as a source of mythology parallel to the classical and the Christian, so did Crantz's account of the indigenous Greenlanders. Crantz believed—and again we might compare some of the sources Blake drew on—that these people retained 'the small remains of the truth of the patriarchal religion' (1: 203) as did the American Indians and Asiatic Tartars. Crantz tells how in times of dearth at sea an Angekok, or sorcerer, with his *torngak*, or familiar spirit, journeys to

---

[5] John Beer, *Coleridge's Poetic Intelligence* (London: Macmillan, 1977), p. 61. Some inner contradictions regarding the relative roles of reason and superstition in this passage are well discussed by Robert Sternbach in an essay also important for establishing Miltonic parallels: 'Coleridge, Joan of Arc, and the Idea of Progress', *ELH*, 46 (1979): 248–61.

[6] As H. W. Piper and others have pointed out, Coleridge's Monads, which are elements of energy, are not Leibnizian. See *Active Universe*, pp. 39–40; Beer, *Coleridge's Poetic Intelligence*, pp. 59–63; and Ian Wylie, *Young Coleridge and the Philosophers of Nature* (Oxford: Clarendon Press, 1989), p. 45.

[7] David Crantz, *The History of Greenland: Containing a Description of the country and its Inhabitants* (2 vols., London, 1767). Crantz's book was translated from German and printed for the Moravian Brethren's Society for the furtherance of the Gospel among the Heathen.

liberate the fish and other sea creatures. Coleridge recounts how this 'Greenland Wizard' descends in a trance state to the bottom of the sea, where he encounters a dreadful female monster and, by the power of the Spirit of Good, forces her 'to unchain the foodful progeny / Of the Ocean stream' (113–14). The sea creatures then float up to the surface and provide food for the starving people. The story has suggestions both of messianic deliverance and of the feeding of the Israelites with manna, though these parallels are not developed explicitly. Such myths, 'On the victorious goodness of high God / Teaching Reliance' (115–16), form for Coleridge a system supportive of, not alternative to, Christianity. We then return to a specifically Christian source with the stepping of heavenly truth 'from Bethabra northward' (117), alluding to *Paradise Regained*[8] and creating a parallel between Coleridge's Joan and Milton's Jesus.

Joan's first vision is induced by 'the guardian Power whose ken / Still dwelt on France' (132–3). These 'illusions apt, / Shadowy of Truth' (135–6) begin with a desolate landscape that is almost immediately peopled with abstract personifications by Southey, who wrote lines 148–222. Coleridge then resumes the discourse of the 'tutelary Power' (224), who has come to resemble the similar narrating spirit in Count Constantin de Volney's *Ruins of Empire* (which Coleridge's friend and brother-in-law Robert Lovell borrowed from the Bristol Library on 2 April 1794[9]). A new myth begins with the birth of Love and the creation of life, becoming an allegory concerning the descent of Night to the Cave of Darkness and the return of this 'Hell-hag' (245) with all her personified progeny to the upper world, to be 'in camps and courts adored / Rebels from God and Monarchs o'er Mankind!' (258–9). When Coleridge later annotated and revised his copy of *Joan of Arc*, he wrote 'These are very fine Lines, tho' I say it, that should not; but hang me, if I know or ever did know the meaning of them, tho' my own composition'.[10] However, this is a typical later Coleridgean escape

    [8] See Reeve Parker, *Coleridge's Meditative Art* (Ithaca, NY: Cornell University Press, 1975), p. 49, citing *Paradise Regained*, i. 183–6.
    [9] Lovell's borrowing the book is recorded by George Whalley, in 'The Bristol Library Borrowings of Southey and Coleridge', *Library*, 5th ser., 4 (1949): 122.
    [10] From Coleridge's copy of *Joan of Arc* in the Berg Collection, New York Public Library, p. 53. I am grateful to Professor Paul Magnusson for drawing my attention to the importance of Coleridge's annotations in this copy. This material was first published by J. T. Brown, 'Bibliomania', *North British Review*, 40 (1864): 79–84; then by Brown in *Odds and Ends*, no. 19 (Edinburgh: Edmonston and Douglas, 1867). My quotations from Coleridge's MS notes on *Joan of Arc* are printed by permission of the Berg Collection of English and American Literature, New York Public Library, Astor, Lennox, and Tilden Foundations.

strategy—that the remark occurs in a manuscript note should not obscure the fact that others were meant to read it—for its general significance is clear enough. The rising of Love on gorgeous wings and the view of the first form of life ('the PROTOPLAST', with its implications of the birth of Venus 'on Confusion's charmed wave', 235–6) result in a temporary paradisaical state with the flight of Beldame Night. Once more there are biblical parallels, this time with Revelation (which is quoted in a note shortly afterwards). The Hell-hag combines the roles of Satan and the Whore of Babylon: Satan, chained for a thousand years, breaks out one last time (Rev. 20: 3); the Whore commits fornication with the kings of the earth (Rev. 17: 2). These will rule for a while but will be overthrown.

Coleridge's Revelation note is attached to Joan's auditory vision of music, which is troped into that of 'The white-rob'd multitude of slaughtered Saints' at line 308:

Revel. vi. 9, 11: And when he had opened the fifth seal, I saw under the altar the souls of them that were slain for the word of God and for the Testimony which they held. And white robes were given unto every one of them; and it was said unto them, that they should rest yet for a little Season, until their fellow-servants also, and their Brethren that should be killed, as they were, should be fulfilled.

In Coleridge's verse the music making is in honour of 'some martyr'd Patriot' (310), and 'patriot' is a term that could apply both retrospectively to one of Joan's contemporaries and in the political discourse of the 1790s to a British radical. As in Coleridge's Bristol lectures of 1795, the languages and typologies of religion and of politics have no point of distinction. The reader is of course expected to know that immediately after the passage quoted from Revelation comes the apocalyptic destruction that sends the kings of the earth hiding in dens from the wrath of the Lamb (6: 12–17). The vision that follows involves a ploughman turning up skulls and bones (we may recall Blake's prophecies of the 1790s with their emphasis on the bones of the dead). A female form, anticipating Hope in Shelley's *Mask of Anarchy*, appears.[11] Her temples are olive-wreathed, and 'where she trod, /Fresh flowrets rose, and many a foodful herb' (325–6). Although she is wan, a 'Pale

[11] For Shelley's familiarity with *Joan of Arc*, see his letter to Elizabeth Hitchener dated 25 July 1811 (*The Letters of Percy Bysshe Shelley*, ed. F. L. Jones (2 vols., Oxford: Clarendon Press, 1964), 1: 126).

Convalescent' (330), her future millennial reign is parenthetically prophesized:

> (Yet some time to rule
> With power exclusive o'er the willing world,
> That blest prophetic Mandate then fulfill'd,
> PEACE be on earth!)
>
> (330–3)

However, that end is not yet. Apocalypse succeeds the bracketed hoped-for millennium. Black clouds rise, redden, and turn into warriors who fight in the sky, raining blood upon the earth. Such war, the tutelary Spirit explains, echoing the belief shared by radicals as diverse as Paine and Godwin, is caused solely by monarchs. More terrible conflict must take place before the realization of millennial peace.

The visionary sequence reaches the American and French Revolutions at line 397. A vapour rises, guided by OPPRESSION wielding a sceptre. Identified in a simile with Egypt and pestilence, this vapour sails westward. Then a 'brighter Cloud' (407) appears and follows the vapour. The situation is complicated because, in three lines claimed by Southey (409–11), we are told that the cloud is guided by ENVY masked like JUSTICE, 'doom'd to aid the fight / Victorious 'gainst OPPRESSION' (410–11). The colonization of America by the British is to be opposed with the help of royal France, not for love of freedom, but as part of the conflict of one empire with another. The cloud then returns to 'the Plain' of its origin, France (414). This is once more in accord with a general radical view, as we have seen in the figuration of revolution in Dr Price's *Discourse on the Love of Our Country* and in Blake's *America*. Like Price and Blake, Coleridge also uses the imagery of light in figuring the transmission of revolution from America to France:

> But long time pass'd not, ere that brighter Cloud
> Return'd more bright: along the Plain it swept;
> And soon from forth its bursting sides emerg'd
> A dazzling Form.
>
> (413–16)

This incarnation of Liberty, still laurel-crowned, is no longer wan of cheek and of 'footsteps insecure' (327), but 'broad-bosom'd, bold of Eye' (416), to be compared with the Apollo Belvedere—and also with 'Gallic Liberty' in the sonnet 'To Earl Stanhope': 'her, who from the Almighty's bosom leapt / With whirlwind arm, fierce minister of

Love!'[12] (Coleridge's penchant for physically powerful female personifications of Revolution will be discussed with respect to lines 18–23 of 'To a Young Lady with a Poem on the French Revolution' and the second strophe of 'France: An Ode'.) She will make short work of 'the locust Fiends that crawl'd / And glitter'd in CORRUPTION's slimy track' (421–2), lines which anticipate the first description of the creatures of the deep in 'The Rime of Ancient Mariner'[13]). However, the resistance of 'AMBITION's ghastly throng' (420) leads to violence qualifying what has up to this point been an unreserved endorsement of revolutionary France:

> Warm'd with new Influence the unwholesome Plain
> Sent up its foulest fogs to meet the Morn:
> The Sun, that rose on FREEDOM, rose in blood!

(431–3)

This view of revolutionary France is consistent with Coleridge's other statements close to the time. In 'A Moral and Political Lecture', delivered in Bristol in 1795, he declares: 'The Example of France, is indeed a "Warning to Britain". A nation wading to their Rights through Blood, and marking the track of Freedom by Devastation!' (*Lectures 1795*, p. 210). There is of course something double-edged about such imagery, for, as Coleridge explicitly says, it is 'a warning'—if violent revolution is to be avoided, peaceful change must be effected. In *The Watchman* for 1 March, 1796 he used the *Joan of Arc* lines themselves to illustrate the argument that 'the excesses of the French' were to be blamed partly on 'the indignation and terror excited by the Combined Forces' as well as on 'the natural effects of Despotism and Superstition'.[14] Nevertheless, in *Joan of Arc* Coleridge condemns the judicial murders of Brissot and of Madame Roland: in a passage of Book III claimed by him, these 'Martyr'd patriots' are addressed as having 'Sow'd . . . seed' that 'by your blood manur'd' will grow into 'That Tree beneath whose vast and mighty shade / The sons of men shall pitch

---

[12] *Poems on Various Subjects* (London, 1796), p. 54, ll. 9–10 and n. Coleridge later disclaimed this sonnet, striking through the text in Sara Hutchinson's copy of his *Poems* of 1803 and claiming, 'It was written in ridicule of Jacobinical Bombast' (Cornell University Library, no. 1722, p. 103). However, both in style and in sentiment it is in keeping with Coleridge's other poems of the period.

[13] As pointed out by Wylie, *Young Coleridge*, pp. 149–50.

[14] *Watchman*, p. 33. As Lewis Patton remarks in his Introduction, this was 'a commonplace among the Friends of Freedom' (p. 33 n.).

their tents in peace' (73–8).[15] Thus, in an image which had (ironically, considering this context) been popularized in a speech by Bertrand Barère arguing the case for the execution of Louis XVI to the National Convention in January 1793,[16] the apocalyptic spilling of blood leads to a re-creation of the millennium.

After the last vision, Coleridge's 'Preternatural Agency' continues for only eleven lines. The tutelary Spirit, once more employing the imagery of light that characterizes revolutionary sympathies at this time, predicts a transition from 'stormy Morning into cloudless Noon' (437), and Joan addresses God as 'Nature's vast ever-acting ENERGY!' (443), in a passage that was later to trouble Coleridge for theological reasons (*CPW* 1: 142 n.). Southey then resumes the narrative at line 453. This was the end of 'Preternatural Agency' in more ways than one, for it did not appear in later editions of *Joan of Arc*. Coleridge now had to decide what to do with what he called '*my Epic Slice*'.[17]

Characteristically, he decided to make it longer. In expanded form, it was to be published in the second edition of his *Poems* and given pride of place at the beginning of the volume as 'the progress of European Liberty, a vision'.[18] On 17 December 1796 he sent John Thelwall some loose sheets including 'a Joan of Arc . . . as I am printing it in my second Edition, with very great alterations & an addition of four hundred lines, so as to make it a complete & independent Poem—entitled The Progress of Liberty—or the Visions of the maid of Orleans' (*CL* 1: 285). Shortly after this he sent the new poem to Charles Lamb for

---

[15] Coleridge claimed lines 73–82 among other scattered passages in books I, III, and IV (*CPW* 2: 1027–30). This would mean that he broke into a sentence begun by Southey at line 72 with 'BRISSOT murder'd'. In a letter to Grosvenor Charles Bedford dated 11 Nov. 1793, Southey speaks of the 'murder of Brissot' (*New Letters of Robert Southey*, ed. Kenneth Curry (2 vols., New York and London: Columbia University Press, 1965), 1: 33). In the first *Watch-man*, in an article dated 15 Feb. 1796, Coleridge printed a passage comprising a variant of part of line 74 and lines 76 through part of 82; but in this context 'Th'imperishable seed' becomes the unsuccessful motions for peace with France. Woodring (*Politics in the Poetry of Coleridge*, p. 34) suggests that the original *Joan of Arc* passage refers to the reformers who died after being sentenced to transportation by Lord Braxfield.

[16] See Leo Gershoy, *Bertrand Barère: A Reluctant Terrorist* (Princeton: Princeton University Press, 1962), p. 145. Barère is quoted as saying: 'As a classical author said, the tree of liberty grows only when it is watered by the blood of all species of tyrants'. Some six years earlier, Thomas Jefferson wrote in a private letter: 'The tree of liberty must be refreshed from time to time with the blood of patriots & tyrants. It is it's natural manure' (letter to William Stephens Smith dated 13 Nov. 1787, in *The Papers of Thomas Jefferson*, ed. Julian P. Boyd (Princeton: Princeton University Press, 1955), 12: 356.

[17] To Thomas Poole, 5 May 1796; *CL* 1: 207.

[18] Letter to Thomas Poole, 1 Nov. 1796; *CL* 1: 243.

comments, an act which had unanticipated results. Lamb had admired *Joan of Arc* and especially 'Preternatural Agency', but after reading the new part of the poem, he criticized what he saw as its lowness of subject-matter and over-generalizing language. Although on 13 February 1797 Lamb turned about and praised what he had previously condemned, this had less to do with his critical judgement than his perception of how deeply Coleridge was attached to the poem, as Lamb's parallel with not objecting to a friend's choice of a wife must have made painfully clear. Besides, Lamb's second letter continued to make criticisms, and one of these applied to the enterprise as a whole. Joan is, Lamb objects, 'roused into a state of mind proper to receive visions emblematical of equality; which what the devil Joan has to do with, I don't know, or indeed with the French and American revolutions'. Such comments from a valued friend were bound to undermine Coleridge's confidence in the work.[19]

'The lines which I added to my lines in the "Joan of Arc"', Coleridge wrote to Joseph Cottle *c.*10 February, 'have been so little approved by Charles Lamb . . . that although I differ from him in opinion, I have not the heart to finish the poem' (*CL* 1: 309). Writing to his publisher again in late June, he blamed his failure to complete it for the second edition of *Poems* on 'my anxieties and my slothfulness' (*CL* 1: 259). However, before the end of the year he regained confidence to the extent of publishing 'The Visions of the Maid of Orleans' in the *Morning Post* for 26 December.[20] Identified as 'A Fragment, by S. T. Coleridge', this passage of 148 lines begins with line 120 of 'Preternatural Agency'—'If there be beings of higher class than Man'—but soon becomes an entirely different poem, telling the story of Joan's peaceful early years (a considerably different past than Southey had given her) and then drawing upon material that Coleridge had reprinted in *The Watchman* to describe her discovery of a family of dead refugees, frozen after escaping from their burning village.[21] Joan's first vision is just beginning when the fragment breaks off. Coleridge intended to continue from this point: on 18 February 1798 he tells Cottle, 'I am going on with the 387 Visions' (*CL* 1: 233), and on 7 March that he still intended to prefix 'the Maid of Orleans' to

---

[19] *Letters of Charles and Mary Lamb*, 1: 94–5; 101–2.

[20] This first publication was overlooked by E. H. Coleridge in *CPW*. For a list of variants between the 'Fragment' and the corresponding lines of 'The Destiny of Nations', see David V. Erdman, 'Unrecorded Coleridge Variants', *Studies in Bibliography*, 11 (1958): 144–53.

[21] *Watchman*, no. 7 (19 Apr. 1796): 239–41. Patton (*Watchman*, p. 238 n.) identifies the source as *An Accurate and Impartial Narrative of the War, by an Officer of the Guards* (2 vols., London, 1795).

a collection of his poems (*CL* 1: 391). However, this material was not to appear again in print until 1817, when, cobbled together with a rearranged and revised 'Preternatural Agency', it was published in *Sibylline Leaves* as 'The Destiny of Nations'.

In contemplating the gap between Coleridge's intentions in 1798 and the publication of 'The Destiny of Nations' as an incomplete poem in 1817, we must consider factors other than the author's self-proclaimed anxieties and slothfulness. In 'Preternatural Agency' Coleridge had produced a series of apocalyptic visions that exploded like rockets over the sere landscape of Southey's epic. Apocalypse, in the form of the French Revolution, was, as we have seen, to be followed by millennium. Coleridge pursued that vision in subsequent poems of the 1790s, until he was forced to abandon it by the recalcitrance of events. As we shall see, the themes of apocalypse and millennium, central to Coleridge's poems of the early and middle 1790s, had virtually disappeared from his work by the next decade. The reason for their re-emergence in *Sibylline Leaves* lies only partly in Coleridge's need to fill space. Coleridge must have been reluctant to abandon a work at least part of which he had characterized as written 'with vast exertion of all my Intellect'.[22] It is true that upon rereading *Joan of Arc* to note his own contributions in 1814, Coleridge remarked on how bad the work was. In a marginal note to Southey's Book III passage, in which Joan describes how she grew up, naturally religious, in the forest, Coleridge wrote: 'How grossly unnatural an anachronism thus to *transmogrify* the fanatic votary of the Virgin into a Tom Payne in Petticoats, a novel-palming Proselyte of the age of Reason'.[23] As George Whalley points out, however, Coleridge is referring to Southey's work here, rather than to his own.[24] In the *Biographia* (as Whalley observes) Coleridge speaks of 'the lines which are now adopted in the introductory part of the VISION in the present collection in Mr. Southey's Joan of Arc, 2nd book, 1st edition' as being 'not more below my present ideal in respect of the general tissue of the style, than those of the latest date' (1: 25–6). Politically the poem was hardly threatening to Coleridge's conservatism, as by the time it appeared in *Sibylline Leaves* the figurative extension of the Joan of Arc story to the modern political world, assumed in the original,

[22] Letter to Robert Southey dated 13 Nov. 1795; *CL* 1: 172.
[23] *Joan of Arc*, Berg Collection, p. 110. Cf. Coleridge's letter to J. J. Morgan dated 16 June 1814; *CL* 3: 510.
[24] Whalley, 'Coleridge, Southey, and "Joan of Arc"', *Notes and Queries*, 199 (1954): 67–9.

could simply be ignored. Joan's visions would have little immediate meaning to a readership not accustomed to thinking in terms of the radical imagery of the mid-1790s. The poem had been recontextualized by history.[25] 'Rebels from God and Monarchs o'er Mankind!' (*Joan of Arc*, 2: 259) became 'Rebels from God and Tyrants o'er Mankind!' ('Destiny of Nations', 314); however, on the whole, few changes had to be made for purely political reasons. The same is true of the poem's theological aspect. Here again, Coleridge's changed views (which, characteristically, he insisted were for the most part unchanged) resulted in little actual rewriting. For example, he marked lines 2: 444–5 of the Berg Collection copy, being troubled by 'Nature's vast ever-acting ENERGY! / In will, in deed, IMPULSE of All to all'. Coleridge noted:

Tho' these lines may bear a sane Sense, yet they are easily & more naturally interpretable [*sic*] into a very false & dangerous one. But I was at that time one of the *mongrels*, the *Josephidites* [Josephides = the Son of Joseph—a proper name of distinction from those who believe *in*, as well as believe, Christ, the only begotten Son of God before all Time.] (p. 65)

Nevertheless, the lines were carried into 'The Destiny of Nations' with only changes in capitalization.[26] Similarly, Coleridge noted in a copy of *Sibylline Leaves* now in the Houghton Library that a passage beginning 'But properties are God' (p. 282) 'Must be altered as false in philosophy and subversive of religion', and he proceeded to draft a twelve-line revision—which was not used in later editions.[27] Such details could always be rationalized away in the spirit of Coleridge's remark *c.*1814 to Joseph Cottle about a similarly offensive passage in 'Religious Musings': 'I was very young when I wrote that poem, and my religious feelings were more settled than my theological notions'.[28]

Most of Coleridge's revisions are stylistic, especially those involving the elimination of personified abstractions. Sometimes both motives may operate at once, as in the excision of lines 397–401, in which OPPRESSION grasps a sceptre, musing on Vengeance. Here in his copy

[25] See Gary Dyer, 'Unwitnessed by Answering Deeds: "The Destiny of Nations" and Coleridge's *Sibylline Leaves*', *Wordsworth Circle*, 20 (1989): 148–55.
[26] As Brown observes, 'Bibliomania', p. 83.
[27] As pointed out by Mary Lynn Johnson, 'How Rare is a "Unique Annotated Copy" of Coleridge's *Sibylline Leaves*?', *Bulletin of the New York Public Library*, 76 (1975): 479–80.
[28] *CL* 3: 467. The reference is to 'The SUPREME FAIR sole Operant' (Coleridge, *Poems on Various Subjects*, p. 143) which was unchanged save for capitalization when the poem appeared in the *Poetical Works* of 1834 (see *CPW* 1: 56).

of *Joan of Arc* Coleridge marked the passage for deletion, remarking: 'These Images imageless, these *small-capitals* constituting Personifica-tions, I despised even at that time; but was forced to introduce them, to present the connection with the machinery of the Poem, previously adapted by Southey' (p. 62). The deepest changes undergone by 'Preter-natural Agency' in its transition to *Sibylline Leaves*, are, however, broader. One was contextual. 'The Destiny of Nations' did not appear in the group designated 'Poems Occasioned by Political Beliefs or Feelings Connected with Them', but, muting whatever political meaning the poem might yet have conveyed in 1817, as the last of the 'Odes and Mis-cellaneous Poems' at the end of the volume. Even more important was Coleridge's decision to break up its structure. We can follow him in the act of doing so in the text of page 135 of his copy (Berg Collection), enclos-ing in parentheses a passage from the middle of line 136 to the middle of 140, with the notation 'Transcribe'. This is the passage that breaks off at the end of 'The Destiny of Nations' on the last page of *Sibylline Leaves*:

> And first a Landscape rose,
> More wild, and waste, and desolate, than where
> The white bear, drifting on a field of ice,
> Howls to her sundered cubs with piteous rage
> And savage agony.[29]

By moving these lines to the end of the poem, Coleridge presented 'The Destiny of Nations' as a Romantic fragment.[30] His structural changes so affected the work that, as Joseph Cottle, who was the first to call attention to its origins in print, observed, it could now make little sense to the reader. 'Who the maid is, no one can tell', wrote Cottle; the result was 'an incoherent mass of imagery and unorganized senti-ment'.[31] An alternative would have been to publish 'Preternatural Agency' as originally written save for Southey's easily-excised passages and some revision of the 'Images imageless'. The poem would then have been complete in itself, ending at line 452 with the final line of Joan's prayer: 'Glory to Thee, Father of Earth and Heaven!' Although such a poem may not now seem to us to indicate the true direction of Coleridge's development, we might bear in mind Norman Fruman's

[29] Coleridge, *Sibylline Leaves: A Collection of Poems* (London, 1817), p. 303.
[30] As Gary Dyer observes in 'Unwitnessed by Answering Deeds', p. 152.
[31] Joseph Cottle, *Early Recollections; Chiefly Relating to the Late Samuel Taylor Coleridge During His Long Residence in Bristol* (London, 1837), 1: 228, 232 n. Cottle proceeded to reprint the original text (2: 241–62), indicating which lines were by Southey.

remark that 'Had he eventually written the great epic that ever floated before him in his working reveries, both "Religious Musings" and the equally long and discursive "Destiny of Nations" would today be seen, not as inconsequential diversions from the mainstream of his genius, but as the inevitable stumblings of youth on the road to Parnassus'.[32] 'Preternatural Agency' would then be considered Coleridge's narrative exploration of the interrelated themes of apocalypse and millennium, while 'Religious Musings', begun shortly after its completion, would be recognized as its discursive counterpart.

These Promised Years

As with 'Preternatural Agency', Coleridge redefined 'Religious Musings' after the failure of his millennial hopes. In this instance he did so not by restructuring and revision but by redefinition, presenting the poem as a youthful indiscretion rather than as a highly promising work begun when Coleridge was 23. We all remember the episode in *Biographia Literaria* where the young Coleridge, selling subscriptions to *The Watchman* in Birmingham, addresses 'a rigid Calvinist, a tallow chandler by trade' (1: 180–1). The description is worthy of Dickens, combining in one grotesque image the physical and moral characteristics of the unfortunate 'taper man of lights'. The tallow chandler combines political radicalism and religious apocalypticism in a way characteristic of late eighteenth-century Dissent: 'He was . . . a true lover of liberty, and . . . had proved to the satisfaction of many, that Mr. Pitt was one of the horns of the second beast in the Revelations, *that spoke like a dragon*'. This man's apocalyptic interests strike a responsive millenarian chord in the young Coleridge, here represented, as so often by the older Coleridge, as a harmless eccentric:

I argued, I described, I promised, I prophecied: and beginning with the captivity of nations I ended with the near approach of the millenium [sic], finishing the whole with some of my own verses describing that glorious state out of the Religious Musings:

> Such delights,
> As float to earth, permitted visitants!
> When in some hour of solemn jubilee
> The massive gates of Paradise are thrown

[32] Norman Fruman, *Coleridge: The Damaged Archangel* (New York: Braziller, 1971), p. 256.

> Wide open, and forth come in fragments wild
> Sweet echoes of unearthly melodies,
> And odours snatch'd from beds of Amaranth,
> And they that from the chrystal river of life
> Spring up on freshen'd wings, ambrosial gales![33]

This use of 'Religious Musings' to cap a passage of ridicule is not the first mention of the poem in the *Biographia*. The poem is dismissed near the very beginning of the book (1: 6–7) in Coleridge's discussion of the early poems published in his volumes of 1796 and 1797: 'The critics of that day, the most flattering, equally with the severest, concurred in objecting to them, obscurity, a general turgidness of diction, and a profusion of new coined double epithets'. 'Religious Musings' is singled out on this account:

I forgot to enquire, whether the thoughts themselves did not demand a degree of attention unsuitable to the nature and objects of poetry. This remark however applies chiefly, though not exclusively, to the *Religious Musings*. The remainder of the charge I admitted to its full extent, and not without sincere acknowledgement to both my private and public censors for their friendly admonitions. In the after editions, I pruned the double epithets with no sparing hand, and used my best efforts to tame the swell and glitter both of thought and diction; though in truth, these parasite plants of youthful poetry had insinuated themselves into my longer poems with such intricacy of union, that I was often obliged to omit disentangling the weed, from the fear of snapping the flower.

These problems may well have been among Coleridge's reasons for deprecating the poem and leaving it out of the *Biographia's* companion volume of poetry, *Sibylline Leaves*. It is true that Coleridge had voiced similar misgivings in similar language as early as the second edition of his *Poems* in 1797.[34] Although Humphry House considered 'Religious Musings' one of the 'more rich and interesting' of Coleridge's very early poems, and G. Wilson Knight called it 'Coleridge's greatest religious utterance',[35] Coleridge's later objections are to some degree true. It does display some turgidity of diction; it does contain too many

---

[33] *BL* 1: 181. This passage corresponds to *CPW* 1: 122, lines 343–51. There are some variants between the passage quoted in *BL* and that of *CPW*, which uses as its copy-text the *Poetical Works* of 1834, and greater differences between the passage in *BL* and that in the 1st ed. (1796).

[34] *Poems by S. T. Coleridge* (Bristol and London, 1797), p. vii.

[35] Humphry House, *Coleridge* (London: Rupert Hart-Davis, 1953), p. 59; G. Wilson Knight, *The Starlit Dome: Studies in the Poetry of Vision* (London: Methuen, 1964), p. 131.

double epithets. Aspiring to sublimity by what Thomas McFarland has characterized as 'an overlaying of the Miltonic model by the bardic style of Gray', it too often achieves what McFarland terms 'the hysterical sublime'.[36] These are, however, likewise characteristics of 'The Destiny of Nations', which, as we have seen, Coleridge did find it possible to print in *Sibylline Leaves*. And if the objection is, as Coleridge says in the *Biographia*, that the poem is an inadequate vehicle for philosophy (especially for a philosophy in which he no longer believed), is this not also true of another poem to be found in *Sibylline Leaves*, 'The Eolian Harp'? Furthermore, 'Religious Musings' had once been Coleridge's favourite; it had been more praised than censured,[37] and was considered by some early reviewers the most sublime of Coleridge's poems; and although after the *Poems* of 1803 the poem did not reappear until 1828, it continued to be remembered by some writers and to be mentioned by them. It was, furthermore, the very millennial vision that is derided in the *Biographia* that Coleridge and his circle had valued most about this ambitious work.

Coleridge had struggled long and hard to achieve a version of the poem that would even partially fulfil his high hopes for it. He subtitled the first published version 'A Desultory Poem, Written on Christmas Eve, in the Year of Our Lord, 1794', but this date can only indicate a beginning. On 29 December he wrote to Southey that he was writing a poem 'in blank Verse on the Nativity'.[38] By October 1795 'The Nativity' numbered 'not quite three hundred Lines' (*CL* 1: 162–3). In March 1796 he announced to his publisher Joseph Cottle that the poem was 'finished' (*CL* 1: 187); but, according to Cottle, Coleridge continued to work on the poem while the book was in press.[39] Ninety-nine lines appeared as 'The Present State of Society' in the second number of The *Watchman*[40] that same month, and at last the whole poem was published in *Poems on Various Subjects* on 16 April 1796.

From the first, Coleridge displayed great pride in this ambitious work, while at the same time maintaining enough critical distance to respond to his friends' private criticisms. 'It has cost me much labor in

---

[36] Thomas McFarland, *Romanticism and the Forms of Ruin: Wordsworth, Coleridge, and the Modalities of Fragmentation* (Princeton: Princeton University Press, 1981), p. 245 n.

[37] Engell and Bate remark that 'C is oversensitive to the adverse criticism of his compound epithets, which appeared in the *Analytical* and esp. *English Review* XXVIII 172–5' (*BL* 1: 6n. 1). However, the *Analytical* did not single out 'Religious Musings' in criticizing Coleridge's compound epithets (see below).

[38] *CL* 1: 147. On the dating of the poem, see also Kathleen Coburn, *CN* 1 (notes): 30.

[39] See *CL* 1: 187 n.   [40] *Watchman*, pp. 64–7.

polishing', he wrote to Cottle in October 1795, 'more than any poem I ever wrote—and I believe, deserves it more' (*CL* 1: 162–3). To his friend, Thomas Poole, he first declared: 'I pin all my poetical credit on the Religious Musings' (11 April 1796 *CL* 1: 203), but less than a month later with greater detachment: 'The "Religious Musings" has more *mind* than the Introduction of B. IId of *Joan of Arc* but it's versification is not equally rich: it has more passages of sublimity, but it has not that diffused air of severe Dignity which characterizes *my Epic Slice*' (5 May 1796, *CL* 1: 207). He admitted to Poole that there were instances of 'vicious affectation in the phraseology', giving as an example 'Unshudder'd unaghasted', which, as E. L. Griggs notes, he later revised. Perhaps the severest strictures that Coleridge received were from his friend John Thelwall, to whom he had declared, as to Poole in April 1796, 'I build all my poetic pretentions on the Religious Musings' (*CL* 1: 205). Thelwall, however, found the religious passages 'the very acme of abstruse, metaphysical, mistical rant', and the whole poem 'infected with inflation & turgidity'.[41] The last word seems to have been picked up by Coleridge himself, but the effect of Thelwall's criticism must have been mitigated by his statement that 'perhaps there is near half the poem that no poet in our language need have been ashamed to own'. Coleridge must have felt further strengthened in his valuation of 'Religious Musings' by the opinion of William Wordsworth that two passages in it were 'the best in all the Volume—indeed worth all the rest'.[42] Interestingly, the passages Wordsworth so valued were both from the apocalyptic conclusion of the poem—on the resurrection of the illustrious dead (387–402) and the descent of the Throne of God with its aftermath (422–46). And early the following year, Charles Lamb called 'Religious Musings' 'the noblest poem in the language, next after the Paradise Lost', adding '& even that was not made the vehicle of such grand truths'.[43] Far from being discouraged, Coleridge was moved to revise and expand the poem. While the second edition was being prepared in 1797, Coleridge wrote to Cottle: 'The Religious Musings, I have altered monstrously, since I read them to you, and received your criticisms' (*CL* 1: 309); and in July he sent his publisher more revisions, although he knew that copy had already been printed

---

[41] For the text of Thelwall's letter, dated 10 May [1796], see Warren E. Gibbs, 'An Unpublished Letter from John Thelwall to S. T. Coleridge', *Modern Language Review*, 25 (1930): 85–90.
[42] 13 May 1796; *CL* 1: 215–16.   [43] 5–6 Feb. 1797; *Letters*, 1: 95.

(*CL* 1: 331–2). And after the *Poems* of 1797 had been published, he promised Cottle that for a third edition, 'My alterations in the Religious Musings will be considerable, & will lengthen the poem' (*CL* 1: 391).

The reviewers of the 1790s for the most part shared the high value that the poet had put on his work. The *Monthly Review* astutely linked it with Coleridge's previous long poem:

> Its subject, and the manner of treating it, place it at the very top of the peak of sublimity. It is, indeed, that in which we chiefly recognize the author of the Maid's vision in Joan of Arc; possessing the same characteristic excellencies and defects. Often obscure, uncouth, and verging to extravagance, but generally striking and impressive to an extreme degree, it exhibits that ungoverned career of fancy and of feeling which equally belongs to the poet and the enthusiast. The Book of Revelation may be a dangerous font of prophecy, but it is no mean Helicon of Poetic inspiration.[44]

This high praise moved Coleridge to a paroxysm of exclamation marks. 'The Monthly', he wrote to John Prior Estlin, 'has at least done justice to my Religious Musings—They place it "on the very top of the scale of Sublimity.["]—!—!—!' (4 July 1796; *CL* 1: 224). Joseph Johnson's *Analytical Review*, as might be expected from its publisher's radical and Unitarian sympathies, was also highly appreciative, remarking on the 'ardour' of the poet's sentiments and pointing out that he was also the author of the anti-war tract *Conciones ad Populum*.[45] Even during the twenty-five-year period after 1803 in which 'Religious Musings' was not in print, its millennial vision was remembered by some readers. In 1817 a Unitarian wrote in an open letter to Coleridge: 'You too must recollect the "Religious Musings," or you are the only one who could ever forget them. . . . This beautiful poem . . . is full of bright visions, half unveiled—of unbounded and indistinct prospects—of all kinds of imaginary excellence'.[46] After the poem was at last republished in 1828, it continued to be praised, usually in eighteenth-century aesthetic terms. Reviewing the *Poetical Works* of 1828, where 'Religious Musings' was placed among 'Juvenile Poems', the *British Critic* said: 'Of his Juvenile Poems', his 'Religious Musings are transcendently the best', going on to quote a long section as 'a sublime and beautiful meditation', and

---

[44] *Monthly Review*, 2nd ser., 20 (1796): 197–8. The reviewer has been identified as Dr John Aitken; see R. Haven, J. Haven, and M. Adams, *Samuel Taylor Coleridge: An Annotated Bibliography* (Boston: G. K. Hall, 1976), p. 2, no. 11.

[45] *Analytical Review*, 23 (1796): 610–12.

[46] SND, 'To Samuel Taylor Coleridge, Esq'., *Metropolitan Literary Journal*, 1 (1824): 231–9.

to call the poem as a whole 'one of his sublimest conceptions'.[47] Shortly after Coleridge's death, his one-time idol William Lisle Bowles called it 'by far the most correct, sublime, and beautiful of his poems'.[48]

It is true that Coleridge received some criticism of 'Religious Musings' from friends and from reviewers, and that he did revise the work immediately after its first publication in 1796. However, despite the impression given by the *Biographia*, the poem was not singled out for abuse by the critics. On the contrary, from its first publication on, it received a remarkably good press. Of course, it is significant that Coleridge's remarks on 'the swell and glitter of thought and diction' first appear during the period of intense discussions with Wordworth that eventuated in their collaboration on the *Lyrical Ballads*. A poetic programme that would soon advocate the use of language really spoken by men would leave as little room for 'Religious Musings' as for *Descriptive Sketches*. However, throughout his career Coleridge practised several types of poetry at the same time. His *Poems* of 1803 included 'Religious Musings', and, as we have seen, he thought his '*Epic Slice*' worth revising as 'The Destiny of Nations' for *Sybilline Leaves*. It required a very strong motive for Coleridge to omit his second longest complete poem from that volume. What disabled 'Religious Musings' for him in the period just after the Anglo–French wars was the millennial vision, explicitly stated and uncloaked by allegory, at its core. This poem had its roots all too plainly in the millenarianism of the 1790s, according to which the French Revolution was seen as a fulfilment of biblical prophecy—a tradition from which Coleridge was now especially anxious to distance himself.

Beginning with a meditation on the birth of Christ, 'Religious Musings' passes on to an apocalyptic view of the present historic moment. In its sweep through world events, this part of the poem, as H. W. Piper has observed, with its denunciation of the war against France, the slave-trade, the partition of Poland, and other evils, is indebted to Gilbert Wakefield's 1794 pamphlet *The Spirit of Christianity compared with the Spirit of the Times*.[49] It is, however, a mistake to conclude, as Norman Fruman does, that in using an expression like 'the Moloch Priest' (205) Coleridge is indebted to Wakefield's 'worshippers of Baal', or that Wakefield's reference to Revelation in a footnote denouncing the

---

[47] *British Critic*, 16 (1834): 398–9. The reviewer has been identified as Joseph Sortain; see Haven *et al.*, *Samuel Taylor Coleridge: An Annotated Bibliography*, p. 84, no. 605.
[48] William Lisle Bowles, 'Coleridge a Private Soldier', *Athenaeum*, 16 Aug. 1834 (no. 355): 614n.   [49] See Piper, *Active Universe*, pp. 29–59.

slave-trade is responsible for Coleridge's citations of Revelation in 'Religious Musings'.[50] Coleridge participates with Wakefield and other radical Dissenters in a community of discourse, a discourse that we have already encountered in Blake, in which contemporary events are cast in Prophetic and apocalyptic terms. For the reading audience Coleridge envisaged, such similarities of expression are confirmatory of the underlying rightness of the views presented. The second part of the poem, beginning at line 218, ranges through time, first tracing the terrible events already described to the accumulation of wealth at a 'dateless' point in 'the primeval age'. At first innocent, wealth leads to avarice, social inequality, poverty, luxury, and war. This present state of society, as Coleridge called it in the *Watchman* fragment, will inevitably be destroyed by a violent apocalyptic event—the French Revolution— to be followed by a millennial society that will be terminated only at the Last Judgement. Apocalypse and millennium are seen as inextricably linked historical events, the first already having begun, the second imminent.

In his expectation of apocalypse and millennium, Coleridge derived much intellectual support from the fact that David Hartley, whose associationist psychology and necessitarianism were so important to him in the 1790s, was also a millenarian. In the second part of *Observations on Man*, which Coleridge cites in a note added to the 1797 'Religious Musings',[51] Hartley discusses the millennium under the rubric 'It is probable that all present civil Governments will be overturned'. Hartley draws upon biblical prophecies:

such as those concerning the destruction of the image, and four beasts, in *Daniel*; of Christ's *breaking all nations with a rod of iron, and dashing them in pieces like a potter's vessel,* &c., and from the supremacy and universal extent of the fifth monarchy, or kingdom of the saints, which is to be set up.[52]

Hartley then goes on to assert that 'It is probable, that the present Forms of Church Government will be dissolved', that the Christian religion will be accepted by all nations, and that the Jews will be restored to Jerusalem. Christ will reign for a thousand years on earth,

[50] See Fruman, *Coleridge: The Damaged Archangel*, pp. 243–4.
[51] *CPW* 1: 110 n. 2. For citations of 'Religious Musings', I generally use the text of 1796, 1st ed. with due attention to changes made in the 2nd ed., *Poems by S. T. Coleridge*. The original 1796 version is conveniently available in John Beer's Everyman edition of *Poems* by Samuel Taylor Coleridge (London: J. M. Dent; 'new edition', 1993), pp. 78–95.
[52] Hartley, *Observations on Man*, 2: 366.

and this will be followed by a general conflagration and a general resurrection.[53] Hartley does not venture to predict, however, when these
events might occur, or to give biblical prophecy any specific contemporary application. The young Coleridge saw unmistakable signs of
these impending events in the revolutions of his own times, and in this
he followed his fellow Unitarians Richard Price and Joseph Priestley.
Price had written that the American Revolution meant that 'the old
prophecies be verified, that the last universal empire upon earth
shall be the empire of reason and virtue, under which the gospel of
peace (better understood) *shall have free course and be glorified*'; and that
American independence was 'one of the steps ordained by Providence
to introduce these times [the millennium]'.[54] As we have seen in
Chapter 1, Price's 1789 address to the Revolution Society, *A Discourse on
the Love of Our Country*, so important both in itself and for Burke's attack
upon it and its author, represented the light kindled in America as
'reflected to FRANCE, and there kindled into a blaze, that lays despotism
in ashes, and warms and illuminates EUROPE!'[55] Coleridge, like Blake,
shared with Price the imagery of fiery revolution-as-apocalypse. After
Price's death, Joseph Priestley became Price's successor, not only as
minister to the Gravel-Pit Meeting, but also as the leading
hermeneutist of apocalyptic-historical events.[56] Coleridge almost certainly read, and may even have reviewed, Priestley's fast-day sermon of
28 February 1794, *The present State of Europe compared with Antient Prophecies*.[57] Ranging widely through the Bible, Priestley stresses the violence
of revolution, 'frequently represented by *earthquakes*',[58] and its destructive power, features that could be taken by readers such as Coleridge to
explain, though not to justify, the all too recent Terror. In an appendix,
Priestley declared that the leading ideas of his sermon were derived
from Hartley's *Observations on Man*, extracts from which are printed.
Thus the chief sources of Coleridge's own millenarianism, including, of
course, the Bible itself, were drawn together in Priestley's text.

[53] Hartley, *Observations on Man*, 2: 370–81.
[54] Richard Price, *Observations on the Importance of the American Revolution* (London, 1784),
pp. 6–7. See Jack Fruchtman, *The Apocalyptic Politics of Richard Price and Joseph Priestley: A Study
in Late Eighteenth Century English Republican Millennialism, Transactions of the American Philosophical
Society*, 73, part 4 (Philadelphia, American Philosophical Society, 1983), pp. 1, 83.
[55] Richard Price, *A Discourse on the Love of Our Country* (London, 1789), p. 50.
[56] See Kathleen Coburn, in *CN* 1: 50 n.
[57] See Clarke Garrett, 'Joseph Priestley, the Millennium, and the French Revolution',
Journal of the History of Ideas, 34 (1973): 51–66.
[58] Joseph Priestley, *The present State of Europe compared with Ancient Prophecies* (London, 1794),
p. 6.

In 'Religious Musings' Coleridge declares his affinity with Priestley by making him one of the Saints who rises 'To Milton's Trump' at the millennium:

> Lo! Priestley there, Patriot, and Saint, and Sage,
> Whom that my fleshly eye hath never seen
> A childish pang of impotent regret
> Hath thrill'd my heart. Him from his native land
> Statesmen blood-stain'd and Priests idolatrous
> By dark lies mad'ning the blind multitude
> Drove with vain hate: calm, pitying he retir'd,
> And mus'd expectant on these promis'd years.
>
> (395–402)

The last lines are particularly interesting, as they express precisely the tone Priestley takes in his letters from America to such correspondents as the Unitarian ministers Theophilus Lindsey and Thomas Belsham in 1795:

The more I think on the subject, the more I am persuaded that the calamitous times foretold in the Scriptures are at hand; and I fear they will be of long continuance, and that England has much to dread from them. I am now giving much attention to the prophecies, but I do not see my way so clearly as I wish.[59]

We find Priestley reading works by Increase Mather, Joseph Bicheno, and even Richard Brothers (undecided about the first, approving of one point in the second, non-committal about the third). The millennium will come, but exactly how and when is a subject for speculation. 'I find the greatest difficulty in . . . the *eleventh chapter of Daniel*: and the more I think, the more puzzled I am.'[60] The attitude here is considerably less definite about the precise application of Scripture than in *The Present State of Europe*, and the appropriateness of 'mused expectant' suggests that Coleridge may have known something about these letters.

In 'Religious Musings' the idea of the millennium is embedded in a scenario in which it is framed on one side by the apocalypse and on the other by the descent of the heavenly throne. Early in the poem the apocalyptic events are foreshadowed by echoes from Revelation of 'the SEVEN SPIRITS, who in the latter day / Will shower hot pestilence on the sons of men' (91–2) and the paradoxical notion of these Spirits filling

---

[59] See *The Theological and Miscellaneous Works of Joseph Priestley*, ed. John Towill Rutt (Hackney, 1817–31; New York: Kraus Reprint Co., 1972), 1, part 2: 289.

[60] Ibid. 1, part 2: 307.

'their Seven Vials with salutary wrath' (98) at the mercy-seat of God.
Coleridge's note (p. 170) quotes from Revelation 16: 1 at this point: 'And
I heard a great voice out of the Temple saying to the Seven Angels pour
out the vials of the wrath of God upon the earth.' That the world has
reached an apocalyptic moment is shown in passages on the slave
trade, the expansionistic tyrannies of Russia and of Austria, the war
against France, and domestic poverty. Then, after a long period of suffering, the day of retribution is announced in an allusion to Revelation
6: 9: 'The Lamb of God hath open'd the fifth seal' (324). John of Patmos's text virtually becomes part of Coleridge's, first in another note
quoting a long passage of Revelation 6, beginning with Death on a pale
horse, then with a rewriting of Revelation 6: 13 and 6: 15:

> And lo! the Great, the Rich, the Mighty Men,
> The Kings and the Chief Captains of the World,
> With all that fix'd on high like stars of Heaven
> Shot baleful influence, shall be cast to earth,
> Vile and down-trodden, as the untimely fruit
> Shook from the fig-tree by a sudden storm.
>
> (329–34)

Yet, although the tendency of such discourse might be to urge radical
action, in 'Religious Musings' the victims of the atrocities described in
the preceding part of the poem need do nothing to bring on the overthrow of the mighty; indeed, they are urged: 'Rest awhile, / Children of
Wretchedness!' (327–8). The outcome will be the fulfilment of a pattern
embedded in history.

In lines 329–42 the French Revolution (specifically identified by the
poet in a note), is represented in terms of storm, whirlwind, and earthquake, the last recalling Priestley's mention of biblical earthquakes in
connection with revolutionary violence. Revelation 17, as duly noted
by Coleridge, is the source of a long passage immediately following, in
which the Church Establishment is represented as the Whore that sitteth on many waters, with Mystery written on her forehead. Here is
another instance of Coleridge's participation in a shared tradition of
the application of apocalyptic imagery. 'It is very true', Hartley had
written, 'that the church of Rome is *Babylon the great, and the mother of
harlots, and of the abominations of the earth. But all the rest must have copied her
example, more or less.*[61] Similarly, Coleridge added to his note in 1797 'I am

---

[61] Hartley, *Observations on Man*, 2: 30.

convinced that the Babylon of the Apocalypse does not apply to Rome exclusively; but to the union of Religion with Power and Wealth, wherever it is found.'[62] The figural conjunction is very like that of Blake's Rahab with the rulers of the world in Night the Eighth of *The Four Zoas*:

John saw these things Reveald in Heaven
On Patmos Isle & heard the Souls cry out to be delivered
He saw the Harlot of the Kings of Earth & saw her Cup
Of fornication food of Orc & Satan pressed from the fruit of Mystery . . .[63]

For She hath fallen
On whose black front was written MYSTERY;
She that reel'd heavily, whose wine was blood;
She that work'd whoredom with the DAEMON POWER . . .

('Religious Musings', 350–3)

Coleridge also uses such figures in his prose of 1795, as in the fifth of his *Lectures on Revealed Religion*, when he asks of the Church of Rome and the Church of England: 'Are they not both decked with gold and precious stones? Is there not written on both their Foreheads Mystery!' (*Lectures 1795*, p. 210). In such a scenario the earthly paradise must be regained after the fall of Mystery, and this is what happens in 'Religious Musings', as also in Night the Ninth of *The Four Zoas*.

With the advent of the Saviour at line 380, the millennium commences. The situation is very much like that in Orc's great speech, already quoted in Chapter 1, in Blake's *America*, concluding 'For Empire is no more, and now the Lion & Wolf shall cease'. In a note added for the 1797 edition, Coleridge makes it clear that this millennium is a physical state in which 'Man will continue to enjoy the highest glory, of which his human nature is capable'.[64] At one point he considered giving this transformation a scientific basis drawn from Erasmus Darwin's speculations about meteorological change in *The Botanic Garden*:

Millennium, an History of as brought about by a progression in natural philosophy—particularly, meteorology or science of airs & winds—

Quaere—might not a Commentary on the Revelations be written from late philosophical discoveries?[65]

[62] Coleridge, *Poems*, ed. Beer, p. 89n.
[63] E 385–6. Erdman dates Night VIII as later than the renewal of war with France in 1804, and possibly much later (E 817).
[64] Coleridge, *Poems*, ed. Beer, p. 90n.   [65] See *CN* 1: 133 and 133n.

However, in the end he did not use such material except for a line and a half that appears only in the 1796 *Poems*: 'And soft gales wafted from the haunts of Spring /Melt the primæval North!' (383–4). As in Revelation 20: 4–5, the first resurrection occurs miraculously, and 'whoe'er from earliest time / With conscious zeal had urg'd Love's wond'rous plan' (385–6) rise again; Milton, Hartley, Newton, and Priestley are named in the text and notes. A community is imagined which in its Christian radicalism owes much, as Nigel Leask has suggested, to James Harrington and 'Commonwealth' ideology.[66] However, as is frequently the case in poetry of the millennium, little space is taken up by the perfected state of society. From 'these promis'd years' (402) we rush to the final destruction. Outside history, as Carl Woodring puts it, 'The post-millennial blaze of God's throne comes like dawn after stormy darkness'.[67]

Some aspects of this scenario may have troubled Coleridge even at the time of its first publication. He had begun 'Religious Musings' less than six months after the fall of Robespierre, an event that had caused Wordsworth to hope for the return of golden times (see Chapter 3 below). Then there followed the Thermidorean Reaction and the abolition of the Law of the Maximum, resulting in vast price increases and inflation. Less than a month after the poem was begun, French troops were in Amsterdam; on 1 October 1795 France annexed Belgium. Events were hardly going in a millennial direction. In *The Watchman* of 27 April 1796, published in the same month as *Poems on Various Subjects*, appeared Coleridge's 'Remonstrance to the French Legislators' (*Watchman*, pp. 269–73) showing his disturbance about France's aggressive wars, refusal to negotiate, and restraints on freedom of the press. Revolutionary events were no more accommodating to Coleridge's vision than to Blake's. As we have seen, Coleridge was working on 'Religious Musings' virtually to the time of publication, and the sense of rushing from the millennium to an extra-historical finale may have resulted from the refusal of history to work out according to Coleridge's plan. By 15 October 1796 he was trying out the figure 'snapped my squeaking baby-trumpet of sedition'—as George Watson points out,

[66] Nigel Leask, *The Politics of Imagination in Coleridge's Political Thought* (Basingstoke: Macmillan, 1988), pp. 32, 37. On this aspect of Coleridge's thought, see also Peter J. Kitson, 'The electric fluid of truth: The Ideology of the Commonwealthsmen in Coleridge's *The Plot Discovered*', *Prose Studies*, 13 (1990): 36–62.

[67] Woodring, *Politics in the Poetry of Coleridge*, p. 75.

almost two years before his use of these words in a better-known letter to his brother, George.[68] This image contains references, whether conscious or not, to Milton's trump in 'Religious Musings' as well as to the seven trumpets of Revelation.[69] It also anticipates Coleridge's later strategy of trivializing——in this instance miniaturizing——his previous radical pursuits. Yet in the autumn of 1796 Coleridge was not yet ready to give up his Prophetic stance, and in a group of poems written over the course of the decade we can trace the interplay of his millennial hopes and apocalyptic forebodings.

The Cottag'd Dell and the Tyrant-Quelling Lance

In his 'Preternatural Agency' Coleridge presented the story of Joan of Arc, or rather a visionary interpretation of it, as proleptic of the Anglo–French conflict of his own time, with apocalyptic war to be followed by a period of millennial peace. 'Religious Musings' gave a discursive framework to this subject, ranging through human history from the origins of inequality to the French Revolution, and culminating in a millennial resurrection followed by the descent of the heavenly throne. In a number of shorter poems written in the 1790s, Coleridge represents contemporary history according to the same model of history. At first apocalypse, comprising both revolutionary violence and the war against France, is seen as a prelude to millennium—an era that would follow France's compelling the nations to be free—but as Coleridge's confidence in that process waned, so did the millenarian element. We can see this happening in a spectrum of poems written in the 1790s until the apocalyptic alone remained.

In its earliest manifestations, Coleridge's millennial thought is bound up with the project of Pantisocracy.[70] He recognized this himself after the scheme had been abandoned, when, in a letter to Robert Southey of August 1795, he referred to the realization of Pantisocracy as 'perhaps a miraculous Millennium' (*CL* 1: 158), but in September 1794, he still hoped to realize it on the banks of the Susquehanna.

[68] See George Watson, 'The Revolutionary Youth of Wordsworth and Coleridge', *Critical Quarterly*, 18 (1976): 54 (citing *CL* 1: 240).

[69] I owe this suggestion to Anne Goldman.

[70] On which see J. R. MacGillivray, 'The Pantisocracy Scheme and its Immediate Background', in *Studies in English by Members of University College Toronto*, collected by Principal Malcolm W. Wallace (Toronto: University of Toronto Press, 1931), 131–69.

Interestingly, he tried to combine both aspects of Pantisocracy, literary and communitarian, in a revision of his 'Monody on the Death of Chatterton', first written in entirely different form when the poet was still a student at Christ's Hospital.[71] Into the latter part of the poem he inserted the octave of a sonnet on Pantisocracy that he had written with his fellow Pantisocrat, Samuel Favell, culminating:

> Sublime of Hope I seek the cottag'd dell
> Where VIRTUE calm with careless step may stray;
> And, dancing to the moon-light roundelay
> The wizard PASSIONS weave an holy spell!
>
> (122–5)

The poetic imagination is to be combined with the ideal of domesticity represented by 'the cottag'd dell' (cf. 'To the Reverend W. J. H.', first published in the *Poems* of 1796: 'In Freedom's UNDIVIDED dell, / Where *Toil* and *Health* with mellow'd *Love* shall dwell' (p. 13)). Here Coleridge is anticipating a suggestion that Charles Lamb would later make to him in a letter of 8 January, 1797: 'In the vast & unexplored regions of fairy-land, there is ground enough un-found & uncultivated; search there, and realize your favourite Susquehanah [sic] scheme'.[72] This incorporation of poetic spirit and communitarian ideal is guaranteed, as it were, by appropriating 'wizard PASSIONS' from Collins's ode 'The Manners'.[73] In including Collins's expression, Coleridge performs an act of integration: Collins's poetry was especially important to him at this time, as indicated by the fact that two poems of his 1796 volume appear in manuscript in his copy of J. Langhorne's edition of the *Poetical Works of Mr. William Collins* (London, 1781; BL Add. MS 47552). In 'The Manners' Collins says farewell to subject-matter represented by 'magic shores', in order to 'read in man the native heart' (lines 6, 26), and Langhorne hypothesizes that Collins wrote the poem about the time he left the university and 'commenced the *scholar* of *humanity*, to study nature in her works, and man in society' (p. 174). This is very much the way in which Coleridge sees his own enterprise, one for

---

[71] On the three versions of this poem, see I. A. Gordon, 'The Case-History of Coleridge's "Monody on the Death of Chatterton"', *RES* 18 (1942): 49–71. My text for the 'Monody' is *Poems on Various Subjects*, pp. 1–11, with citations by line number.

[72] *Letters of Charles and Mary Lamb*, 1: 88. Nevertheless, Lamb did not like this particular addition; see his letter to Coleridge dated 31 May 1796 (1: 11).

[73] As suggested by J. C. C. Mays in the notes to his forthcoming edition of the *Poetical Works* for *The Collected Works of Samuel Taylor Coleridge*.

which he wishes to appropriate the idea of Chatterton via the mediation of Collins. Despite Coleridge's will to combine the millennial with
the domestic, however, he is unable even in imagination to bring Chatterton over the ocean into the Pantisocratic community. The elements
are too disparate, and the poetic spirit that Chatterton represents can
therefore be commemorated only by the erection of a cenotaph
'Where Susquehannah pours his untam'd stream' (p. 10, l. 137). The
integration of poetic imagination and communitarian ideal turns out
to be unrealizable, even as a fantasy.

While Coleridge was still engaged in the Pantisocracy scheme, he
was also seeking a millenarian scenario in the wide field of contemporary events. Here he found something already familiar to him from
his study of John of Patmos, Milton,[74] and the third and fourth books of
Thomas Burnet's *Sacred Theory of the Earth*: there is no millennium without an apocalypse to precede it. In the Europe of the mid-1790s such
signs of the times were not far to seek. Coleridge had already written a
schoolboy 'Ode on the destruction of the Bastile [*sic*]' in which he had
introduced some of the images that would recur in his later treatments
of the French Revolution: the triple chain of Tyranny, the personification of Freedom 'rous'd by fierce Disdain' that 'wildly' (ll. 7–8) breaks it,
and the opposing array of 'Power's blood-stained streamers' (54 (34)).[75]
In September 1794, he transformed the allegorized Freedom of 1789
into a powerful mythical figure, as he worked lines 7–8 of the earlier
poem into the text of 'To a Young Lady, with a Poem on the French
Revolution', published in the *Poems* of 1796: 'When slumb'ring FREEDOM
rous'd by high DISDAIN / With giant fury burst her triple chain!' (p. 37,
ll. 17–18). Once more we are reminded of Erasmus Darwin's 'Giant-
form' waking from sleep 'on Gallia's plains' and rending his 'steely
rivets'.[76] As we have seen, Blake, too, adapted Darwin's lines in his
personification of Revolution, the 'hairy youth' Orc, who breaks his
'tenfold chains' in the 'Preludium' of *America*. But for Coleridge, Revolution is female, and in 'To a Young Lady' he daringly reverses tenor
and vehicle from a trope in the Song of Solomon 6: 4 ('Thou art

---

[74] See Peter Kitson, 'Coleridge, Milton, and the Millennium', *Wordsworth Circle*, 18 (1987):
61–6.

[75] This poem exists only in fragmentary form. The MS is in the Ottery Copy Book, BL
Add. MS 47551 (here quoted); Coleridge first published it, revised, in the *Poetical Works* of
1834. The fragment appears in *CPW* 1: 10–11.

[76] See Ch. 1 above. The comparison between Coleridge and Darwin is made by Patton,
Watchman, p. 28 n.

beautiful, O my love, as Tirzah, comely as Jerusalem, terrible as an army with banners'):

> Fierce on her front the blasting Dog-star glow'd;
> Her Banners, like a midnight Meteor, flow'd;
> Amid the yelling of the storm-rent skies
> She came, and scatter'd battles from her eyes!

$$(19-22)$$

Amazonian demi-goddesses like these are typically associated with the French Revolution by Coleridge, as we have already seen in the figures of Liberty in 'Preternatural Agency' and Gallic Liberty in 'To Earl Stanhope'. Another example is Alhadra, the heroine of the drama *Osorio*, written in 1797, who at the end of the play says: 'This arm should shake the kingdoms of this world', and goes on to invoke the messianic rider on the white horse of Revelation 6: 2:

> And all that were and had the spirit of life,
> Sang a new song to him who had gone forth,
> Conquering and still to conquer![77]

Such heroic female figures do not merely suffer and expostulate like Blake's Oothoon but, anticipating Shelley's Cythna, take an active role in bringing on human freedom. Eliciting both male fear and desire, they combine beauty and terror in a politicized version of the sublime that momentarily combines the allure of the revolutionary ideal with its fearful violence.

In such a field of force, what is the representation of the poet himself? He is a Bardic celebrant, a seer of visions, a roving ambassador of Sensibility, but seldom a participant. A highly interesting exception occurs in 'To a Young Lady':

> Red from the Tyrants' wound I shook the lance,
> And strode in joy the reeking plains of France!

$$(25-6)$$

These lines introduce the poet as Tyrant-killer. His weapon, 'the lance', is probably a pike like those distributed to the French municipalities in the autumn of 1792.[78] This idea can be reinforced by

---

[77] *CPW* 2: 596–7. Cf. Rev. 6: 2: 'And I saw, and behold a white horse: and he that sat on him had a bow; and a crown was given unto him: and he went forth conquering, and to conquer'. Coleridge's preceding line echoes Rev. 5: 9: 'And they sung a new song, saying, Thou art worthy to take the book, and to open the seals thereof . . .'

[78] As Mays suggests (notes to his forthcoming edition of Coleridge's *Poetical Works*).

referring to the role of the pike in British radical iconography. The pike was regarded as the weapon of freedom, as it would be in Shelley's *Revolt of Islam* (1817), where the people of the Golden City arm themselves with pikes against counter-revolutionary assault. The enemies of Liberty, too, had a special place for pikes in their imaginations: the stockpiling of pikes emerged as an accusation in the State Trials of 1794. There is something equivocal, however, about just what the poet does with his weapon. Does he shake the lance, red with blood, free of a dead body? Or is 'shook' a gesture of joy made with the reddened lance as the poet strides? In either case, there is a disturbing association with the Crucifixion: 'But one of the soldiers with a spear pierced his side, and forthwith came there out blood and water' (John 19: 34). That there is guilt on the poet's part, or at least ambivalence, is shown by line 28: 'And my heart akes, tho' MERCY struck the blow'. When Coleridge wrote this poem in September 1794, the Terror had come to an end, and indeed the 'Poem on the French Revolution' is the Coleridge–Southey collaboration, *The Fall of Robespierre*. Yet the events referred to in 'To a Young Lady' are not very recent; the 'battles scatter'd from her eyes' are surely those in which the Duke of Brunswick's invading army was stopped and turned back in the later summer and early autumn of 1792. This could be 'the Tyrants' wound',[79] or the reference could be to the execution of Louis XVI on 21 January 1793, thus involving the poet in regicide. There is an in-built semantic wobble in which the words suggest now the one, now the other. The point is not, of course, whether Coleridge consciously meant to implicate himself in the execution of the King. 'Tyrant' can be taken as a collective representation of what Blake would call Urizen, or Nobodaddy. Rather, there is an *association* of regicide that Coleridge could have decided to avoid but did not, and that association accounts for the complexity of 'my heart

[79] In Coleridge's letter to Southey of 21 Oct. 1794, the reading is 'Tyrants' wounds' (these two words are printed as 'Tyrant's wounds' in *CL* I: 118, but in the original manuscript letter the first word ends in an *s* followed by an apostrophe, although the apostrophe is reversed, i.e., c-shaped). The Quarto Copy Book reads 'Tyrants' wound'; and the Estlin Copy Book 'Tyrants' Wound'. I am grateful to the Pierpont Morgan Library for permission to quote from the manuscript letter to Southey (MA 1848) and from the Quarto Copy Book (MA 1916), to the Bristol Central Library for permission to quote from the Estlin Copy Book, and to Miss D. Dyer for providing me with a photocopy.

Mays (private communication) considers Coleridge's *s* to be singular when the apostrophe is close to the *s*, as it is in these three early manuscripts. The three earliest printed versions read as follows: *Watchman* (1 Mar. 1796, p. 15): 'Tyrants' wound'; *Poems 1796*: 'Tyrants' Wound'; *Poems 1797*: 'Tyrants' Wound'. In the *Poetical Works* of 1828, 1829, and 1834, the reading became 'Tyrant's wound'.

2. Samuel Taylor Coleridge, page from a manuscript of 'To a Young Lady,
with A Poem on the French Revolution' in a letter to Robert Southey,
21 October 1794

akes, tho' MERCY struck the blow' and contributes to the poet's with-drawal from the sphere of public events at the end of the poem.

'The reeking plains of France' also invites reflection. Presumably the reek comes from the carcasses of the dead. However, there is another possibility, though its basis is an annotation made by Coleridge later, in 1802, to William Godwin's *Thoughts Occasioned by the Perusal of Dr. Parr's Spital Sermon* (London, 1801). In describing the early response to the French Revolution, Godwin had written: 'Where was the ingenuous heart which did not beat with exultation at seeing a great and culti-vated people shake off the chains of one of the most oppressive political systems in the world, the most replenished with abuses, the least molli-fied and relieved by an infusion of liberty?' Coleridge replied in his note:

Had this been the fact, which the whole History of the French Revolution in its first workings disproves a posteriori, it would have been a *priori* impossible that such a revolution could have taken place. No! it was the discord & con-tradictory ferment of old abuses & recent indulgences or connivances—the heat & light of Freedom let in on a half-cleared, rank Soil, made twilight by the black fierce Reek, which this Dawn did itself draw up.[80]

We cannot, of course, just transfer this 'black, fierce Reek' to 'the reeking plains of France' in a poem of 1794. Yet there is a certain resonance between the two, and a suggestion that something is rotten in the state of France in 'To a Young Lady, with a Poem on the French Revolution', as in 'Preternatural Agency' when 'Warm'd with new Influence the unwholesome Plain / Sent up its foulest fogs to meet the Morn' (431–2).

In his poetry of the 1790s Coleridge characteristically oscillates between the public and the domestic. In the last part of 'To a Young Lady', such a swing occurs as the poet, 'With wearied thought once more' seeks the shelter of domestic life, and approaches 'the shade, / Where peaceful Virtue weaves the MYRTLE braid' (29–30), emblematic of marriage. To emphasize this point, in the copy of the poem Coleridge sent to Robert Southey (Morgan Library), Coleridge drew a little picture of a cottage at the end of line 35. Although this cottage signifies a withdrawal from the public sphere, it is not necessarily the antithesis of the millennial, for it is at least potentially a millennium in microcosm, as 'the cottag'd dell' of the Chatterton poem. The relation between the domestic and the millennial can nevertheless be uneasy, as is seen in two better-known poems of the mid-1790s.

---

[80] *Marginalia*, 2: 845–6.

'Reflections on Having Left a Place of Retirement' was probably written *c.* March 1796, at about the time that Coleridge was putting the last touches (for the time being) to 'Religious Musings'. It is a more personal statement on the subject of the poet's place in the world as described in the longer poem. Coleridge recognized it as belonging to a certain sub-genre, first by calling it 'A Poem, which affects not to be Poetry' when it was first published in the *Monthly Magazine* (October 1796), then by subtitling it '*Sermoni propriora*—HOR.' when it appeared in the *Poems* of 1797 (p. 100). In explanation of the term which he was also to apply to 'Fears in Solitude' (see *CPW* I: 257 n.), he later wrote to William Sotheby: 'There are moods of mind, in which they [formal similes] are natural—pleasing moods of mind, & such as a Poet will often have, & sometimes express; but they are not his highest, & most appropriate moods. They are "Sermoni propiora" which I once translated—"*Properer* for *a Sermon*"' (*CL* 2: 864). When one examines the Latin tag in context, it is clear that it is meant to disarm the reader: 'First', writes Horace, 'I will take my own name from the list of such as I would allow to be poets. For you would not call it enough to round off a verse, nor would you count anyone poet who writes, as I do, lines more akin to prose. If one has gifts inborn, if one has a soul divine and tongue of noble utterance, to such give the honour of that name'.[81] If the reader wishes to apply the term at face value to Coleridge's poem, good; if he or she reflects that it is no bad thing to be in company with Horace, so much the better. It should also be remembered that 'a Sermon' did not connote to Coleridge what it perhaps may to his readers today. The Sermon is one of the weapons with which the poet intends 'to fight the bloodless fight/Of Science, Freedom, and the Truth in CHRIST' (61–2). It was, in other words, a personal statement, though a public one. As Mays suggests in the notes to the forthcoming *Poetical Works*, the poem's original title, 'Reflections on Entering into Active Life', refers to the life of a Dissenting minister as a realization of the programme envisaged at the end of 'Religious Musings'.

---

[81] From Horace, *Satires*, I. iv. See *Horace: Satires Epistles, and Ars Poetica*, trans. H. Rushton Fairclough (London: W. Heinemann, 1926), pp. 51–3. C. R. Watters suggests that Coleridge was making a pun on the Latin *propiora/propriora*—'"A Distant 'Boum' Among the Hills": Some Notes on Coleridge's "Fears in Solitude"', *Charles Lamb Bulletin*, 59 (1987): 89. For Coleridge's possible knowledge of John Foster's discussion of the term in *An Essay on the Different Nature of Accent and Quantity*, see Richard T. Martin, 'Coleridge's Use of *sermoni propriora*', *Wordsworth Circle*, 3 (1972): 71–5; and Woodring in *TT* I: 314 n. 1.

It should be noted that the word as used by Horace and followed in Coleridge's letter is *propiora*, while the word in the epigraph in the *Poems* of 1797 is *propriora*.

'Reflections on Having Left a Place of Retirement' has three foci: 'the pretty Cot' of line 1, the 'VALLEY of SECLUSION' (9) that surrounds it, and 'the bleak Mount' (29) above. As the juxtapositions of 'The Eolian Harp' are similar in some respects—a point Coleridge himself emphasized by printing the 'Reflections' immediately after it in the *Poems* of 1797—a comparison is informative. In the earlier poem,[82] the poet leaves the flower-overgrown Cot to climb, at least in imagination, 'the midway slope / Of yonder hill' (26–7), where he stretches his limbs and envisions the unity of all living things. From this trance-like state he is recalled to the domesticity of the Cot by Sara Coleridge's 'more serious eye' (41). As Nigel Leask remarks, 'The central drama and tension of the poem remains that between the poet's hubristic and visionary egalitarianism, and Sara's "mild reproof".'[83] Furthermore, the two poles are conceived in terms of the sublime and the picturesque, the vision of 'animated nature' versus the domesticity of 'PEACE, and this COT, and THEE, heart-honor'd Maid!' (36, 56). In contrast, 'Reflections' presents its basic elements not in opposition but as parts of an aesthetic whole, Cottage and valley occupy the first movement of the poem (1–26), the mountain the second (26–42). From the vantage-point of the mountain the poet can see what appears to be 'the whole World' (39), but this does not obviate the centrality of the cottage in the valley. Both are joined in the first line of the third and last movement of the poem: 'Ah quiet dell! dear Cot! and Mount Sublime!' (44). These three embody all three modes of late eighteenth-century visual aesthetics: the sublime (mountain), the beautiful (dell), and the picturesque (cottage). As Tim Fulford astutely points out, the climax 'transforms the picturesque scene into a sublime vision'.[84] All must reluctantly be left behind for the realization of 'the active life', which is the subject of the rest of the poem.

Up to its third movement, 'Reflections' is notable for its imagery of nature—the thick jasmine that twines across the cottage porch, 'The bare bleak mountain speckled thin with sheep!' (31). The third movement is indeed 'sermoni propriora', in that it abandons such imagery

---

[82] Coleridge dated 'The Eolian Harp' as 'Composed August 20th, 1795, At Clevedon, Somersetshire'. See *CPW* 1: 100n. The poem was first published as 'Effusion XXXV' in the *Poems* of 1796. 'Reflections', though dated 1795 by E. H. Coleridge, must, as Mays argues in the forthcoming *Poetical Works*, be contemporary with or later than the Coleridges' removal from Clevedon in March 1796. I have used the text of the *Poems* of 1797 in citing both poems.

[83] Leask, *Politics of Imagination*, p. 89.

[84] Fulford, *Landscape, Liberty, and Authority: Poetry, Criticism, and Politics from Thomson to Wordsworth* (Cambridge: Cambridge University Press, 1996), p. 227.

for rhetorically structured statements about the poet's anticipated future role, with the prison reformer John Howard (d. 1790) as role model and hero of Sensibility. At the end, as in 'The Eolian Harp', the Cot with its attendant flowers returns, but here as a touchstone of the communitarian ideal once represented by Pantisocracy: 'Ah—had none greater! And that all had such!' (70). As Carl Woodring remarks, '"Reflections" ends in a quieter vein than *Religious Musings* but is also millenarian: the Pantisocratic millennium becomes also the New Jerusalem'.[85] However, as in 'Religious Musings', 'The time is not yet' (71), though in the last line the poet prays for its advent: 'Speed it, O FATHER! Let thy Kingdom come!'

The year 1796 saw the publication of Coleridge's *Poems* by Joseph Cottle, the launching of *The Watchman* and its abandonment after ten issues—but not the coming of the Kingdom. In the world of public events there were abortive peace negotiations with France, continued war, and the threat of invasion of England itself. Near the end of the year, Coleridge was again moved to write a poem describing history in apocalyptic terms, but now for the first time without presenting the possibility of a millennium to come. His 'Ode on the Departing Year'[86] is a terribly bleak poem in contrast to those so far discussed. For it, Coleridge needed not one but two vatic personae, one the imagined speaker of the verse, the other the speaker of a Greek epigraph. These are united in their self-contradiction, as if prophecies that would not be believed or that the prophetic speaker hoped would fail could be a buffer against the horror of a virtually unmitigated apocalyptic vision.

The 'Ode' begins with an epigraph, a fact important to Coleridge, who wrote of this one to John Prior Estlin on 30 December 1796: 'You know, I am a *mottophilist*, and almost a *motto-manist*' (*CL* 1: 293). When he republished the 'Ode' in the *Poems* of 1797, the poet had to struggle with Joseph Cottle to insert the Greek motto from Aeschylus's *Agamemnon*. On the two separate title-pages of the poem among the manuscript material and annotated pages of *Poems* 1797, now known as British Library, Ashley 408, Coleridge wrote: '"The Motto! where is the

  [85] Woodring, *Politics in the Poetry of Coleridge*, p. 73.
  [86] The poem was originally published as 'Ode for the Last Day of the Year, 1796' in the *Cambridge Intelligencer* for 31 Dec., 1796; and, at about the same time, as a quarto pamphlet entitled *Ode on the Departing Year*. By the time of the 'deathbed edition' of 1834, which was used by E. H. Coleridge for his principal text, the title had become 'Ode to the Departing Year'. However, this does not make sense: the being addressed in line 1 as 'Spirit, who sweepest the wild Harp of Time', is certainly not the Departing Year, which is seen in vision and described but not addressed. My text for the poem is the 1796 quarto.

Motto?" I would not have lost the *motto* for a kingdom twas the best part of the Ode' (fol. 58ᵛ). 'I beseech you, let the Motto be printed; and printed accurately' (fol. 66ᵛ). A master of the recontextualized quotation, Coleridge was able to use the words spoken by Cassandra in several ways:

Ha, ha! Oh, oh, the agony! Once more the dreadful throes of true prophecy whirl and distract me with their ill-boding onset. . . .

What is to come, will come. Soon thou, present here thyself, shalt of thy pity pronounce me all too true a prophetess.[87]

Several points are notable about these lines. First, they are spoken by yet another prophetic female, but this time by one far from powerful, occupying the position of the poet who can describe but not effect. Second, to emphasize the idea of the poet-prophet's powerlessness, the quotation is the beginning and end of a long speech made while Agamemnon is about to be murdered out of sight of the audience. Third, the whirling and the distraction to be found in the 'Ode' itself can be associated with true prophecy. Furthermore, as a prophetess whom no one will believe, Cassandra is an appropriate persona for the poet whose dithyrambic utterances mask a certain equivocation about what he is saying.

Coleridge may also have had in mind the fate of a prophet from whom he was anxious to distinguish himself. Richard Brothers, as we have seen in Chapter 1, had made a remarkable stir in the mid-1790s with his denunciations of war and empire but had been confined since his arrest in 1795 to a private madhouse. Coleridge had sympathy for Brothers, but at the same time he feared confusion between Brothers's prophetic stance and his own. We sense this when in the fourth of his *Lectures on Revealed Religion* Coleridge contrasts St Paul's account of his appeal to King Agrippa (see Acts 25–6) to an imagined report by Brothers's parliamentary disciple Nathaniel Brassey Halhed to Chief Justice Eyre.[88] The purpose of this ironical passage is to show that while Paul would be believed because Agrippa would confirm his testimony, Halhed and Brothers would not because Eyre would not confirm theirs. The whole passage seems invented to show that its author

---

[87] *Aeschylus*, trans. Herbert Weir Smyth, Loeb Classical Library (London: William Heinemann, 1926), pp. 107, 109.

[88] Coleridge, *Lectures 1795 on Politics and Religion (CC* 1), ed. Lewis Patton and Peter Mann (Princeton: Princeton University Press, 1971), p. 178. On Coleridge and Brothers, see Paul M. Zall, 'The Cool World of Samuel Taylor Coleridge', *Wordsworth Circle*, 4 (1973): 25–30.

shared the norms of evidence with his opponents and therefore is, though a millenarian, not a madman. In a letter written shortly after Brothers's arrest, Coleridge commiserates, but once again in such a way as to bring out the difference between them: 'Poor *Brothers!* They'll make him know the *Law* as well as the *Prophets!*'[89] Like Cassandra, Brothers was considered insane; yet this did not vitiate the prophetic import of their messages. Coleridge wished to avoid their fates by defining his role as that of a reluctant apocalypticist who took no pleasure in the burden of prophecy.

In the statements Coleridge made about the poem early on, this idea of non-responsibility is further stressed. 'You, I am sure', he wrote to Thomas Poole in the letter prefaced to the 1796 quarto, 'will not fail to recollect, that among the Ancients, the Bard and the Prophet were one and the same character; and you *know*, that although I prophesy curses, I pray fervently for blessings' (p. 4). This prophet would rather be a Jonah than a Jeremiah. While the *Poems* of 1797, including the 'Ode', were in press, Coleridge wrote on 10 March 1797, to Joseph Cottle: 'Public affairs are in strange confusion—I am afraid that I shall prove at least as good a prophet as bard—O doom'd to fall, enslav'd & vile:— but may God make me a foreboder of evils never to come!' (*CL* 1: 313). The quotation is of course from the 'Ode' itself (line 129 in the 1796 quarto). It makes us all the more conscious of the contrast between Coleridge's self-presentation as shrinking from his own apocalyptic vision and the extraordinary violence of that vision. In the 'Ode on the Departing Year', there are only traces of millennial imagery; and, instead of being a prelude to millennium, apocalypse threatens to become the only reality.

The subject-matter of the 'Ode' is the present state of Europe, and particularly the role of England. The poem is deliberately antithetical to the New Year's odes delivered annually by the Poet Laureate, James Henry Pye.[90] This is true not only of the sentiments expressed, but also of the language. For example, in Pye's 'Ode to the New Year' for 1793 (*London Chronicle*, 1–3 January 1793, p. 12) the Laureate contrasts France, 'Where Anarchy's insatiate brood / Their horrid footsteps mark with blood', to 'shores where temperate freedom reigns / . . . Where BRITAIN's grateful sons rejoice in GEORGE's sway'. In his 'Ode for the New Year 1795', Pye hoped for Concord or, alternatively, 'dismay to

---

[89] To George Dyer, 10 Mar. 1795; *CL* 1: 156.
[90] As Woodring suggests (*Politics in the Poetry of Coleridge*, p. 175).

Gallia's scatter'd host' (*London Chronicle*, 30 Dec. 1794–1 Jan. 1795, p. 1). Inflated rhetoric, luridness of diction, and frequent personification seem endemic to the sub-genre, and in these respects Coleridge was all too ready to match his rival.

The poetic mode that Coleridge chose for this poem, the English Pindaric ode in the manner of Thomas Gray, was one in which he had little experience.[91] The four extant stanzas of the early 'Ode on the destruction of the Bastile' indicate that this was a regular, controlled piece of verse. The 'Monody on the Death of Chatterton' could be considered an ode, but in its 1794 form it consists mainly of couplets, which produces an effect of control. But in the 'Ode on the Departing Year', Coleridge announced that he was striving for 'that Impetuosity of Transition, and that Precipitation of Fancy and Feeling, which are the *essential* excellencies of the sublimer Ode' (p. 4). Sympathetic readers were disposed to grant him this. Charles Lamb declared, 'The opening is in the spirit of sublimest allegory',[92] and Thomasina Dennis, a governess in the Wedgwood household, expressed the kind of response the poet desired when she found part of the poem 'as energetic, and almost as sublime in my opinion as Gray's Bard'.[93] However, this response was far from universal, and in a letter to Cottle, 10 February 1797, Coleridge referred to the poem as 'an "Ode" ... which some people think superior to "the Bard" of Gray, and which others think a rant of turgid obscurity' (*CL* 2: 309). The problem is that in taking up a mid-eighteenth-century mode with its attendant conventions, Coleridge sought to move beyond his model by intensifying its wilder aspects. In so doing he unwittingly moved the poem a certain degree from the sublime towards the grotesque. He may have intended an effect like Dante's vision of Philip the Fair embracing the Whore of Babylon, but he sometimes achieved something closer to the caricatures of Gillray and Isaac Cruikshank.[94]

[91] Coleridge was, however, the author of a Greek 'Ode on Astronomy' written at Cambridge in 1793 (for Southey's translation of it, see *Poems*, ed. Beer, pp. 17–20). His earlier, prize-winning Greek ode on the subject of slavery (1792), was written as the Cambridge rules required, in imitation of Sappho (rather than of Pindar). Part of it was published in a note to 'Preternatural Agency' with an English prose translation. See Anthea Morrison, 'Samuel Taylor Coleridge's Greek Prize Ode on the Slave Trade', in *An Infinite Complexity*, ed. J. R. Watson (Edinburgh: Edinburgh University Press, 1983), pp. 145–60. This essay includes a translation of the entire poem.
[92] 2 Jan. 1797; Lamb, *Letters*, 1: 80.
[93] Letter to Davies Giddy, 25 Aug. 1798; see R. S. Woof, 'Coleridge and Thomasina Dennis', *University of Toronto Quarterly*, 32 (1962): 41–2.
[94] Woodring compares a print by Cruikshank showing the dying Catherine the Great envisioning her crimes against humanity (*Politics in the Poetry of Coleridge*, p. 49).

In the first strophe the poet attempts to establish an Old Testament quality with his vision of 'the skirts of the DEPARTING YEAR' (8),[95] and later (112–24) he undergoes Cassandra-like agonies at witnessing the events of contemporary history in Warsaw, Ismail, Belgium, the Vendée, and Africa. There is a moment of millennial possibility in a myth of Nature in travail and then birth (30–7): 'Her groans are horrible! But ô! most fair / The promis'd Twins, she bears—EQUALITY and PEACE!' Had Coleridge retained a simile from his notebook draft (*CN* 1: 199) of this passage, 'Like a mighty Giantess', the affinity of Nature here to Coleridge's other powerful female personifications of French Revolutionary freedom would be even more marked.[96] However, this short passage concludes the second strophe. Coleridge no longer hoped for a millennium in a France governed by the Directory, although 'the light'ning of thy Lance' (66) could still intimidate the crowned heads of Europe, and the epode begins with a catalogue of horrors centring on Catherine the Great.

Catherine's death on 17 November 1796 may have given Coleridge the initial impetus to write this poem, though he appears to have delayed for a month. Coleridge's inner state during this period, especially as mirrored in his letters to Thomas Poole in December, was as unsettled as the world's. Yet all the public themes addressed are important concerns in *The Watchman* and other Coleridge prose, and it would be a mistake to view the Ode's apocalyptic aspect as merely psychological projection, especially for a poet to whom the public and the private were as closely related as they were for Coleridge. He even glosses line 106—'For ever shall the bloody Island scowl?'—with a footnote (p. 12) from his own *Conciones ad Populum*: 'In Europe the smoking villages of Flanders and the putrified fields of La Véndee [sic]—from Africa the unnumbered victims of a detestable Slave-trade—in Asia the desolated plains of Indostan and the million whom a rice-contracting Governor destroyed by famine—in America the recent enormities of our scalp-merchants—the four quarters of the globe groan beneath the intolerable iniquity of this nation!'[97] Coleridge's prophetic sweep across the

---

[95] Though admired by Lamb (*Letters*, 1: 80), 'skirts' was replaced by 'train' in *Sibylline Leaves* and the *Poetical Works* of 1828, 1829, and 1830.

[96] Instead, Coleridge demythologized the passage in later versions of the poem. 'The whole Childbirth of Nature is at once ludicrous and disgusting', he wrote to John Thelwall on 6 Feb. 1797 (*CL* 1: 307).

[97] From 'On the Present War', in *Lectures 1795*, 1: 46, 58. There are some minor variations of text, but one important one: 'our scalp-merchants' for 'their Scalp-Merchants' emphasizes the collective responsibility of the community.

four continents (as then considered) of the globe is similar to that of Blake's Continental Prophecies of 1794–5. In both instances the poet's desire is to exhibit a world groaning to be delivered from the wrongs of empire, and in both the deliverance comes in an apocalyptic moment. For Blake, its agent is the incarnation of revolutionary energy, Orc, who helps the fierce Americans overthrow their governors, frees the slaves, drives the kings of Asia from their dens, and will next flame in the vineyards of France. In the 'Ode', it is the SPIRIT of the EARTH, who at the end of antistrophe II cries, 'Rise, God of Nature, rise! Why sleep thy Bolts unhurl'd?' (110).

The second epode begins with the Cassandra-like torments of the prophetic poet as he denounces his own country as 'doom'd to fall, enslav'd and vile' (129). In a beautiful pastoral passage, a millennial gleam seems to fall across the land:

> O ALBION! O my mother Isle!
> Thy valleys, fair as Eden's bowers,
> Glitter green with sunny showers.
>
> (130–2)

England is seen as potentially a spatial extension of the nook or dell; what follows, however, is not an expansion of this theme but rather a turning-away from the millennial. First we are given what Woodring terms 'one of the most apocalyptic of all the images in Coleridge's political poetry',[98] that of DESTRUCTION, the 'Fiend-hag' troped to vulture and dragon. This monster is at once an extension of the reference to Catherine the Great (the 'insatiate Hag' of line 45), a female version of the Great Red Dragon of Revelation, and an epitome of the female monsters in Coleridge's poems. She dreams 'Of central flames thro' nether seas upthund'ring' (150), a reference to the end of the world derived from Thomas Burnet.[99] However, Burnet's description of the final conflagration is followed by an extensive exposition of the millennium, an element conspicuously lacking in Coleridge's Ode.

In the last movement of the poem, the poet separates himself from the state of England. At first this passage may look superficially like the closures of poems such as 'The Eolian Harp' and 'Lines on Having Left a Place of Retirement', but it is the solitariness of the poet that is

---

[98] Woodring, *Politics in the Poetry of Coleridge*, p. 178.

[99] See J. Livingston Lowes, *The Road to Xanadu: A Study in the Ways of the Imagination* (Princeton: Princeton University Press, 1986 [1927]), pp. 458–9 n. 28, referring to book 3 of the *Sacred Theory of the Earth*, 'Concerning the Conflagration'.

emphasized here. There is no cottage twined with flowers, no heart-honoured Maid. Instead, the poet, 'unpartaking of the evil thing' (163), is imagined as apart from any community with others.

> Now I recenter my immortal mind
> In the long sabbath of high self-content;
> Cleans'd from the fleshly Passions that bedim
> God's Image, Sister of the Seraphim.
>
> (167–70)

This last line is related to one of the many fragments Coleridge stored in his notebook in the autumn and early winter of 1796.[100] In this instance, as in several others, the source has been noted by Kathleen Coburn as a sermon by Jeremy Taylor: 'First, if we consider what the soul is in its own capacity to happiness, we shall find it to be an excellency greater than the sun, of an angelical substance, sister to a cherubin, an image of the Divinity, and the great argument of that mercy whereby God did distinguish us from the lower form of beasts, and trees, and minerals' (*CN* 1: 276g and n.). However, in the poem, Coleridge takes the last words not from Taylor's sermon, but from Richard Crashaw's poem 'The Flaming Heart', in which St Teresa is addressed as 'Fair sister of the SERAPHIM!'[101] Coleridge's choice of Crashaw's 'Seraphim' over Taylor's 'cherubin' is significant, for the soul is here akin to angels of love rather than to angels of knowledge. Nevertheless, this does not involve any human community. The poet is left in purity, but it is the purity of isolation. Such an imagined solution could not long be a stable one.

Coleridge was proud of his 'Ode on the Departing Year', as he had been of 'Religious Musings', and he had it placed first in the 1797 edition of his *Poems*. At the same time, he began making revisions almost as soon as the poem first appeared in 1796. Responding[102] to separate criticisms from Thelwall, Lamb, and Wordsworth,[102] Coleridge made alterations in the syntax and diction. These stylistic changes have little

---

[100] See especially the notebook entries and related notes in *CN* 1: 175, 259(a), 272(g and u), 273. The chief sources are Jeremy Taylor, the Bible, and the Apocrypha; the themes, as Coburn points out, are divine wrath and punishment. See also Fruman, *Coleridge: The Damaged Archangel*, pp. 235–42.

[101] See *The Poems English Latin and Greek of Richard Crashaw*, ed. L. C. Martin, 2nd edn. (Oxford: Clarendon Press, 1957), p. 327. Coleridge later quoted this line again in the *Philosophical Lectures*, p. 316.

[102] See letters to Joseph Cottle, 6 Jan. 1797, *CL* 1: 297–8; to John Thelwall, 6 Feb. 1797, *CL* 2: 307; and to Joseph Cottle, 8 June 1797, *CL* 1: 325.

to do with the political content, and Coleridge even added a fierce diatribe from Nahum 3 (p. 15n.) to his own denunciation of England in the *Poems* of 1797, reinforcing that element of his poem with expressions like 'all thy strong-holds shall be like fig trees . . . if they be shaken, they shall ever fall into the mouth of the Eater. . . . Thy crowned are as the locusts and thy captains as the great grasshoppers'. Later, however, some changes were made as part of Coleridge's programme of political self-rehabilitation. In the *Sibylline Leaves* of 1817, England became '*Not yet* enslav'd, *not wholly* vile' (p. 56, emphasis mine), and in *On the Constitution of the Church and State* an altered version of the entire passage was printed to illustrate the argument that 'It is the chief of many blessings derived from the insular character and circumstances of our country, that our social institutions have formed themselves out of our proper needs and interests'.[103] Here a passage intended as a radical critique has actually been adjusted so as to idealize the *status quo*! Of greater literary interest is the manner in which Coleridge placed the ode in 1817 so as to form part of a continuum illustrating his political and poetic development.

When Coleridge published *Sibylline Leaves* in 1817, he placed the 'Ode on the Departing Year' first among 'Poems Occasioned by Political Events or Feelings Connected with Them'. The second poem in this group was 'France: An Ode', originally published as 'The Recantation' in the *Morning Post* for 16 April 1798, and next in the *Fears in Solitude* volume (London: Joseph Johnson, 1798), which is the text of 'France' cited here. By placing the two odes in sequence in *Sibylline Leaves*, Coleridge made the second answer the first, signalling the poet's abandonment not only of his former political convictions, but also of his apocalyptic interpretation of history and of the millennial hope that had at one time accompanied it.

The international-political circumstances behind 'France' have been reconstructed in a seminal essay by C. Bonnard, setting the poem in relation to British journalistic reaction to France's invasion of Switzerland.[104] On 30 January Daniel Stuart's *Morning Post* condemned France for the first time, because of that invasion. But in February, its line was that the invasion was Swiss-inspired and justified. Then on 19 March, the editor vehemently condemned the French. By the end of

---

[103]   ed. John Colmer, *CC* 10 (Princeton: Princeton University Press, 1976), pp. 22–3.
[104]   C. Bonnard, 'The Invasion of Switzerland and English Public Opinion (January to April 1798): The Background to Samuel Taylor Coleridge's *France*', *English Studies*, 1 (1940): 1–26.

March 1798, only the *Courier* among the dailies defended the French, and the *Monthly Review* among the monthlies. 'Even the *Morning Post*', writes Bonnard, 'gave expression to feelings of compassion and indignation in a leading article of the 2nd of April, in its news columns of the 3rd, 10th, and 11th, and crowned it all by the publication of Coleridge's "France: An Ode"'. Bonnard concludes that 'the final conversion of Coleridge to anti-revolutionary views was but one manifestation, among many others, of a very deep and very general movement of public opinion'. Coleridge dated his poem February 1798, although it was written in late March or early April, in order to make its political wisdom seem more acute. (In the collected editions of 1828, 1829, and 1834, it is dated February 1797, making the author seem actually prescient.)

'France' begins with the situation envisaged at the end of the 'Ode on the Departing Year'—the poet alone in the natural world. Here the situation is much less bleak, being positively valorized by key words that would once have been applied to the political realm, but are now applied to Nature: 'control', 'eternal laws', 'imperious branches', 'free', and 'divinest liberty'.[105] In contrast to the 'Ode on the Departing Year', not a single personification is introduced in the first stanza, as if to show the reader that we are now on a more common plane of reality. Formally, too, the new ode contrasts with the old: instead of 'wild', irregular rhyming, we now have a carefully structured 21-line stanzaic rhyme scheme—*abbacdcdeefgfghihjjij*—followed throughout. In style, as well as substance, the reader is assured of the poet's mastery of his subject.

Nevertheless, we encounter the familiar figure of the Amazon France at the opening of stanza II, as the poet harks back to the situation of 1789 in a momentary echoing of his earlier mode of representation.

> When France in wrath her giant limbs uprear'd,
> And with that oath which smote earth, air, and sea,
> Stamp'd her strong foot and said, she would be free
>
> (22–4)

---

[105] Cf. M. H. Abrams's remark on 'the degree to which English writers, collaterally with their German contemporaries, imported such societal terms as "conflict", "mastery", "tyranny", "submission", "slavery", "equality", and "freedom" into the cognitive realm, to represent the relations between the mind and the natural world, or between the mind and the physical senses, in the act of perception'. Abrams continues: 'This radical shift of emphasis is itself the subject of Coleridge's "France: An Ode . . . "'. (*Natural Supernaturalism: Tradition and Revolution in Romantic Literature* (New York and London: Norton, 1973), pp. 363–4).

There are some undercutting nuances here. It seems as if the Tennis Court Oath is being performed by a petulant child. 'Said, she would be' introduces important qualifications, and 'smote' directs aggression towards 'earth, air, and sea', which have already been declared the proper abodes of Liberty. The poet presents himself as having sung 'amid a slavish band' (of poets like James Henry Pye) as the campaigns against France began. The weapon that figured so prominently in 'To a Young Lady, with a Poem on the French Revolution' reappears as 'the tyrant-quelling lance' (37), but the poet now makes clear that it was his *voice* that contributed to the defeat of the tyrant, presumably at Valmy in September 1792.

The third strophe introduces the elements of 'blasphemy' and drunken intoxication to refer to the events of 1793–4: 'Blasphemy's loud scream' (43) could signify the instauration of Reason in Notre Dame Cathedral or, equally, its displacement by the cult of the Supreme Being. The 'dance more wild' (46), though in part metaphorical, is also literal, for the *farandole* was indeed danced at revolutionary festivals, the ruins of the Bastille being a favourite place. Coleridge pictures such an event as a Dionysiac orgy, much like Blake's rendering of the crushing of human grapes to make the wine of Luvah (typically identified with France in *The Four Zoas*). The storms that follow, hiding the sun, are probably the Terror, which 'ceas'd' (50) with the execution of Robespierre and his confederates at the end of July 1794. Then, after the Thermidorean Reaction, 'all *seem'd* calm and bright' (50, emphasis mine) under the Directory. France militant now appears as a gigantic female apocalyptic manifestation: 'her front deep scar'd and gory, / Conceal'd with clust'ring wreaths of glory' (51–2), echoing Milton's description of the fallen Satan, with its images of the sun shining through misty air and 'his face / Deep scars of Thunder had intrencht' (*Paradise Lost*, i. 594–5, 600–1). Once more the effect is to undercut the poet's rationalizations and questions—'And what (I said)' (43); 'And soon (I said)' (59). 'Reason, indeed, began to suggest many apprehensions', Coleridge wrote in the 'Argument' that he added to make everything perfectly clear in 1802 (*CPW* i: 244).

Stanza III continues with another Miltonic allusion in rendering the military gains of the Directory abroad and its consolidation of power at home:

> When insupportably advancing,
> Her arm made mock'ry of the warrior's ramp,
> While, timid looks of fury glancing,

> Domestic treason, crush'd beneath her fatal stamp,
> Writh'd, like a wounded dragon in his gore;
>
> (53–7)

Curiously, in 1799, Coleridge was accused of having plagiarized this passage from Milton by a reviewer[106] who called attention to its source in *Samson Agonistes*:

> When insupportably his foot advanc't,
> In scorn of thir proud arms and warlike tools,
> Spurn'd them to death by Troops. The bold *Ascalonite*
> Fled from his Lion ramp; old Warriors turn'd
> Thir plated backs under his heel;
> Or grov'ling soil'd their crested helmets in the dust.
>
> (136–41)

Coleridge was, as we sadly know, capable of plagiarism; but the 'insupportably advancing' France is surely meant to suggest Samson, just as a few lines earlier she was meant to suggest Satan. (In Sir George Beaumont's copy of the 1798 *Fears in Solitude*, Coleridge marked lines 135–6 and wrote '*Milton* "Samsons [*sic*] Agonistes". /S.T.C.'.[107]) The intertextuality reinforces her ambiguity. Satan or Samson? The poet presents himself as having naïvely hoped that France would choose the positive alternative and create a millennium by example, 'Till love and joy look round, and call the earth their own!' (63). This process was, moreover, to be non-violent. France would 'compel the nations to be free', but only by example, 'conqu'ring by her happiness alone' (61). (In the *Morning Post* version published on 14 October 1802, 'compel' was changed to 'persuade' so as to leave no doubt.) As both poet and reader now know this was not to be, the time span of the poem having reached the present, stanza IV begins the recantation proper.

Coleridge expressed his new political attitude in a letter to his brother George on 10 March 1798: 'I have snapped my squeaking

---

[106] Anonymous review of *Fears in Solitude* (1798), *New London Review*, 1 (1799): 98–100; repr. in *The Romantics Reviewed*, ed. Donald R. Reiman (3 vols. in 9, New York and London: Garland, 1972), part A, 2: 794–5. In the *Morning Post* version of 1802, Coleridge showed sensitivity to this charge by changing 'insupportably' to 'irresistibly', but he restored the original reading *in Sibylline Leaves*, and kept it in the three later editions of his collected poems. (Textual information from J. C. C. Mays.)

[107] I am grateful to the Pierpont Morgan Library for permission to quote from these annotations (PML 47225). In his editorial apparatus for the forthcoming *Poetical Works*, Mays dates them *c*.1807.

baby-trumpet of Sedition & the fragments lie scattered in the lumber-room of Penitence' (*CL* 1: 397). This would be more convincing had Coleridge not, as we have seen, used the same expression to Charles Lloyd, Senior, in a letter dated 15 October 1796 (*CL* 1: 240). Once again, trivialization is used as a rhetorical technique to fictionalize Coleridge's political past. The harmless poet could never have accomplished much with such a little trumpet. Similarly, in 'France: An Ode' all he has to feel guilty about are 'dreams' (64). Helvetia's wrongs are presented in grim detail, but a sensitive reader might well be expected to wonder why a poet who had only 'hop'd', 'feared', 'sung', and conversed with himself should feel so guilty.

The poet of 'France' has renounced millennial dreaming, but not prophetic denunciation, and he applies to France the figure of sexual transgression that Jeremiah does to Jerusalem: 'O France! that mockest heav'n, adult'rous, blind' (78). France has joined the kings of the earth, Nimrod figures who 'Yell in the hunt, and share the murd'rous prey' (82). She is 'patriot'[108] only 'in pernicious toils!' (79), in contrast to the poet, a 'patriot' in his feelings for England (34) and to the Swiss, 'A patriot race' (74). The distinction is important because of the importance of the word in the discourse of British radicalism. Before 1789, 'patriot' had connoted not merely love of country but also resistance to arbitrary power; after that date its meaning expanded to include support of the goals of the French Revolution, as in 'the patriot fire' of 'To a Young Lady, with a Poem on the French Revolution' (23). In *The Prelude* (1805–6) Wordsworth tells how he

> did soon
> Become a Patriot; and my heart was all
> Given to the People, and my love was theirs.

> (ix. 124–6)

And in line 554, Michel Beaupuy is Wordsworth's 'patriot Friend'. In 'France' this kind of patriotism is now viewed as a deception by which the loyalties of English radicals, including the poet's, had been ensnared. True patriotism is, at least by implication, the love of one's country alone. This new definition prepares the way for the poet's attempt to redefine Liberty in the last stanza.

---

[108] In the two *Morning Post* printings, the word is 'patient'. In the Beaumont copy of *Fears in Solitude* (Morgan Library, p. 17), Coleridge noted: '—I wrote it "patient"—who altered it, I know not, but it seems to me an improvement'.

Coleridge claimed that there had been an intermediary stanza between the present IV and V, one that 'alluded to the African Slave Trade as conducted by this Country, and to the present Ministry and their supporters' (*CPW* I: 247 n.). In its original *Morning Post* printing of 1798, the last stanza begins with a distinction between the 'patriot zeal' of '*these*'—presumably referring to the ministers—and that of the poet, followed by an address to 'Afric' in which 'They' are likened to hyenas. All this seems to refer to a passage on slavery not extant in any text. When Coleridge revised 'France' for the *Fears in Solitude* volume of 1798, he began the last stanza with four considerably stronger lines that retain an echo of the anti-slavery subject in their metaphorical images. Here the image of the chain is especially important. The threefold chain of 'To a Young Lady, with a Poem on the French Revolution' turns out not to have been burst so easily after all. 'At Genoa', Coleridge had jotted in his notebook, 'the word, Liberty, is engraved on the chains of the galley-slaves, & the doors of Prisons'.[109] In 'France' the resumed chain makes the Orwellian statement that Freedom is Slavery: 'They burst their manacles, and wear the name / Of freedom graven on a heavier chain!' (85). As Coleridge now sees the revolutionists, they are creatures of licence (cf. the orgiastic imagery of stanza III), with traces of the British stereotype of the 'light' French or the 'confident and over-lusty French' of *Henry V*. Furthermore, they embrace what Blake would call 'a Philosophy of five senses'. Therefore the poet turns away from them, as he had turned away from England and its allies in his 'Ode on the Departing Year'.

The fact that the publisher of the *Fears in Solitude* quarto was Joseph Johnson shows how much Coleridge's recantation accorded with the views of liberals and even radicals in 1798. The reviewer for Johnson's own *Analytical Review*, 'D.M.S.', found that 'the poet reconciles to the strictest consistency, his former attachment to french [*sic*] politics, with his present abhorrence of them'.[110] As might be expected, conservative critics preferred to concentrate not on the poet's new attitudes, but on his old ones. The Tory *British Critic* said of line 27, 'We should like to

---

[109] *CN* I: 206; see Woodring, *Politics in the Poetry of Coleridge*, pp. 183–4.

[110] *Analytical Review*, 28 (1798): 591; repr. in *Romantics Reviewed*, part A, I: 11. In 'The Politics of "Frost at Midnight" ' (*Wordsworth Circle*, 22 (1991): 3–11), Paul Magnuson hypothesizes that Johnson's motive in publishing and promoting the volume was his need to establish good character while awaiting the sentencing phase of his trial for having sold a seditious pamphlet by Gilbert Wakefield. Magnuson ascribes Coleridge's motive to a need to counter the attacks upon him in the *Anti-Jacobin*.

know *where this slavish band* existed. There are none of that description in this country.'[111] A more interesting question was raised by the *Critical Review*, which had been hospitable to Coleridge to the point of reviewing all his books to date. The reviewer, who may have been Southey, asked of the ending: 'What does Mr. Coleridge mean by liberty in this passage? or what connexion has it with the subject of civil freedom?'[112] This cut close enough for Coleridge to reply, though not for publication. In Sir George Beaumont's copy of the *Fears in Solitude* volume he wrote that '*unfounded* Objections' had made it seem 'as if I had confounded moral with political Freedom—but surely the object of this stanza is to show, that true political Freedom can only arise out of moral Freedom' (p. 18). Interesting as this proposition may be in its own right, it is not the argument of the last stanza. Liberty 'nor ever / Didst breathe thy soul in forms of human pow'r' but rather 'speedest on thy subtle pinions, / To live amid the winds, and move upon the waves!' (91–2, 97–8). 'The resolution of this poem is intelligible', M. H. Abrams maintains, '*only* if we recognize that it turns on the conversion of the political concepts, slavery and liberty, into the metaphors of the mind in relation to nature'.[113] However, this conversion does involve a rejection of the political realm and a semantic juggling of 'Liberty' on Coleridge's part. In the poem's end is its beginning, with the poet alone on the sea cliff experiencing the unity of his own being with the forces of Nature. Significantly, he does not link these, as he does in the 'Monody on the Death of Chatterton', with a human community. His situation is much like that at the end of the 'Ode on the Departing Year', with the forces of Nature now substituted for the purely spiritual ones of the earlier ode. The ideal of domesticity has disappeared, the apocalyptic become historicized in the past, the millennial shown to be an illusion.

This is also the situation at the beginning of 'Fears in Solitude', composed shortly afterwards and published as the first poem of the 1798 quarto volume: the poet is alone in the natural world. Some familiar elements of earlier poems also appear with 'A GREEN and silent spot amid the hills! / A small and silent dell!' (1–2) and 'a quiet spirit-healing nook!' (12). In this seeming paradise regained,[114] the poet hears the lark

[111] *British Critic*, 13 (1799), 663; repr. in *Romantics Reviewed*, part A, 1: 127.
[112] *Critical Review*, 26 (1799): 474; repr. in *Romantics Reviewed*, part A, 1: 312.
[113] Abrams, *Natural Supernaturalism*, p. 363.
[114] As Kelvin Everest remarks, the dell or vale is almost synonymous with 'family, friendship, and marriage' (*Coleridge's Secret Ministry: The Context of the Conversation Poems* (Hassocks,

and 'dreams of better worlds' (26). This budding millennial scene is, however, not allowed to develop further, because the next verse paragraph turns to the subject-matter of the subtitle: 'Written, April 1798, During the Alarms of an Invasion'. The feared invasion is seen as an apocalyptic punishment of the ills of British society. Chief among these is slavery, troped as 'a cloud that travels on, / Steam'd up from Cairo's swamps of pestilence' (48–9). National corruption is denounced in a moralized discourse reminiscent of Young's *Night Thoughts*, seeming to cry out for a Blake to illustrate it:

> We have been drinking with a riotous thirst
> Pollutions from the brimming cup of wealth,
> A selfish, lewd, effeminated race.

> (55–7)

Once more the image is of the Whore in Revelation with her cup of abominations: 'For all nations have drunk of the wine of the wrath of her fornication, and the kings of the earth have committed fornication with her, and the merchants of the earth are waxed rich through the abundance of her delicacies' (Rev. 18: 3). The poet, suffering in a community of guilt with his countrymen, uses the first person plural—'We have offended very grievously' (43), but as he alone appears aware of the guilt, he suffers in solitude.[115]

Much of 'Fears in Solitude' is devoted to a denunciation of England's role in the French wars, but the French themselves are seen, as in 'France: An Ode', as 'still promising / Freedom, themselves too sensual to be free' (139–40). The result is a sense of void, eloquently described by Clement Carlyon, to whom Coleridge recited the poem while in Germany: 'The trammels of Pantisocracy were falling from him, and he was struggling to devise an outlet from the storm, which had already gathered around the nations, and was overwhelming with still increasing darkness, the visions of Utopian felicity with which the drama of the French Revolution opened, and of which he had himself drunk so deeply.'[116] In this diminished world, the British are called upon to repel

---

Sussex: Harvester, 1979), p. 41). For a somewhat different perspective on the dell in this poem as 'a centre of magnetic attraction', see Peter Larkin, 'Fears in Solitude: Reading (from) the Dell', *Wordsworth Circle*, 22 (1991): 11–14.

[115] In Coleridge's partial republication of the poem in *The Friend* for 8 June 1809, the title is given as 'Fears of Solitude'. See *CPW* I: 257n. and *The Friend*, ed. Barbara E. Rooke (2 vols., Princeton; Princeton University Press, 1969), 2: 25.

[116] Clement Carlyon, *Early Years and Late Reflections* (London, 1836), I: 141–2.

the imagined invaders, but domestic political change is rejected as irrelevant, since evil derives 'From our own folly and rank wickedness' (167). The poet's own role is seen as bardic but no longer prophetic: 'I walk with awe, and sing my stately songs, / Loving the God that made me!' (193–4).[117] Nearing its end, 'Fears in Solitude' makes the now familiar turn from the public world to the private as the poet goes from the 'soft and silent spot' (205) to the brow of the hill to encounter a picturesque 'burst of prospect' (212).[118] Here, from what Tim Fulford aptly terms 'Coleridge's spiritual high ground',[119] the poet can imagine a community amongst the trees, comprising his friend Thomas Poole in his mansion and his own wife and baby in their cottage. This may constitute an embryonic millennial world, but it is hard to disagree with Nicholas Roe's judgement that at the end of this poem 'Coleridge's indulgence is self-deception, but it arises from a need to believe in the benificent influence to moral good that the poem has significantly failed to answer'.[120]

As we have seen, the role of the millennium in these poems of 1798, compared to its prominent place in 'Religious Musings' and other works of just a few years before, is severely reduced. Having abandoned his millenarian theme, Coleridge has problems in finding a viable substitute, whether it be nature, as in 'France: An Ode', or friendship and domesticity, as in 'Fears in Solitude'. He still envisages apocalyptic subjects; but, without its millennial counterpart, the apocalyptic tends to become grotesque. This is precisely what happens in several poems published in the *Morning Post* from 1798 to 1800: 'Fire, Famine, and Slaughter', 'The Devil's Thoughts', and 'The Two Round Spaces on the Tombstone'. In entering the two-dimensional realm of the apocalyptic grotesque, Coleridge gained (though anonymously) a much larger audience, for the first two of these caused a minor sensation among contemporary readers.

---

[117] Coburn points out that these lines come from the Gutch Notebook (*CN* 1: 268 and n.) and that their source is Ecclus. 47: 8.

[118] The term 'burst' is frequently used in this sense in William Gilpin's *Observations*, as pointed out in *The Prose Works of William Wordsworth*, ed. W. J. B. Owen and J. W. Smyser (3 vols., Oxford: Clarendon Press, 1974), 2: 429.

[119] Fulford, *Landscape, Liberty, and Authority*, p. 236.

[120] Nicholas Roe, *Wordsworth and Coleridge: The Radical Years* (Oxford: Clarendon Press, 1988), p. 267.

The Apocalyptic Grotesque

Apocalyptic foreboding—the sense of historically imminent catastrophe—linked with the expectation of a consequent millennial society is, as we have seen, a major theme of Coleridge's poetry in the decade following the French Revolution. In 'Preternatural Agency' it is embodied in a series of allegoric visions; in 'Religious Musings' it is part of a scenario that culminates in the descent of the heavenly throne; and, as we have also seen, the theme is modulated as the poet's faith in a millennial outcome weakens. However, the apocalyptic did not disappear from Coleridge's poetry at quite the same time as the millennial. After he had abandoned millennial hope, Coleridge still saw the world as driven by enormous forces beyond the control of ordinary human beings. When represented in relation to the millennial, the aesthetic mode of the apocalyptic is sublime; but with the disappearance of any accompanying millennial element, the sublime merges into the grotesque.[121] This can be seen in three poems mentioned above, poems that might be called 'apocalyptic satires'[122] While none of these would be published under their author's name for a long time to come, two of them were among the poems of Coleridge best known to his contemporaries. All three reveal a strain of *diablerie* that he seldom expressed elsewhere, as if working in the mode of the apocalyptic grotesque gave free play to an otherwise dormant aspect of his imagination.

'Fire, Famine, and Slaughter' was the third of Coleridge's poems to be published in the *Morning Post*, appearing there on 8 January 1798. It may have been composed a year or more earlier, for '*The Scene [is] a desolated tract in La Vendee [sic]*', where a war in which it is estimated that 140,000 died[123] had ended in 1796. In the 'Introductory Essay' to *The Watchman*, Coleridge had stated that the Methodists 'shudder with pious horror at defending [Christianity] by famine, and fire, and blood'; and, as Lewis Patton observes, there are many references in

---

[121]   As I have argued with respect to British painting in *The Apocalyptic Sublime* (New Haven and London: Yale University Press, 1986), pp. 42, 45, 63, 65, 68, 90–7, 184–6.

[122]   For 'Fire, Famine and Slaughter' and 'The Devil's Thoughts' the texts cited are those of the original *Morning Post* printings; for 'The Two Round Spaces on the Tombstone' the text is that of Coleridge's letter to Humphry Davy dated 9 Oct. 1800, as printed in *CL* 1: 632–3. On the relation between satire and the grotesque, see Wolfgang Kayser, *The Grotesque in Art and Literature*, trans. Ulrich Weisstein (New York: Columbia University Press, 1981 [1957]), pp. 37, 41.

[123]   See Emmet Kennedy, *A Cultural History of the French Revolution* (New Haven and London: Yale University Press, 1989), p. 405 n. 6.

The Watchman to bloodshed in the Vendée and in Ireland, 'both enormities being chargeable, directly or indirectly, Coleridge felt, to the
English ministry' (*Watchman*, p. 13 and n. 1). If, however, David V. Erdman is correct in ascribing to Coleridge two *Morning Post* articles of
January 1798—'Ireland and La Vendée' and 'Pitt and Buonoparte'
(*EOT* 3: 11–15)—the poem may be as close in date to these prose pieces
as it is in spirit. The occasion for publishing it at the beginning of 1798,
like that of 'Parliamentary Oscillators', which appeared in the *Cambridge Intelligencer* on 6 January, was the passage of Pitt's war taxes by
the House of Commons on 4 January. Both poems are signed
'Laberius'[124]—a name with thematic resonance.

The story of P. Decimus Laberius, a Roman knight and 'a blunt and
outspoken man',[125] is known chiefly through the *Saturnalia* of Macrobius. Laberius was a writer of mimes and satires during the time of
Julius Caesar. 'Invited' by Caesar to appear in one of his own pieces,
which was considered a degradation for a man of his class, Laberius
inserted into his prologue the line 'Many he needs fear whom many
fear'. According to Macrobius, 'at those last words, the audience as one
man turned and looked at Caesar, thus indicating that this scathing
gibe was an attack on his despotism'.[126] The choice of Laberius as a
pseudonym, then, has a double function. It presents the poet as a
satirist who defies dictatorial authority, but it also points up his vulnerability to that authority. This double aspect contains the germ of the
later 'Apologetic Preface', in which Coleridge would argue that his
poem had never threatened authority at all. Actually, it is one of
Coleridge's most aggressive fantasies, although this does not necessarily vitiate the poet's argument about personification in the 'Apologetic
Preface'.

'Fire, Famine, and Slaughter' is indeed one of Coleridge's 'political
pop-ups', as Carl Woodring has called them,[127] a two-dimensional
projection with affinities to Gillray's caricatures. One might compare
Gillray's *Presages of the Millennium* (published 4 June 1795), in which Pitt
is represented as Death on the pale horse from Revelation 6: 8.[128] Like

---

[124] On Coleridge's use of this pen-name, see Woodring, *Politics in the Poetry of Coleridge*,
pp. 228–9.
[125] Macrobius, *The Saturnalia*, trans. Percival Vaughan Davies (New York: Columbia
University Press, 1969), p. 180.   [126] Ibid., p. 181.
[127] Woodring, *Politics in the Poetry of Coleridge*, p. 129.
[128] See my discussion of this print in *Apocalyptic Sublime*, pp. 184–6. Also cf. Richard
Newton's caricature entitled 'The Devil's Darling', dated 5 May 1797, in which a grotesque

Gillray's work, Coleridge's displays a certain genius in its conflation of the political, the apocalyptic, and the grotesque. The subtitle 'A War Eclogue' is itself grotesque, signifying an impossible genre. For this Coleridge may have been indebted to Southey's 'Botany Bay Eclogues', although the poems themselves are very different in nature.[129] More of a model for Coleridge's combination of comic viciousness and doggerel verse is the conversation of the three witches at the beginning of Act I, scene iii, of *Macbeth*. There is at the same time a suggestion of the four riders of the Apocalypse, who were given power 'over the fourth part of the earth, to kill with sword, and with hunger, and with death, and with the beasts of the earth' (6: 8), with Pitt as the absent fourth.

The macabre jokes of the poem are based on ironical hyperbole. Fire forbids the naming of Pitt because ''Twill make a holiday in Hell'—it happened once before, and the damned were so full of glee that they became uncontrollable. Therefore he who sent the three sisters must be denoted by unspecified 'Letters four', thus becoming like one of those dashes used in eighteenth-century satire not to obscure but to identify. Somewhere in the background there is a suggestion of 'the bottomless pit' of Revelation, a play on words Coleridge makes in 'A Moral and Political Lecture'.[130] Famine flew from the battlefield because she could not endure the sight of the carrion-eaters enjoying their feast. Slaughter is grateful for the blood of 'thrice ten hundred thousand men', a figure afterwards reduced (probably for the sound value) to 'thrice three hundred thousand'. Fire appreciates the irony of seeing Irish cottagers shot by the light of their own burning houses. All three figures are conceived dramatically—asking and answering, chorusing, verbally recreating their acts of destruction. This aspect of the poem was appreciated by John Bowring in the *Westminster Review* when he later imagined it 'got up as a theatrical interlude' with Edmund Kean in the role of Fire'.[131] At the dramatic climax

---

Devil dandles Pitt, dressed as a baby, on one knee. The caption reads: 'Never man beloved worse / For sure the Devil was his nurse'.

[129] Although none of the 'Botany Bay Eclogues' were published before 1797, Coleridge could have seen them in manuscript as early as September 1794. See Southey, *New Letters*, 1: 80.

[130] 'He [Pitt] has digged a pit into which he himself may be doomed to fall' (*Lectures 1795*, p. 12). Cf. Rev. 9: 1, 2, 11; 11: 7; 17: 8; 20: 1 and 3.

[131] Repr. from *Westminster Review*, 12 (1830), in J. R. de J. Jackson, ed., *Coleridge: The Critical Heritage* (London: Routledge and Kegan Paul, 1970), p. 137.

there occurs a possibility that Coleridge had raised in 1795—that famine might bring down the government—but only to be turned into a final irony.

In 'A Letter from Liberty to Her Dear Friend Famine' prefixed to *Conciones ad Populum*, Coleridge had presented a grotesque array of personifications, including a picture of Religion based on Revelation 18: 4–5: 'a painted patched-up old Harlot . . . arrayed in purple and scarlet colour, and decked with precious stones and pearls, and upon her forehead was written "Mystery"' (*Lectures 1795*, p. 30). Since neither Religion, nor Gratitude, nor Prudence, nor Conscience will help her, Liberty appeals to Famine to plead her cause to the viceregents of Heaven, 'so that they may listen to your first pleadings, while yet your voice is faint and distant, and your counsels peaceable' (p. 31). Things have gone much further in 'Fire, Famine, and Slaughter', and Famine's counsels are no longer peaceable:

> Wisdom comes with lack of food.
> I'll gnaw, I'll gnaw the multitude,
> Till the cup of rage o'erbrim:
> They shall seize him and his brood—

With the overflowing of the apocalyptic cup of wrath (Rev. 14: 10), Slaughter eagerly assents: 'They shall tear him limb from limb!' The poem seems to be shifting into a political-prophetic mode, but in an exquisite touch Fire accuses Famine and Slaughter of ingratitude to a benefactor who has 'richly catered' for them for 'Full many moons'— presumably since the beginning of the Anglo–French war.[132] *Prima inter pares*, Fire dismisses her sisters:

> —Away! away!
> I alone am faithful! I
> Cling to him everlastingly.

This witty denouement keeps the poem in the realm of the apocalyptic grotesque, and its faithfulness to genre allowed it to transcend topicality and to be admired long after its composition and in some surprising quarters, ranging from William Hazlitt, who praised its

---

[132] 'Ninety months' in subsequent versions, beginning with Southey's *Annual Anthology* for 1800; however, the specification of eight years that follows is present in all versions. William Empson argues: 'We need not puzzle much on the oracular utterance "eight years", as there was no attempt to adapt the date when reprinting' (Introduction to *Coleridge's Verse: A Selection*, ed. William Empson and David Pirie (New York: Schocken Books, 1973), p. 86).

'grotesqueness of fancy',[133] to Mary Shelley,[134] who recited it in Switzerland, to Sir Walter Scott. At first Coleridge's authorship had been known only to a few friends, but it became public knowledge at a social gathering that probably took place in 1803,[135] where the poet found himself listening to Scott reciting 'Fire, Famine, and Slaughter'. The incident seems so STC-ish that one is grateful for Scott's independent corroboration: 'I was in company at the same time, the house being that of our mutual friend, Mr William Sotheby; indeed, I was the person who first mentioned the verses which introduced the discussion'.[136] After Sotheby condemned the unknown author, Coleridge felt obligated to offer a defence, which he later amplified in written form. This essay was published in *Sibylline Leaves*, when, despite the advice of Charles Lamb, who urged Coleridge to leave out 'Fire, Famine, and Slaughter' because 'it is the most popular among a sort of people I dont care for pleasing', the poem appeared in that collection.[137] Partly self-exculpatory and partly theoretical, the 'Apologetic Preface' has largely been regarded as yet another instance of Coleridge's political hypocrisy, and its more serious claims have received little attention.[138]

It is understandable that Coleridge's critics would concentrate on statements like 'There was never a moment in my existence in which I should have been more ready, had Mr Pitt's person been in hazard, to interpose my own body, and defend his life at the risk of my own' (*CPW* 2: 1101). This sort of defence was likely to please no one, including the poem's admirers. The conservative John Wilson, writing as 'Christopher North', regarded 'Fire, Famine, and Slaughter' as 'the most spirited and powerful of his poetic writings', but he thought the preface showed that Coleridge ought to be treated 'with pity and

---

[133] William Hazlitt, *Select British Poets* (London, 1824), p. xiii.
[134] See John William Polidori, *The Diary of Dr. John William Polidori*, ed. William Michael Rossetti (London: Elkin Mathews, 1911), p. 113; discussed in Ch. 5 below.
[135] E. H. Coleridge (*CPW* 2: 1097 n.) based this conjecture on the presence of Coleridge and Scott in London in the spring of that year.
[136] Letter to Mrs Eliza Fletcher, 18 Dec. [?1830], in Sir Walter Scott, *The Letters of Walter Scott*, ed. H. J. C. Grierson (12 vols., London: Constable, 1932–7), 11: 442.
[137] 20 or 21 Aug. 1815, in *Letters*, 3: 187–8. David Erdman, noting that Leigh Hunt reprinted the poem in *The Examiner* (24 Nov. 1816), suggests that Coleridge's inclusion of it in *Sibylline Leaves* 'was in effect calculated to forestall or draw the teeth of the Radicals' use of it' (*EOT* 1: p. clxxi, n. 3).
[138] Two exceptions are Reeve Parker, *Coleridge's Meditative Art*, pp. 86–8; and Steven Knapp, *Personification and the Sublime: Milton to Coleridge* (Cambridge, Mass.: Harvard University Press, 1985), pp. 32–6.

contempt'.[139] On the other hand, the *Monthly Review* praised the 'energy' of the poem, but maintained that no one would believe the preface because Coleridge had been right about 'that obnoxious minister' in the first place.[140] The *Monthly Magazine* also deplored the preface, though it called 'Fire, Famine, and Slaughter' 'the poet's master-piece'.[141] Although the poem was appreciated by critics of very different persuasions, virtually all condemned the preface. Nevertheless, Coleridge's discussion of his poem deserves to be taken seriously.

Imagining himself as a reader, Coleridge says of the poem's images and feelings: 'I should judge that they were the product of his [the poet's] own seething imagination, and therefore imprinted with that pleasurable exultation which is experienced in all energetic exertion of intellectual power; that in the same mood he had generalized the causes of the war, and then personified the abstract and christened it by the name which he had been accustomed to hear most often associated with its management and measures' (*CPW* 2: 1100–1). In this respect we might compare Blake's apocalyptic painting *The spiritual form of Pitt, guiding Behemoth* (Tate Gallery), in which Pitt holds on a lead the man-eating monster of war, while a city burns in the background and refugees rush away among flames. Blake presented Pitt not as an individual but as an archetypal force, which may be taken as a hallmark of the apocalyptic mode, and the same may be said of one aspect of 'Fire, Famine, and Slaughter'. In neither instance is the satirical thrust blunted because its object is not the 'real' William Pitt. Both are examples of the process by which, as Steven Knapp puts it, 'an agent associated with the causal operation of an institution or event becomes its personal representative'.[142]

The reception of 'Fire, Famine, and Slaughter' must have prompted Coleridge's next expedition into the apocalyptic grotesque, 'The Devil's Thoughts'. This was a collaboration with Southey, who wrote four of the fourteen stanzas of the poem published in the *Morning Post* of 6 September 1799. The *Post*'s publisher, Daniel Stuart, later commented

---

[139] Repr. from *Blackwood's Edinburgh Magazine*, 2 (1817), in Jackson, (ed.), *Coleridge: The Critical Heritage*, p. 343.

[140] Repr. from vol. 8 (1819) in ibid., p. 410. Interestingly, the reviewer says: 'Fire, Famine and Slaughter, most of our political readers will remember'.

[141] Repr. from vol. 44 (1817) in ibid., p. 392.

[142] Knapp, *Personification and the Sublime*, p. 36. In a similar vein, Coleridge wrote a late marginal note to *Conciones ad Populum*, saying he had little to regret in it 'with exception of some flame-coloured Epithets applied to Persons, as Mr. Pitt & others, or rather to Personifications (for such they really were to me)' (*Lectures 1795*, p. 25 n.).

on its extraordinary success, linking it with Coleridge's prose essay on Pitt (19 March 1800):

I never knew two pieces of writing so wholly disconnected from daily occurrences, produce so lively a sensation. Several Hundred sheets extra were sold by them, and the paper was in demand for days and weeks afterwards.[143]

'Our "Devil's Thoughts" have been admired far & wide—most *enthusiastically* admired!', Coleridge wrote to Southey on 10 November 1799 (*CL* 1: 550). The poem then led a subterranean life of transcripts, recitations, and unauthorized printings. Mrs Henry Sandford remarked astutely in 1888:

In its original shape 'The Devil's Walk' [*sic*] went up to the *Morning Post* and created a great sensation. It is grotesque and rather in the manner of Southey than Coleridge's own manner, but there is a searching quality in the irony of which Southey possessed not the secret, and a fantastic extravagance in the wit, which has a great deal more of Coleridge's fling than of Southey's fancy in it.[144]

As in the case of 'Fire, Famine, and Slaughter', Coleridge did not admit authorship in print until the 'Apologetic Preface' of 1817. He was probably concerned about the circulation of the poem as the work of the classicist Richard Porson, who had died in 1808, leaving a copy among his papers; but even so, Coleridge did not include the poem itself in *Sibylline Leaves*. By 1827, when he had decided to include it in his *Poetical Works*, he did not even have a copy, and had to write to Daniel Stuart asking for one (*CL* 6: 672). Even the appearance of 'The Devil's Thoughts' as Coleridge's, however, did not prevent the subsequent publication of *The Devil's Walk* [sic] as 'by Professor Porson', delightfully illustrated by R. Cruikshank, in 1830. Remonstrating with the volume's editor, H. W. Montagu, in April 1830, Coleridge emphasized the wide knowledge of his own authorship: 'Sir Walter Scott and half a Score other men of Rank and Literary Name knew that Mr Coleridge was the principal author from it's first appearance in the Morning Post' (*CL* 6: 830). Accordingly, Montagu brought out a second edition with Coleridge and Southey named as the authors and an 'Advertisement' stating that '*The Devil's Walk* has now put forth its fiftieth thousand copy'.[145]

[143] Daniel Stuart, 'Anecdotes of the Poet Coleridge', *Gentleman's Magazine*, NS 9 (1838): 488.
[144] Mrs Henry Sandford, *Thomas Poole and His Friends* (London, 1888), 1: 307.
[145] *The Devil's Walk*, 2nd edn. (London, 1830), p. v.

The extraordinary popularity of 'The Devil's Thoughts', which earned the sincerest form of flattery from Byron and from Shelley (see Chapter 5), is easy to understand. The poem exploits the grotesque possibilities of the apocalyptic, toying with the idea of a corrupt society nearing its final end. In the fourth stanza of the original *Morning Post* version, the Apocalypse is invoked as an apothecary rides by on a white horse—'And the Devil thought of his old friend /Death, in the Revelation'. Lest the reader miss this allusion, the reference to Revelation 6: 8 is glossed in an authorial footnote. In 1830 H. W. Montagu observed a further parallel with 'West's celebrated painting', remarking that 'There is a touch of great sublimity in that awful image, Death in the Revelations'.[146] Montagu was referring to West's very large *Death on the Pale Horse* of 1817, but West had exhibited a smaller version entitled *The Opening of the Seals* at the Royal Academy in 1796, and it had been widely discussed.[147] Coleridge and West were personally acquainted by 1814,[148] but whether or not he knew West by 1799, Coleridge may well have known that painting.

The Devil in his visit makes a transit of the institutions of a venal England that is virtually crying out for apocalyptic consummation. In a stanza written by Southey he is introduced to the plight of the prisoners in Cold Bath Fields,[149] where 'a solitary cell /. . . gave him a hint / For improving the prisons of Hell' (31-3). Cold Bath Fields then housed, among others, mutineers from the Nore and state prisoners, including Colonel Edward Marcus Despard (imprisoned there on charges prior to his alleged treason). Despard was no doubt meant to be the occupant of the solitary cell, for in January 1799 the *Morning Post* had given considerable coverage to his circumstances. On 5 January it printed Lord Suffolk's statement to Parliament that Despard 'was confined in a cell seven feet square, debarred of light, open to the cold, and without a table or chair'. On the 9th it reported Sir Francis Burdett's visit to the prison and the fact that he had been banned from entering it again. Other stories concerning Despard's situation appeared on 8, 16, and 17 January. This stanza, then, was a verse allusion to circumstances reported by the same newspaper (and others) earlier in the year.

---

[146] Ibid., p. 19.   [147] See Paley, *Apocalyptic Sublime*, pp. 22-4.
[148] See Coleridge's letter to Daniel Stuart dated 12 Sept. 1814; *CL* 3: 534.
[149] The original *Morning Post* text printed '——fields'. The name of the prison is given in Southey's draft MS in the British Library (BL Add. MS 47887) and in his fair copy MS (University of Rochester, A S727), as well as in the version in Sara Hutchinson's commonplace

In the Devil's perambulation of British institutions, religion is not ignored.

> He met an old acquaintance
> Just by the Methodist Meeting;
> She held a consecrated flag,
> And the Devil nods a greeting.

In Southey's draft manuscript (and also in his fair copy MS) the 'old acquaintance' turns out to be 'Religion', and 'She held a consecrated *Key*' (emphasis mine), alluding to St Peter's keys of the kingdom; but in the *Morning Post* this became a more topical consecrated flag.[150] The practice of consecrating regimental banners was commonly attacked by Dissenters, as it was by Blake in *Jerusalem* (67. 30), where the soldiers fight 'Beneath the iron whips of their captains & their consecrated banners'. Coleridge's line has been linked with his notebook entry on Archbishop Randolph's consecration of the banners of the Duke of York in 1795.[151] Hazlitt, in a bitter attack on the later Coleridge, recalled Coleridge's preaching against the practice in 1798: 'He talked of those who had inscribed the cross of Christ on banners dripping with human gore'.[152] The consecration of banners, like the drinking from the poisoned cup of wealth in 'Fears in Solitude', is for Coleridge a parody of a sacramental act, part of a topsy-turvy world in which the rites of the Church parallel those of the kingdom of Hell.

Having made a progress through the social institutions of 1799, the Devil scurries back to Hell, because, in a bit of end-time cartooning, he mistakes 'General——'s burning face' for 'the General Conflagration' (54, 57). There have been numerous candidates for General——, of which the most likely are Isaac Gascoigne and Banastre Tarleton, whose respective names Henry Crabb Robinson and Derwent Coleridge wrote in their transcripts of the poem. Both were involved in England's brutal suppression of Ireland, and both were public

book (Dove Cottage Library). It was printed in the *Poetical Works* of 1828, 1829, and 1834. The relevance of this prison is discussed by Woodring in *Politics in the Poetry of Coleridge*, p. 146. I have benefited from conversations with Dr David Worrall on this subject, and I am grateful to Peter Dzwonkosi for a photocopy of the Rochester MS.

150 When this stanza was finally included in the *Poetical Works* of 1834—it had been left out in 1828 and 1829—the 'consecrated Key' reading was retained.

151 See E. H. Coleridge, *CPW* I: 323 n. and *CN* I: 174 (18) and n. Coburn notes that this took place at Bath on 27 Nov. 1795.

152 William Hazlitt, *The Complete Works*, ed. P. P. Howe (London and Toronto: J. M. Dent, 1932), 7: 128, from *Examiner*, 12 Jan. 1817.

opponents of the abolition of slavery.[153] Coleridge himself inserted in Sara Hutchinson's commonplace book the name of General Burrard, one of the three generals who agreed to the Convention of Cintra—a name appropriate in 1809–10,[154] but hardly in 1799. The General's face was plastic enough to bear numerous identities. Coleridge deliberately begged the question in a note in the *Poetical Works* of 1828:

> If anyone should ask who General— meant, the Author begs leave to inform him, that he once did see a red-faced person in a dream whom by the dress he took for a general; but he might have been mistaken, and most certainly he did not hear any names mentioned. In simple verity, the author never meant any one, or indeed any thing but to put a concluding stanza to his doggerel. (*CPW* 1: 321 n.)

Here Coleridge reacts against his own fantasy, attempting to footnote it into innocuousness. Perhaps more to the point is a note that he jotted down about one of his own prose writings: 'The one Side is all too hugely beangel'd, the other all too desperately bedevil'd: yet in spite of the Flattery and spite of the Caricature both are *Likenesses*'.[155] The Falstaffian general was based on an individual but appeals to the imagination as a type. In this respect, as in others, the life of 'The Devil's Thoughts' and of 'Fire, Famine, and Slaughter' comes from snatching the perpetual from the occasional.

In 'Fire, Famine, and Slaughter' and 'The Devil's Thoughts' there is not a trace of the millennial. Apocalypse, lacking any relation to Millennium, has gone from the sublime to the grotesque, and in these two poems the reader is invited to enjoy its macabre effects. The same is true of the third poem in this mode, 'The Two Round Spaces on the Tombstone', which also appeared in the *Morning Post*.

Published on 24 November 1799, 'The Two Round Spaces' is Coleridge's satirical response to a visit to Grasmere by Sir James Mackintosh. Since his reply to Burke's *Reflections*, *Vindiciae Gallicae* (1791), Mackintosh had, like Coleridge, altered his view of the French Revolution, and his 'Introductory Discourse' to a series of 'Lectures on the Law of Nature and of Nations' had been praised in 'highly flattering'

---

[153] Information on Gascoigne from J. C. C. Mays; on Tarleton from Woodring, *Politics in the Poetry of Coleridge*, p. 252 n. 20.

[154] As conjecturally dated by George Whalley, *Coleridge and Sara Hutchinson* (Toronto: University of Toronto Press, 1955), p. 20.

[155] See Griggs's note in *CL* 1: 532 n. and Erdman, *EOT* 3: 14 n. 2). Erdman compares Coleridge's technique in his 'Pitt and Buonaparte' (*Morning Post*, 17 Jan. 1798) and 'Fire, Famine, and Slaughter'.

terms by Pitt on 3 January 1799.[156] Coleridge attended when the lectures were given a second time in the following the year, after the poem had been written, but he no doubt already had an idea of their contents. Actually, he would have found much to agree with, as, for example, Mackintosh's view that:

France had been deluged with blood, and Europe overrun by hostile armies. Very wild and irrational opinions, some of them destructive of the very foundations of civil society, had, in pretty extensive classes, gained considerable currency. The friends of liberty, though unshaken in their final hopes, saw the wished-for termination removed to a great, and a very uncertain, distance. The difficulty now was, not to give an impulse to the torpor of political indifference, but to check the madness of wild and irrational projects of change. Men of feeling turned away from the abused name of liberty, which they were almost tempted to abjure.[157]

However, Coleridge was anxious to distinguish his own position, as expressed, for example, in 'France: An Ode', from what Stephen Gill has called Mackintosh's 'crude reversal' and what Hazlitt termed 'his envenomed tooth'.[158] He sent his poem in a letter to Humphry Davy under the title 'Skeltoniad/(to be read in the Recitative *Lilt*)'; it is unclear whether he himself gave it to the *Morning Post* or whether Davy or some other did—much later, Coleridge thought he had not sent it, while Daniel Stuart thought he had not published it![159] Nevertheless, published it was, and although it did not become as famous as its two predecessors, it was, according to Coleridge, 'printed repeatedly in magazines' (*CPW* 1: 354 n.). It was first included in Coleridge's *Poetical Works* in 1834. There remained some family resistance to this aspect of the poet: Derwent and Sara Coleridge excluded it from their edition of 1852 as 'a piece of extravagant humour' that had been 'printed for the first time among the Author's works in 1834, rather it would appear with his acquiescence, than by his desire'.[160] In addition to the difficulties of applying such a view consistently, this ignores the fact that one of

---

[156] See Robert James Mackintosh, *Memoirs of the Life of the Right Honourable Sir James Mackintosh* (2 vols., London: Moxon, 1835), 1: 104. Ch. 3, 1: 99–124, summarizes parts of the lectures.   [157] Ibid. 1: 123.

[158] Stephen Gill, *William Wordsworth: A Life* (Oxford: Clarendon Press, 1989), p. 172, citing Hazlitt's *Spirit of the Age* (*Works*, 11: 98).

[159] See Coleridge's Prefatory Note, *CPW* 1: 354 n.; Stuart, 'Anecdotes of the Poet Coleridge', p. 486; and Griggs, in *CL* 1: 628 n.

[160] *The Poems of Samuel Taylor Coleridge*, ed. Derwent and Sara Coleridge (London: Moxon, 1854 [1852]), p. xii.

the magazines in which the poem was reprinted was *Fraser's* (in February 1833 and again in May 1833), whose editor, Coleridge's friend William Maginn, was unlikely to reprint the poem twice without the poet's approval.

Coleridge's designation of 'Two Round Spaces' as 'a Skeltoniad' is worth notice. As the poet knew, Skelton's favourite verse-form, with its short lines, rushing rhythms, and doggerel lines, is called the Skeltonic; and, as he also must have known, Skelton frequently claimed divine inspiration and prophetic status in his poetry.[161] With a longer, galloping line, and a grotesque treatment of apocalyptic content, Coleridge invents a form that he playfully christens with a Greek epic suffix.

The 'Skeltoniad' begins in good, thumping measure with an allusion to the Second Coming:

> The Devil believes, that the Lord will come
> Stealing a March without beat of Drum
> About the same Hour, that he came last,
> On an old Christmas Day in a snowy Blast.

As the subject shifts to the Last Judgement, the verse becomes outrageous doggerel:

> Till he bids the Trump sound, nor Body nor Soul stirs,
> For the Dead Men's heads have slipped under their Bolsters.

Attention then centres on one particular grave, its occupant identified in a descriptive passage (13–19) that includes his 'black Tooth in front' (presumably because Mackintosh was Daniel Stuart's brother-in-law, these lines were not printed in the *Morning Post*). The poet then puns 'Apollyon *scotch* him for a Snake', alluding to the king of monstrous locusts and 'angel of the bottomless pit' of Revelation 9: 11. 'Apollyon' was later changed to 'the Devil', slightly diluting the fun, as there is enough of the devil in the poem already, and he will reappear 'with his Grannam' at the end—'Expecting and hoping the Trumpet to blow: / For they are cock-sure of the Fellow below!'

When Coleridge was assembling his poems for *Sibylline Leaves* and composing the *Biographia* in the year of Waterloo, the idea of apocalyptic destruction still had a reality for him, but that of a political millennium had become entirely foreign to his thought. He could use the language

---

[161] On this aspect of Skelton's poetry, see Stanley Fish, *John Skelton's Poetry* (New Haven and London: Yale University Press, 1965), pp. 13–16, 153–5, 172–5.

of Revelation in his account of the civil wars of the seventeenth century, as when he writes: 'And now it might have been hoped, that the mischievous spirit [of religious persecution] might have been bound for a season, and "a seal set upon him that he might deceive the nations no more" '; but that instead, fanaticism 'emptied its whole vial of wrath on the miserable covenanters of Scotland'.[162] This language is, however, figurative, not figural. Recognizing the strict division of tenor and vehicle, it is typical of Coleridge's later apocalyptic language in leavening a secular exposition with yeasty eschatological tropes. Coleridge still defends the authenticity of Revelation in his *Lay Sermon* of 1817, but declares: 'It has been most strangely abused and perverted from the Millenarians of the primitive Church to the religious Politicians of our own times'.[163]

This is not to say that Coleridge had abandoned the application of Revelation to history. There is, indeed, much to indicate the contrary. As Elinor Shaffer points out, Coleridge's marginalia to J. G. Eichhorn's commentary on Revelation 'cluster about the climactic point in the history, that is, around Rev. ix: 13–15, the second of the three woes when the sixth angel sounds its trumpet'.[164] The attitude expressed in the Eichhorn marginalia is significant of a broader change in Coleridge's views. Coleridge's dissociation from the millenarianism of the 1790s was accompanied by a different mode of apocalyptic utterance and, eventually, by a different notion of the relationship of Revelation to history. In the notes to Eichhorn Coleridge suggests similarities between the situation preceding the fall of Jerusalem, supposedly alluded to by John, and the French Revolution. 'The 4 first Trumpets', he writes of Revelation 8: 13, 'denote the Evils that preceded and prepared the way for, the Outbreak of the Zelotae, Terorists, and Septembrizers of Jerusalem, with anticipation of their horrors during the War & Siege'.[165] The star that fell to earth in Revelation 9: 1 'must assuredly signify some one of the Nobles or Archiereis (the Princely or Pontifical Houses) who like the Duke of Orleans in the early part of the French Revolution had encouraged the Terrorists'.[166] Coleridge now considers

[162] *BL* 1: 198. Cf. the seven angels and their vials in Rev. 16.

[163] *Lay Sermons*, ed. R. J. White, *CC* 6 (Princeton: Princeton University Press, 1982), p. 157 n.

[164] Elinor Shaffer, '*Kubla Khan' and The Fall of Jerusalem* (Cambridge: Cambridge University Press, 1972) p. 98.

[165] Coleridge, *Marginalia*, 2: 509–10. George Whalley (2: 503) dates the notes to Eichhorn as written in Feb. 1826, and observes that some of Coleridge's remarks here are similar to those in the 1817 *Lay Sermon*, pp. 142, 146–7.

[166] *Marginalia* 2: 509–10.

John's text as providing parallels to recent history, rather than as a model of present and future events. Such analogies can even be said to work through intermediate texts: in Revelation 9: 7, 'on their heads were as it were crowns like gold' suggests to Coleridge Milton's Death in *Paradise Lost* and 'Burke's masterly accomodation [*sic*] of the Passage [in the *Reflections*] to the first Constitution of the French Demagogues, the Zelotae of Paris'.[167] Apocalypse has become a matter of intertextuality, while Millennium is nowhere to be seen, as the marginalia end with the disasters of Revelation 16.

[167] Ibid., p. 511.

3

Wordsworth

In the 'Conclusion' to Wordsworth's *Ecclesiastical Sonnets*, written in 1820, the poet imagines cyclical time sleeping 'as a snake enrolled, /Coil within, coil at noon-tide', while the river of 'living Waters' rolls towards 'the eternal City'.[1] It is indeed, as has been argued, 'an apocalyptic vision that postulates a potential return to a modified Edenistic state'.[2] The last stanza of the *Salisbury Plain* of 1793 includes, as Stephen Gill puts it, 'the whole world in its apocalyptic vision'.[3] *Home at Grasmere* (1800) celebrates the millennial peace experienced by the poet and his Emma in a Cottage in a Vale. In a long passage in Book II of *The Excursion*, the Solitary describes a vision of a city in the clouds, with implications of the New Jerusalem, including a comparison to visions of the Hebrew prophets (827–81), and in Book III he talks about the fall of the Bastille and its aftermath in millennial terms:

> I beheld
> Glory—beyond all glory ever seen,
> Confusion infinite of heaven and earth,
> Dazzling the soul. Meanwhile, prophetic harps
> In every grove, were ringing, 'War shall cease;
> Did ye not hear that conquest is abjured?
> Bring garlands, bring forth choicest flowers, to deck
> The tree of Liberty'.[4]

Earl Wasserman justly terms the above an assertion that 'For many, the millennium promised by the Book of Revelation was at hand'.[5]

[1] *The Poetical Works of William Wordsworth*, ed. E. de Selincourt and Helen Darbishire, 2nd edn. (5 vols., Oxford: Clarendon Press, 1966–7), 3: 407.

[2] See Anne L. Rylestone, *Prophetic Memory in the Ecclesiastical Sonnets* (Carbondale: Southern Illinois University Press, 1991), p. 105.

[3] Stephen Gill, 'Introduction', *The Salisbury Plain Poems of William Wordsworth* (Ithaca, NY: Cornell University Press, 1975), p. 6.

[4] Wordsworth, *Poetical Works*, 3: 71–2 (ii. 827–81), 101 (iii. 719–26).

[5] Earl K. Wasserman, *Shelley: A Critical Reading* (Baltimore and London: Johns Hopkins University Press, 1971), p. 25. See also M. H. Abrams, *Natural Supernaturalism* (New York and

Throughout Wordsworth's poetic career, as scholars have long recognized, his productions are charged with the apocalyptic and the millennial. However, the work in which the *relationship* between the two comes to the fore is Wordsworth's greatest long poem, *The Prelude*.

In the first two Books of *The Prelude*, adumbrations of the apocalyptic and the millennial prepare for their fuller development later on. The famous episode of the stolen boat results in what seems to the boy Wordsworth an apocalyptic moment:

> When from behind that craggy Steep, till then
> The bound of the horizon, a huge Cliff,
> As if with voluntary power instinct,
> Uprear'd its head . . .

> (i. 406–9)[6]

Although the explanation for this perception is entirely natural, a perspectival illusion, the child responds as if to something beyond the natural word:

> . . . in my thoughts
> There was a darkness, call it solitude,
> Or blank desertion, no familiar shapes
> Of hourly objects, images of trees,
> Of sea, or sky, no colours of green fields;
> But huge and mighty Forms that do not live
> Like living men mov'd slowly through my mind
> By day and were the trouble of my dreams.

> (i. 421–8)

A parallel to the millennial equally exists in the boy's perception of an Edenic nature in Cumbria:

> A Child, I held unconscious intercourse
> With the eternal Beauty, drinking in
> A pure organic pleasure from the lines
> Of curling mist, or from the level plain
> Of waters colour'd by the steady clouds.

> (i. 590–4)

London: Norton, 1973), p. 331: 'In expressing the response of the Solitary to the "unlooked-for dawn" of a "new world of hope" in France, Wordsworth set forth the turbulent expectations (compounded of elements from Isaiah, Revelation, and Virgil's fourth eclogue) of the English radicals of the day, himself included.'

[6] i. 406–9. My text, unless otherwise noted, is the AB-Stage Reading Text printed in

And the adult Wordsworth whom we meet at the beginning is much like Blake's Adam returning to Paradise:

> 'Twas Autumn, and a calm and placid day,
> With warmth as much as needed from a sun
> Two hours declined towards the west, a day
> With silver clouds, and sunshine on the grass
> And, in the shelter'd grove where I was couch'd,
> A perfect stillness.

(i. 74–9)

Much as in Coleridge's 'Reflections on Having Left a Place of Retirement', the poet imagines a microcosm of the millennium in terms of a cottage in a valley:

> I made a choice
> Of one sweet Vale whither my steps should turn
> And saw, methought, the very house and fields
> Present before my eyes

(i. 81–4)

Such moments as these anticipate deeper explorations, as *The Prelude* continues, in a series of five visionary moments. Each of these involves an encounter of the poet with something outside himself that also turns out to be, whether another person or an aspect of the natural world, within him; each establishes a different relationship between the apocalyptic and the millennial; and each is marked by the crossing of a threshold.

The Discharged Soldier

The first of these episodes, that of the Discharged Soldier in Book IV, was, as is well known, first written as an individual poem in 1798.[7] When Wordsworth placed a revised version in *The Prelude*, he made it

Mark Reed's edition of *The Thirteen-Book Prelude* (Ithaca, NY, and London: Cornell University Press, 1991), vol. 1.

[7] For the several texts of the 1798 poem, see Beth Darlington, 'Two Early Texts: *A Night-Piece* and *The Discharged Soldier*', in *Bicentennial Wordsworth Studies in Memory of John Alban Finch*, ed. Jonathan Wordsworth (Ithaca, NY, and London: Cornell University Press, 1970), pp. 425–48. In citing line references to this poem, I use Darlington's text with an equal sign designating the corresponding place in the A-B State Reading Text (on which see n. 6 above).

follow immediately after the description of his consecration as a poet in the summer vacation of 1789:

> I made no vows, but vows
> Were then made for me; bond unknown to me
> Was given, that I should be, else sinning greatly,
> A dedicated Spirit.
>
> (iv. 341–4)

It is important that the narrator is an incipient poet, one who can appreciate the *unheimlich* quality of what is to come. He is, moreover, in the peculiar state of poetic receptivity that we have learned to call 'Wordsworthian': 'Tranquil', his sense 'listless' and 'Quiescent', all the more 'dispos'd to sympathy' (376, 380). He is absorbed in the ground before him, as he will be on Mount Snowdon in Book XIII, 'With forehead bent / Earthward' (29–30); compare an interim MS reading of *The Discharged Soldier*: 'My eyes upon the earth I moved along'.[8] As he proceeds in this passive state, there is a transition from the quotidian world to the realm of imagination:

> I slowly mounted up a steep ascent
> Where the road's watry surface, to the ridge
> Of that sharp rising, glitter'd in the moon.
>
> (iv. 370–2)

The imagery of shining is, as so often in Wordsworth, liminal. The young poet is at a threshold as, again, he will be in climbing Mount Snowdon, 'When at my feet the ground appear'd to brighten / And with a step or two seem'd brighter still' (xiii. 36–7). There, the object of his vision will be universal, or at least the vast moon-illuminated sea of mist that Wordsworth chose as his great culminating image. In Book IV, beyond the threshold is a particular figure, one who is Other, yet familiar.

On a natural level, the Discharged Soldier could be one of the marginalized people of Wordsworth's *Lyrical Ballads* or *Salisbury Plain* poems, a soldier who had fought against the French in the West Indies and then been dumped at some English port to find his way home; and the meeting could be viewed as what Alan Bewell, using an anthropological model, aptly calls a 'primitive encounter'.[9] Yet, other details

---

[8] Inserted, then deleted, in the *Christabel Notebook*, lines 25/6; see Darlington, 'Two Early Texts', p. 438.

[9] Alan Bewell, *Wordsworth and the Enlightenment* (New Haven and London: Yale University Press, 1989), pp. 81–93.

suggest the supernatural or at least the preternaturnal. 'Lank and lean', 'meagre', 'ghastly in the moonlight', he could be a terrestrial Ancient Mariner, ready to inculcate unsought-for self-knowledge in his normative listener. (We remember the 'long, and lank, and brown' that Wordsworth contributed to that image.) In the original *Discharged Soldier* his apartness is further accentuated; he is

> a man cut off
> From all his kind, and more than half detached
> From his own nature.
> (58–60 (preceding = 415))

Perhaps Wordsworth removed this because it was too obvious. The Soldier is established as Other by his appearance, his behaviour, and his language. With respect to the last, the 'murmuring sounds' that issue from his lips seem at first *pre*-linguistic, and though it turns out he can indeed speak, he is not allowed to tell his own story (as he is in the original poem). He is, to use Jonathan Wordsworth's term, one of those who dwells at 'the borders of vision'.[10]

In his capacity as preternatural visitant, the Soldier has an iconic quality. He is first seen propped by a milestone—a detail that Wordsworth thought worth repeating in the original poem (94 = 440), and when he takes up his 'Traveller's Staff' (461), he seems a languid version of the emblem of a traveller, like the one in Blake's (later) ninth wood engraving for Thornton's *Virgil*. He might, like the Leech Gatherer, become 'a Man from some far region sent, / To give me human strength, and strong admonishment'.[11] However, this short excursion into the apocalyptic is cut short, as we pass back into the natural world, first encountering, as it were, the liminal imagery from the other side:

> every silent window to the moon
> Shone with a yellow glitter. 'No one there,'
> Said I, 'is waking; we must measure back
> The way which we have come . . .'
>
> (452–5)

---

[10] Jonathan Wordsworth, *William Wordsworth: The Borders of Vision* (Oxford: Clarendon Press, 1982), *passim*. Here (p. 13) it is suggested that in describing this encounter the poet has in mind the ghost in his own *The Vale of Esthwaite* and Satan's meeting with Death in *Paradise Lost*, ii. 666 ff.

[11] 'Resolution and Independence', lines 118–19. See *Poems, in Two Volumes*, ed. Jared Curtis (Ithaca, NY: Cornell University Press, 1983), p. 128.

The situation now becomes humanized with the introduction of the Labourer, who

> will not murmur should we break his rest
> And with a ready heart will give you food
> And lodging for the night.
>
> (457–9)

This proto-Steinbeckian theme that only the poor can be counted on to help each other (to disappear by *1850*) contains a germ of millennium, emphasized as the poet now refers to the Soldier as 'My Comrade'. At the same time, such domestication threatens to diminish the stranger's stature as a visitant: far from bringing strong admonishment, the Soldier is admonished by the youth not to linger in the roads. To this the Soldier, whose very 'mildness' is 'ghastly' (493), gives a reply worthy of one of the *Lyrical Ballads* subjects: ' "My trust is in the God of Heaven / And in the eye of him that passes me" ' (494–5). Appealing as he does to one of Wordsworth's and Coleridge's favourite themes, the power of the eye,[12] the Soldier avoids becoming altogether an object of commiseration, so retains his alterity for the reader. What one senses as his unrealized potential as an initiator into another realm of being will be taken up by another, in some respects similar figure in Book V.

The Stone and the Shell

In the Five-Book *Prelude*, the connection between these two episodes is even clearer, because what became lines 1–48 of Book V, written in the first part of 1804, was once a continuation of Book IV.[13] The apocalyptic presentiment which once followed the encounter with the Soldier now precedes the meeting with the Arab, who will initiate Wordsworth further into apocalyptic knowledge:

> A thought is with me sometimes, and I say,
> Should earth by inward throes be wrench'd throughout,
> Or fire be sent from far to wither all

---

[12] See Lane Cooper, 'The Power of the Eye in Coleridge', in *Studies in Language and Literature in Celebration of the Seventieth Birthday of James Morgan Hart* (New York: H. Holt, 1910), pp. 78–121.

[13] See *The Prelude 1799, 1805, 1850*, ed. Jonathan Wordsworth, M. H. Abrams, and Stephen Gill (New York and London: Norton, 1979), p. 152 n. 1. (This edition will hereafter be cited as the Norton *Prelude*, with *1850* indicating the 1850 version of *The Prelude* reproduced

Her pleasant habitations, and dry up
Old Ocean in his bed left sing'd and bare,
Yet would the living Presence still subsist
Victorious: and composure would ensue,
And kindlings like the morning; presage sure,
Though slow perhaps, of a returning day!

(v. 28–36)

This reader appears to have been absorbed not in Cervantes (introduced in line 60), but in Thomas Burnet's *Theory of the Earth*, which Wordsworth evidently had been reading at about this time.[14] After having explained what seemed to him to have been the mechanism of the Deluge, Burnet went on to postulate the future destruction of the world by fire, placing great emphasis on the physical details of this future destruction, citing 2 Thessalonians 1: 7–8 ('. . . when the Lord Jesus shall be revealed from heaven with his mighty angels, In flaming fire taking vengeance on them that know not God . . .') and the 'one general Fire' of Lucan's *Pharsalia*.[15] There is also something both in Burnet and in Wordsworth's account of the so-called little apocalypse of 2 Peter 3: 12, 'hasting unto the coming of the day of God, wherein the heavens being on fire shall be dissolved, and the elements shall melt with fervent heat'. Such a blueprint for world destruction accords with God's covenant with Noah that 'neither shall all flesh be cut off any more by the waters of a flood; neither shall there any more be a flood to destroy the earth' (Gen. 9: 11). The poet's concern is that the destruction by fire will threaten 'The consecrated works of Bard and Sage', which, having been given physical embodiment, must necessarily 'lodge in shrines so frail' (41, 48). The dream that follows encapsulates this anxiety, although the medium of threatened destruction changes.

As is now well known, the dream derives in part from a dream of Descartes, probably transmitted via Adrien Baillet's *Vie de Descartes* (1691), and the dreamer was in all manuscripts prior to the corrected D (1839) 'a Friend', revised in the C-Stage to 'a Philosophic Friend'.[16]

---

in it.) The editors note that in *1850*, v. 75, the Arab when he first appears is called 'an uncouth shape', linking him with the Soldier, also called 'an uncouth shape' in the A-B Stage Reading Text, iv. 402.

[14] See Duncan Wu, *Wordsworth's Reading 1800–1815* (Cambridge: Cambridge University Press, 1995), pp. 36–7.

[15] Thomas Burnet, *Theory of the Earth*, 3rd edn. (2 vols., London, 1967), 2: 75, 81.

[16] See Jane Worthington Smyser, 'Wordsworth's Dream of Poetry and Science: *The Prelude*: V', *PMLA* 71 (Mar. 1956): 269–75; *The Prelude*, ed. E. de Selincourt and H. Darbishire, 2nd edn. (Oxford: Clarendon Press, 1959), p. 539; *Thirteen-Book Prelude*, ed. Reed, 276n.

However, Descartes' dream contained no Stone or Shell; and whether or not the philosophic friend was Coleridge, the *poem* is Wordsworth's. It is indeed in the genuinely dreamlike transmutation of images that much of the power of the episode lies. The objects are at the same time a Stone and a Shell, and yet 'both were Books' (113), reminding us of the 'books in the running brooks' and 'Sermons in stones' praised by Duke Senior in the Forest of Arden.[17] The bearer of these objects maintains the dream's double significations, being both 'an Arab of the Desert' and Don Quixote.[18] In both these roles he is shown by his strange appearance and demeanour to be Other than the normative narrator, to whom he acts as the initiator of apocalyptic insight through poetry as he commands holding the Shell to the ear:

> I did so;
> And heard that instant in an unknown Tongue
> Which yet I understood, articulate sounds,
> A loud, prophetic blast of harmony,
> An Ode, in passion utter'd, which foretold
> Destruction to the Children of the Earth,
> By deluge now at hand.

> (93–9)

Once more we have the dreamlike double signification with a language of vatic utterance that is both unknown and understood. The understanding of 'an unknown Tongue' brings to mind the Apostles at Pentecost who 'were all filled with the Holy Ghost, and began to speak with other tongues, as the Spirit gave them utterance' (Acts 2: 4), suggesting that the dreamer too may become filled with the Spirit. The Shell that makes this possible is presumably a conch shell of the kind that an allegorical figure might blow in a Renaissance painting, and it may also be compared to the one that will appear in Shelley's *Prometheus Unbound*.

> that curved shell which Proteus old
> Made Asia's nuptial boon, breathing within it
> A voice to be accomplished.[19]

However, the Arab's Shell brings no future hope. The 'mighty music' of Asia's 'many-folded Shell' will announce the advent of the

---

[17] Shakespeare, *As You Like It*, II. i. 16–17.

[18] J. Hillis Miller notes that Cervantes' novel adopts the fiction that it was written by an Arab. See 'The Stone and the Shell: The Problem of Poetic Form in Wordsworth's Dream of the Arab', in *Mouvements premiers: Études critiques offertes á Georges Poulet* (Paris: Corti, 1972), p. 130.

[19] III. iii. 65–7.

Promethean age, while what the poet hears in the Arab's Shell is a prediction of apocalypse without millennium.[20]

Adding to the burden of anxiety, the form of destruction is not fire as
anticipated earlier, but one that would violate God's compact with
Noah and humanity. We recognize the two icons as the 'consecrated
works' that had been the objects of the narrator's concern, and the des-
perate quest of the Arab Quixote to bury them as an attempt, in dream
logic, to preserve the frail shrines in which knowledge and poetry must
lodge. Just as the poet thought of the Discharged Soldier by the end of
the encounter as his 'Comrade', the narrator now moves closer to the
Other:

> A wish was now engender'd in my fear
> To cleave unto this Man, and I begg'd leave
> To share his errand with him.
>
> (115–17)

However, the appearance of 'A glittering light' (129) marks, as in Book
IV, the transition to another realm of being, and the Arab must ride off,
like an inversion of Moses, 'With the fleet waters of the drowning
world /In chace of him' (136–7). Lapsing into his normative self, the
narrator awakes to find the sea before him and *Don Quixote* by his side.

The narrator's after-meditation emphasizes both the otherness of
'This Arab Phantom . . . This Semi-Quixote' (141–2) and a desire for
fellowship with him. As Jonathan Wordsworth points out, there is a
'disproportionate intensity' in the transformation of the Arab into a
maniac whose mind is 'the blind and awful lair /Of such a madness'
(151–2).[21] A quest like the Arab's would involve a sundering from the
human community—'Their Wives, their Children, and their virgin
Loves' (154)—and yet the poet thinks he could do it, 'Could share that
Maniac's anxiousness, could go /Upon like errand' (i. 60–1). It is as if
the Wedding Guest felt an inclination to join the Ancient Mariner in
his wandering. The Arab now seems a possible Wordsworth; but the
poet, now initiated into the apocalyptic, fears the aspect of himself he
recognizes in the Other, and so when the dreamer awakes, it is 'in
terror' (137).

---

[20] As Mary Jacobus puts it, the sound heard in the Shell is a 'disordering blast or destructive ode [that] restores originary speech to poetry in an apocalyptic logocentricity which
destroys the need of texts' (*Romanticism, Writing and Sexual Difference: Essays on* The Prelude
(Oxford: Clarendon Press, 1989), p. 101.

[21] Jonathan Wordsworth, *William Wordsworth*, pp. 207–8.

This last detail brings in another aspect of the episode in the Stone and the Shell. It is in some respects a Last Man narrative, and a very early one. One might compare Byron's 'Darkness', written twelve years later, which will be discussed in Chapter 4. Beginning 'I had a dream, which was not all a dream', 'Darkness' goes on to describe the destruction of life on earth.[22] The typical Last Man narrative employs either a dream or some other buffer to shield the reader from a direct encounter with Lastness.[23] In the first such narrative, Jean-Baptiste F. X. Cousin de Grainville's *Le dernier homme* (Paris, 1805; published in English in 1806 as *Omegarus and Syderia: A Romance in Futurity*), the buffering device is a magic mirror in which the narrator sees future events displayed. In Mary Shelley's *The Last Man* (1826) it is the sibylline leaves of a manuscript that has to be assembled and translated. Wordsworth uses the device of a dream that generates apocalyptic terror until the point where the sleeper wakes up. It is interesting that the dreamer is at first disturbed at his solitude and then overjoyed at the sudden appearance of the Arab.

> he fancied that himself
> Was sitting there in the wide wilderness,
> Alone, upon the Sands. Distress of mind
> Was growing in him when, behold! at once
> To his great joy a Man was at his side
>
> (72–6)

The dreamer's joy stems from the discovery that he isn't the Last Man; but although the Arab is Other, he is not *an* other, but rather an aspect of the poet, one with which he makes brief contact, only to become separated again in a quotidian world in which everything is rationally explicable, with 'the Sea before me; and the Book, / In which I had been reading, at my side' (138–9).

A dream of a Deluge that threatens to destroy humanity and overwhelm its achievements can be seen as related to the poetic imagination in various ways. Geoffrey Hartman argues that 'the dream is sent by Imagination to lead the poet to recognize its power, and that what the dreamer desires and fears is a direct encounter with Imagination'.[24]

---

[22] Lord Byron, *The Complete Poetical Works*, ed. Jerome J. McGann (7 vols., Oxford: Clarendon Press), vol. 4 (1986), p. 40.

[23] See Morton D. Paley, '*Le dernier homme*: The French Revolution as the Failure of Typology', *Mosaic: A Journal for the Interdisciplinary Study of Literature*, 24 (1991): 67–76.

[24] Geoffrey H. Hartman, *Wordsworth's Poetry 1787–1814* (New Haven and London: Yale University Press, 1964), p. 229.

Jonathan Bishop sees the dream's message as threatening: 'If you choose poetry as a way of life, as you have done and are bound to do, you run the severe risk of being overwhelmed by the unconscious forces from which your poetry must derive its vital inspiration, and the signifi- cant portion of its subject matter; if you lose your nerve, you will find yourself "burying" your talent to escape the emotional turmoil it brings upon you'.[25] Jonathan Wordsworth argues: 'It is surely a threatened engulfment *of*, not by, imagination that causes the terror', going on to cite the near-contemporary *Prelude*, xi. 335–6, in which the hiding- places of Wordsworth's power close when he approaches them.[26] Alan Bewell, who links geological theories of catastrophism with post- revolutionary anxiety, suggests that the encounter allows Wordsworth 'to link his own melancholy *postrevolutionary* hauntings with the *postdiluvian* trauma of the world's first men and their anxiety about the impending return of the Flood'.[27] These divers views are in one respect not as deeply opposed as may at first appear, and it would not be yield- ing up interpretive questions in despair to say that they could be viewed as providing several related vantage-points on the 'deluge now at hand'.[28] They have in common the idea of the Imagination as either an apocalyptic force itself or a perceiver of apocalyptic forces. What was imagined by the poet as destruction by fire at the beginning of the book is imagined by the dreamer as destruction by flood later on. Wordsworth is, furthermore, very much of his time in rendering the apocalypse as deluge, because by the late eighteenth century the Flood had achieved a special status in painting as the ultimate sublime sub- ject, with Nicholas Poussin's much-imitated *Winter, or the Flood* (Louvre) as its supreme example.[29] In both literature and art the Deluge

[25] Jonathan Bishop, 'Wordsworth and the Spots of Time', in *Wordsworth, 'The Prelude': A Casebook*, ed. W. J. Harvey and Richard Gravil (London: Macmillan, 1972), pp. 134–54.

[26] Jonathan Wordsworth: *William Wordsworth*, p. 194.

[27] Bewell, *Wordsworth and the Enlightenment*, p. 259.

[28] I recognize, of course, that it is also possible to emphasize the differences among these interpretations. In particular, Bewell's general argument is that in Enlightenment catas- trophist geology placed the apocalypse at the beginning rather than the end of time, and that 'In Wordsworth's poetry, apocalyptic imagery has a similar primal status, and is always struc- tured as a return to an original, prehuman environment in which man is separated from nature, with a consequent unleashing of the powers in nature that human life has sought to control' (ibid., p. 257). In my view, this makes a valuable contribution to the subject, but is at the same time too limited a view, equating 'apocalypse' with catastrophe and not with vision.

[29] See my *The Apocalyptic Sublime* (New Haven and London: Yale University Press, 1986), pp. 8–16.

occupies a special place at the meeting-point of the apocalyptic with the natural.

What of the two objects that the Arab goes to bury? They have been identified in the text of the dream itself, but they are also linked to the meditations that frame it. In his opening lines, Wordsworth speaks of human creations, 'Things worthy of unconquerable life' (19) as doomed to perish when 'the immortal being / No more shall need such garments' (22–3). The garment is of course a traditional image. In Paul's Epistles, 'putting off the old man' and 'putting on the new man' signifies a spiritual rebirth (cf. Eph. 4: 22, 24; Col. 3: 9). In Neoplatonism, as in interpretations of Porphyry's *Cave of the Nymphs*, the garment is the body itself, woven before physical birth to accommodate the pre-existent spirit. Blake uses these alternative figurations in *Milton*, *The Four Zoas*, and *Jerusalem*. Wordsworth, in what has become a celebrated passage in the third *Essay on Epitaphs*, makes a sharp distinction between words as the incarnation of thought and as 'only a clothing for it', declaring that the latter will 'prove an ill gift; such a one as those poisoned vestments, read of in the stories of superstitious times, which had power to consume and to alienate from his right mind the victim who put them on'.[30] However, the oppositions in the *Prelude* text are not quite the same as they are in this passage. Wordsworth was, after all, a poet, not a systematic philosopher. The 'garments' needed by 'the immortal being' are not here contrasted with an incarnational state. Rather, the poet wishes that while 'garments' are needed, there were some substance more durable (than, for example, the materials of which books are made) on which the mind could stamp its image, like a die stamping a coin or medal. Wordsworth does not specify what such a substance might be, and the results of thought remain lodged in frail shrines that would easily succumb to fire or flood.

That the Arab seeks to bury his 'strange freight' would not make sense in waking logic, as there will be no one to read 'The consecrated works of Bard and Sage' (41) after the children of the earth have been destroyed. This again has a corollary in Last Man narratives, which are typically related by beings who would have no business knowing their stories of the destruction of humankind, did not their authors invent

---

[30] Wordsworth, *Prose Works*, ed. W. J. B. Owen and Jane Worthington Smyser (3 vols., Oxford: Oxford University Press, 1974), 2: 85. See Frances Ferguson, *Wordsworth: Language as Counter-Spirit* (New Haven and London: Yale University Press, 1977); Jonathan Wordsworth, *William Wordsworth*, pp. 210–12, 436–7.

ingenious ways of bending time back upon itself in order to make this possible. We do not know whether the Arab's enterprise will succeed, but the sudden wish of the narrator to join him in it seems to valorize the attempt. In the meditation that follows, Wordsworth returns to the idea of a volume as a physical object with 'Poor earthly casket of immortal Verse!/Shakespeare, or Milton, Labourers divine' (164–5). 'Immortal Verse' echoes Milton's *L'Allegro*, 137, and *Comus*, 516, as de Selincourt and Darbishire note;[31] while Shakespeare has already been introduced with the quotation from Sonnet 64—'Might almost "weep to have" what he may lose'—embedded in line 25. The latter also has a thematic relevance. Two major subjects in Shakespeare's Sonnets are mortality and mutability and the question of whether the poem may survive both. In Sonnet 64 the poet meditates upon the destructive power of various forces, one of which is the 'hungry ocean' (5), while in Sonnet 65 he hopes for the 'miracle' that 'in black ink my love may still shine bright'.[32] Sonnets 55 and 107 are more confident in asserting their ability to outlast marble, gilded monuments, and tombs of brass. Wordsworth's 'Poor earthly casket of immortal verse' (164) is a jewel box (perhaps suggested by 'Time's chest' in Sonnet 65) that may protect its contents for a while but that, like the 'shrines so frail' of the preliminary meditation, can survive neither conflagration nor deluge.

The dream of the Stone and the Shell takes us very much farther into the apocalyptic than the episode of the Discharged Soldier. In the dream we are brought into contact with apocalyptic forces associated with the End Time of the earth. No millennium follows, though there is, as in the previous episode, a hint of it. The geometrical Stone, which figures less prominently than the poetic Shell, 'wedded man to man by purest bond /Of nature undisturb'd by space or time' (105–6). It therefore holds the possibility of human community through the recognition of universal natural laws, something which, if extended, could lead to a millennium through reason in its most exalted mood.[33] This theme is not pursued further here, though a related one will figure prominently later in the poem. First, however, we will move even closer to the very nature of Apocalypse in Book VI.

---

[31] *The Prelude*, ed. de Selincourt and Darbishire, p. 540.

[32] *William Shakespeare: The Complete Works*, ed. Peter Alexander (London and Glasgow: Collins, 1951), p. 1319.

[33] In the C-Stage Reading Text, 'nature' has become 'Reason' (*Thirteen-Book Prelude*, ii. 78).

The Simplon Pass

In Book VI, the poet's visionary recollection of crossing the Alps in the summer of 1790 is preceded by a trail of false hints of the millennium. He and his friend Jones land at Calais 'on the very Eve / Of that great federal Day' on which the first anniversary of the Revolution was celebrated.[34] The poet is indeed aware that this historical moment could have been described in millennial terms:

> 'twas a time when Europe was rejoiced,
> France standing on the top of golden hours,
> And human nature seeming born again.
>
> (352–4)

The implied image is of a cast figure posed on top of a clock the hands of which are at noon.[35] Yet with the Revolution figured as a clock face, we are reminded that the hands may—indeed must—descend from noon, at which point the emphasis of line 354 will be on 'seeming'. And, as in the case of the imagery of enchantment to come in Book X, the descriptions of revolutionary celebration are self-undermining. 'Gaudy with reliques of that Festival' appropriates diction typical of English Protestant denunciations of Papist idolatry, and the 'Flowers left to wither on triumphal Arcs' (362–3) testify to a failure to appropriate nature to a political cause. Delegates returning from the great festival in Paris are troped to a swarm of bees, which could be taken as a semi-millennial, Georgic image, if that meaning were not unsettled by the context:

> Like bees they swarm'd, gaudy and gay as bees;
> Some vapour'd in the unruliness of joy
> And flourish'd with their swords, as if to fight
> The saucy air.
>
> (398–401)

These are very much in line with the British stereotype of confident

---

[34] On the provincial celebrations, see Alan Liu, *Wordsworth: The Sense of History* (Stanford, Calif.: Stanford University Press, 1989), pp. 14–15; and Nicholas Roe, *Wordsworth and Coleridge: The Radical Years* (Oxford: Clarendon Press, 1988), pp. 21–2.

[35] Marjorie Levinson argues that 'By transforming the "golden hours" of the Revolution [1. 340] into "a psychic and metaphysical postulate", Wordsworth ... suppresses the militant, apocalyptic thrust of that traditionary reading' (*Wordsworth's Great Period Poems: Four Essays* (Cambridge: Cambridge University Press, 1986), p. 92). This whole essay is important for Wordsworth's supposed rejection of 'the Revolution's millennial thrust'.

and over-lusty Frenchmen, and 'their great Spousals newly solem-
niz'd/At their chief city in the sight of Heaven' (396–7) seem more
likely to have taken place in Pandemonium than in the New Jerusalem.
Once in Switzerland, the two Englishmen encounter 'Enticing
Vallies' (438), again suggestive of the millennium (just as the image of
the 'dell' is a microcosmic millennium in Coleridge's 'Lines on Having
Left a Place of Retirement'). The first of these, later located by Dorothy
Wordsworth as above Martigny,[36] is described as 'A green recess, an
aboriginal vale' (449), all the more demi-paradisaical for having simple
riverside huts that could be compared to Indian cabins. Next, the
valley of Chamonix is described as a place of eternal summer:

> There doth the Reaper bind the yellow sheaf,
> The Maiden spread the hay-cock in the sun,
> While winter like a tamed lion walks
> Descending from the mountain to make sport
> Among the cottages by beds of flowers.
>
> (464–8)

There appears something willed about these lines, even apart from the
fact that Wordsworth wrote them during the summer and had not
experienced the winter there. Coleridge (who had of course created
his own fictionalized Chamonix) objected that the ideas that the lion
had been tamed and that it descended from the mountain to make
sport were incompatible.[37] One senses a desire to furnish materials
for a view of humankind and the natural world in harmony that will
justify the variant on the traditional idea of the Book of Nature that
follows:

> With such a book
> Before our eyes we could not chuse but read
> A frequent lesson of sound tenderness,
> The universal reason of mankind.
>
> (473–6)

---

[36] In his edition of *The Prelude*, de Selincourt, p. 558, notes that Dorothy Wordsworth so
placed it in her *Tour of the Continent* of 1820, remarking that William told her that a certain
'shady deep recess, the very image of pastoral life, stillness, and seclusion . . . was the same
dell, that *aboriginal vale*, that *green recess*, so often mentioned by him—the first of the kind that
he had passed through in Switzerland' (citing *The Journals of Dorothy Wordsworth*, ed. E. de
Selincourt (Oxford: Clarendon Press, 1941), p. 280).

[37] *The Prelude*, ed. de Selincourt, p. 558, quoting Coleridge's note in MS B, which
Coleridge read after returning from Malta.

As in Book V, we have here a 'book' that binds human beings together, once again embodying the possibility of a millennial society. Yet these limp verses fail to carry conviction, and the Book of Nature will shortly be superseded or transformed by a book that will fully claim the reader's attention—the Apocalypse.

The 'two brother pilgrims' (478) push on to the Simplon Pass, where they famously miss the object of their pilgrimage. A peasant whose language they do not know becomes, as it were, the ghost of Wordsworth's previous initiators into the apocalyptic, informing them 'that we had cross'd the Alps' (524). At this point, as the Norton editors point out, Wordsworth wrote the great passage beginning 'As when a traveller hath from open day' (which later was transferred to Book VIII, where it became lines 711–41), in reaction against the anticlimactic experience.[38] This passage comprises an enormous extended simile of a cavern in which details are gradually discerned only to prove disappointing when they can really be seen 'in perfect view, / Exposed and lifeless as a written book' (726–7). This is far from the meaning of the previous images of books that we have seen, and it will also bear an interesting relation to some later ones. After the traveller has gone through the process a second time, with no more satisfying results, the scene shifts to the *now* of poetic composition, with its exhilarating rewards, to be followed by the discovery of an apocalypse in nature, as Wordsworth recollects the Gondo gorge.

There is something intrinsically difficult for Wordsworth about describing the sudden manifestation of his own imagination:

> Imagination! lifting up itself
> Before the eye and progress of my Song
> Like an unfather'd vapour
>
> (525–7)

Vapour is one of those material things that appears close to being immaterial, and it is 'unfather'd' because it seems to have no natural progenitor; but the metaphor seems awkward, nevertheless. De Selincourt calls 'eye and progress' a 'doublet' of the sort used by Shakespeare, giving an example from *King John*.[39] But there it is 'the eye

---

[38] See the Norton *Prelude*, pp. 216n. and 304n. MS WW (DC MS 43), in which this draft appears, is discussed by Mark Reed, *Thirteen-Book Prelude*, 1: 19–21, and reproduced photographically in 1: 329–66. See also Jonathan Wordsworth, *William Wordsworth*, p. 189.

[39] *The Prelude*, ed. de Selincourt, p. 559. Hartman, *Wordsworth's Poetry 1787–1814*, p. 46n., gives another instance of the same 'doublet' from *Much Ado About Nothing*.

and prospect', which combines a metaphorical and a literal noun, each of which means the same thing. That isn't true of 'eye and progress'. Evidently aware of the problem, Wordsworth tried to correct it in the manuscript page known as the Trevenen fragment by substituting:

> Imagination—lifting up herself
> In sudden apparition like a cloud
> Whose fleecy substance mounts upon the wind
> Into a vacant sky or like the form
> Ghostly and wan of some unfathered mist[.][40]

We see that here the doublet has been eliminated, but that Wordsworth wants to keep the image of the most tenuous of substances with, metaphorically, no natural origin. He was, however, reluctant to do without 'vapour' and pencilled it in next to 'mist'; and the *1850* reading is 'unfathered vapour'.[41] In *1850* 'the mind's abyss' (594) is the place from which the vapour comes, making it clear that the source is internal and at the same time introducing a psychological parallel to the Gondo gorge. This last revision also clarifies Wordsworth's use of the term 'Imagination' by differentiating its meaning, as Coleridge had in the *Biographia*, from the traditional one of the image-making faculty. Imagination here becomes 'the Power so called / Through sad incompetence of human speech' (592–3), an 'awful', ultimately incomprehensible power—but so it has been throughout the 1805–6 *Prelude*. It is this that associates it so closely with the apocalyptic. As the passage continues, signs typical of the threshold phenomenon appear in the imagery of light. When the poet tells his soul, 'I recognize thy glory' (532), on one level what he recognizes is a nimbus like Christ's at the Transfiguration. Likewise, the 'flashes that have shewn to us / The invisible world' (535–6) are liminal. The glimpse of forces beyond the veil is for the moment presented as a triumph,[42] at which point

---

[40] This MS leaf is said to have been a separate sheet pasted into the album of Emily Trevenen, who visited the Wordsworths at Rydal Mount in September 1829. The album is now in the Cornell University Wordsworth Collection, but the sheet bearing these lines is no longer part of it, and is now unlocated. The variant passage is known through a transcription published by Anne Treneer in 'Emily Trevenen's Album', *West Country Magazine*, 2 (1947): 171–8, from which this quotation is taken. (The variant is printed by Reed, *Thirteen-Book Prelude*, ii. 108 n.) It is of course interesting that, for the moment at least, Wordsworth gendered Imagination as female.

[41] See Treneer, 'Emily Trevenen's Album', p. 176; *1850*, line 595. The doublet does not return in *1850*.

[42] Liu, in his *Wordsworth: The Sense of History*, pp. 27–31, discusses this passage as a displaced version of Napoleon's crossing of the Alps.

apocalypse is succeeded by an internalized millennium, with the mind 'Strong itself, and in the access of joy / Which hides it like the overflowing Nile' (547–8). Unlike the 'waters of the deep' in Book V, the Nile's annual overflow is a millennial image, renewing life and making possible an abundant harvest. One can see why Coleridge in reading this passage in manuscript noted an urge to change what he called 'this faultless line' to 'Spread o'er it, like the fertilizing Nile'.[43] The line indeed became in *1850* 'To fertilise the whole Egyptian plain', but the idea of fertilization is already implicit in 'the overflowing Nile', and the change merely spells out what is already there. Geoffrey Hartman takes these lines as an illustration of Wordsworth's supposed propensity 'to bend back the energy of his poem and of his mind to nature', in support of the argument that 'An unresolved opposition between Imagination and Nature prevents him from becoming a visionary poet'.[44] However, it must be remembered that the fertilization of the Nile created the rich harvests that made Egyptian civilization possible. Viewed from such a perspective, the succession of unfathered vapour to overflowing Nile is yet another Romantic attempt at transition from apocalypse to millennium, attempts that seldom prove wholly successful, but that often result, nevertheless, in great poetry.

The 'usurpation' of the quotidian self by Imagination, making the poet for the moment analogous to the Pauline new man, makes it possible for him to re-envisage the scene perceived in 1790. What he now sees is a universe of process, but process far different from the optimistically perceived 'something evermore about to be' of line 542. These goings-on are powerful and threatening, embodied by violent present participles: 'thwarting', 'shooting', 'drizzling', 'raving'. These phenomena assume 'the features of the same face' (568–9), but a face such as never was seen in the human world, something like the reality that Melville's Ahab hopes to reveal by striking through the mask of the visible in *Moby Dick*. Wordsworth's previous image of the book then returns, but in a far different sense:

> Characters of the great Apocalyps,
> The types and symbols of Eternity,
> Of first, and last, and midst, and without end.
>
> (570–2)

---

[43] See *The Prelude*, ed. de Selincourt, p. 558.
[44] Hartman, *Wordsworth's Poetry 1787–1814*, p. 39.

'Types' can be related to the idea of the mind stamping her image in Book V: printer's type functions through pressure, as does a die. There is a play of meaning upon *archetypes* here, as when Blake wrote, 'Therefore I print; nor vain my types shall be', alluding both to his 'Giant forms' and to the plates from which he printed.[45] A third stratum of meaning is contributed by the meaning of *type* as something in the Old Testament that prefigures something in the New. The phenomena seen in the Simplon Pass are at the same time archetypal forms, the letters of an alphabet, and typological signifiers. What they signify is 'the great Apocalyps[e]' because it is the thing itself and not an intermediate text. The Book of Revelation is obviated because Wordsworth himself is now in the position of John on the isle of Patmos.[46]

Yet in another sense, Revelation cannot be obviated, since it presents the model that Wordsworth is both following and departing from. It has been pointed out that line 572—'Of first and last, and midst, and without end'—echoes the prayer of Adam and Eve in *Paradise Lost*, Book V, 'Him first, him last, him midst, and without end';[47] but this in turn alludes to the words in John's first vision: 'I am Alpha and Omega, the beginning and the ending, saith the Lord, which is, and which was, and which is to come, the Almighty' (Rev. 1: 8). Apocalypse affirmed, a form of millennium will soon follow. It is a variant of the 'aboriginal vale' encountered earlier:

> And Como, thou a treasure by the earth
> Kept to itself, a darling bosom'd up
> In Abyssinian privacy, I spake
> Of thee, thy chestnut woods and garden plots
> Of Indian corn tended by dark-eyed Maids.
>
> (590–4)

It was in *Descriptive Sketches* that Wordsworth had spoken of Como, but in this later passage the proximity of 'Abyssinian' to 'Maids' stirs unavoidable associations of the Abyssinian maid of Coleridge's 'Kubla Khan', and with her other images of a secret paradise in Abyssinia—

---

[45] *Jerusalem*, 3, E 145.

[46] For an interesting discussion of the language of prophecy and the language of apocalyptic, see Elinor Shaffer, '"Secular Apocalypse": Prophets and Apocalyptics at the End of the Eighteenth Century', in *Apocalypse Theory and the End of the World*, ed. Malcolm Bull (Oxford: Blackwell, 1995), pp. 137–58.

[47] Norton *Prelude*, p. 218 n.; see Jonathan Wordsworth, *William Wordsworth*, pp. 192–3. On the interrelationship of Wordsworth and Milton in this passage, see Jacobus, *Romanticism, Writing and Sexual Difference*, pp. 9–11.

Mount Amara in *Paradise Lost*, the Happy Valley of *Rasselas*.[48] At the same time, this quasi-millennial site does not seem adequate to the powerful apocalyptic passage that preceded it. It is, to put it in Blakean terms, a Beulah (that sweet and pleasant rest from the labours of Eternity), not an Eden with its interchange of powerful human energies. The millennial theme is further undermined by what happens shortly afterwards. At Gravedona the travellers get the time wrong, start out in the middle of the night, wander and get lost, and find the landscape anything but unfallen:

> An open place it was, and overlook'd
> From high the sullen water underneath,
> On which a dull red image of the moon
> Lay bedded, changing oftentimes its form
> Like an uneasy snake.

$$(634-8)$$

As if to protect itself from those who have seen characters of the great Apocalypse through its 'hollow rent' (559), nature closes itself against them. Tormented by stinging insects and terrified by the cries of nocturnal birds, they find that they have as little place in the natural world as they did in the political world at the beginning of Book VI. The expedition thus ends in a second anticlimax, in what might be called a parody of the millennial. Book VI does not close, however, without a hint, irrelevant as Wordsworth makes it seem, of things to come:

> We cross'd the Brabant Armies, on the fret
> For battle in the cause of Liberty.

$$(691-2)$$

At the time, the poet was touched 'with no intimate concern' at sights like this of troops on their way to fight for their republic, not yet knowing that the French Revolution would bring his next encounter with the apocalypse and the millennium.

The French Revolution

Wordsworth's most extensive treatment of the millennial theme is presented in Books IX, X, and XI, largely written about events beginning

---

[48] The parallels with Milton and with Johnson are made by, respectively, the editors of the Norton *Prelude*, p. 220 n. 9, and by Reed, *Thirteen-Book Prelude*, i. 191 n.

with Wordsworth's return to France late in 1791. These are presented not as a scenario of apocalypse followed by millennium, but rather with both suspended as alternative possibilities. As these Books were written retrospectively, the millennial is necessarily seen as a forlorn hope, the apocalyptic as revealing only an inexorable cycle of history. That cycle is mimed by the poet's two crossings of Paris, first in late November or early December 1791, then about a year later.[49] In the first instance, the population seem inhabitants of Milton's Pandemonium, while their 'hubbub wild' comes out of Chaos:

> I stared and listen'd with a stranger's ears
> To Hawkers and Haranguers, hubbub wild!
> And hissing Factionists with ardent eyes,
> In knots, or pairs, or single, ant-like swarms
> Of Builders and Subverters.
>
> (ix. 55–9)[50]

Formerly the French had swarmed like bees, now like ants. Behind both similes is the image of Satan's fallen angels entering their hall:

> As bees
> In spring-time, when the Sun with Taurus rides,
> Pour forth their populous youth about the hive
> In clusters; they among fresh dews and flowers
> Fly to and fro. . . .
> . . . .
> . . . so thick the aery crowd
> Swarmed and were straitened.[51]

The verb 'swarm', typically threatening to Wordsworth, recurs as he likens France to ancient Egypt during the plagues: 'The land all swarm'd with passion, like a Plain / Devoured by locusts' (178–9). We seem to be at the threshold of apocalypse. Instead, a guide is introduced who would take his willing pupil directly into millennium.

From the first, Michel Beaupuy is presented in terms less appropriate to a general than to a saint:

---

[49] For the dates, see Mark Reed, *Wordsworth: The Chronology of the Early Years, 1770–1799* (Cambridge, Mass.: Harvard University Press, 1967), pp. 124–7, 137.

[50] De Selincourt compares *Paradise Lost*, ii. 951–2, where Satan in Chaos hears 'a universal hubbub wild' (*Prelude*, p. 587).

[51] *Paradise Lost*, i. 768–76.

A meeker Man
Than this lived never, or a more benign,
Meek though enthusiastic to the height
Of highest expectations.

(298–301)

As Nicholas Roe has shown, Beaupuy, far from being 'with an oriental loathing spurn'd' (297) by his fellow officers, was an important and respected figure who commanded a unit sympathetic to the Revolution.[52] Perhaps Wordsworth misremembered some twelve years later, or perhaps he deliberately chose to make Beaupuy in at least one respect a marginal figure like the Discharged Soldier and the Arab. What is important is that Beaupuy is a typological figure, even perhaps a type of Christ:

Injuries
Made him more gracious, and his nature then
Did breathe its sweetness out most sensibly
As aromatic flowers on Alpine turf
When foot hath crush'd them.

(301–5)

Even the word 'enthusiastic' marks him, for Wordsworth (like Blake, when he wrote 'That Enthusiasm & Life may not cease'[53]) knew this would provoke a certain class of reader because of its religious associations. Beaupuy's 'radiant joy' (322) also marks him as a Romantic *schöne Seele*, a being who, like the German-Romantic conception of Hamlet, acts rightly through his very nature. The charismatic Beaupuy will initiate the poet into the apocalypse of the French Revolution and a revelation of the millennium beyond it. Wordsworth's conversion to the revolutionary cause is not immediately presented as a revelation, but rather as a dialogue using some of the terms of the Burke–Paine debate, terms that would have been instantly recognizable to the contemporary readers of the poem (and we must remember that the 1805–6 *Prelude* had only a chosen few).

With him did I discourse about the end
Of civil government, and its wisest forms,
Of ancient prejudice, and charter'd rights,
Allegiance, faith, and laws by time matured.

[52] Roe, *Wordsworth and Coleridge*, p. 56.   [53] *Jerusalem*, 9: 31, E 152.

> Custom and habit, novelty and change,
> Of self-respect and virtue in the Few
> For patrimonial honour set apart,
> And ignorance in the laboring Multitude.[54]
>
> (329–36)

When they talked 'Of ancient prejudice, and charter'd rights' (331), they touched on points fiercely contested in England following the publication in 1790 of Burke's *Reflections on the Revolution in France*. There Burke had dared to defend 'the great influencing prejudices of mankind', asserting that 'Prejudice is of ready application in the emergency. . . . Prejudice renders a man's virtue his habit. . . . Through just prejudice, his duty becomes part of his nature'.[55] To radicals of almost every description, however, *prejudice* meant what it commonly means today. William Godwin would state, for example, that 'Public education has always expended its energies in the support of prejudice; it teaches its pupils, not the fortitude that shall bring every proposition to the test of examination, but the art of vindicating such tenets as may chance to be established'.[56] As for charters, we have seen in Chapter 1 how what for Burke were guarantors of liberty going back at least to Magna Carta and forward to the charters of cities and corporations were viewed by Blake, following Thomas Paine, as conferring special privilege on the few at the expense of the rights of the many. Similarly, when Wordsworth says '[I] thus did soon / Become a Patriot' (124–5) he uses the word in the sense that, as we have seen, it had acquired of one who opposed the arbitrary power of government on behalf of the rights of the people.[57]

---

[54] James Chandler remarks that 'Although these topics happen to resemble those listed by Burke in certain parts of the *Reflections*, Wordsworth seems to invite us, probably not unreasonably, to regard them as constituting a predictable litany for the 1790s' (*Wordsworth's Second Nature: A Study of the Poetry and Politics* (Chicago and London: University of Chicago Press, 1984), p. 49).

[55] Edmund Burke, *Reflections on the Revolution in France*, ed. Conor Cruise O'Brien (Harmondsworth: Penguin, 1984), pp. 275, 183. It's interesting that *1850* line 324 substitutes 'loyalty' for 'prejudice' an alteration made by the time of the C-Stage Reading Text, though not incorporated into it (see *Thirteen-Book Prelude*, ii. 164).

[56] William Godwin, *Enquiry Concerning Political Justice and its Influence on Modern Morals and Happiness*, ed. Isaac Kramnick (Harmondsworth: Penguin, 1985), p. 614. I am not, of course, suggesting that Wordsworth is echoing Godwin's text of 1793 here (though we must remember that Wordsworth's own text dates from 1804), but am rather presenting Godwin's statement as representative of radical usage during the period. See also Chandler, *Wordsworth's Second Nature*, pp. 148–9.

[57] Cf. Coleridge's use of the term in 'Preternatural Agency', as well as *Prelude*, ix. 296 and ix. 501.

It is further interesting that the dialogue of Wordsworth and Beaupuy, though presumably conducted in French, is carried on in the terms of a then ongoing controversy in England. Of course such conceptions and even terms were shared by French and British writers, and we do not know whether 'the master Pamphlets of the day' (97) that Wordorth tells us he read were French, as de Selincourt assumes, or English, as the Norton editors and Reed do.[58] What is important is that Wordsworth is at pains to emphasize the *Englishness* of his new revolutionary faith,[59] his conversion to republicanism having been prepared both by his upbringing in the Lake District (218–26) and by his years at Cambridge (226–42). The Lake District has of course been represented all along as the site of individual freedom and social equality, but in the 'Retrospect' of the book immediately preceding this one, that representation achieves a millennial intensity with:

> Man free, man working for himself, with choice
> Of time, and place, and object; by his wants,
> His comforts, native occupations, cares,
> Conducted on to individual ends
> Or social, and still follow'd by a train
> Unwoo'd, unthought-of even, simplicity
> And beauty, and inevitable grace.

> (viii. 152–8)

Nigel Leask makes an excellent distinction when he remarks that 'it seems that the mountain republic does not echo the untried perfection of pre-lapsarian Eden so much as the millennial perfection of Christ's reign on earth'.[60] Here (in contrast to the Abyssinian privacy of Como) we have Blake's Eden, not his Beulah. Furthermore, during his residence at Cambridge, Wordsworth now sees he found something scarcely mentioned in the book of that title: something 'holden up to view / Of a republic' (ix. 229–30). Previously, Wordsworth's verdict was that his Imagination had slept at Cambridge, but now he can see a

---

[58] See *Prelude*, ed. de Selincourt, p. 585; Norton *Prelude*, p. 316 n., and *Thirteen-Book Prelude*, p. 234. De Selincourt points out that in the Wordsworth library sale (1859), one lot was 'Pamphlets and Ephemera—French; a bundle'.

[59] A point stressed by Chandler, who remarks, for example, on how Wordsworth regarded his English background as providing him with a defence against the arguments of the Royalist officers earlier (*Wordsworth's Second Nature*, p. 50).

[60] Nigel Leask, *The Politics of Imagination in Coleridge's Political Thought* (Basingstoke: Macmillan, 1988), p. 42.

correspondence between the notion of a community of scholars and that of a larger human community. The passage then links the Lakes and Cambridge, with 'fellowship with venerable books / . . . and mountain liberty' (240–2), the latter being a kind of seal of authenticity, echoing as it does Milton's 'mountain-nymph, sweet Liberty' (*L'Allegro*, 36).

The particular moment of the poet's conversion bears a peculiar resemblance to one of the famous 'spots of time' that appear in Book XI of the 1805–6 *Prelude*. (As is well known, this passage, part of Wordsworth's original conception in the Book I of 1799, was rewritten and repositioned for the Five-Book *Prelude* and again for *1805–6*.) Part of the experience below the Penrith Beacon is related in the 1805–6 Reading Text as follows:

> [I] saw
> A naked Pool that lay beneath the hills,
> The Beacon on the summit, and more near
> A Girl who bore a Pitcher on her head
> And seem'd with difficult steps to force her way
> Against the blowing wind.
>
> (303–8)

The time-spot is at least potentially apocalyptic in that it hovers at the edge of forces sensed as active just beyond perception:

> It was, in truth,
> An ordinary sight; but I should need
> Colours and words that are unknown to man
> To paint the visionary dreariness
> Which, while I look'd all round for my lost Guide,
> Did at that time invest the naked Pool,
> The Beacon on the lonely Eminence,
> The Woman, and her garments vex'd and toss'd
> By the strong wind.
>
> (xi. 308–16)

On one of Wordsworth's philosophical walks with Beaupuy, they encounter a scene interesting in both its similarity to and difference from the one above:

> We chanced
> One day to meet a hunger-bitten Girl
> Who crept along, fitting her languid self
> Unto a Heifer's motion, by a cord

Tied to her arm . . .
     . . . while the Girl with her two hands
Was busy knitting, in a heartless mood
Of solitude.

(ix. 511–19)

What the two passages have in common is obvious; the difference is, that in its larger context, the former scene possesses the 'renovating Virtue' (xi. 260) that characterizes the spots of time, while the latter is merely a sign—albeit a sign vividly remembered. This scene is not apocalyptic but epiphanic, revealing in a momentary observation an entire condition of being. What is as striking about the 'hunger-bitten Girl' as her physical condition is her apathy, and both will be described in the following verses as socially remediable. Also, unlike the boy below the Penrith beacon, the young man does not have to seek his guide:

                    and at the sight my Friend
     In agitation said, "Tis against that
     Which we are fighting'.

(518–20)

In response, the poet, with Beaupuy, envisions a world in which poverty will soon be wiped out, the privileges of the upper class abolished along with 'cruel power' whether of king or aristocracy, and the people empowered to participate in law making. In the Loire valley in the spring or summer of 1792, it was possible to envisage millennium without apocalypse. However, by 1804 such a vision could not be reconstituted without being coloured by after-knowledge, and in Book X it is dissipated. Now millennial visions coexist with apocalyptic ones, in no order of cause and effect, but as alternative possibilities, each of which threatens to displace the other.

Book X begins with yet another natural microcosm of millennium, the valley of the Loire with its 'scenes / Of vine-yard, orchard, meadow-ground and tilth' (5–7), but this is immediately contrasted with 'the fierce Metropolis' to which Wordsworth must now return. The dramatic international events of the past two months are summarized in quasi-biblical terms: the 'congregated Host, / Dire cloud' might as well have burst upon the plain of Shinar as 'on the Plains of Liberty', and their being troped to 'a band of Eastern Hunters' (14–15) brings in associations of the biblical 'mighty hunter' Nimrod (Gen. 10: 9), whom

Dante put into Hell and Milton's Michael prophetically describes as an imperialistic tyrant:

> Of proud, ambitious heart, who, not content
> With fair equality, fraternal state,
> Will arrogate Dominion undeserv'd
> Over his brethren, and quite dispossess
> Concord and law of Nature from the Earth;
> Hunting (and Men not Beasts, shall be his game)
> With War and hostile snare such as refuse
> Subjection to his Empire tyrannous.
>
> (*Paradise Lost*, xii. 25–32)

But the advance of the Duke of Brunswick's army had been stopped at Valmy on 20 September 1792:

> ... themselves
> Had shrunk from sight of their own task, and fled
> In terror.
>
> (18–20)

These are, in Blake's terms, the stars who threw down their spears in the tyrannical Urizen's account in *The Four Zoas*:

> I hid myself in black clouds of my wrath
> I calld the stars about my feet in the night of councils dark
> The stars threw down their spears & fled naked away
> We fell.[61]

The defensive victory celebrated by the young Wordsworth and by Blake had, however, been preceded by bloody events of another kind. On 10 August, the Tuileries had been attacked and captured by a Revolutionary crowd, and the defending Swiss Guards were afterwards murdered in violation of the accord that had ended the fighting. Then, during the massacres of the first week of September, perhaps 3,000 prisoners had been murdered. These events, the poet hopes, were 'Ephemeral monsters'; but a walk 'Through the wide City' (41) and across the Place du Carrousel, where the dead of the Tuileries had been

---

[61] 64: 25–8, E 344. On the application of these lines, on one level of meaning to the Battle of Valmy, see David V. Erdman, *Blake: Prophet Against Empire: A Poet's Interpretation of the History of his own Times*, rev. edn. (Princeton: Princeton University Press, 1969), p. 194.

heaped up and burned, leads to different thoughts. The familiar image of the book now reappears, but in a different sense than previously:

> . . . upon these
> And other sights looking as doth a man
> Upon a volume whose contents he knows
> Are memorable, but from him lock'd up,
> Being written in a tongue he cannot read;
> So that he questions the mute leaves with pain
> And half upbraids their silence.
>
> (48–54)

In contrast to the Shell in Book V that was also Euclid's elements (understandable to Wordsworth through his Cambridge education) and the apocalyptic text that became intelligible in the visionary moment of Book VI, the volume of contemporary history is unreadable. The volume 'from him lock'd up' is, in the words of Isaiah 29: 11 'as the words of a book that is sealed, which men deliver to one that is learned, saying, Read this, I pray thee: and he saith, I cannot; for it is sealed', as well as the book 'sealed with seven seals' of Revelation 5: 1. Wordsworth had once thought he could read the 'Characters of the great apocalypse', but history has obscured their meaning.

In his return to Paris, Wordsworth has himself performed a cycle, within which is the smaller cycle of his traversing the central part of the city a second time (cf. ix. 40–62), and outside of which is the larger cycle of his imminent return to England. It is interesting that two Shakespearian allusions in this passage have to do with murdered kings. 'Divided from me by a little month' (65), referring to the September Massacres, echoes Hamlet's 'a little month' as separating the death of his father and Gertrude's remarriage; the voice that cries to the city ' "Sleep no more" ' (77) comes from Macbeth's guilty conscience after the murder of Duncan. Louis XVI had been dethroned on 10 August, and in his walk Wordsworth had passed 'the Prison where the unhappy Monarch lay' (42). These allusions do not, of course, endow Wordsworth with prescience—the King was yet to be tried and would not be executed until 21 January 1793—but we must again remember that, vivid as it is, the poetry was written after the fact. Of course Wordsworth's political associations were with the Gironde, which on the whole opposed the King's death, but he could nevertheless have felt a sense of guilt at the turn of events. It no longer appears certain to him that the bloody events of August and September in Paris were ephemeral monsters. A kind of folk wisdom, placed in quotation marks, instructs him otherwise:

> 'The horse is taught his manage and the wind
> 'Of heaven wheels round and treads in his own steps,
> 'Year follows year, the tide returns again,
> 'Day follows day, all things have second birth;
> 'The earthquake is not satisfied at once.'
>
> (70–4)

As Reed notes, the National Convention (the 'National Synod' of ix. 47) met at a former riding school, the Manège.[62] Many of the most dramatic scenes of the Revolution occurred at this place where horses had once been put through their paces—that is, taught their manage—around a riding ring. Historical recurrence will bring back earthquakes and whirlwinds, typically associated with violent revolution, and 'second birth' here seems a ghastly parody of the belief in a New Birth of the soul among Moravians, Methodists, and others who based their belief on Christ's words to Nicodemus that 'Except a man be born again, he cannot see the kingdom of God' (John 3: 3). Here, however, it is some rough beast that slouches towards Paris to be born. Paris seems 'Defenceless as a wood where tigers roam' (82), an image shared at the time by authors as diverse as William Blake ('The Tyger' was written and revised during 1792–3) and Sir Samuel Romilly ('One might as well think of establishing a republic of tigers in some forest of Africa').[63] The apocalypse once glimpsed behind nature is now glimpsed behind history.

In reaction to this, the poet muses on last things, hoping that France might experience a descent of the Holy Spirit like that at the first Pentecost:

> . . . that throughout earth upon all souls
> Worthy of liberty, upon every soul
> Matured to live in plainness and in truth,
> The gift of tongues might fall, and men arrive
> From the four corners of the winds to do
> For France what without help she could not do,
> A work of honour.
>
> (118–24)

---

[62] *Thirteen-Book Prelude*, i. 269 n. De Selincourt (*Prelude*, p. 595) compares *As You Like It*: 'His horses are bred better . . . they are taught their manage' (I. i. 13).

[63] For the drafts of 'The Tyger', see E 794–5; on Romilly, see Morton D. Paley, *Energy and the Imagination* (Oxford: Clarendon Press, 1970), p. 52 n. 2.

It is important to notice that the episode in Acts 2 to which reference has previously been made leads to an apocalyptic prophecy. After 'cloven tongues of fire' fall upon the apostles and disciples and they begin speaking strange languages, there come 'Jews, devout men out of every nation under heaven'—Wordsworth's 'men . . . / From the four corners of the winds'—whose nations are then enumerated in a long list. Some marvel, while others think the speakers in tongues must be drunk. Peter then rises, cites the prophet Joel, and makes a declaration about the 'last days':

And I will shew wonders in heaven above, and signs in the earth beneath; blood, and fire, and vapour of smoke; The sun shall be turned into darkness, and the moon into blood, before that great and notable day of the Lord come. (Acts 2: 19–20)

Wordsworth's hope is not, of course, realized; and from here to the end of Book X his visions of apocalypse and of millennium are delivered not as a sequence, but in loosely connected fragments. History, at least for the time being, is seen without a structure, oscillating between apocalyptic terror and millennial hope.

After Wordsworth's return to England, he experiences a traumatic shock at seeing Britain's preparations for war with France, in which the psychological is rendered in terms of the political—a 'revolution' (237) in which his inner being undergoes 'subversion' (233). This insurrection in the little world of Man leads him to become an Outsider, or, perhaps more precisely, to realize the Outsider that has been one of his incipient identities all along. Like an apocalypticist whom no one will believe, he sits silent in church, feeding 'on the day of vengeance yet to come' (274). What he perceives are alternative glimpses of apocalypse and millennium, without any structured relationship, befitting the confusion and turmoil both within and around him. At one moment the Revolution appears to promise something like the coming of Christ. In an anticipation of what in the 1930s would be called 'the higher loyalty', he explains how 'a higher creed' seemed to its British sympathizers to supersede the claims of patriotism just as the love of Christ did that of John the Baptist—'Like the Precursor when the Deity / Is come, whose Harbinger he is' (282–3). (These tropes may have stimulated Coleridge to employ them for himself and Wordsworth in 'To William Wordsworth', the great poem he wrote after hearing the poet read *The Prelude* through.[64]) However, in the next verse paragraph we see

[64] See my *Coleridge's Later Poetry* (Oxford: Clarendon Press, 1996), p. 23.

how wrong they were, with the Jacobins' taking the occasion of
Britain's participation in the war to rationalize the Terror—'Tyrants,
strong before / In devilish pleas' (309–10) echoing Milton's Satan's use
of 'necessity, the tyrant's plea'.[65] Adding to the allusive nature of the
narrative is 'the goaded land waxed mad' (312), probably a reference to
Coleridge's 'Recantation', a political verse fable of 1798 in which a
playful ox is driven mad by persecution.[66] There follows an enormous
sentence (315–26) cataloguing the different types of misguided revolutionists, in which the piling up of multiple subjects gives the sense of all
meaning being overwhelmed. It is now seen that millenarianism can be
a form of collective insanity, in 'the hopes of those / Who were content
to barter short-lived pangs / For a paradise of ages' (319–21). These
'short-lived pangs' are of course their euphemism for the 'Domestic
carnage' (329) of the Terror, and Wordsworth dreams of himself as one
of its victims, pleading 'before unjust Tribunals' (377). At this point
Wordsworth could have said with Joyce's Stephen Dedalus, 'History is
a nightmare from which I am trying to awake'.

Yet, with all this chaos before him, Wordsworth experiences a
growth in prophetic empowerment that sustains him, enabling him to
denounce apocalyptic wrath upon the world.

> But as the ancient Prophets were enflamed
> Nor wanted consolations of their own
> And majesty of mind, when they denounced
> On Towns and Cities, wallowing in the abyss
> Of their offences, punishment to come;
> Or saw, like other men, with bodily eyes,
> Before them in some desolated place
> The consummation of the wrath of heaven.
>
> (401–8)

If Wordsworth does not find a Nietzschean joy in asserting such
destruction, he at least experiences, amid the 'rage and dog-day heat'
of 'evil times', consolation in 'the order of sublimest laws' (411–13). This
great apocalyptic passage culminates with an image recalling the 'Deluge now at hand' of Book V. Denying the claim of 'Scoffers in their
pride', that the Terror was a result of 'popular Government and Equality', Wordsworth asserts the true cause:

---

[65] Noted by de Selincourt, *Prelude*, pp. 597–8.   [66] *CPW* I: 299–303.

> It was a reservoir of guilt
> And ignorance, fill'd up from age to age,
> That could no longer hold its loathsome charge,
> But burst, and spread in deluge through the Land.
>
> (436–9)

This time there is not even a Semi-Quixote to attempt to rescue what was best in the order about to be destroyed.

It is important, however, to keep in mind that what led Wordsworth to Godwinism, and subsequently to his crisis of 1795, was not the failure of the French Revolution to preserve a republic, let alone to lead to a millennium, but rather the entry of England into the war and his consequent psychological self-exclusion from the community. He was still capable of celebrating, once more in terms of biblical archetypes, the fall of Robespierre and his supporters. The representation of Robespierre as the 'chief Regent' of 'this foul tribe of Moloch' (468–9) is linked with Milton's 'Moloch, horrid king, besmeared with blood/Of human sacrifice, and parents' tears' and beyond to the god of the Ammonites to whom children were sacrificed in the Old Testament.[67] Wordsworth takes his place with poets like Blake and Allen Ginsberg who have used Moloch as a symbol with significance for their own time. The scene in which Wordsworth learns the news seems full of the promise not so much of the millennium as of the immediate advent of the New Jerusalem:

> ... beneath a genial sun
> With distant prospect among gleams of sky
> And clouds, and intermingled mountain tops
> In one inseparable glory clad,
> Creatures of one etherial substance, met
> In Consistory, like a diadem
> Or crown of burning Seraphs, as they sit
> In the Empyrean.
>
> (476–83)

Words like 'gleams' and 'glory', in a context of interwoven Miltonic passages, seem to promise a breakthrough into the supernal.[68] Significantly, 'the great Sea, meanwhile,/Was at safe distance, far

---

[67] *Paradise Lost*, i. 392–3; cf. Lev. 18: 21, 20: 1–5. Jonathan Wordsworth, *William Wordsworth*, p. 257, points out that 'the atheist crew' comes from *Paradise Lost*, vi. 370.

[68] For the Miltonic sources, see de Selincourt, *Prelude*, p. 600.

retired' (529). Deluge no longer threatens. The poet can yield to an impulse once more to invoke the millennium:

> 'Come now ye golden times',
> Said I, forth-breathing on those open Sands
> A Hymn of triumph.

(541–3)

The 'golden times' recall the image of 'France standing at the top of golden hours' of vi. 353, and this is followed by the image, much like Blake's in *America*, of a millennial dawn:

> '... as the morning comes
> Out of the bosom of the night, come Ye:
> Thus far our trust is verified...'

(543–5)

This hymn of triumph concludes by asserting that '"Earth / [will] March firmly towards righteousness and peace"' (551–2), echoing Isaiah's prophecy of the future kingdom where 'the work of righteousness shall be peace; and the effect of righteousness quietness and assurance for ever' (32: 17). Yet, unrealized as it obviously was, this prediction could not be left as the final statement about the French Revolution in *The Prelude*. At this point Wordsworth needed to formulate his former revolutionary hope, yet show a belated recognition that the 'mighty renovation' that he had thought, as late as August 1794, 'would proceed' (556) had never occurred. He achieved this in his fullest treatment of the French Revolution as millennium—the famous passage in Book X (lines 689–727) beginning 'O pleasant exercise of hope and joy!' that was first published in Coleridge's *Friend* for 26 October 1809.[69] Even in 1804 the emphasis is retrospective (further qualifications would appear in *1850*), especially in Wordsworth's enlistment of the vocabulary of Romance to achieve a mixture of results. Before discussing these, we may look back at the Romance imagery of Book IX, as applied first to Beaupuy and then to Wordsworth himself. Beaupuy, who has been presented as a unique, almost supernal being, appears to move through history as through the text of *The Faerie Queene*:

---

[69] Coleridge, *The Friend*, ed. Barbara E. Rooke (2 vols., Princeton: Princeton University Press, 1969); and for collation *Thirteen-Book Prelude*, pp. 285–7 n.

> He thro' the events
> Of that great change wander'd in perfect faith,
> As through a Book, an old Romance or Tale
> Of Fairy, or some dream of actions wrought
> Behind the summer clouds.

(ix. 305–9)

Beaupuy has earned this knight-errant quality by his meekness, benignity, and love of humanity, sealed by his heroic death (lines 431–2). Wordsworth is not as kind to his own past self when describing the reveries he sometimes fell into between their philosophic dialogues (445 ff.). In his fantasies hermits stray from sheds and caves, a 'devious Traveller' is transformed into Ariosto's Angelica or Tasso's Erminia (recalling Wordsworth's Italian studies at Cambridge), knights joust, and satyrs dance orgiastically about an abducted woman.[70] There is something of Scott's Waverley about this young man, something in his mixture of 'real fervour' with 'that / Less genuine and wrought up within myself' (474–5) that warns the reader against taking at face value his perceptions of events around him. It also prepares us for the evocation of the Revolution as 'a Country in Romance' (x. 696). Of course, the yoking of this with Reason is a deliberate yoking of antitheses. Yet what are we to make of Reason as 'A prime Enchanter', when *the* prime enchanter in Spenser is the diabolical Archimago? Are the best candidates for directing a new society 'They who had fed their childhood upon dreams, / The Play-fellows of Fancy' (709–10)? Or are these, too, Waverleys who will mistake the nature of historical experience because of their own romantic preconceptions? Are they capable of creating a millennial society outside the realm of fiction,

> Not in Utopia, subterraneous fields,
> Or some secreted Island Heaven knows where;
> But in the very world which is the world
> Of all of us, the place on which in the end
> We find our happiness, or not at all.

(723–7)

The passage is both lyrical and eloquent, yet it makes us wonder as to the possibility of the new society whose imminent existence seems so

---

[70] Reed, *Thirteen-Book Prelude*, i. 243 n. identifies allusions to *The Faerie Queene*, I. vi. vii–xix, III. x. xliii–xliv, VI. viii. xxxv–li, and VI. x. xxxix–xi. xxiv.

strongly asserted. Looking back on the events, inner and outer, of the period, Wordsworth could say:

> A veil had been
> Uplifted; why deceive ourselves? 'Twas so,
> 'Twas even so, and sorrow for the man,
> Who either hath not eyes wherewith to see,
> Or seeing hath forgotten.
>
> (855–9)

Apocalypse had left behind a residue of bitter insight, millennium a recollection of a dreamlike wish-fulfilment fantasy. The only way that Wordsworth could find to bring them together again was to locate them outside history at the poem's Conclusion.

Mount Snowdon

In the Five-Book *Prelude* Wordsworth had made the ascent of Snowdon, previously the subject of lines 492–511 of *Descriptive Sketches*, the climax of his poem, and it retained that privileged position in 1805–6 and beyond. One can see why. Although the experience dated from 1790, and so antedated the subject-matter of the books immediately preceding it, by re-creating it at this point Wordsworth hoped for a thematic resolution bringing together the themes of apocalypse and millennium. The way it does this is unique, in that the two are neither presented alternatively, as in the 'France' books, nor sequentially, the second being born of the first, but simultaneously. Yet they do not fuse their identities as in *The Marriage of Heaven and Hell*, but exist in a perpetual interchange with each other. This representation of the two as intermixed is given in the first 65 lines, and is then the subject of a long meditation that gradually fades into a longer coda to the work as a whole. However, despite Wordsworth's seeming assurance that he has rendered 'The Soul, the Imagination of the Whole' (65), some doubts may persist for the reader, and perhaps even for the poet, as to whether the merging of apocalypse and millennium provides an adequate resolution.

With Robert Jones, who also shared the crossing of the Alps, and 'the Shepherd, who by ancient right/Of office is the Stranger's usual Guide' (7–8), Wordsworth set out to walk up Mount Snowdon. They started from 'Bethkelet' (Beddgelért, now as then a starting-point for

the ascent of Snowdon), whose 'huts' (3, meaning old tufted cottages[71])
suggest an aboriginal place appropriate to the primal experience that
is to come. What the walkers first experience is something like the
crossing of the Alps in reverse. The sullenness of nature that in Book VI
had followed their mountain experience now precedes it. As if Nature
were trying to protect herself against any penetration of her mystery,

> It was a Summer's night, a close warm night,
> Wan, dull, and glaring, with a dripping mist
> Low-hung and thick that cover'd all the sky,
> Half-threatening storm and rain.

(xiii. 10–13)

J. C. Maxwell suggests that 'glaring' is used in the sense of the northern
dialect 'glarry' or 'glaurie', meaning dull, rainy, sticky, clammy,[72] and
this, with the rest, recalls the night spent (or in linear time *to be* spent)
outside Gravedona in Book VI. Pressing on with Jones and their shepherd guide, Wordsworth now seems like Dante labouring up Mount
Purgatory:

> With forehead bent
> Earthward, as if in opposition set
> Against an enemy, I panted up
> With eager pace.

(xiii. 29–32)

Without realizing it, the poet is approaching a threshold of the apocalyptic, like the boy who

> slowly mounted up a steep ascent
> Where the road's wat'ry surface, to the ridge
> Of that sharp rising, glitter'd in the moon.

(iv. 370–2)

And once more the characteristic vocabulary of light indicates that
the threshold has been crossed:

> For instantly a Light upon the turf
> Fell like a flash: I look'd about, and lo!
> The Moon stood naked in the Heavens, at height

---

[71] See Norton *Prelude*, p. 458 n. 1. Compare the 'naked huts' of vi. 450, at Martigny.
[72] *The Prelude*, ed. J. C. Maxwell, 2nd edn. (Harmondsworth: Penguin, 1972), p. 564. He
compares 'the glaring hill' in *An Evening Walk*, l. 54.

> Immense above my head, and on the shore
> I found myself of a huge sea of mist,
> Which meek and silent, rested at my feet.
>
> (xiii. 39–44)

What follows is a passage in which the poet perceives the world as a perpetual ongoing process of interaction of apocalyptic and millennial elements. The sea of mist upon which 'the Moon look'd down . . . In single glory' (xiii. 52–3) has the beauty and peace of the millennial, while the power and sublimity of the apocalyptic manifests itself in the 'roar of waters, torrents, streams / Innumerable, roaring with one voice' (xiii. 58–9).

As previous scholars have pointed out, there are in this passage remarkable echoes of Milton's account of the Creation in Book VII of *Paradise Lost*.[73] Recollecting what he saw (and rewriting lines 492–511 of the *Descriptive Sketches*), Wordsworth seems to be in the very act of creating the hills, vapours, headlands, and chasm that are his text. The apocalyptic elements here are contained within the framework of nature. The 'blue chasm, a fracture in the vapour' (56) has something in common with 'the hollow rent' of vi. 559, both seeming at the point of revealing supernal forces beyond. The 'voice of waters' that comes through is 'homeless', yet this is made unthreatening by the finality with which the poet asserts that in 'That dark, deep thoroughfare, had Nature lodged / The soul, the imagination of the whole' (64–5). Such accommodation of the apocalyptic to the natural leads to Hartman's well-known comment: 'Wordsworth sees Imagination by its own light and calls that light Nature's, and this deception or transference, a greatest avoidance of apocalypse, is still the best possible ending for *The Prelude*'.[74] Another way of putting it is that this is the only possible ending for *The Prelude*. Throughout the poem apocalypse and millennium have alternated irregularly and in uneasy relationship. In his depiction of forces that in the Simplon Pass seemed uncontrollable but are now represented as the thought processes 'of a mighty mind' (69) in direct relationship with his own imagination—Wordsworth has his apocalypse and his millennium engaged in a perpetual ongoing transaction. It has been remarked how in the 'meditation' (66) that follows, Wordsworth strongly asserts that his imagery is equal to his conceptions, in expressions like 'the express / Resemblance, in the fullness of

---

[73] See Norton *Prelude*, p. 460 n. 4; Jonathan Wordsworth, *William Wordsworth*, p. 324.
[74] Hartman, *Wordsworth's Poetry*, p. 254.

its strength / Made visible, a genuine Counterpart' (86–8).[75] Yet the urgency with which Wordsworth thrusts on the reader the complete adequacy of these visible signs as he presents them suggests a sense of difficulty about this outcome.

Wordsworth's displacement of apocalypse and millennium is both a model for, and a prime example in, M. H. Abrams's powerful argument that, first sought in the political world and then in external nature, both come to exist internally as a secularized version of Milton's 'Paradise within thee, happier far'.[76] The passage is certainly one of the grandest in Wordsworth's *œuvre*, especially in the 1805–6 Reading Text, before the poet's later religious scruples led to substantial changes for the worse.[77] Yet there is also something about it that recalls the objections to Wordsworth made by those intolerant contemporaries William Blake and John Keats. It is often wondered what these two poets would have thought of Wordsworth's greatest long poem had they had a chance to read it. How would their judgement of Wordsworth have been affected by passages like this one? It appears likely that, if anything, their (needless to say) partial views would have been reconfirmed, and the ascent of Snowdon in Book XIII would have been a prime example. It embodies precisely what Blake meant in his misreading of the *Poems* of 1815, when he wrote 'I see in Wordsworth the Natural Man rising up against the Spiritual Man Continually', and in another sense, Keats's distinguishing 'the poetical Character' from 'the wordsworthian or egotistical Sublime; which is a thing per se and stands alone'.[78] One need not endorse Blake's bifurcation of the Natural and the Spiritual to see that in the Snowdon episode there is a blurring, rather than a synthesis, of the two. Wordsworth is the man alone, gazing into the landscape like one of the solitary figures of Kaspar David Friedrich (whose paintings, interestingly, are now frequently taken as parallels), while at the same time he gazes into his memory and his previous text. Although the passage begins in the first person plural, it quickly shifts into the singular. The youthful friend and the shepherd guide who were his companions in the early lines of Book XIII have

[75] See Theresa M. Kelley, *Wordsworth's Revisionary Aesthetics* (Cambridge: Cambridge University Press, 1988), p. 130.

[76] *Paradise Lost*, xii. 586–7; p. 467.

[77] For the textual history of this passage, see the appendix to the Norton *Prelude*, pp. 516–17.

[78] Annotations to Wordsworth's *Poems*, E 665; *The Letters of John Keats*, ed. H. E. Rollins (2 vols., Cambridge, Mass.: Harvard University Press, 1958), 1: 386–7.

been forgotten. This is the poet as, in Coleridge's harsh words, 'a spectator ab extra of nature and society', one who 'felt for, but never sympathized with, any man or event'.[79] There is in the Snowdon vision no human community (though Wordsworth does, perhaps in compensation, name his significant others in the coda). Relocating the millennial in the psyche deprives it of its meaning for society, something that should lead us to question Abrams's argument that his three-phase model represents the best possible outcome for poetry; and, while making the apocalyptic an object of meditation may provide a temporary relief from the anxieties it causes, the forces that Melville's Ahab glimpsed behind the unreasoning mask of Nature cannot be so convincingly tamed.

[79] *TT* 1: 306 (21 July 1832).

4

Byron

Travelling beyond Interlaken in September 1816, Lord Byron noted in his journal: 'Arrived at the foot of the Mountain (the Yung-Frau—i.e. the Maiden)—Glaciers—torrents—one of these torrents *nine hundred feet* in height of visible descent—', and then continued: 'the torrent I spoke of . . . is in shape curving over the rock—like the *tail* of a white horse streaming in the wind—such as it might be conceived would be that of the "*pale* horse" on which *Death* is mounted in the Apocalypse'.[1] The image was too good to let go, and it emerges in *Manfred*:

> . . . the sunbow's rays still arch
> The torrent with the many hues of heaven,
> And roll the sheeted silver's waving column
> O'er the crag's headlong perpendicular,
> And fling its lines of foaming light along
> And to and fro, like the pale courser's tail,
> The Giant steed, to be bestrode by Death,
> As told in the Apocalypse.[2]

This image and Byron's use of it tell us something about the place of the apocalyptic in Byron's imagination. His cognition of it is genuine. The image registers on his senses, and he is impelled to work it into a superb passage of Alpine description, extending it beyond the natural. At the same time, this fragment of the apocalyptic is (despite the descent in II. iv to the Hall of Arimanes, who rules the destructive forces of tempests, earthquakes, volcanoes, Pestilence, and War) subordinate to the main concern of *Manfred*, which is with Manfred and Astarte. This is often the case in Byron's major poems, in which strong apocalyptic elements will extrude themselves without becoming the central subjects. At the field of Waterloo in *Childe Harold's Pilgrimage* the narrator remarks, 'How that

---

[1] Byron, *Letters and Journals*, ed. Leslie A. Marchand (12 vols., Cambridge, Mass.: Belknap Press of Harvard University Press, 1973–82), 5: 101.

[2] II. ii. 1–8, in *Byron*, ed. Jerome J. McGann (Oxford and New York: Oxford University Press, 1986), p. 289. References to Byron are to this edition unless otherwise noted.

red rain hath made the harvest grow!' and the battlefield becomes a col-
lective Golgotha—'this place of skulls, / The grave of France, the deadly
Waterloo!'[3] This apocalyptic imagery continues with an allusion to
Napoleon and 'Europe's flowers long rooted up before / The trampler
of her vineyards'.[4] Such images would not seem out of place beside
Blake's Orc in the vineyards of red France or his Wine-press on the
Rhine. Byron ambiguously equates Rousseau with the Delphic Oracle:

> For then he was inspired, and from him came,
> As from the Pythian's mystic cave of yore,
> Those oracles which set the world in flame,
> Nor ceased to burn till kingdoms were no more.[5]

Despite the destruction they caused, Rousseau 'and his compeers'
acted upon an urge for apocalyptic knowledge with which the poet can
identify: 'the veil they rent, / And what behind it lay, all earth shall view'
(ll. 772–3). Byron can also intuit terrible forces moving behind the surface of the natural world, as after the shipwreck in Canto II of *Don Juan*.

> 'Twas twilight, and the sunless day went down
> Over the waste of waters; like a veil,
> Which, if withdrawn, would but disclose the frown
> Of one whose hate is masked but to assail.[6]

It is an image that Captain Ahab could have understood.

Although not at the centre of either *Childe Harold* or *Don Juan*, apocalyptic forces are at times evoked in both poems, displaying an important aspect of Byron's poetic sensibility.[7] What of the millennial? That
element manifests itself in two very different ways. One is through
Byron's ruthless satire on its would-be prophets, as in the prose preface
to *Don Juan*, where in the course of his attack upon Wordsworth, Byron
writes: 'This Man is the kind of Poet, who, in the same manner that
Joanna Southcote found many thousand people to take her Dropsy for
God Almighty re-impregnated, has found some hundreds of persons to
misbelieve in his insanities, and hold him out as a kind of poetical
Emanuel Swedenborg—a Richard Brothers—a parson Tozer—half

---

[3] Canto III, ll. 151, 154–5, p. 109.   [4] iii. 174–5, p. 109.
[5] iii. 761–4, p. 128.   [6] ii. 385–8, p. 445.
[7] One might call 'The Devil's Drive' of 1813, like Shelley's 'The Devil's Walk', an imitation of Coleridge and Southey's 'The Devil's Thoughts', mock-apocalyptic, but it is a
broader burlesque lacking the bite of either the original or Shelley's imitation. (For a more
positive view of Byron's poem, see Frederick L. Beaty, *Byron the Satirist* (DeKalb, Ill.: Northern Illinois University Press, 1985), pp. 77–8.)

Enthusiast and half Impostor'.[8] Byron takes the reader into the joke, the assumption being that the millennial is *per se* ridiculous. Wordsworth's *Excursion* is in *Don Juan* compared with the messianic child that Joanna Southcott had proclaimed she would bear:

> But Wordsworth's poem, and his followers, like
>   Joanna Southcote's Shiloh, and her sect,
> Are things which in this century don't strike
>   The public mind, so few are the elect;
> And the new births of both their stale virginities
> Have proved but dropsies, taken for divinities.[9]

Shiloh, the name of the miraculous child not to be born, is derived from Genesis 49: 10: 'The sceptre shall not depart from Judah, nor a lawgiver from between his feet, until Shiloh come; and unto him shall the gathering of the people be'.[10] Significantly, Shiloh was a nickname Byron used for that unregenerate millenarian Percy Bysshe Shelley.[11] However, the millennial also appears in Byron's poetry in an entirely different way. We glimpse it in *Childe Harold* III in the beautiful lines on the dead at Ardennes, which offer a post-apocalyptic peace:

> And Ardennes waves above them her green leaves,
>   Dewy with nature's tear-drops, as they pass,
> Grieving, if aught inanimate e'er grieves,
>   Over the unreturning brave,—alas![12]

The natural world in Byron's poetry can be seen as potentially millennial, although that promise is never fulfilled. The Rhine, 'this paradise' in *Childe Harold* III, would be like the river of the New Jerusalem if man could leave it untouched by his conflicts:

> ... then to see
> Thy valley of sweet waters, were to know
> Earth paved like Heaven.[13]

---

[8] ll. 24–9, in *Don Juan*, ed. Leslie Marchand (Cambridge, Mass.: Houghton Mifflin, 1958), p. 2. On William Tozer, disciple of Joanna Southcott and author of *Scriptural and Hieroglyphic Observations* (1812), see J. C. F. Harrison, *The Second Coming: Popular Millenarianism 1780–1850* (New Brunswick, NJ: Rutgers University Press, 1979), pp. 52, 126. Byron calls Tozer 'Parson' because he was a Southcottian preacher; he was not an ordained minister.

[9] iii. 851–6, p. 514.

[10] Shiloh is a name with millennial associations in Blake's *Jerusalem*, as, e.g., when Jerusalem says 'I seek for Shiloh' in *Jerusalem* (79: 10, E 234).

[11] See Byron's letter to Richard Belgrave Hoppner, 10 Sept. 1820, in Byron, *Letters and Journals*, 7: 174.

[12] ll. 235–8, *Byron*, p. 111.   [13] ll. 508, 447–9.

And he shewed me a pure river of water of life, clear as crystal, proceeding out of the throne of God and of the Lamb. In the midst of the street of it, and on either side of the river, was there the tree of life.   (Rev. 22: 1–2)

Juan and Haidee at the beginning of their love inhabit a world reminiscent of Blake's regained Eden, 'for to their young eyes / Each was an angel, and earth paradise'.[14] Whether such tropes imply a return to Eden or a progression to the millennial world is hardly significant, for in theological tradition these were frequently identified; as Burnet put it, after the Conflagration 'a new face of Nature will accordingly succeed, *New Heavens* and a *New Earth, Paradise* renew'd'.[15] However, Byron sceptically undermines this later in Canto III with the long description of the sophistication and artifice of the lovers' banquet in stanzas 62–77, to be followed in Canto IV by Juan's expulsion and the death of his beloved. For Byron, the millennial is either an imposture or a dream.

When in certain poems Byron makes apocalypse his central subject, it is unaccompanied by millennium, although he may play upon the expectation by the reader of a millennium to follow. This is indeed the case in the three works by Byron that concentrate most upon the apocalyptic: 'Darkness', *Cain*, and *Heaven and Earth*. 'Darkness', originally published in the *Prisoner of Chillon* volume of 1816, came to great prominence in the wake of a literary controversy shortly after Byron's death, a controversy that both tells us a great deal about contemporary critics' (and presumably readers') attitudes toward the apocalyptic and also links 'Darkness' with several near-contemporary literary projects involving the closely related subject of the Last Man. For these reasons it is interesting to consider Byron's poem not only for its own considerable literary interest but also as part of the cultural construction of Lastness in the Romantic period.

Imagining Lastness

In 1823 Thomas Campbell published in the *New Monthly Magazine* a poem entitled 'The Last Man'. Reviewed when it appeared in Campbell's volume *Theodoric, a Domestic Tale: with Other Poems*, it became the subject of a debate not so much about its particular quality as about the

---

[14] iii. 1631–2.
[15] Thomas Burnet, *Theory of the Earth*, 3rd edn. (2 vols., London, 1697), 1: 223.

validity of its subject. This controversy began innocuously enough with Francis Jeffrey's review of *Theodoric* in the *Edinburgh Review*. 'There is a very striking little poem entitled "The Last Man"', Jeffrey remarked, 'the idea of which has probably been borrowed from a very powerful sketch of Lord Byron's to which he gave, we think, the title of "Darkness"; and the manner in which the subject is treated by those two great authors is very characteristic of the different turns of their genius.' Campbell could not bear even this gentle insinuation, and he published an open letter to Jeffrey claiming not only that the idea of a Last Man poem was originally his but also that it was he who, fifteen or more years earlier, had suggested to Byron the subject of 'a being witnessing the extinction of his species and of the creation, and of his looking, under the fading eye of nature, at desolate cities, ships floating at sea with the dead'. The publication of 'Darkness', Campbell declared, had discouraged him from pursuing the theme. 'But', he continued, 'I was provoked to change my mind, when my friend Barry Cornwall informed me that an acquaintance of his intended to write a long poem entitled the "Last Man". I thought this hard!'[16]

Byron's 'Darkness' was not the first literary work to envisage the last man on earth. That distinction belongs to a little-known French novel, or rather prose epic: *Le dernier homme* by Jean François Xavier Cousin de Grainville.[17] Grainville's book was translated into English and published anonymously in 1806 as *The Last Man, or Omegarus and Syderia, a Romance in Futurity*.[18] Something of a mystery attaches to how this came about less than a year after the book's virtually unnoticed début in Paris; the intermediary may perhaps have been Sir Herbert Croft, best known for *Love and Madness* (London, 1780), who was a great admirer of Grainville and who lived in France at this time. It may be, as Eugen Kölbung argued in 1898, that both Byron and Mary Shelley read the English version.[19] Apart from any possible literary sources, however,

---

[16] For Jeffrey, see *Edinburgh Review*, 61 (1824–5): 284. Campbell's letter is repr. in Cyrus Redding's *Literary Reminiscences and Memoirs of Thomas Campbell* (2 vols., London: Charles J. Skeat, 1860), 1: 304–8.

[17] *Le dernier homme* was first published privately in Paris in 1805. A 2nd edn., with a preface by Charles Nodier, appeared in 2 vols. in Paris in 1811.

[18] [Cousin de Grainville], *The Last Man, or Omegarus and Syderia* (2 vols., London: R. Dutton, 1806).

[19] See *Lord Byrons Werke in Kritischen Texte mit Einleitung und Anmerkungen*, ed. Eugen Kölbung (Weimar, 1896), 2: 136–52, 206–27, 396–404. Ernest Hartley Coleridge accepted this view in his edition *The Works of Lord Byron* (13 vols., London: John Murray, 1898–1905), 4: 42–3. Neither Kölbung nor Coleridge was aware of Grainville's original authorship.

the extraordinary climatic conditions during the summer of 1816, when Byron wrote his poem, must have turned his imagination to Last Things. The year 1816 became known as 'the year without a summer' because of its unusual cold and darkness, not then known to have been caused by the great Tambora volcanic eruption of the year before.[20] According to Richard B. Strothers, during the lunar eclipse of 9–10 June 1816, 'the moon (which should have been visible by earthlight) was seen to vanish entirely, under clear observing conditions' by astronomers in London and in Dresden.[21] In New York during the spring and summer of the same year, sunspots were visible to the naked eye. In the city of Geneva the summer of 1816 was the coldest recorded for the period 1753–1960, according to data published by Henry and Elizabeth Stommel in *Scientific American*; crops failed, and in the following winter critical food shortages were reported.[22] Byron himself remarked in 1822 when asked 'how he could have conceived such a scene as that described in his poem called "Darkness"', that 'he wrote it in 1815 [*sic*] at Geneva, when there was a celebrated dark day, on which the fowls went to roost at noon, and the candles were lighted as at midnight'.[23]

'Darkness' is spoken by an imagined spectator of the end of life on earth. However, it is typical of Last Man scenarios that they be rendered intermediately. This kind of buffering is provided in Grainville's narrative by having future events displayed by a celestial spirit in a magic mirror in a cave. In Byron's poem it is rendered in the first line: 'I had a dream, which was not all a dream'. The dreamer is in the position of the Last Man; what he sees is 'not all a dream' because, like the vision Grainville's spirit shows in the magic mirror, it may be predictive of future reality. The sun is dark, and the moon (as in Grainville) is gone. As a consequence, every possible source of warmth is exploited: men ignite forests for fuel, burn their own homes and dwell 'within the eye /Of the volcanos, and their mountain-torch' (16–17). These efforts

---

[20] See Anthony Rudolf, *Byron's Darkness: Lost Summer and Nuclear Winter* (London: Menard Press, 1984); and Brian Aldiss, Introduction to *The Last Man* by Mary Shelley (London: Hogarth Press, 1985). Byron also may have known of a prophecy, attributed to an Italian astronomer and reported in the British press, saying that the sun would burn out on 18 July. See Jeffrey Vail, '"The bright sun was extinguish'd"', *Wordsworth Circle*, 28 (1997): 183–92.

[21] R. B. Strothers, 'The Great Tambora Eruption and Its Aftermath', *Science*, 224 (1984): 1191–8.

[22] H. and E. Stommel, 'The Year without a Summer', *Scientific American*, 240 (1979): 176–86.

[23] Ernest J. Lovell, Jr. ed., *His Very Self and Voice* (New York: Macmillan, 1954), p. 299. Byron could misremember the year, but the atmospheric conditions were unforgettable.

at survival are no more successful than those in *Omegarus and Syderia*. Men behave much as the cannibals in Omegarus's vision of the posterity wisely denied to the Last Man:

> each sate sullenly apart
> Gorging himself in gloom . . .
>
> . . . .
>
> and the pang
> Of famine fed upon all entrails—men
> Died, and their bones were tombless as their flesh;
> The meagre by the meagre were devoured.
>
> (40–6)

In 'an enormous city' the last two survivors, enemies, each bearing a Cain-like mark upon his brow upon which 'Famine had written Fiend' meet and die 'Even of their mutual hideousness' (67–9). The earth's devastation can be expressed only by telling what is *not* there—'Seasonless, herbless, treeless, manless, lifeless—' (71). The final lines of the poem continue this process, pronouncing inanimate natural forces and objects 'dead'—tides, moon, winds, clouds—and concluding 'Darkness had no need / Of aid from them—She was the universe' (81–2). This culminating personification owes something to the last line of Pope's *Dunciad* ('And Universal Darkness buries All'), but it seems significant that Byron, as Grainville before (and Mary Shelley after) him, makes the dominating destructive personification female, turning it from an abstraction into a mythical being.

From the first, 'Darkness' was recognized as an unusual poem. Most of the contemporary reviews[24] of the *Prisoner of Chillon* volume (1816) mention 'Darkness' favourably, but one senses the critics employing strategies of categorization and comparison in an attempt to familiarize the unfamiliar, pursuing the reassurance of classification. The disturbing effect of 'Darkness' could be moderated by invoking sublimity, as did the *Dublin Examiner*—'absolutely sublime' (2 (1816): 126)—and the *Eclectic Review*—'a sort of spectral sublimity' (2nd ser., 7 (1817): 301). The *Critical Review* was reminded of 'an effusion by Mr Coleridge, entitled "The Ancient Mariner"' (5th ser., 4 (1816): 580), and in the *Quarterly* Sir Walter Scott compared it with 'the wild, unbridled, and fiery imagination of Coleridge' (16 (1816): 204). The sense of spiritual

---

[24] Unless otherwise indicated, reviews of Byron's 'Darkness' are quoted from *The Romantics Reviewed*, ed. Donald H. Reiman (New York and London: Garland, 1972), part B, vols. 1–4. References are cited in the text.

vastation in Coleridge's poems is certainly germane, evoked by details like 'Ships sailorless lay rotting on the sea, / And their masts fell down piecemeal; as they dropped / They slept on the abyss without a surge—' (75–7). Nevertheless, the Ancient Mariner is in the end reunited (intermittently) with human community, while in 'Darkness' the subject is the destruction of that community itself. 'Darkness' may be characterized as an example of the Burkean sublime, and its horrors compared with those of Coleridge's poem, but it retains unique and disturbing qualities not explained by these comparisons.

Another way of 'placing' the unfamiliar is by analogy. Parallels with painting could serve this purpose. The *British Lady's Magazine* said that 'Darkness' seemed 'intended for a fancy painting in the horrible style' (5 (1817): 23). Two comparisons were more specific. 'It is Fuseli out-Fuselied', said the *Eclectic Review* (2nd ser., 7 (1817): 301), and the *Monthly Magazine* called it 'a sketch with a pen which our great dealer in hobgoblins, Fuseli himself, might be eager to transfer to his canvas' (81 (1816): 436–7). Fuseli was of course identified with the terrible sublime, and his psychologically disquieting pictures do at times border on the apocalyptic. Nevertheless, Fuseli's most celebrated paintings, such as *The Nightmare*, frequently display wit among their shadows, and one senses in the reviewers' parallel a desire to mitigate the effect of 'Darkness' by turning it into a quasi-Gothic tale. Yet, the subject of Byron's poem is after all not 'hob-goblins' but the end of life on earth. It was precisely because 'Darkness' could not be accommodated to conventional categories that some critics were troubled. The *British Lady's Magazine* qualified its praise by saying: 'It is difficult to confine one's ideas to such a catastrophe exclusively'. This point was also made in the two most important contemporary reviews: Francis Jeffrey's and Walter Scott's. Jeffrey said in the *Edinburgh Review*: 'The very conception is terrible above all conception of known calamity—and is too oppressive to the imagination, to be contemplated with pleasure, even in the faint reflection of poetry' (27 (1816): 308). Scott in the *Quarterly* elaborated a similar argument:

To speak plainly, the framing of such phantasms is a dangerous employment for the exalted and teeming imagination of such a poet as Lord Byron, whose Pegasus has ever required rather a bridle than a spur. The waste of boundless space into which they lead the poet, the neglect of precision which such themes may render habitual, make them, in respect to poetry, what mysticism is to religion. (16 (1816): 205)

In Scott's judgement, it would be better not to undertake such a subject at all. 'The strength of poetical conception, and beauty of diction', Scott continued, 'is as much thrown away as the colours of a painter, should he take a cloud of mist, or a wreath of smoke for his canvass'. Scott's view is that the imagination cannot successfully engage such a subject. His analogy with painting is reminiscent of a scathing remark about Turner quoted by Hazlitt in 'On Imitation': 'pictures of nothing and very like'.[25] Having come to value such pictures of nothing, we may not immediately apprehend the force of Scott's argument. For him, as for Jeffrey, the danger lies in trying to imagine what cannot be imagined—in this instance the 'waste of boundless space' that will succeed at the end of the world.

One further, near-contemporary article should be mentioned here because of the further dimension of meaning it supplies to 'Darkness' and, by extension, to Campbell's 'The Last Man'. In 1828 a correspondent of the *Imperial Magazine* (10: 699–70), signing himself 'R. L. L.', published a letter headed 'The Bible and Lord Byron'. There R. L. L. demonstrated some striking resemblances between parts of Byron's poem and certain passages in Jeremiah, Isaiah, and Ezekiel. He did this by printing these passages *seriatim*, to create in effect a prose poem that, as a partial quotation may indicate, reads very much like 'Darkness':

I beheld the earth, and, lo, it was without form and void; and the heavens, and they had no light. I beheld the mountains, and, lo, they trembled, and all the hills moved lightly. I beheld, and, lo, there was no man, and all the birds of the heaven were fled. I beheld, and, lo, the fruitful place was a wilderness, and all the cities thereof were broken down. For this shall the earth mourn, and the heavens above be black, the stars thereof shall be dark; I will cover the sun with a cloud, and the moon shall not give her light. All the bright lights of heaven will I make dark over thee, and set darkness upon thy land. Every city shall be forsaken, and not a man dwell therein.

(Jer. 5: 23–9; Is. 5: 25, 30; 50: 3; 61: 6; Ezek. 28: 20)

To the parallels printed by R. L. L. may be added a few others. The entire poem is in a sense a reversal of Genesis 6: 3: 'And God said, Let there be light: and there was light.' Also important is Revelation 6: 12:

And I beheld when he had opened the sixth seal, and lo, there was a great earthquake; and the moon became black as sackcloth of hair, and the moon became as blood.[26]

[25] *The Complete Works of William Hazlitt*, ed. P. P. Howe (London and Toronto: J. M. Dent, 1932), 4: 76 n. Hazlitt may not have been the author of the expression, as he frames it in quotation marks.

[26] See R. J. Dingley, ' "I had a Dream …" ': Byron's "Darkness" ', *Byron Journal*, 9 (1981): 20–33.

What is most significant about Byron's working in of such biblical passages is, however, not quite what R. L. L. had in mind. It is true, as he says, that 'the celebrated poet had come forth from the prophetic "chamber of imagery", furnished with those uncommon and awful conceptions of which he has constructed one of the most remarkable poems to be found in the English language'. For R. L. L. this shows that even unbelievers 'are often indebted to that holy book for some of the brightest truths, and sublimest conceptions, which adorn their pages'. This may have been a comforting way of viewing a disquieting poem, but it significantly avoids mentioning what Byron did *not* take from the Bible.

As we have seen throughout this study, the invocation of apocalypse leads to the expectation of a millennium. 'Darkness' does indeed raise for a moment the vision of a world in which, in the terms of Isaiah, 'they shall beat their swords into plowshares, and their spears into pruning-hooks: nation shall not lift up sword against nation, neither shall they learn war any more' (2: 4). However, this hope is brutally dissipated: 'And War, which for a moment was no more,/Did glut himself again' (38–9). Another residue of millenarian prophecy is found when 'vipers crawl'd/And twined themselves among the multitude,/Hissing, but stingless' (35–7). One of the features of Isaiah's messianic age is: 'the sucking child shall play on the hole of the asp' (11: 8), and the characterization in 'Darkness' of 'the wildest brutes' as 'tame and tremulous' (34–5) parallels 'The wolf also shall dwell with the lamb, and the leopard shall lie down with the kid' in Isaiah 11: 6. However, Byron's brutes and vipers are greedily devoured by the remaining humans in an orgiastic feast. Millennial associations are consistently invoked in order to be bitterly frustrated, as they would also be in Campbell's 'The Last Man'. In the year without a summer, which was also the year after the Congress of Vienna and the reinstitution of the old political order in Europe, nature must have seemed to parallel the world of human events. Unlike apocalyptic poems of the 1790s like Coleridge's 'Religious Musings' and Blake's *America*, 'Darkness', a true product of post-revolutionary awareness, presents apocalypse but no millennium.

Thomas Campbell's poem,[27] despite some superficial similarities, is really a poem of a different order from Byron's. It introduces, as does 'Darkness', an observer who mediates the condition of lastness:

[27] 'The Last Man', in *The Poetical Works of Thomas Campbell*, ed. William Michael Rossetti (London: Moxon, 1871), pp. 261–5.

I saw a vision in my sleep,
That gave my spirit strength to sweep
Adown the gulph of Time!
I saw the last of human mould,
That shall Creation's death behold,
As Adam saw her prime!

Unlike Byron, however, Campbell sounds a conventionally religious note that is in discord with the subject. Campbell's Last Man remains constant in his faith, allowing the visionary who dreams of him to conclude:

Thou saw'st the last of Adam's race
On Earth's sepulchral clod,
The darkening universe defy
To quench his Immortality,
Or shake his trust in God!

Introducing theodicy into the Last Man *topos* creates problems that Byron avoided, and Campbell's poem is perhaps less interesting in itself than for the dispute that his public letter engendered. As we have seen, the disturbing nature of Byron's subject prompted some critics to deny that it could be treated successfully, and some to wish that it had not been treated at all. There were, of course, some parodies—no British figure was exempted from these—beginning with the anonymous 'Despair: A Vision' in 1820[28]—but on the whole Byron's prestige, and perhaps the memory of *English Bards and Scotch Reviewers*, had a moderating effect on the tone of most reviews. Campbell enjoyed no such immunity. In the critical discussion of his 'Last Man' and his claims for its priority, we see in undisguised form the defensive strategies of categorizing, familiarizing, trivializing, and burlesquing that were adopted to prevent or deflect the imagining of Lastness. The production of lampoons on the subject soon became a cottage industry of literary journalism.[29]

Campbell's claim was dismissed by the *London Magazine* (NS 1 (1825): 588–90), 'the idea of the Last Man being most particularly obvious, or rather absolutely common-place, and a book with the taking title of

---

[28] See William Hamilton, ed., *Parodies of the Works of English and American Authors* (6 vols., London: Reeves and Turner, 1886), 3: 228.

[29] For an extensive survey of these, see Arthur McA. Miller, 'The Last Man: A Study of the Eschatological Theme in English Poetry and Fiction from 1806 through 1839' (Ph.D. diss., Duke University, 1966).

Omegarius [sic], *or the Last Man,* having gone the rounds of all circulating libraries for years past'. 'Had the idea in question been that of a *Last Poem*', the author added, 'indeed the very originality of so extravagant a thought might perhaps have been worth discussing'. According to such buffoonery, Lastness supposes a reader who cannot, by definition, be the last and whose existence therefore precludes the subject from being Last as well. *Blackwood's Edinburgh Magazine* (21 (1827): 54, 57), found Campbell's poem 'of a very low order . . . the very idea being in itself absurd', and asserted:

There is no such thing as the Last Man, or the Last Grosset [sic], or the last Dew-drop, or the Last Rose of Summer, or the Last Kick to a Cockney, or the Last Pot of Porter, or the Last Long Sermon,—but the class of objects to which they one and all do severally belong, goes off after quite another fashion,— men, grossets, dew-drops, sparks, roses, kicks, and sermons, all perish, not by a consecutive series of deaths, but by simultaneous extinction.

The *Monthly Magazine* (NS 2 (1826): 137–43) approached this subject more generally and more philosophically. In an essay called 'The Last Book: with a Dissertation on Last Things in General', the examples of *The Last of the Mohicans* and *The Lay of the Last Minstrel* are cited, as well as 'Mr. Campbell's prior and poetical candidate' and 'Mrs. Shelley's subsequent and sibylline one' (Mary Shelley's novel *The Last Man* appeared early in 1826). The insufficiency of language in this respect is deplored, and the author argues: 'A term should be invented comprehensive enough to include those superlatively late comers that usually follow the last . . . But, as words are at present, last things are generally the last things in the world that are last'.

The bitterness of the Last Man controversy caused at least one work on the subject not to be written. The acquaintance who Barry Cornwall told Campbell was planning such a work was the young poet Thomas Lovell Beddoes. Beddoes had indeed been projecting a verse play on the Last Man, but, in view of the acrimony Campbell had introduced, he gave it up, at least for the time being. On 25 March 1825 he wrote caustically to his friend Thomas Forbes Kelsall, 'I will do the Last Man before I die . . . Meanwhile let Tom Campbell rule his roast & mortify the ghost of [Thomas] Sternhold: It is a subject for Michael Angelo, not for the painter of the Marquis of Granby on the sign post'.[30] Despite his offhand tone, however, Beddoes had become

---

[30] *The Works of Thomas Lovell Beddoes,* ed. W. H. Donner (London: Oxford University Press, 1935), p. 600. All subsequent quotations from Beddoes are cited from this edition.

almost as preoccupied as Campbell by the question of whose *Last Man* was first. Upon learning that the artist Francis Danby had complained to friends that his idea of painting the Deluge had been appropriated by John Martin, Beddoes compared the situation to 'Campbell and Lord B.', and suggested that Danby, already becoming celebrated as a painter of apocalyptic subjects, ought to paint a Last Man.[31] (In the event, it was Martin who depicted a rather grumpy-looking Last Man brooding over a desolate landscape, exhibiting his painting with lines from Campbell's poem in the accompanying catalogue entry.) When Beddoes learned that Mary Shelley, whom he had met in the spring of 1824, had published her *Last Man*, his response was generous if patriarchal: 'I am very glad', he wrote to Kelsall on 1 April 1826, 'that Mrs. S. has taken it [the Last Man subject] from the New Monthly Fellow [Campbell]—and I am sure that in almost every respect, she will do much better than either of us: indeed she has no business to be a woman by her books'.[32] Despite his seeming to yield the subject, Beddoes did not quite give it up. A memorandum that H. W. Donner conjectured to have been written *c.*1837 shows Beddoes's continued interest, but also displays a confusing variety of possibilities:

Death and the Gods—The last man—to serve Death (whose character is to be new-modelled—see the Devil in Meph.) in some way so that the latter promises not to take his life—After the world is over he goes to heaven and behaves saucily to the Gods—Or make Death a woman and enamoured of Orion the last one &c.[33]

This scenario begins in a manner close to Goethe's *Faust* only to depart disconcertingly into a prefiguration of Jean Cocteau's *Orpheus*. There is a bit of Grainville here (in the idea of Death's vow), nothing of Mary Shelley, but a conclusion much in the vein of *Prometheus Unbound*:

Chorus describing the ruins of Olympus & melancholy Jove—And then a dialogue between the sun, moon, and seven stars about the state of the Earth's health. One of the dramatis personae an incarnation of the world's destruction.

---

[31] Letter postmarked 7 Mar. 1826, in *Works*, p. 615. On Danby's allegations, see Paley, *The Apocalyptic Sublime* (New Haven and London: Yale University Press, 1986), pp. 177–8.
[32] Letter of 1 Apr. 1826, in *Works*, p. 618. Mrs Shelley was a friend of Beddoes, and in her *Last Man* quotes some lines of his *Bride's Tragedy*.
[33] Beddoes, *Works*, pp. 525–6.

Some of the passages intended for Beddoes's *Last Man* went into his *Death's Jest-Book*, while others remained in manuscript.[34] It is clear that this Last Man would have been cosmic in scope and stamped with Beddoes's characteristically macabre irony; but, apart from that, these fragments do not give any coherent idea of what the whole would have been like. Beddoes seems to have been deterred from working up his play because the subject had become controversial, over-familiar, and even ludicrous.

In January 1826 Mary Shelley's novel *The Last Man* was published by Henry Colburn. Now there were at least four Last Men, not counting the one hidden in Beddoes's manuscript. Burlesques of the theme began to proliferate, and since Last Man narratives share certain common characteristics, it is sometimes hard to tell which author or authors a writer may have had in mind. Early in 1826 *Blackwood's* (19 (1826): 284–6) printed a sketch entitled 'The Last Man' in which the narrator awakens (both Byron's 'Darkness' and Campbell's 'Last Man' involve dream visions) to find himself in a cave (the source of revelation in both Grainville's and Mary Shelley's novels). He sees a desolate landscape that seems to combine elements of all Last Man narratives: 'I looked around on that inclosed glen as far as my eye could reach, but all was dark and dreary, all seemed alike hastening to decay. The rocks had fallen in huge fragments, and among these fragments appeared large roots and decayed trunks of trees.' The sun appears 'a dark round orb of reddish flame', exhibiting 'the symptoms of decay and dissolution'. On finding himself alone on earth, the narrator is driven to a paroxysm of despair by 'thoughts of never-ending darkness and cold', but then 'I gave one wild shriek—one convulsive struggle—and awoke—and there stood my man John, with my shaving-jug in the one hand, and my well-cleaned boots in the other—his mouth open, and his eyes rolling hideously at thus witnessing the frolics of his staid and quiet master'. The appearance of quotidian John saves the author not only from being the last man but also from continuing his attempt to convey the state of lastness.

Other authors base their satire upon deflections in which a play upon 'Last' comes to the rescue. In 'The Last Man in Town', published in the *Literary Souvenir for 1830*, the narrator is condemned to stay in London in July when all polite society has gone to the country.[35] He

---

[34] See Letter to Kelsall postmarked 27 Feb. 1829, in *Works*, p. 642. Donner (ibid., pp. 236–53) identifies four manuscript fragments of 1823–5.

[35] *The Literary Souvenir for 1830* (London: Longman, Rees, Orme, Browne, and Green, 1829), pp. 183–92.

wanders through a city abandoned by the upper classes (Kensington Gardens echoes to 'no gentle footsteps', opera rows are untenanted, even Almack's is about to close), which may be intended as a parallel to the desolate London of Mary Shelley's novel, although *Omegarus and Syderia* and John Wilson's verse drama *The City of the Plague*[36] also have descriptions of deserted cities. The piece is prefixed by the lines

> The last—the last—the last!
> Oh, by that little word
> How many thoughts are stirred!

One senses that, by this time, the subject had become more or less exhausted.

Among these divers parodies and lampoons, Thomas Hood's poem 'The Last Man' has a special status. Published in Hood's *Whims and Oddities*,[37] it displays no strong resemblance to its predecessors, though as a literary journalist and editor in London, Hood was no doubt familiar with all of them.[38] Somewhat archly he compares the two drawings he made to accompany his poem with Byron's 'Darkness', hoping 'that his sketches may look interesting, like Lord Byron's Sleeper,—"with all their errors"'.[39] His 'Last Man' is not a parody of anything except, possibly, itself. Its theme may perhaps be taken from an aphorism in La Bruyère's *Les Caractères de Théophraste*: 'Je suppose qu'il n'y ait que deux hommes sur la terre, qui la possèdent seuls, et qui la partagent toute entr'eux deux: je suis persuadé qu'il leur naître bientôt quelque sujet de rupture, quand ce ne serait pour les limites'.[40] Hood's treatment of the theme is jaunty. His speaker is by trade a hangman, and the poem begins on (literally) a note of gallows humour:

> 'Twas in the year two thousand and one,
> A pleasant morning of May,
> I sat on the gallows-tree, all alone,

[36] John Wilson, *The City of the Plague and other Poems* (Edinburgh: Constable, 1816).

[37] Thomas Hood, *Whims and Oddities* (London: Lupton, Rolfe, 1826), pp. 23–32.

[38] Hood knew about Mary Shelley's *Last Man*, for he mentions it in an early, unpublished version of his 'Ode to Malthus' in Feb. 1826. See *Selected Poems of Thomas Hood*, ed. John Clubbe (Cambridge, Mass.: Harvard University Press, 1970), p. 353.

[39] Hood, *Whims and Oddities*, p. ix.

[40] Jean de La Bruyère, *Les Caractères de Théophraste*, in *Oeuvres complètes*, ed. Julian Benda (Paris: Pléiade, 1975), p. 164. ('I suppose that there are only two men on earth, who possess it alone, and who share it all between them; I am persuaded that there will arise between them some subject of conflict, be it only for the sake of [establishing] limits.') Walter Jerrold first noted this resemblance, in his edition of Hood's *Poetical Works* (London: Oxford University Press, 1906), p. 738.

A chaunting a merry lay,—
To think how the pest had spared my life,
To sing with the larks that day!

But the hangman is not allowed to enjoy his lastness for long. Up comes a beggar, 'his old duds / All abroad in the wind, like flags' (9–10). Obviously, there can't be two Last Men; the situation could almost be viewed as an allegorization of Campbell's claim for his poem. The hangman is consumed with rage toward this co-survivor who keeps him from being 'King of the earth', and he broods until the obvious recourse presents itself. He practices his trade upon the only available candidate. For a moment he feels triumphant: 'So there he hung, and there I stood, / The LAST MAN left alive'. Pursued by wild dogs and haunted in dreams by the beggar man, the hangman passes, ironically, to self-pity: 'But I never felt so lone!' At the end of the poem he is depicted as a drunkard longing for his own death, a sufferer from what might be called terminal Lastness.

As we can see, in the literary atmosphere of 1826 any reasonable critical evaluation of a serious work on the theme of the Last Man was not to be expected. The threatening nature of the subject combined with the defensive strategies of critics and journalists had made this impossible. It comes, then, as no surprise that Mary Shelley's *The Last Man* was attacked by the reviewers. As I have discussed this subject elsewhere,[41] one example will suffice here. In reviewing Hood's *Whims and Oddities*, *Blackwood's Edinburgh Magazine* (21 (1827): 45–60) contrasted the poem, which it printed in full, with the novel. 'Had the verses been published two years ago, they surely would have saved Mrs. Shelley from the perpetration of her stupid cruelties', wrote the anonymous critic. Hood's poem was worth 'five hundred of Mrs. Shelly's [*sic*] abortion' (p. 54). Of course, praising Hood's comic-grotesque poem was in itself a way of disparaging the Last Man theme, and the rhetorical overkill, typical of the reviews of Shelley's novel, seems yet another attempt to erase the conception of Lastness. Later in the nineteenth century, several minor writers attempted their own versions of the Last Man,[42] but these achieved no wide readership. Even had mediocre works such as T. J. Ouseley's poem 'The Last Man' (1833), George

---

[41] Morton D. Paley, '*The Last Man*: Apocalypse without Millennium', in *The Other Mary Shelley: Beyond Frankenstein*, ed. Audrey A. Fisch, Anne Mellor, and Esther H. Schor (New York and Oxford: Oxford University Press, 1993), pp. 107–23.

[42] See Miller, 'The Last Man', pp. 238–58.

Dibdin Pitt's play *The Last Man* (1833), and Edward Wallace's *The Last Man: A Poem in Three Cantos* (1839) been considerably better than they were, it remains unlikely that they would have escaped the fate of their predecessors. The reviewers had succeeded in protecting readers from imagining lastness by making the Last Man a ridiculous subject. *Omegarus and Syderia* was forgotten; Beddoes's play remained unwritten; Campbell's poem was derided; Mary Shelley was apprehensive that the failure of her novel might cause Henry Colburn to reject her next work; and Byron's 'Darkness' long remained one of the least discussed of his major poems.

Mysteries

'What think you of Lord Byrons last Volume?', Percy Bysshe Shelley asked John Gisborne in a letter dated 26 January 1822. 'In my opinion it contains finer poetry than has appeared in England since the publication of Paradise Regained—Cain is apocalyptic—it is a revelation not before communicated to man.'[43] Shelley was in this respect Byron's ideal audience as Cain is Lucifer's, for each is in quest of apocalyptic knowledge (though it must be said that in his evaluation of the knowledge actually gained, Cain is the more realistic of the two). When Cain first encounters Lucifer, he immediately begins asking questions. Their dialogue soon assumes the form of question and answer much like that between Asia and Demogorgon in the previously completed *Prometheus Unbound*.

> CAIN. And ye?
> LUCIFER.   Are everlasting.
> CAIN.   Are ye happy?
> LUCIFER. We are mighty.
> CAIN.   Are ye happy?
> LUCIFER.   No: art thou?[44]

Like Demogorgon, Lucifer doesn't really answer the questions, although, unlike Demogorgon, he is motivated by bad faith. Cain's last question (136) 'And what is that [you are]?' prompts Lucifer's long pseudo-Promethean speech (137–66), making God seem very much like Blake's Urizen 'on his vast and solitary throne' (147–8). Then, in his

---

[43] Shelley, *Letters of Percy Bysshe Shelley*, ed. F. L. Jones (2 vols., Oxford: Clarendon Press, 1964), 2: 388.   [44] Byron, *Cain*, I. i. 121–2.

next speech (196–205), in which Lucifer shrewdly echoes Cain's words from lines 36–7 and 72–4, he also reverses the situation and becomes the questioner, well knowing the answers he will elicit and the further questions from Cain these will generate. Questions remain important controlling structures throughout this part of the play.

At first Cain's motive may seem simply a resolute quest for knowledge. 'But thou canst not', he tells Lucifer,

> Speak aught of knowledge which I would not know,
> And do not thirst to know, and bear a mind
> To know.[45]

He can also appear a Romantic over-reacher. Early in their journey through space, he replies to Lucifer's 'wouldst thou be as I am?' with:

> I know not what thou art: I see thy power,
> And see thou show'st me things beyond *my* power,
> Beyond all power of my born faculties,
> Although inferior still to my desires
> And my conceptions.[46]

This is a Faustian Cain; although, as is well known, Byron denied having read *Faust* at this time, he had read Mme. de Staël's *De l'Allemagne*, which contains a detailed account of *Faust*, in 1813 and he had heard Matthew Lewis read aloud some of his own translation of it in 1816.[47] What is truly characteristic of Cain's desire is his willingness to risk destruction for an unmediated perception of the ultimate. When Cain wants to see the dwellings of God and of Lucifer, Lucifer sneers in his 'Manichean' vein:

> Thy human mind hath scarcely grasp to gather
> The little I have shown thee into calm
> And clear thought; and *thou* wouldst go on aspiring
> To the great double Mysteries! the *two Principles*!
> And gaze upon them on their secret thrones!
> Dust! limit thy ambition; for to see
> Either of these, would be for thee to perish![48]

---

[45] Byron, *Cain*, I. i. 246–9.   [46] II. i. 79–83.

[47] See Byron, *The Complete Poetical Works*, vol. 6, ed. Jerome J. McGann and Barry Weller (Oxford: Clarendon Press, 1991), p. 651; and Philip W. Martin, *Byron: A Poet before His Public* (Cambridge: Cambridge University Press, 1982), pp. 125–6. However, it is not my purpose here to enter the well-trodden ground of Byron's sources unless they particularly concern the apocalyptic or millennial.

[48] II. ii. 401–7. Once more, I assume that Byron's use of supposed Manichean doctrines is a familiar subject. For a succinct summary, see Truman Guy Steffan, *Lord Byron's Cain:*

Cain's reply is that of the resolute apocalyptist: 'And let me perish, so I see them!' (408). However, his quest, in this, as in so many other things, is thwarted by his guide, with 'That sight is for the other state' (410). Before the sacrifice in Act III, Cain, as described by Abel, is transformed in a way very reminiscent of Coleridge's 'Kubla Khan':

> Thine eyes are flashing with unnatural light—
> Thy cheek is flush'd with an unnatural hue—
> Thy words are fraught with an unnatural sound—[49]

Byron had been instrumental in getting 'Kubla Khan' published by John Murray, and here he is evidently recalling 'And all should cry, Beware! Beware! / His flashing eyes, His floating hair!'[50] Interestingly, Cain shares this power of the eye with Lucifer; 'in his eye', says Adah, 'There is a fascinating attraction which / Fixes my fluttering eyes on his' (I. i. 409–11, p. 896). However, it is a power that serves different ends: for Lucifer, it establishes his domination, but for Cain, even as we approach the tragic moment of his crime, it is the non-volitional power of the apocalyptic visionary.

It is of course on their journey through space that Lucifer offers, or seems to offer, what Shelley called a revelation not before communicated to man. Exploiting the accordion-like nature of Time, Lucifer asserts 'we / Can crowd eternity into an hour, / Or stretch an hour into eternity'.[51] Although it has been suggested that Byron may have been following Shelley's *Queen Mab* here, both were probably following Volney's *Ruins*. Shelley was true to the optimistic spirit of his source, which leads to a vast conclave of humanity assembled for the purpose of discovering truth, while Byron recontextualizes it to suit his purpose. Lucifer's invitation to Cain appears to be very much in the spirit of Volney's voyage of instruction.:

> but fly with me o'er the gulf
> Of space an equal flight, and I will show
> What thou dar'st not deny, the history
> Of past, and present, and of future worlds.[52]

Twelve Essays and a Text with Variants and Annotations (Austin, Tex., and London: University of Texas Press, 1968), pp. 262–3.

[49] III. i. 185–7, p. 927.   [50] *CPW* 1: 298, ll. 49–50.

[51] I. i. 535–7, p. 900. The resemblance to Blake's 'Hold . . . Eternity in an hour' ('Auguries of Innocence', E 490) must be due either to coincidence or to an unknown common source.

[52] II. i. 22–5, *Byron*, p. 90. See Steffan, *Lord Byron's Cain*, pp. 301–2.

Early in Volney's *Ruins*, the narrator reports his encounter with a
Phantom or Genius, who promises, 'I will unfold to thy view that truth
thou invokest; I will teach thy reason the wisdom thou seekest; I will
reveal to thee the wisdom of the tombs and the science of ages'.[53]
'Suddenly', the narrator continues, 'a celestial flame seemed to dissolve
the bands which held us to the earth; and like a light vapour, borne up
on the wings of Genius, I felt myself wafted to the regions above'. Once
in outer space, Cain exclaims:

> Can it be?
> Yon small blue circle, swinging in far ether,
> With an inferior circlet near it still,
> Which looks like that which lit our earthly night?
> Is this our Paradise?[54]

'Under my feet', says Volney's narrator, 'floating in the void, a globe
like that of the moon, but less large and less luminous, presented to me
one of its phases; and that phase had the aspect of a disk dappled with
large spots'. The Genius tells him, 'They are the seas and continents . . .
and those of the very hemisphere which you inhabit'.[55] The source as
a mere fact is, as usual, not very important in Byron; but the parallel
raises expectations in the reader that will deliberately be left unfulfilled.

The world that Lucifer shows Cain is 'The phantasm of the world; of
which thy world / Is but the wreck'.[56] The idea of an anti-world can give
scope for the play of imagination, as in Vladimir Nabokov's brilliant
Ada, and it can allow the exploration of alternate possibilities, as in
Shelley's *Prometheus Unbound*:

> For know, there are two worlds of life and death:
> One that which thou beholdest, but the other
> Is underneath the grave, where do inhabit
> The shadows of all forms that think and live
> Till death unite them, and they part no more;
> Dreams and the light imaginings of men
> And all that faith creates, or love desires,
> Terrible, strange, sublime, and beauteous shapes.[57]

---

[53] Constantin-François Chasseboeuf, comte de Volney, *A New Translation of Volney's* Ruins,
with an introduction by Robert D. Richardson, Jr. (2 vols., New York and London: Garland,
1979), 1: 26. The text is a reprint of an edition published in Paris in 1802. According to Richardson (p. vii), the new translation was begun by Thomas Jefferson and finished by Joel Barlow.
[54] II. i. 28–32, p. 902.   [55] *Volney's* Ruins, 1: 27.   [56] II. i. 152–3, p. 902.
[57] I. 195–202, in *Shelley's Poetry and Prose*, ed. Donald H. Reiman and Sharon B. Pavers
(New York and London: W. W. Norton, 1977), p. 141.

A plurality of worlds implies a plurality of Edens, with, Lucifer's hints, other serpents in them (72–3), answering (in a way) both Cain's question and Thomas Paine's 'Are we to suppose that every world, in the boundless creation, had an Eve, an apple, a serpent, and a redeemer?'[58] The particular world they approach has much in common with the earth of Byron's 'Darkness':

> CAIN.   'Tis a fearful light!
> No sun, no moon, no lights innumerable.
> The very blue of the empurpled night
> Fades to a dreary twilight . . . .
>
>   . . . .
> All here seems dark and dreadful.[59]

As they approach the gates of Hades, Lucifer cries 'Behold!' and Cain responds, 'Tis darkness'.[60] Thus, self-referentially, Byron leads them into a ruined world.

In his Preface to *Cain*, Byron calls attention to the fact that 'the author has partly adopted in this poem, the notion of Cuvier, that the world had been destroyed several times before the creation of man'.[61] This adaptation of, to use Stephen Jay Gould's terms, Time's Cycle in preference to Time's Arrow,[62] consistent with Byron's pessimistic interpretation of history, enables the poet to invest with scientific prestige the idea of cyclical recurrence. Baron Cuvier's geological work was indeed based upon field research, including the evidence of fossils. In the first English edition of his *Essay on the Theory of the Earth*, Cuvier presents himself almost as the editor and translator of a hitherto unknown text, 'obliged to learn the art of deciphering and restoring those remains, of discovering and bringing together . . . the scattered and mutilated fragments of which they are composed'.[63] It is interesting that Cuvier frequently uses the term 'revolutions', while disclaiming any political parallel, in describing his project of 'collecting, amidst the darkness which covers the infancy of the globe, the traces of those revolutions which took place anterior to the existence of all nations'.[64] This creates an involuntary parallel with Volney in statements proving

---

[58] Thomas Paine, *The Age of Reason* (London: Daniel Isaac Eaton, 1794), p. 46.
[59] II. i. 177–80, 190, p. 906.   [60] II. i. 196, p. 907.   [61] *Byron*, p. 882.
[62] Stephen Jay Gould, *Time's Arrow, Time's Cycle: Myth and Metaphor in the Discovery of Geological Time* (London: Penguin, 1991).
[63] Baron Cuvier, *Essay on the Theory of the Earth*, trans. Robert Kerr, introduction and notes by Professor Robert Jameson (Edinburgh, 1813), pp. 1–2.
[64] Ibid., p. 3.

'that such Revolutions have been numerous'. In describing his project, Cuvier can even sound like Byron's Lucifer: 'Would it not also be glorious to burst the limits of time, and, by a few observations, to ascertain the history of this world, and the series of events which preceded the birth of the human race?'[65] Our species is, however, exempted but Byron circumvents this by remarking, 'The assertion of Lucifer, that the pre-adamite word was also peopled by rational beings much more intelligent than man, and proportionately powerful to the mammoth, etc., etc., is of course a poetical fiction to help him to make out his case'.[66]

However, the pre-Adamites do not exist merely in Lucifer's discourse. Cain describes them as 'mighty phantoms' that do not 'wear the form of man', but are 'mighty yet and beautiful'.[67] As has been recognized, here Byron is following not Cuvier but the marvellous fantasy of William Beckford's *Vathek*, where, in the Halls of Eblis, the caliph encounters the pre-Adamite sultans.

A funereal gloom prevailed over the whole scene. Here, upon two beds of incorruptible cedar, lay recumbent the fleshless forms of the pre-Adamite kings, who had been monarchs of the whole earth. They still possessed enough of life to be conscious of their deplorable condition. Their eyes retained a melancholy motion; they regarded one another with looks of the deepest dejection, each holding his right hand, motionless, on his heart.[68]

As Byron knew, Cuvier had found no human bones in a fossil state.[69] There is one curious aspect to Cuvier's argument, for he does speculate about a possible exception. 'He [man]', Cuvier writes,

may have then inhabited some narrow regions, whence he went forth to repeople the earth after the cessation of those terrible revolutions and overwhelmings. Perhaps even the places which he then inhabited may have been sunk into the abyss, and the bones of that destroyed human race may yet remain buried under the bottom of some actual seas; all except a small number of individuals who were destined to continue the species.[70]

Cuvier chooses not to pursue this possibility, which is not to be confused with the Deluge of 5,000 or 6,000 years ago, which he does

---

[65] Baron, Cuvier, *Essay on the Theory of the Earth*, p. 4.   [66] *Byron*, pp. 882–3.
[67] II. i. 43–62, pp. 908–9.
[68] William Beckford, *Vathek*, in *Three Gothic Novels*, ed. Peter Fairclough with an introduction by Mario Praz (Harmondsworth: Penguin, 1970), pp. 247–8. On the link with *Vathek*, see McGann and Weller's note in *Complete Poetical Works*, 6: 655.
[69] Cuvier, *Essay on the Theory of the Earth*, pp. 127–8. Cuvier makes it clear that he does not refer to remains in peat deposits or turf bogs.   [70] Ibid., p. 131.

proceed to discuss, and which will become Byron's subject in *Heaven and Earth*. In *Cain*, he followed Cuvier's view that there were no fossilized human remains, and he wrote to Thomas Moore, 'I have, therefore, supposed Cain to be shown, in the *rational* Preadamites, beings endowed with a higher intelligence than man, but totally unlike him in form, and with much greater strength of mind and person'.[71] These beings are described by Cain in terms of what they are not:

> They bear not
> The wing of seraph, nor the face of man,
> Nor form of mightiest brute, nor aught that is
> Now breathing; mighty yet and beautiful
> As the most beautiful and mighty which
> Live, and yet so unlike them, that I scarce
> Can call them living.[72]

Byron may here be thinking of Cuvier's assertion that mythological monsters are not to be found in nature. 'We might as well endeavour to find the animals of Daniel, or the beasts of the Apocalypse, in some hitherto unexplored recesses of the globe,' he wrote.[73] The poem could not go against this and remain *au courant*, for, although the anti-world is not earth, it is an exhibition hall for what once existed on earth. The pre-Adamites can be described only in terms of what they are not, just as at the end of 'Darkness' the earth is described only in terms of what it is not.

Cuvier's catastrophist theory leaves no room for a millennium, for the 'revolutions' he describes are, as the term he chooses implies, cyclical; and he explicitly rejects the notion, endorsed by Burnet and so attractive to millenarians like Shelley, that slow motions such as changes in the ecliptic could be the source of the dramatic changes— 'those revolutions and catastrophes'—of which the earth's crust bears testimony.[74] Of course Byron had not been converted to this view by Cuvier. What he found in the *Essay on the Theory of the Earth* appeared to be scientific confirmation of his deeply held conviction that the millennial was either a fraud or a fantasy. What of the apocalyptic? The veil has indeed been lifted for Cain, but with the result that he is 'sick of all / That dust has shown me' (II. ii. 109–10). Lucifer insists, 'thou now

---

[71] Letter of 19 Sept. 1821, in *Byron's Letters and Journals*, 8: 215–16; see McGann and Weller's note in *Complete Poetical Works*, 6: 660.

[72] II. ii. 56–62, p. 909.

[73] Cuvier, *Essay on the Theory of the Earth*, p. 75.   [74] Ibid., p. 37.

beholdest as / A vision that which is reality' (107–8), but it is hard for the reader not to sympathize with Cain's complaint that he has not gained knowledge of the ultimate (172). To fob him off, Lucifer shows him the earthly globe in space, with 'The past leviathans' (190) and an immense serpent with a 'dripping mane' (191). Cain is now in the situation of the narrator Blake watching, with the Angel, the approach of Leviathan in *The Marriage of Heaven and Hell*, but there is no political-psychological meaning here, just a conjuror's trick, much like the entertainment that Mephistopheles provides for Faust in Marlowe's *Dr. Faustus* (which Byron had not, according to his own statement, read[75]). The knowledge Cain has achieved has only the effect that Lucifer—and Byron—intended: 'Alas! I seem /Nothing' (420–1).

Reunited with Adah and the sleeping Enoch at the beginning of Act III, Cain has a momentary glimpse of the microcosm of the millennium offered by domestic life, as we have seen, at certain points in the works of Blake, Coleridge, and Wordsworth. 'Why wilt thou always mourn for Paradise?', Adah asks. 'Can we not make another?' (37–8). But such a possibility is not allowed, any more than is the larger alternative of Eden's being proleptic of life on earth in an imagined future. Cain must inexorably go on to utter his surly prayer, to see his 'shrine without victim' (266) overthrown by a meat-eating God, and to discover his identity, as Leonard Michaels aptly puts it, 'as none other than Cain, the infamous Biblical murderer'.[76] 'That which I am, I am', he says, anticipating God's words 'I AM THAT I AM' to Moses in Exodus 3: 14 and contrasting with Lucifer's evasive 'I seem that which I am' (II. i. 88). Authenticity has been Cain's hallmark throughout, and he bears it with him eastward from Eden at the end of the poem. Yet he is diminished not merely by his transgression but by the demands of the scenario. The quester for ultimate knowledge, the furious rebel, has become an anguished, guilt-possessed man, as the story demands he must. This is not a fault in this wonderfully concentrated work. Exploring the limits of the apocalyptic, and free of the potential pitfalls in attempting to connect with the millennial, *Cain* also demonstrates just how far apocalypse can be taken without its complement. Taking it further incurs the risk of mere reiteration, as if 'Darkness' could have a sequel.

A sequel, however, is what Byron attempted to provide, in *Heaven and Earth*, like *Cain* subtitled *A Mystery*. 'Mystery' to Byron meant, as he

---

[75] See letter to John Murray, 12 Oct. 1817, in *Byron's Letters and Journals*, 5: 268.
[76] Leonard Michaels, 'Byron's Cain', *PMLA* 84 (1969): 71.

explained to John Murray, 'a tragedy on a sacred subject'.[77] (Although Byron could have read some of the mystery plays, there is nothing to indicate that he did.[78]) Written in October 1821, just a month following the completion of *Cain*, *Heaven and Earth* incorporated an important aspect of Cuvier's theories that had not received much attention in the earlier play, and it also capitalized on Richard Laurence's recent translation into English of the apocryphal Book of Enoch.[79] Byron called the reader's attention to the original in a note regarding his reference to 'The scroll of Enoch' in scene iii, line 275: 'The Book of Enoch, preserved by the Ethiopians, is said by them to be anterior to the Flood'.[80] As E. H. Coleridge observes, a fragment of the Book of Enoch, 'Concerning the Watchers', was published by J. J. Scaliger in 1606, and in this fragment appear the names of the two seraphs of Byron's poem, Semjâzâ and Azâzêl, as well as Raphael.[81] Byron may have been interested in the Book of Enoch's account of the angels' lubricity, more detailed than the two terse lines of Genesis 6: 1–2, but there is no evidence that he had read Laurence's translation; nor did he claim to have done so.

Cuvier, however, is another matter, for the *Essay on the Theory of the Earth* once again gave scientific sanction to Byron's imagination of disaster. Cuvier was a diluvian, which is to say that he was a catastrophist of a special sort: he denied the importance of volcanic eruptions in making profound changes to the earth's crust but posited a series of floods, coming round in what Gould terms 'Time's Cycle'. 'All nations', Cuvier wrote, 'which possess any records or ancient traditions, uniformly declare that they have been recently renewed, after a grand revolution in nature.'[82] The biblical Flood Cuvier calculates to have occurred 'rather less than five thousand years before the present day', and the countries left dry afterwards 'had been formerly

---

[77] Letter dated 10 Sept. 1821, in *Byron's Letters and Journals*, 8: 205.

[78] McGann and Weller (*Complete Poetical Works*, 6: 653), note that the Chester and Coventry cycles had been published by Byron's time. Philip W. Martin suggests that Byron may have read about the Mysteries in Thomas Warton's *History of English Poetry* and Robert Dodsley's commentary in *A Select Collection of Old Plays*, and he points out that both these sources stress the licentiousness of these dramas. See *Byron, A Poet Before His Public*, p. 165.

[79] *The Book of Enoch the Prophet*, trans. Richard Laurence (Oxford: Oxford University Press, 1821).

[80] *Heaven and Earth*, in *Complete Poetical Works*, 6: 362, 687. Further references to *Heaven and Earth* are to this edition.

[81] See Coleridge, ed., *Works of Lord Byron*, 5: 279–82, 303. Byron calls the seraphs Samiasa and Azaziel.

[82] Cuvier, *Essay on the Theory of the Earth*, p. 164.

inhabited at a more remote era, if not by men, at least by land animals'.[83] Despite that 'if not', Cuvier makes it clear that humans were victims of the previous Deluge:

In order to discover some truly historical traces of the last grand *cataclysma*, or universal deluge, we must go beyond the vast deserts of Tartary, where in the north-east of our ancient continent, we meet with a race of men differing entirely from us, as much in their manners and customs, as in their form and constitution.[84]

Curiously, this was precisely the view of Emanuel Swedenborg, according to whom 'that ancient Word, which was in Asia before the Israelitish Word' was 'still preserved among the people who live in Great Tartary'.[85] Byron would not have been impressed by any view of Swedenborg's, but he seized upon Cuvier's, featuring, for example, the fossil evidence for the Deluge in the Chorus's lines in scene iii, lines 238–40.

The wave shall break upon your [the mountains'] cliffs; and shells,
    The little shells, of ocean's least things be
    Deposed where now the eagle's offspring dwells—

John Martin would incorporate this detail in *The Eve of the Deluge*, one of a triad of paintings deeply influenced by Byron's poem,[86] by showing sea creatures left on a mountain side by receding waters.

Byron distinguished his second Mystery from its predecessor by referring to it in a letter to John Murray as an 'Oratorio'[87] and by writing to Douglas Kinnaird, 'It is *choral* and mystical—and a sort of Oratorio on a sacred subject'.[88] *Heaven and Earth* does at its very best exhibit oratorio-like characteristics, as when the Chorus of Spirits presents the Deluge as the undoing of the Creation: 'The fountains of the great deep shall be broken, /And heaven set wide her windows' (iii. 490–1). Again, when in iii. 883–4 the voice of a 'A Mortal' emerges from the Chorus of Mortals with 'Blessed are the dead / Who die in the Lord'—a quotation from Revelation 14: 13[89]—there is the sense of a

[83] Cuvier, *Essay on the Theory of the Earth*, pp. 148, 172.   [84] Ibid., p. 159.
[85] Emanuel Swedenborg, *True Christian Religion*, trans. John Clowes (London, 1781), nos. 265 and 278. Swedenborg also asserts that these people possess three lost books of the Old Testament.   [86] See Paley, *Apocalyptic Sublime*, pp. 140–1.
[87] Letter of 24 Oct. 1822, in *Byron's Letters and Journals*, 10: 18.
[88] Letter of 14 Dec. 1821, ibid. 9: 81.
[89] 'And I heard a voice from heaven saying unto me, Write, Blessed are the dead which die in the Lord from henceforth . . .'.

soloist and a massed choir. Such moments are unfortunately few. Much of the rhyming is slipshod, as in 'All shall be void, /Destroy'd' (iii. 94–5), which Matthew Arnold singled out for derision.[90] There is a failure of imagination in lines like these, and there are a great many of them in *Heaven and Earth*. Byron attempts to bring in the type of anti-millennium he had exploited in 'Darkness' with another parody of Isaiah's vision:

> . . . even the brutes, in their despair,
> Shall cease to prey on man and on each other,
> And the striped tiger shall lie down to die
> Beside the lamb as though he were his brother[91]

The reprise of 'Darkness' continues with Japhet's address to the fading sun:

> The sun! the sun!
> He riseth, but his better light is gone;
> And a black circle, bound
> His glaring disk around,
> Proclaims earth's last of summer days hath shone![92]

These details seem merely mechanical here. *Heaven and Earth* is merely a disaster scenario, and the sequel that Byron envisaged[93] appears even less promising. Perhaps Byron relied too much on a general sense that, as a *Blackwood's* reviewer wrote of Thomas Moore's *Loves of the Angels*, 'Everything antediluvian is poetical. The flood washed away a world from life into imagination.'[94] The diluvial is indeed first cousin to the apocalyptic, but the failure of millennium to follow apocalypse, brilliantly exploited in 'Darkness', has a second-hand feeling in *Heaven and Earth*; and the failure of Cain to be helped by the revelation he receives could not be a feature of the sequel. Taken together, these three works exemplify both the possibilities and the limitations of the theme of apocalypse without millennium.

---

[90] See Andrew Rutherford, ed., *Byron: The Critical Heritage* (London: Routledge and Kegan Paul, 1970), p. 449.

[91] iii. 177–80.   [92] iii. 738–42.

[93] According to Tom Medwin, it would have involved interplanetary travel, a return to earth, and a disastrous ending for both the seraphs and their human lovers. See Ernest J. Lovell, Jr. ed., Medwin's *Conversations of Lord Byron* (Princeton: Princeton University Press, 1966), p. 157.

[94] *Blackwood's*, 13 (Jan. 1823): 63.

5

Shelley

Percy Bysshe Shelley's imagination had a virtually lifelong engagement with apocalypse and millennium, and some of the poems written near the beginning of his career anticipate the deep commitment to these themes that marks his later poetry. The tone of some of these early poems can be difficult to establish. At times they are in the vein of Coleridge's apocalyptic grotesque; at other times they insist stridently upon their seriousness of purpose. Veering from sardonic *diablerie* to erotic fantasy to near-hysterical (or pseudo-hysterical) Gothicism, some of these also show Shelley's desire to forge links with the radicalism of the previous generation, frequently a strong and important motive in his works. Poems like the *Posthumous Fragments of Margaret Nicholson* and 'The Devil's Walk' can be read as premonitions of what is to come, but they also offer some interest of their own, perhaps in their very willingness to be outrageous.

The *Margaret Nicholson* poems[1] were written in the persona of a woman who had been confined to Bedlam after menacing George III with a knife in 1786 (and who was very much alive when the book was published in 1810). Several of the six poems present unassimilated apocalyptic and millennial elements, beginning with the first, untitled poem, which foretells the end of monarchy at 'the last eventful day' (59)—an ambiguous expression that could refer either to the end of the world or to the outcome of revolution. Full of personifications of Gothic horror like 'giant Fear, / With War, and Woe, and Terror in his train' (68–9), the poem nevertheless ends with a projection of millenarian hope in the form of a murmuring sound that tells:

> That heaven, indignant at the work of hell,
> Will soon the cause, the hated cause remove,
> Which tears from earth peace, innocence, and love.

(86–8)

---

[1] *The Poems of Shelley*, ed. G. M. Matthews and Kelvin Everest (London and New York: Longman, 1989), 1: 113–28.

The polarization of imagery notable in the untitled first poem is also characteristic of the second, which shows a certain brilliance in its conception and title: 'Fragment. Supposed to be an Epithalamium of Francis Ravaillac and Charlotte Cordé'.[2] For example, there is a sharp contrast between the opening passage on 'the ceaseless rage of Kings' (l. 6) envisioned in the murky air at midnight during a thunderstorm and 'Enthroned in roseate light, a heavenly band / Strewed flowers of bliss that never fade away' (37–8). The latter seems somewhere beyond this world, in an unspecified space in which the marriage of Francis and Charlotte takes place. Just as sharply contrastive are the passages in which Satan welcomes despots to Hell (60–8) and those in which Francis and Charlotte's 'endless night' (101) of love making is evoked. Of the six poems, 'The Spectral Horseman'[3] is the one with the most intensely apocalyptic elements. 'A white courser bears the shadowy sprite' (28) anticipates the figure of Anarchy riding a white horse 'like Death in the Apocalypse' in *The Mask of Anarchy*[4] (30–3); and the 'dragon, who chained in the caverns / To eternity' (47–8), though from Irish mythology, inescapably recalls 'the dragon, that old serpent' who is 'bound for a thousand years', during which the millennium will take place in Revelation 20: 2. These apocalyptic and millennial elements in *Posthumous Fragments of Margaret Nicholson* are not set in any relation to each other. They are nevertheless pronounced, giving an idea of certain aspects of the Shelleyan imagination that will later find more fully defined expression.

Another early poem that in some ways foreshadows *The Mask of Anarchy* is 'The Devil's Walk', written in Keswick in late December 1811 or early January 1812 after Shelley's encounter with Robert Southey there. Shelley was in Keswick by early November 1811, and stayed for about three months; he had met Southey by 26 December. Despite their political differences, Shelley was at first impressed by what seemed to him Southey's conscientiousness, regarding him as 'an advocate of liberty and equality', but by the following January he wrote that Southey had lost his good opinion.[5] In the mean time, Southey did his best to act as (to use his own word) Shelley's 'physician' and to cure his philosophical and political maladies.[6] Regarding Shelley as 'just

[2] Ibid. 1: 117–22.   [3] Ibid. 1: 125–7.

[4] See *Shelley's Poetry and Prose*, ed. Donald H. Reiman and Sharon B. Powers (New York and London: Norton, 1977), p. 302.

[5] Letters to Elizabeth Hitchener, 26 Dec. 1811 and ?16 Jan. 1812; *Letters of Percy Bysshe Shelley*, ed. F. L. Jones (2 vols., Oxford: Clarendon Press, 1964), 1: 211 and 1: 233.

[6] Ibid. 1: 219 n. 10.

what I was in 1794', Southey evidently tried to impress him with the resemblance by showing the young poet a production partly his own from the radical 1790s—'The Devil's Thoughts'.

'The Devil's Thoughts', to the original of which Southey had contributed only four stanzas, had been appropriated and greatly expanded by him over a period of years. He was continuing to revise the poem as late as 1826, when he wrote to Caroline Bowles that 'It now contains 49 stanzas, 30 of which have now been added, and 4 of the others since it was first written and printed',[7] and the version he published in 1838 had fifty-seven stanzas.[8] The fact that 'The Devil's Walk' first appears in draft form in a letter sent by Shelley from Keswick[9] strongly suggests that Southey had read or shown him the earlier poem, or an amplified version of it. (Similarly, Shelley sent Elizabeth Hitchener a transcription from memory of parts of Wordsworth's 'A Poet's Epitaph', following a long account of a conversation with Southey.[10]) If Southey thought 'The Devil's Thoughts' would strike a responsive chord, he was correct: 'I was once rather fond of the Devil', wrote Shelley in introducing his own poem.[11]

What text of Coleridge's poem would Shelley have seen? Southey had made a rough draft (BM Add. MS 47887, fols. 6–8), which is now in the British Museum along with some of his expanded drafts, and a fair copy (University of Rochester). Even in its greatly expanded form, the poem maintains the point of view of the Devil throughout, and the mode remains ironic. It has been observed that some details included by Shelley, such as the Devil's walking into London, are present in Southey's longer poem but not in the original.[12] Interestingly, Southey presents Richard Brothers at this point:

> He walk'd into London leisurely,
> The streets were dirty and dim:
> But there he saw Brothers the Prophet,
> And Brothers the Prophet saw him.[13]

As we have seen earlier, Southey showed considerable interest in Brothers and some of his followers in *Letters from England*, and he adds a

[7] *New Letters of Robert Southey*, ed. Kenneth Curran (2 vols., New York and London: Columbia University Press, 1965), 2: 308.

[8] *Poetical Works of Robert Southey* (10 vols., London: Longman, 1837–8), 3: 87–100.

[9] Letter to Elizabeth Hitchener ?16 Jan. 1812; *Letters*, 1: 235–7.

[10] 2 Jan. 1812; *Letters*, 1: 217.

[11] Letter to Elizabeth Hitchener, ?16 Jan. 1812; *Letters*, 1: 235.

[12] See *Poems of Shelley*, 1: 233 n.   [13] Southey, *Poetical Works*, 3: 90.

note here citing the source of the encounter: '"After this I was in a vision, having the angel of God near me, and saw Satan walking leisurely into London"—*Brothers' Prophecies*, part I, p. 41'. It is of course possible that Southey showed Shelley more than one manuscript, for, whatever state Southey's reworking may have reached by 1811–12, it is likely that the older poet would have also produced an early version in order to impress the young man whom he regarded as a version of his useful self. In its economy, the initial poem is certainly more effective, and that kind of economy seems at first to have been what Shelley desired.

The draft of the poem that Shelley was to publish in revised and expanded form under the title 'The Devil's Walk' comprises nine stanzas totalling forty-nine lines—close to the fifty-seven lines of the original 'Devil's Thoughts'. It is close in other ways too. Line 2 of 'The Devil's Thoughts'—'A walking the Devil is gone'—is echoed in Shelley's opening line. Shelley's stanza 5 is mostly plagiarized from the earlier poem's stanza 3. Both poems represent the Devil as a promenading beau and as a gentleman farmer who inspects his livestock with a view to improvement, and both poems satirize religion. As Steven Jones remarks, the indebtedness of Shelley's poem to its source is meant to be seen, to establish a sense of connection.[14] There are also some significant differences. 'The Devil's Thoughts', though shorter, is wider in scope, its attacks extending to taxation, genteel ostentation, booksellers, apothecaries, the military, and especially the prison system. It does not, however, burlesque the monarchy, while 'a Brainless King' is a target for Shelley. In its draft form, 'The Devil's Walk' is a *jeu d'esprit* very much in the manner of 'The Devil's Thoughts' and with similar, though not identical, political motives.

When Shelley expanded the poem to thirty stanzas, he did not much increase the scope of its satirical elements, except to include three stanzas burlesquing the Prince Regent. Here he may possibly have been indebted to another Coleridge poem, the third of the 'Nehemiah Higgenbottom' sonnets that originally appeared in the *Monthly Magazine* for November 1797 (and that would be reprinted in the *Biographia*). Southey, who had once considered himself one of the objects of Coleridge's satire, no doubt had copies. The third sonnet concludes with the image of the knight's 'hindward charms' gleaming through his tattered brogues, like 'the full-orb'd harvest moon' shining through broken clouds;[15] similarly, the Prince's 'pantaloons are like half-moons, / Upon each brawny haunch' (74–5). The satire on the Regent may have followed the lead of Leigh Hunt's *Examiner* article (22 March 1812) insulting the Regent, for which Hunt would be prosecuted and imprisoned.[16] However, most of the new material in the broadside version is not in this comic vein. What made 'The Devil's Thoughts' such a success was its coolness. It scored its points by being genuinely funny, down to the mock apocalypse of the General's florid face at the end. Shelley started out by imitating its method, but when he more than doubled the size of his 'Ballad', most of what he introduced was straightforward rhetorical denunciation and invective that weakened the effect of his satire.

One further point of both resemblance and difference between 'The Devil's Thoughts' and 'The Devil's Walk' is that both were published anonymously—though it was a different kind of anonymity. Coleridge's was a journalistic convention. Much newspaper writing was anonymous or pseudonymous, and the more politically offensive, defamatory, or otherwise contentious a piece, the more likely it was to appear without the author's real name. This might give the author some protection as a private person, but it would not protect him from a government eager to prosecute its critics, as Leigh Hunt learned. The opposition had to stay on the windy side of the law, and radical journalists became expert at doing so. Anonymity in the case of Shelley's broadside was another matter. The lack of any name at all on a publication was *de facto* actionable, even had it not abused the sovereign and the Prince Regent. Great care had therefore to be taken about distribution, as the arrest of Shelley's servant Dan Healy (or Hill) for posting the broadside and Shelley's *Declaration of Rights* in August 1812 attests. However much 'The Devil's Walk' may have been printed to look like a popular ballad, it was far from popular, and we owe the preservation of the text to the diligence of the Home Office.

'The Devil's Walk' is of course an apprentice work. It expresses an embryonic feeling for the apocalyptic grotesque, one that would mature brilliantly in the first part of *The Mask of Anarchy* in 1819. It also reflects another of Shelley's ongoing concerns: bridging the gap

---

[15] *BL* 1: 28.
[16] As suggested by Donald H. Reiman and Neil Freistat in a note to their electronic text of 'The Devil's Walk' (*Romantic Circles*, World Wide Website).

between the radicalism of his own time and that of the previous generation. Robert Southey in his personal role appeared to do this for only a very short time, but the poem to which he introduced Shelley provided, none the less, an important moment in his poetic development. At the same time Shelley had begun a much more ambitious project, a long poem largely devoted to putting forward his idea of the millennial.

Queen Mab

Queen Mab is a rarity in English poetry—a long millennial (not millenarian) poem, projecting the slow growth of human society to a state of perfection. Poetically, its chief models are Southey's long poems *Joan of Arc, Thalaba the Destroyer*, and *The Curse of Kehama*.[17] Philosophically, it draws upon a veritable anthology of eighteenth-century thought, including D'Holbach, Condorcet, Volney, and Godwin.[18] Shelley is in this respect heir to the Enlightenment's confident combination of philosophy and science, as we see in Shelley's notion, central to the subject of millennium in *Queen Mab*, of the precession of the equinoxes. This idea occurs in vi. 39–46 and in Shelley's note to the passage.

> How sweet a scene will earth become!
> Of purest spirits a pure dwelling-place,
> Symphonious with the planetary spheres;
> When Man, with changeless Nature coalescing,
> Will undertake regeneration's work,
> When its ungenial poles no longer point
> To the red and baleful sun
> That faintly twinkles there.

---

[17] Shelley mentioned *Thalaba* as an important influence in his letter to Thomas Jefferson Hogg dated 7 Feb. 1813, *Letters* 1: 352–3; it was also noticed by a critic in the *Literary Gazette and Journal of Belles Letters* in 1821 (repr. in Newman Ivey White, *The Unextinguished Hearth: Shelley and his Contemporary Critics* (New York: Octagon Books, 1972 [1938]), 56); and another critic wrote in the *Monthly Magazine* in the same year: 'It is in the *Thalaba* style, which has been so bepraised by the poetasters of the present day' (*Unextinguished Hearth*, p. 60).

[18] The most complete background is that given in Shelley's own prose notes to the poem (see *Poems of Shelley*, 1: 360–424). Among scholarly studies, K. N. Cameron's *The Young Shelley: Genesis of a Radical* (New York: Collier, 1962 [1950]) remains the most comprehensive, and invaluable contributions to the eighteenth-century political background are made by Gerald McNiece in *Shelley and the Revolutionary Idea* (Cambridge, Mass.: Harvard University Press, 1969), and to the religious setting by Bryan Shelley's *Shelley and Scripture: The Interpreting Angel* (Oxford: Clarendon Press, 1994).

Shelley's note identifies the red and baleful sun as 'the north polar star, to which the axis of the earth, in its present state of obliquity, points'.[19] Shelley continues, citing Laplace, Cabanis, and Bailly, that 'this obliquity will gradually diminish, until the equator coincides with the ecliptic: the nights and days will then become equal on the earth throughout the year, and probably the seasons also', and he speculates that this would be accompanied by a parallel moral and physical improvement in the human species. This notion of a change in the angle of the earth's axis is found in *Paradise Lost*, where changes from the perfection of nature may have been a result of the Fall of Man:

> Some say he bid his Angels turn askance
> The Poles of Earth twice ten degrees and more
> From the Sun's Axle; they with labor push'd
> Oblique the Centric Globe: Some say the Sun
> Was bid turn Reins from th'Equinoctial Road
> Like distant breadth to *Taurus* with the Sev'n
> *Atlantic Sisters*, and the *Spartan* Twins
> Up to the *Tropic* Crab; thence down amain
> By *Leo* and the *Virgin* and the *Scales*,
> As deep as *Capricorn*, to bring in change
> Of *Seasons* to each Clime; else had the Spring
> Perpetual smil'd on Earth with vernant Flow'rs,
> Equal in Days and Nights.[20]

According to Thomas Burnet, the Primitive Earth differed from the post-diluvian in that there was 'a perpetual Æquinox all the Earth over', because its axis was parallel to the plane of the ecliptic. At the Deluge, the Earth's centre of gravity shifted, and its poles presented an oblique axis to the ecliptic. The longevity of the ancients was due to the steadiness of the weather.[21] Coleridge's association with the scientists Beddoes and Davy led him to jot down the speculation:

Millennium, an History of, as brought about by progression in natural philosophy—particularly meteorology or science of airs & winds—Quaere—might not a commentary on the Revelations be written from late philosophical discoveries?[22]

---

[19] *Poems of Shelley*, 1: 373.
[20] *Paradise Lost*, x. 668–80, p. 254. Hughes's note in Milton, *Complete Poems and Major Prose* (New York: Odyssey, 1957) tracks the sun through the constellations.
[21] Thomas Burnet, *Theory of the Earth*, 3rd edn. (2 vols., London, 1697), 1: 133.
[22] *CN* 1: 133. Coburn in her note calls attention to a similar passage in Erasmus Darwin's *Botanic Garden*, Part I: *The Economy of Vegetation* (London: J. Johnson, 1791), I. iv. 308.

If the angle of the earth's axis was going to be restored to the plane of the ecliptic, as Shelley thought it would, the millennium became not only possible but inexorable,[23] and this idea leads to the long millennial passage of part VIII, beginning 'The habitable earth is full of bliss' (58), in which even the poles are temperate. This conviction reinforces, and is in turn reinforced by, the necessitarian and perfectibilitarian doctrines that Shelley had derived from his reading of Godwin and others.

Necessity, though not a conception peculiar to Godwin, was defined by him for his British contemporaries. 'He who affirms that all actions are necessary', Godwin wrote, 'means that the man who is acquainted with all the circumstances under which a living or intelligent being is placed upon any given occasion is qualified to predict the conduct he will hold, with as much certainty as he can predict any of the phenomena of inanimate nature'.[24] It is a form of determinism, and a forerunner of behaviourism, since 'The character of any man is the result of a long series of impressions, communicated to his mind and modifying it in a certain manner, so as to enable us, a number of these modifications and impressions being given, to predict his conduct'.[25] As 'Man . . . is only the vehicle through which certain antecedents operate',[26] this doctrine in one sense makes humanity appear powerless and devoid of moral agency, as in the interpretation that Wordsworth's Rivers gives it in *The Borderers*:

> —What? in this universe,
> Where the least things controul the greatest, where
> The faintest breath that breathes can move a world;
> What! feel remorse, where, if a cat had sneezed,
> A leaf had fallen, the thing had never been
> Whose very shadow gnaws us to our vitals?[27]

[23] However Matthews and Everest (*Poems of Shelley*, 1: 373 n.) observe that Shelley seems at this time to have been ignorant of Laplace's actual view that the precession was an oscillation (which would make it a cyclical phenomenon) and that the intervals were very long indeed—26,000 years. The discussion of the subject in Thomas Love Peacock's *Headlong Hall* (1815/16) suggests that it was a familiar one in the Shelley circle. See *Headlong Hall*, ed. Michael Baron and Michael Slater (Oxford: Oxford University Press, 1987), pp. 40–1. In *The Last Man*, Mary Shelley satirizes the comforts of the precession of the equinoxes when she has the astronomer Merrival say 'that the joyful prospect of an earthly paradise after an hundred thousand years, was clouded to him by the knowledge that in a certain period of time after, an earthly hell or purgatory would occur, when the ecliptic and the equator would be at right angles' (*Last Man*, ed. Morton D. Paley (Oxford and New York: Oxford University Press, 1994), p. 220).

[24] William Godwin, *Enquiry Concerning Political Justice and its Influence on Modern Morals and Happiness*, ed. Isaac Kramnick (Harmondsworth: Penguin, 1985), pp. 336–7. (This edition is based on Godwin's 3rd edn. (1798).)

[25] Ibid., p. 341.   [26] Ibid., p. 351.

[27] Wordsworth, *The Borderers*, ed. Robert Osborn (Ithaca, NY, and London: Cornell

Indeed, Godwin writes: 'In the life of every human being there is a chain of events, generated in the lapse of ages which preceded his birth, and going on in regular procession throughout the whole period of his existence, in consequence of which it was impossible for him to act in any instance otherwise than he has acted'.[28] However, there is a certain kind of empowerment in attaining the Godwinian ideal of the philosopher 'who regards all things past, present, and to come as links of an indissoluble chain'[29]—like Blake's Bard 'who Present, Past, & Future sees',[30] or like Shelley's idea of poets as 'the mirrors of the gigantic shadows which futurity casts upon the present'.[31] Furthermore, although Shelley may not see moral agency for the individual in necessity, he does envision a long-term moral outcome for the species, indeed, for the entire world, when he addresses 'Necessity! thou mother of the world!' (vi. 198). One of the things seen by both Godwinian philosopher and Shelleyan poet is that necessity makes all human things tend toward perfectibility, the burgeoning of what Shelley calls 'perfection's germ' in v. 147. When Godwin proposes that 'man is perfectible', he makes it clear that he does not mean that man 'is capable of being brought to perfection'.[32] Rather, the word is meant 'to express the faculty of being continually made better and receiving perpetual improvement'. It is a process rather than a state, and it means that 'every perfection or excellence that human beings are competent to conceive, human beings, unless in cases that are palpably and unequivocally excluded by the structure of their frame, are competent to attain'.[33] This is a view that Shelley would push to its furthest ramifications in the millennialism of *Queen Mab*.

Shelley's conception of the millennium is very much like the epitome of Blake's as mediated by Northrop Frye: a garden and a city. It is a special feature of Shelley's imagination that the structural features of both are stressed, as for example in the address to the Spirit of Nature that ends part III, proleptic of the millennial predictions to come in *Prometheus Unbound*:

University Press, 1982), early version (1797–9), III. v. 83–8, p. 216. Godwin states that 'under the system of necessity, the terms guilt, crime, desert and accountableness, in the abstract and general sense in which they have sometimes been applied, have no place' (*Political Justice*, p. 357)—a position satirized in Peacock's *Headlong Hall* (p. 48) when the necessitarian Cranium refuses to give Escot credit for saving his life.

[28] Godwin, *Political Justice*, p. 351.   [29] Ibid., p. 359.
[30] Blake, Introduction to *Songs of Experience*, E 18.
[31] Shelley, *A Defence of Poetry*, in *Shelley's Poetry and Prose*, p. 508.
[32] Godwin, *Political Justice*, p. 144.   [33] Ibid., p. 145.

> Man, like these passive things,
> Thy will unconsciously fulfilleth;
> Like theirs, his age of endless peace,
> Which time is fast maturing,
> Will swiftly, surely, come;
> And the unbounded frame which thou pervadest,
> Will be without a flaw
> Marring its perfect symmetry.

(iii. 233–40)

The tyranny of the old order sacrificing humankind in factory labour and war, is presented in terms almost parodying Revelation's 'Thrust in thy sickle, and reap . . . for the harvest of the earth is ripe' (14: 15):

> They rise, they fall; one generation comes
> Yielding its harvest to destruction's scythe.
> It fades, another blossoms; yet behold!
> Red glows the tyrant's stamp-mark on its bloom,
> Withering and cankering deep its passive prime.

(iv. 227–31)

This is no human harvest preparatory to a Last Judgement as in the Book of Revelation or in Blake's *Milton*. History is experienced as the same kind of cyclical nightmare that Wordsworth had in Paris during the winter of 1792–3. Similarly, God's 'death-blushing chariot-wheels' (vii. 35) suggest cyclical recurrence as they roll over his victims. The necessitarian outcome is revolution, as represented by the felling of the poison tree of the old order:

> Let the axe
> Strike at the root, the poison-tree will fall;
> And where its venomed exhalations spread
> Ruin, and death, and woe, where millions lay
> Quenching the serpent's famine, and their bones
> Bleaching unburied in the putrid blast,
> A garden shall arise, in loveliness.
> Surpassing fabled Eden.

(iv. 82–9)

Burke in the *Reflections* had presented the celebrated image of 'the British oak' sheltering large numbers of great cattle.[34] Shelley in effect

---

[34] Edmund Burke, *Reflections on the Revolution in France*, ed. Conor Cruise O'Brien (Harmondsworth: Penguin, 1984), p. 181.

transforms this into something like Coleridge's poisonous manchi-neel[35] or Blake's Tree of Mystery, and lets the spirit of Thomas Paine loose to lay the axe to its root.[36] The long-term result will be a millen-nium ('where no term can be') marked in true Shelleyan fashion by a work of architecture, a temple dedicated to the Spirit of Nature:

> That wondrous and eternal fane,
> Where pain and pleasure, good and evil join,
> To do the will of strong necessity,
> And life, in multitudinous shapes,
> Still pressing forward where no term can be,
> Like hungry and unresting flame
> Curls round the eternal columns of its strength.

> (vi. 232–8)

This dramatic image concluding part VI anticipates the conclusion of *Prometheus Unbound* in its serpentine curling, the implications of which will be confronted in the later poem.

Apocalypse is present in *Queen Mab*, though subordinated in import-ance to millennium. It is chiefly associated with the figure of the Wan-dering Jew, who had been the subject of two earlier poems (and who would reappear in *Hellas*). 'The Wandering Jew; or the Victim of the Eternal Avenger' (1809–10) is merely a Gothic romance, but 'The Wandering Jew's Soliloquy' (1810–11), invoking biblical imagery of earthquake, pestilence, and fire, has elements of the suffering and defi-ance of Ahasuerus in *Queen Mab*. In a note appended to Canto VII by Shelley, consisting of a prose translation of C. F. D. Schubart's 'Der ewige Jude', this character embodies a kind of *anti*-millennium, 'con-demned to hold for millenniums that yawning monster, Sameness, and Time, that hungry hyena, ever bearing children, and ever devouring again her offspring!'[37] This is the curse of eternal recurrence, as also suffered by the shadowy female of Blake's *Europe*, who laments how she must 'bring forth howling terrors, all devouring fiery kings. / De-vouring & devourd'.[38] Shelley makes Ahasuerus a figure of opposition to

---

[35] 'False and fair-foliag'd as the Manchineel': line 26 of 'To the Rev. George Coleridge', *CPW* 1: 174.

[36] Another possible source of this image, as noted by Matthews and Everest (*Poems of Shelley*, 1: 301 n.), is the upas-tree of Erasmus Darwin's *Botanic Garden*, II. iii. 239–44. Paine wrote: 'Lay then the axe to the root', in *Rights of Man* (ed. Eric Foner (Harmondsworth: Penguin, 1985), p. 58); the ultimate source is Matt. 3: 10.

[37] *Poems of Shelley*, 1: 395. Shelley's sources are discussed in an editorial note, 1: 392.

[38] Blake, *Europe*, 'Preludium', E 61.

tyranny (an element present in Schubart's original), partly modelled on Milton's Satan and prefiguring Shelley's own Prometheus as one who dares tell the truth about a tyrannical God and who must suffer for it:

> Thus have I stood—through a wild waste of years
> Struggling with whirlwinds of mad agony,
> Yet peaceful, and serene, and self-enshrined,
> Mocking my powerless tyrant's horrible curse
> With stubborn and unalterable will,
> Even as a giant oak, which heaven's fierce flame
> Had scathèd in the wilderness, to stand
> A monument of fadeless ruin there;
> Yet peacefully and movelessly it braves
> The midnight conflict of the wintry storm,
> As in the sunlight's calm it spreads
> Its worn and withered arms on high
> To meet the quiet of a summer's noon.

(vii. 254-66)

Ahasuerus's discourse is replete with phrases and images associated with apocalypse: he characterizes war under the sign of Christianity, with a reference to Revelation 14: 20–1, as 'Drunk from the wine-press of the Almighty's wrath' (218); and tells how 'blood-red rainbows' transform the covenant into a harbinger of further massacres.[39] He is empowered to describe and to some extent to embody the apocalyptic, but Ahasuerus's capacity ends at the threshold of millennium. It is therefore after his dismissal at the end of part VII that Queen Mab decisively orders Time 'Tear thou that gloomy shroud' (viii. 9), and with this literally apocalyptic event,

> Joy to the Spirit came.
> Through the wide rent in Time's eternal veil,
> Hope was seen beaming through the mists of fear.

(viii. 11-13)

The millennium arrives on cue, in passages blending elements of Isaiah, the Fourth Eclogue of Virgil, and Pope's *Messiah*, as was noted by an early critic of Shelley's poem, who wrote: 'The wonders of Pope's *Messiah*, from which much of this matter, and all the ideas seem to be gathered, as those of the Messiah from Virgil and the prophets, are to

---

[39] As Matthews and Everest (*Poems of Shelley*, pp. 340–1 nn.) point out, these details point to Shelley's reading of chs. 18–21 of Gibbon's *Decline and Fall*.

be realized in this *new world*.[40] In a setting of sensuous imagery of spring, summer, and autumn (there is no winter), the babe shares his meal with a basilisk (84–7) and the lion sports with 'the dreadless kid' (124–6).[41] An important agent of transformation here is vegetarianism, as Shelley emphasized by printing as a long note to lines 211–12 ('no longer now / He slays the lamb that looks him in the face') a version of his essay *A Vindication of Natural Diet* (published in 1813).[42] Part VIII ends with the words 'paradise of peace' (l. 238), and IX is almost entirely devoted to the millennial world. Earth is now addressed as the 'reality of Heaven!' (ix. 11), but this 'haven of perpetual peace' (ix. 20) has been obtained not by some sudden messianic advent, but by 'the eternity of toil / That framed the fabric of thy perfectness' (ix. 21–2). This is truly a millennialist, not a millenarian, view, as Shelley expressed it in a letter to Elizabeth Hitchener on 19 October 1811: '*My* golden age . . . will be the millennium of Xtians "when the lion shall lay down with the lamb" tho' neither will it be accomplished to complete a prophesy, or by the intervention of a *miracle*'.[43] Time loses its power, although this must refer to the manner in which time is perceived, as mortality still exists, although painless. Law is gone, replaced by 'that sweet bondage which is freedom's self' (ix. 76)—the liberty of the *schöne Seele* to act rightly by instinct alone.

When the the Fairy's millennial vision concludes in part IX, one interesting feature is the recuperation of the image of the chariot. Previously associated with cyclical time, it now becomes, in an anticipation of *Prometheus Unbound*, iv. 270–6, part of the forward thrust toward the millennium:

> All tend to perfect happiness, and urge
> The restless wheels of being on their way,
> Whose flashing spokes, instinct with infinite life,
> Bicker and burn to gain their destined goal.
>
> (ix. 151–4)

Here is an example of what Thomas Burnet called *apocatastasis*, meaning the 'restoration, re-establishment, renovation'.[44] Shelley's

---

[40] *An Answer to Queen Mab* (1821), repr. by White in *Unextinguished Hearth*, p. 64. White (p. 63) suggests that the critic may have been William Johnson Fox, editor of the *Monthly Repository*. [41] See B. Shelley, *Shelley and Scripture*, p. 47; cf. Is. 11: 6, 8. [42] See *The Prose Works of Percy Bysshe Shelley*, ed. E. B. Murray (Oxford: Clarendon Press, 1993), 1: 75–91; for collation, see 1: 502. [43] Shelley, *Letters*, 1: 152. [44] *OED*, s.v. See Introduction, above, citing *Theory of the Earth*, 2: 103, where Burnet cites Acts 3: 21.

temperament, like Blake's, involves recovering images that were formerly associated with the processes of cyclical time; so, near the end of the poem, the emphasis is on the energy of the 'burning wheels' of Mab's chariot drawn by 'enchanted steeds' (ix. 213–17). The wheels of this chariot have much in common with those of Ezekiel (3: 12, 13), Daniel (7: 9), and Milton (*Paradise Lost*, vi. 832), as Bryan Shelley points out,[45] as well as with Blake's 'Chariot of fire' in *Milton* (plate 1, E 76). This is the vehicle that will take us from apocalypse to millennium. Although the means of such a transition, the tenor of this fiery vehicle, are not explored further in *Queen Mab*, it would become a major subject in some of the most ambitious poems that Shelley went on to write.

Apocapolitics

In 1819, the year of 'Peterloo', or the Manchester Massacre, Shelley was deeply concerned with events in England, and in the following year he had the idea of publishing 'a little volume of *popular songs* wholly political, & destined to awaken & direct the imagination of the reformers'.[46] 'A New National Anthem', which would surely have been included, gives a sense of what the tone of this book would have been like. The true Queen of England, Liberty, has been 'murdered', and the poet calls upon God to raise her from 'England's grave', concluding with a deliberately discordant apocalypse:

> Lips touched by seraphim
> Breathe out the choral hymn
>   'God save the Queen!'
> Sweet as if angels sang,
> Loud as that trumpet's clang
> Wakening the world's dead gang,—
>   God save the Queen![47]

---

[45] See *Shelley and Scripture*, pp. 38–9. Shelley provides a list of biblical allusions in *Queen Mab* on pp. 175–6.

[46] Letter to Leigh Hunt, 1 May 1820; *Letters*, 2: 191. For a list of the probable contents of such a volume, see Richard Holmes, *Shelley: The Pursuit* (London: Quartet, 1976), p. 593. Some of these poems are printed as part of an edition of *Shelley's Socialism* by Edward Bibbins Aveling and Eleanor Marx Aveling (London and West Nyack, NY: Journeyman Press, 1975).

[47] *The Complete Poetical Works of Percy Bysshe Shelley*, ed. Thomas Hutchinson (London: Oxford University Press, 1960 [1905]), p. 574. See Timothy Webb, *Shelley: A Voice Not Understood* (Manchester: Manchester University Press, 1977), p. 107.

The image of murdered freedom also appears in the powerful 'Sonnet: England in 1819', which presents another situation ripe for death and resurrection: a king, 'old, mad, blind, despised and dying', and 'leech-like' parasites for princes. In calling Religion 'a book sealed' (line 11), Shelley was probably making an ironical reference to a review of his *Revolt of Islam* by John Taylor Coleridge in the *Quarterly*. Coleridge had written that the Bible to Shelley was 'a sealed book to a proud spirit',[48] alluding to the sealed books in Isaiah 29: 11 and in Revelation 5: 1 (see Chapter 3, p. 181). Shelley returns the favour, saying that the State's religion is one of those sealed books. We suspect we know what will emerge when the seals are broken. All the things on Shelley's list 'Are graves, from which a glorious Phantom may / Burst, to illumine our tempestuous day' (13–14). Shelley had previously used very similar language in the concluding sentence of *An Address to the People on the Death of the Princess Charlotte* (1817), in which his subject is the recent execution of the working men Brandeth, Ludlam, and Turner, as well as the death of the Princess in childbirth: 'Let us follow the corpse of British Liberty, slowly and reverentially to its tomb: and if some glorious Phantom should appear, and make its throne of broken swords and sceptres and royal crowns trampled in the dust, let us say that the Spirit of Liberty has arisen from its grave and left all that was gross and mortal there, and kneel down and worship it as our Queen'.[49] In both contexts Shelley, always interested in the political discourse of the previous generation, may be ringing a change on an image in Burke, who pictured rising out of the tomb of monarchy a 'tremendous, unformed spectre . . . a hideous phantom'.[50] Just as he had returned the metaphor of the sealed book, he reverses Burke's meaning: the phantom that emerges from these graves is not hideous but glorious, the phantom of liberty.

The apocalyptic power of the *Popular Songs* group reaches its greatest intensity in a poem that occupies a curious place in the modern criticism of Shelley's work. Some of those who have written about *The Mask of Anarchy* with the highest interest and the greatest sympathy express serious reservations about it. For Thomas R. Edwards, 'It is a fine

---

[48] See James E. Barcus, ed., *Shelley: The Critical Heritage* (London and Boston: Routledge and Kegan Paul, 1975), p. 134.

[49] *Prose Works*, ed. Murray, 1: 239.

[50] Edmund Burke, *Writings and Speeches*, ed. Paul Langford (9 vols., Oxford: Clarendon Press, 1981–97), 8: 191. Blake too may have had this passage in mind when he wrote of Luvah (in this context France) in *Jerusalem*, 60. 2–3: 'Albions Spectre who is Luvah . . . / Not yet formed but a wretched torment unformed & abyssal' (E 209–10).

poem, in its early parts nearly a great one', but the clash of attitudes between what Edwards terms 'Shelley's overt political intentions' and his 'lurking despair about politics' makes the result a demonstration of 'how a certain kind of poetic imagination can damage its own admirable concern for the public world'.[51] Although Richard Hendrix takes issue with this conclusion, praising *The Mask*'s 'blend of dramatic form . . . with political insight and populist attitudes', he concedes that 'the blend was imperfect'.[52] Michael Scrivener, who illuminatingly discusses *The Mask* in relation to popular radical iconography, finds the poem 'contradictory, at war with itself, not entirely resolved'.[53] Stephen C. Behrendt finds in it an 'ambivalence of voice [that] is potentially dangerous, for the poem implicitly condones a variety of the violence it explicitly condemns'.[54] These positive but uneasy critical judgements are at least in part responses to something deeply embedded in *The Mask of Anarchy*: the unsettled relationship between apocalypse and millennium.

The programme of *The Mask of Anarchy* could be described as a rewriting of the Book of Revelation for England in 1819. As Carl Woodring puts it, '[*The Mask of Anarchy*] treats the mode of prophetic dream—vision as apocalypse, a final uncovering and revelation, at first of horror and then of what horror hides. The sequence follows the movement of Revelation from the seven-headed beast empowered by the great red dragon to the victory and marriage of the lamb.'[55] According to this agenda, apocalypse should be followed by the establishment of a New Jerusalem, and so it is in the longest section of the poem. However, the apocalyptic element comprises a transformation of events actually occurring, while the millennial one consists of a future imagined as possible. Each demands and receives a different poetic mode, but although a brilliant transition is made from one to the other, one is left with the disquieting sense that this sequence may not be inevitable.

Shelley's title introduces a sense of ironical inversion that is characteristic of the entire poem and especially of the dramatic sections that

[51] Thomas R. Edwards, *Imagination and Power: A Study of Poetry and Public Themes* (London: Chatto & Windus, 1971), pp. 161–8.
[52] Richard Hendrix, 'The Necessity of Response: How Shelley's Radical Poetry Works', *Keats–Shelley Journal*, 27 (1978): 68.
[53] Michael Scrivener, *Radical Shelley* (Princeton: Princeton University Press, 1982), p. 199.
[54] Stephen C. Behrendt, *Shelley and his Audiences* (Lincoln, Neb.: University of Nebraska Press 1989), p. 199.
[55] Carl Woodring, *Politics in English Romantic Poetry* (Cambridge, Mass.: Harvard University Press, 1970), p. 266.

I shall call the Triumph and the Agon. Shelley knows what a masque is supposed to be and what anarchy is supposed to be; by linking these words on the analogy of, say, *The Masque of Cupid*, he prepares the reader for the crooked house that he proceeds to construct. Both nouns demand scrutiny, as does their syntactical relation.

'Anarchy' is a word with both political and literary associations. In *Paradise Lost* it is a feature of the realm of Chaos—'Eternal Anarchy' (ii. 896) and 'wild Anarchy' (vi. 873). Following Milton's designation of Chaos as 'the Anarch old', Pope uses 'Anarch' in *The Dunciad*.[56] However, in making Anarchy characterize the governing institutions of society, Shelley is even closer to Byron's 'Imperial anarchs, doubling human woes' in the second canto of *Childe Harold*.[57] In the realm of political discourse, a precedent for transforming the conventional meaning of 'anarchy' may be found in Jeremy Bentham's *Plan of Parliamentary Reform in the Form of a Catechism*, first published in 1817. Bentham sarcastically remarks to his Tory antagonist: 'The same "great characters" by which the monster of anarchy has so happily been crushed in France—by those same exalted persons will the same monster be crushed in Britain'; and he continues in a spirit very much like Shelley's: 'In the language of legitimacy and tyranny, and of the venal slavery that crawls under them, *democracy* and *anarchy* are synonymous terms'.[58] What Shelley effects is a combination of Bentham's unmasking of 'the language of legitimacy' with Byron's ironical reversal of meaning, so that 'Anarchy' redounds on the legitimists themselves.

Such a radical transformation is appropriate to a masque, in which we are aware that all the characters are disguised. But what kind of masque, or mask, did Shelley have in mind? He seems to have attached the same meaning to either spelling, using 'Mask' in manuscript, but 'Masque' in correspondence.[59] (A similar situation exists for Poe's

[56] The uses of 'Anarch' by Milton and by Pope are noted by Donald H. Reiman in *Percy Bysshe Shelley* (New York: Twayne, 1969), p. 108.

[57] Byron, *The Complete Poetical Works*, ed. Jerome J. McGann (7 vols., Oxford: Clarendon Press), 2 (1980): 58. Shelley also uses 'Anarch' in this subversive sense in 'Lines Written Among the Euganean Hills' (l. 152) and *Hellas* (ll. 318, 879, 934).

[58] *The Works of Jeremy Bentham*, ed. John Bowring (11 vols., Edinburgh: W. Tait, 1843), 3: 343a, 447b.

[59] See letter to Leigh Hunt, 14–18 Nov. 1819; *Letters*, 2: 152. 'Masque' is the spelling of the first edition: *The Masque of Anarchy* (London, 1832), edited by Hunt. Donald Reiman suggests that either Hunt or his publisher, Moxon, may have considered the spelling 'Mask' obsolescent in 1832. See Donald H. Reiman, ed., *Percy Bysshe Shelley: The Mask of Anarchy, The Manuscripts of the Younger Romantics*, vol. 2. (New York and London: Garland, 1985), p. xv.

'Masque of the Red Death', where in the story's first and second publications the spelling was 'Mask', but then 'Masque' in the *Broadway Journal*, of which Poe was an editor.[60]) Either spelling could signify a dramatic
performance (*OED*, s.v.), although 'Mask' would be the more ambiguous spelling, as in Shakespeare's 'Degree being vizarded, / Th' unworthi-
est goes as fairly in the maske'.[61] Stuart Curran has shown that Shelley
could have learned about masques from Leigh Hunt's *The Descent of
Liberty:/A Mask* (published in 1815) with its introductory essay,[62] and
Shelley's continuing interest in masque conventions is later displayed in
the scene of *Charles the First* called 'The Masque of the Inns of Court'.

The primary reference of 'Mask' here, then, is, to a dramatic performance, as the 'Pageant' of line 51 and 'the triumph of Anarchy' of line
57 also suggest, but that two other meanings are constantly suggested
as well, and that one of these may at any point become the primary
meaning: 'this ghastly masquerade' (27) and the masks worn by
Castlereagh and his fellow ministers, for example.[63] Even the proposition 'of' creates some semantic wobbling. In addition to suggesting the
title of a masque, the syntactical relation can signify the mask of legit-
imate authority that Anarchy wears and/or a masquerade hosted by
Anarchy. This title immediately introduces a sense of dislocated meaning that characterizes other aspects of the poem as well.

At first *The Mask of Anarchy* may seem itself to embody anarchy. Such
an impression is in part created by a strategy of reversals and of ironical inversions of meaning, in part by the strangely disparate lengths of
its structural units. Nevertheless, this ninety-one-stanza poem does
have an overall structure, albeit a radically skewed one. It begins with
an introductory vision, a single stanza in length, that is followed by the
Triumph and the Agon—the Triumph twenty stanzas long, the Agon
twelve. A 'bridge' of three stanzas then leads to the longest section of
the poem, which I shall call the Hortatory Address. After a two-stanza
apostrophe, this section is divided almost geometrically into three

[60] See *The Complete Poems and Stories of Edgar Poe*, ed. Edward Hayes O'Neill (2 vols., New
York: Knopf, 1946), 2: 1079.
[61] *Troilus and Cressida*, I. iii. 83–4. For editorial discussion of the word in this context, see
New Variorum Shakespeare, vol. 26, ed. Harold N. Hillebrand (Philadelphia and London:
Lippincott, 1953), p. 53.
[62] Stuart Curran, *Shelley's Annus Mirabilis* (San Marino, Calif.: Huntington Library, 1975),
pp. 187–90.
[63] Kenneth Neill Cameron calls attention to the *Examiner's* expression 'Men in the Brazen
Masks of Power' in an editorial on the Peterloo Massacre published on 29 Aug. 1819. See
Shelley: The Golden Years (Cambridge, Mass.: Harvard University Press, 1974), p. 625 n. 8.

parts, as if to call attention to the ungainliness of the previous divisions. That a poem has a plot or plan does not necessarily make it a good poem, but it is important, as a preliminary to further discussion, to realize that *The Mask* does have one.

> As I lay asleep in Italy
> There came a voice from over the Sea[64]

These opening lines with their lulling assonance prepare us for a dream vision of some *locus amoenus*, but our reverie is brutally interrupted by the first line of the next stanza: 'I met with Murder on the way—'. Jarred by this reversal of expectation, our attention is redirected to the beginning. Now these lines no longer seem so innocent. Ought the sleeper in Italy to have been awake in England? In compensation or atonement, he is 'forth led' to experience and communicate his vision. The sleeper does not seem to comprehend the meaning of what he relates: extraordinary events are recounted in a flat, quotidian tone, much as in Blake's 'The Mental Traveller'. This is, as Richard Cronin puts it in his excellent discussion of *The Mask*'s relation to the ballad tradition, 'the assumed voice of the naive balladeer'.[65]

The speaker does not, for example, see any reason for Hope's being a 'maniac maid', and since 'she looked more like Despair', he merely reports her putative identity: 'And her name was Hope, she said'. The mailed Shape who defeats Anarchy is never identified by the speaker; neither is the 'voice' that speaks the last fifty-four stanzas. The reader is left to construe the meaning of what has been said.

The matter-of-factly delivered lines 5–6 introduce another simple— but because simple easy to overlook—aspect of the Triumph that now begins. Murder wears a mask *like* Castlereagh, Fraud an ermined gown *like* Eldon. This is not the usual relation of the disguise to the disguised. To be absurdly simple for a moment: Castlereagh ought to be masked as Murder, not vice versa. Personifications have been reified, taking as their manifestation the identities of British cabinet ministers. (This element would have perhaps been emphasized too literally had Shelley retained the manuscript lines (10ᵛ) in which, after Anarchy's overthrow, 'Fraud, less quickly [*del.*] to be known / Threw off E—'s wig & gown'.[66])

[64] My text for this poem is *Shelley's Poetry and Prose*, pp. 301–10.

[65] Richard Cronin, *Shelley's Poetic Thoughts* (London: Macmillan, 1981), p. 43. See also Edwards, *Imagination and Power*, p. 162; and Hendrix, 'Necessity of Response', p. 33.

[66] All quotations of Shelley's draft MS are from his manuscript notebook in the Henry E. Huntington Library, and grateful acknowledgement is made to the Library for permission to

Anarchy, however, has no occasional identity, but is troped to another representation—'Death in the Apocalypse'—and this double identity is present throughout the Pageant and Agon.

As is widely recognized, these four figures are secularizations of the four riders of the Book of Revelation.[67] Anarchy's correspondence to the rider of Revelation 6: 8 is self-evident:

> Last came Anarchy: he rode
> On a white horse, splashed with blood;
> He was pale even to the lips,
> Like Death in the Apocalypse
>
> (30–3)

And I looked, and behold a pale horse, and his name that sat on him was death, and Hell followed with him.

So graphic is this image that Reiman and Powers suggest the possible influence of Benjamin West's painting *Death on the Pale Horse* (now in the Pennsylvania Academy of Fine Arts).[68] Shelley could indeed have seen this enormous picture exhibited in London before he departed for the Continent in 1817; however, an even better candidate as a pictorial source may be the *Death on a Pale Horse* of John Hamilton Mortimer, as etched by Joseph Haynes. Shelley calls Anarchy 'the Skeleton' (74), and in Mortimer's design Death has the head and neck of a skeleton, while in West's he is a black figure swathed in a dark gown.[69] Furthermore, Mortimer's treatment of the subject has a sense of *diablerie* that is completely lacking in West's but is consonant with the tone of this part of *The Mask*. Shelley's apocalyptic-grotesque conception also has something in common with James Gillray's caricature print *Presages of the Millennium*, where, as in Shelley's 'ghastly masquerade', apocalyptic content and contemporary political reference combine in a macabre yet comical way.[70] It should be remembered that prints such as these,

refer to it. There is a facsimile edn. in Shelley, *The Manuscripts of the Younger Romantics*, vol. 4: *The Mask of Anarchy Draft Notebook*, ed. Mary A. Quinn (New York and London: Garland, 1990).

[67] See, e.g., Carlos Baker, *Shelley's Major Poetry: The Fabric of a Vision* (Princeton: Princeton University Press, 1948), p. 61; and Heinrich Schwinning, 'Der Maskenzug der Anarchie', *Gulliver / Deutsche-englische Jahrbücher*, 1 (1976): 76.

[68] See *Shelley's Poetry and Prose*, p. 302 n. 8.

[69] See Morton D. Paley, *The Apocalyptic Sublime*, (New Haven and London: Yale University Press, 1986), pp. 18, 184–6.

[70] Cf. Woodring, *Politics in English Romantic Poetry*, pp. xiii–xiv, where a parallel between Gillray's print and Shelley's *Swellfoot the Tyrant* is suggested.

though produced long before Shelley's poem, continued to be known by collectors and connoisseurs then as they are today, and there is no reason to limit the history of their reception to the immediate time in which they were produced.

The use of John of Patmos's apocalyptic text as a prototype, which we have seen in the portrayal of Anarchy, continues in a loose, unsystematic, and even playful manner. The 'seven bloodhounds' who follow Murder may indicate the seven nations that joined England in postponing the final abolition of the slave trade;[71] but, more generally, they are associated with all the sevens of Revelation. The Destructions who 'played' disguised 'Like Bishops, lawyers, peers, or spies' (26–9) are analogous to the small flying demons that in the pictorial tradition started by Mortimer hover around the rider on the pale horse like gulls following a fishing boat. (In the Gillray print these become identifiable political figures, Edmund Burke among them.) On Anarchy's forehead the mark of the Beast (Rev. 13: 16) is written in a parody of the inscription borne by the messianic rider of Revelation:

> On his brow this mark I saw—
> 'I AM GOD, AND KING, AND LAW!'
>
> (lines 36–7)

And he hath on his vesture and on his thigh a name written, KING OF KINGS, AND LORD OF LORDS. (Rev. 19: 16)

Much as Blake's Urizen, who announces 'One King, one God, one Law',[72] Anarchy combines elements conventionally associated with the divine with others conventionally associated with the Satanic into a single subversive figuration. The overall effect is of an apocalyptic vision of modern history paralleling that of John's Apocalypse in a complex and sometimes ironical way.

Some of Shelley's phrases from Revelation conflate with other biblical texts. In describing the 'Pageant' of Anarchy 'Drunk as with intoxication / Of the wine of desolation' (48–9), Shelley is not quite echoing John. In the book of Revelation, the Whore of Babylon has a golden cup, 'and all the nations have drunk of the wine of her fornication' (Rev. 18: 3; see also Rev. 17: 12). However, Ezekiel, addressing Jerusalem,

---

[71] See G. M. Matthews's note in *Shelley: Selected Poems and Prose* (Oxford and New York: Oxford University Press, 1964), p. 197.
[72] Blake, *The [First] Book of Urizen*, E 72.

prophesies: 'Thou shalt be filled with drunkenness and sorrow, with the cup of astonishment and desolation' (23: 33). The fact that 'the wine of desolation' sounds like a biblical quotation rather than a new combination of elements both indicates Shelley's success in this mode and prefigures another powerful apocalyptic-political text meant for a wide audience (one that reached the kind of audience Shelley hoped for in his *Popular Songs*): namely, Julia Ward Howe's 'Battle Hymn of the Republic'.

Other biblical passages are ironized to underline the Triumph's grotesqueness. Sidmouth is 'Clothed with the Bible, as with light' (line 22) in emulation of the Lord in Psalm 104: 2: 'who coverest thyself with light as with a garment'. This ironical parallel is appropriate for the Home Secretary who in 1818 got Parliament to appropriate a million pounds for church building[73] and in 1819 defended the Peterloo Massacre. In his notebook manuscript, Shelley had Sidmouth 'Singing Hosannah / With a cold tear in either eye' (23ᵛ, but apparently he decided this was excessive, for he cancelled the lines. Elsewhere in the Pageant a passage from the Gospels provides material for transmutation. Lord Chancellor Eldon weeps big tears because as a judge he had been famous for weeping while pronouncing the harshest verdicts (like Urizen, who 'saw / That no flesh nor spirit could keep / His iron laws one moment. . . . / And he wept, & he called it Pity'[74]). But in one of those animated cartoon-like metamorphoses that characterizes the Pageant and Agon, Eldon's tears

> Turned to mill-stones as they fell.
> And the little children, who
> Round his feet played to and fro,
> Thinking every tear a gem,
> Had their brains knocked out by them.
>
> (lines 17–21)

As Leigh Hunt originally suggested,[75] Shelley is no doubt thinking of the little children of his first marriage, and of Lord Chancellor Eldon, who had distrained him from taking charge of them in 1817, the provocation for 'thy false tears—those millstones braining men' in 'To the Lord Chancellor' (1817).[76] But there is in *The Mask* another

---

[73] See G. M. Matthews's note in *Shelley: Selected Poems and Prose*, p. 197.
[74] Blake, *The [First] Book of Urizen*, E 81–2.
[75] Hunt, Preface to *The Masque of Anarchy* (London, 1832), p. iv.
[76] Line 52, *Complete Poetical Works*, p. 543. See Hendrix, 'Necessity of Response', p. 54.

dimension: a macabre echo of Christ and the little children in Matthew 18: 6, where Jesus says: 'But whoso offends one of these little ones which believe in me, it were better for him that a millstone were hanged about his neck, and that he were drowned in the depths of the sea' (cf. Mark 9: 42 and Luke 17: 2). In an instance of what Hunt called 'the union of ludicrousness with terror',[77] the millstone that was to punish the transgressor against the child is what causes the child's destruction.

The Triumph of Anarchy continues through line 85, where we are again in the apocalyptic-grotesque world of some of Gillray's caricatures. 'Anarchy, the Skeleton' assumes the characteristics of a Regency beau who 'Bowed and grinned to every one', and perhaps of that paragon of Regency beaux, the Regent himself, whose 'education / had cost ten millions to the nation' (76–7).[78] Anarchy's agents are sent to seize the Bank of England and the Tower of London, institutions that had allegedly been the object of a plot in 1817, thus providing a pretext for the suspension of habeas corpus.[79] Anarchy himself goes on 'with intent / To meet his pensioned Parliament' (84–5). The expression 'pensioned Parliament' is especially interesting, for these words occur in one of the radical tracts reprinted in the appendix to a book that, as mentioned early in the present study, was of great interest to Shelley— the Abbé Barruel's *Memoirs of the History of Jacobinism*.[80] The Peterloo Massacre seems to have brought to Shelley's mind the potentially revolutionary applications he had previously seen in Barruel's book. However, as *The Mask of Anarchy* is an apocapolitical poem, not a discursive proposal for an association, revolution comes about in a moment.

The instigator of that revolution is a Cassandra figure, the 'maniac maid' Hope, who appears at line 86, and so begins the Agon. It seems beyond coincidence that her cry concludes 'Misery, oh Misery!': as Shelley well knew, this was the refrain of Martha Ray in Wordsworth's 'The Thorn'.[81] This parallel is more than a verbal echo, because

---

[77] Preface to *The Masque of Anarchy*, p. iv. Reiman observes that Hunt first wrote 'humour with terror', but changed the word in proof (*Manuscripts of the Younger Romantics: Mask of Anarchy*, p. 70). Had it been retained, the frisking of Murder's bloodhounds in Shelley's MS notebook would have been another instance of what Hunt meant.

[78] See P. M. S. Dawson, *The Unacknowledged Legislator* (Oxford: Clarendon Press, 1980), p. 206; Scrivener, *Radical Shelley*, p. 207.

[79] See G. M. Matthews's note in *Shelley; Selected Poems and Prose*, p. 197.

[80] Robert Clifford, 'Note', appended to his translation of Barruel's *Memoirs*, 4: 17.

[81] This verbal parallel is noted by Reiman in *Manuscripts of the Younger Romantics: Mask of Anarchy*, p. 15.

Martha Ray is also a 'maniac' female. She is furthermore a mother with a dead child, like the iconic figure of the woman whose child was trampled to death at Peterloo.[82] Although Martha Ray was suspected of having killed her child, the narrator's animosity—and presumably the reader's—is directed toward her masculine betrayer, a role assumed in *The Mask* by Anarchy and his all-male crew. Thus the Wordsworthian source is conflated by Shelley with imagery of the sort later displayed in the collaborations of George Cruikshank and William Hone.[83]

The dead children of Father Time (among whom lay Hope herself 'naked on a bier' in a cancelled MS reading, 7ᵛ) in lines 94–6 are analogous both to Martha Ray's child and to the child killed in St Peter's Fields. (Shelley's most explicit treatment of this theme among the *Popular Songs* of which *The Mask* was to have been part is the 'Ballad of Young Parson Richards', in which the parson turns away from his gate a mother with a dying child who is, it turns out, his own.[84]) Father Time is 'weak and grey' (90), but Anarchy, incorporating the patriarchal 'GOD, AND KING, AND LAW', is a seemingly powerful ogre father. In a draft stanza copied by Mary Shelley into both the manuscript notebook (26ᵛ) and the intermediate fair copy,[85] he is the trampler of a figurative child:

> And the earth whereon he went
> A cry   Like a trampled infant sent
> A piercing scream of loud lament.

In the absence of a male both potent and protective, Hope lies 'Right before the horses' feet' (99) like a Peterloo victim—when a saviour suddenly appears.

This 'Shape arrayed in mail' shares with some other parts of *The Mask* characteristics of an animated cartoon. Reality here is conveyed in a succession of similes which, as so often in this poem, are the primary vehicle of meaning.

---

[82] See Holmes, *Shelley: The Pursuit*, p. 532.

[83] Cf. George Cruikshank's (later) 'Victory of Peterloo', reproduced in Woodring's *Politics in English Romantic Poetry*, p. 22; see also Scrivener, *Radical Shelley*, pp. 201–3.

[84] Cameron also points out the relevance of a letter by Sir Francis Burdett in the *Examiner*, urging the English 'not to stand idly by while tyrants "rip open the mother's womb"'. See *Shelley: The Golden Years*, p. 625 n. 8.

[85] For details, see *Shelley and his Circle*, ed. Donald H. Reiman (Cambridge, Mass: Harvard University Press, 1973), 6: 892–4.

> A mist, a light, an image rose,
> Small at first, and weak, and frail
> Like the vapour of a vale:
>
> Till as clouds grow on the blast,
> Like tower-crowned giants striding fast
> And glare with lightnings as they fly,
> And speak in thunder to the sky,
>
> It grew—
>
> (lines 103–10)

This dramatic modification recalls the approach of the spectre-bark in
The Rime of the Ancient Mariner:

> At first it seemed a little speck,
> And then it seemed a mist;
> It moved and moved, and took at last
> A certain shape, I wist
>
> . . . .
>
> A speck, a mist, a shape, I wist!
> And still it neared and neared:[86]

Shelley's images of cloud and storm also reveal a biblical prototype. In
1 Kings, in the third year of drought, Elijah demonstrates the Lord's
power to Ahab, sending his servant seven times to the top of Mount
Carmel.

> And it came to pass at the seventh time, that he said, Behold, there ariseth a
> little cloud out of the sea, like a man's hand. And he said, Go up, say unto
> Ahab, Prepare thy chariot and get thee down, that the rain stop thee not. And
> it came to pass in the mean while, that the heaven was black with clouds and
> wind, and there was a great rain. (18: 44–5)

All three supernatural phenomena begin as vapoury configurations—
'the vapour of a vale', 'a mist', 'a little cloud'—and grow into startling
realities—Shape, spectre- bark, storm. In *The Mask*, Anarchy is analogous to the tyrannical Ahab, while the role of Elijah, revealing powers
greater than those of Ahab's kingdom, belongs to the visionary poet
himself.

Three aspects of the giant winged Shape are especially important.
Its mail is 'brighter than the viper's scale' (111), it is associated with the
morning star, and it is ungendered. The first two, taken together, are

---

[86] *CPW* 1: 192.

among *The Mask's* numerous reversals of meaning. The subversion of conventional associations here is like that in the first canto of *The Revolt of Islam*, where after the victory of the blood-red Comet over the Morning Star, 'That fair Star fell', and the triumphant Spirit of Evil entered the world to be worshipped, like Anarchy, 'As King, and Lord, and God'. Consequently,

> his immortal foe,
> He changed from starry shape, beauteous and mild,
> To a dire Snake.[87]

The 'planet, like the Morning's' on the Shape's helm, provides a parallel and contrast to the mark on the brow of Anarchy (lines 36–7), and at the same time links the Shape with the Lucifer of Isaiah 14: 12: 'How art thou fallen from heaven, O Lucifer, son of the morning!' (In manuscript Shelley at one point used the word 'Angel' for the Shape, but evidently decided this was too explicit.) In a world where Anarchy can personify the institutions of the State, it is appropriate that the saviour be represented by the configuration of Lucifer and serpent.

The Shape is almost as indefinite as that 'mighty darkness' of *Prometheus Unbound*, Demogorgon, but is in addition without gender, as if the force that brings about apocalyptic transformation must be beyond sexuality. (As H. Buxton Forman points out in his study of the manuscript, Shelley almost made the mistake of referring to the Shape as 'her' in the thirty-first stanza, but presumably 'saw how inconsistent his phraseology was with the carefully guarded mystery of the quality and sex of "the presence"'.[88]) Attempts to assign an allegorical meaning to this manifestation, from Leigh Hunt's 'the description of the rise and growth of Public Enlightenment' to Hendrix's 'reborn Liberty',[89] do not fully describe what is happening, because the apocalyptic moment cannot be contained in a single denotative meaning.

The Shape's conflict with Anarchy is even shorter than Demogorgon's with Jupiter, and as decisive. Typical of the violent oppositions of *The Mask* is the outcome in which

---

[87] See stanzas 26–8, ll. 360, 367–9, 378, *Complete Poetical Works*, ed. Hutchinson, p. 46.

[88] Shelley, *Note-books of Percy Bysshe Shelley, from the Originals in the Library of W. K. Bixby, Deciphered, Transcribed, and Edited* (3 vols., Boston: Bibliophile Society, 1911), 2: 30, 37.

[89] Hunt, Preface to *The Masque of Anarchy*, p. v; Hendrix,, 'Necessity of Response', p. 58. Cf. Paul Foot, *Red Shelley* (London: Sidgwick & Jackson, 1980), pp. 176–7: 'the spirit of Hope, mingled with the spirit of direct action'.

ankle-deep in blood,
Hope that maiden most serene
Was walking with a quiet mien:

(127–9)

The source of all this blood must give the reader pause. Anarchy the
Skeleton cannot have supplied it. Even the murderers who, we are told
a few lines later, were ground by the hoofs of the white horse, could not
have supplied such a deal of blood. It is the not yet named 'sons of
England' whose blood has 'bedewed' the face of their mother Earth
(lines 140, 144). This linking suggests the relationship of the Pageant
and Agon with the Hortatory Address that follows. The former is the
mythologized version of the latter. Only by heeding the Hortatory
Address can the sons of England actuate the myth that precedes it.

Linking the Agon with the Hortatory Address is a three-stanza
'bridge' that Shelley laboured over in manuscript more than any other
passage except perhaps for that describing the manifestation of the
Shape. As in stanza 1 a voice is heard, and again it is of uncertain
origin. Although there have been attempts to identify this voice as 'the
power inherent in nature', or Hope's, or 'probably Brittania',[90] such
delimitations once more seem unsatisfactory, for the omission appears
both deliberate and effectual. A powerful 'as if' clause now enables the
recovery of the mother–child relationship that has been absent from
the poem so far:

As if their Own indignant Earth
Which gave the sons of England birth
Had felt their blood upon her brow,
And shuddering with a mother's throe

. . . .

Had turned every drop of blood
By which her face had been bedewed
To an accent unwithstood,—

(139–45)

In the two following stanzas, the mother–child relationship is reinforced by the continued personification of Earth as female and the
address to the 'sons of England' as 'Nurslings of one mighty Mother'
(149). (In the notebook, 8^r, a strong link would at one point have been

---

[90] Cameron, *Shelley: The Golden Years*, p. 348; Cronin, *Shelley's Poetic Thoughts*, pp. 43, 47, 49;
Scrivener, *Radical Shelley*, p. 205.

established between Earth and the Shape, who in a cancelled version of stanza 26 'sprung from the earth'.) The kingdom of Anarchy was haunted by the ghosts of dead children and an absent mother ('Misery, oh, Misery!'); this longest section of the poem begins by establishing the seemingly indestructible presences of mother and children.

It should be remarked that Shelley had some eight years earlier introduced a similar figure of Mother Earth in a truly popular song of which he was not the author but the translator: Rouget de Lisle's *La Marseillaise*, which, *c*.19 July 1811, the young poet rendered as 'A Translation of the Marseillaise Hymn'.[91] Shelley's text comprises six stanzas, each followed by a four-line chorus, the last two lines of which are 'And the rank gore of tyrants / Shall water your soil!' This is a pretty close translation of the French 'Qu'un sang impur / Abreuve nos sillons!'[92] Shelley brings more of his own imagination to the text in lines 37–40:

> But if we sink in glory's night
> Our Mother Earth will give ye new
> The brilliant pathway to pursue
> That leads to Death or Victory!

The French line 38 is 'La France en produit de nouveaux'—there is no Mother Earth here. The mother figure does exist in the French lines that call 'ces complices de Bouillé' 'tigres qui, sans pitié / Déchirent le sein de leur mère!' Shelley rendered this as:

> Be death fell Bouillé's bloodhound-meed,
> Chase those unnatural fiends away
> Who on their mother's vitals play
> With more than tiger cruelty.

One might say that in his translation Shelley reinforced the maternal element that was already there, and broadened the song's appeal from a national to a universal one. In choosing to translate it, he showed his appreciation of the enormous appeal of a 'popular song', an appeal that he no doubt hoped could be exerted by *The Mask of Anarchy*.

In addition to their both being addressed by a 'voice', the speaker of the beginning of the poem and the men of England have in common

---

[91] See *The Esdaile Notebook: A Volume of Early Poems*, ed. Kenneth Neill Cameron (New York: Alfred A. Knopf, 1964), pp. 144–6.

[92] See Fréderic Roberts, *La Marseillaise* (Paris: Imprimerie Nationale, 1989), p. 20.

their sleep. Called upon to 'Rise like Lions after slumber', the men of England are told that their chains had fallen on them 'in sleep'. '*Sleep*, in Shelley', G. M. Matthews has written, 'is another over-determined concept which awaits investigation'. It may imply what is now known as hibernation, an artificial state of cold insensibility, or a 'detested trance' like that of winter, but winter is also 'the winter of the world, an era of bondage or apathy in the face of social injustice'.[93] The awakening that is projected has an eschatological dimension affecting both the poet-speaker and the men of England, like that of the 'trumpet's clang' of 'A New National Anthem'.

> Wakening the world's dead gang,—[94]

In both instances a general awakening suggests the resurrection of humankind in a new millennial dawn.

It is time to consider why, when in this poem the men of England are called upon to oppose their enemies with an anticipation of Gandhian *satyagraha*,[95] the vehicle of awakening should be 'Lions after slumber' (151). Although it is possible to see in such a polarization of trope and tenor an 'ambivalence' toward revolution, we should be aware of how the contrast contributes to Shelley's apocalyptic scenario. Shelley's thought about revolution does have two aspects, and they appear in virtually all of his major political writings. He hoped revolution would come; he feared it would come violently, in which case it would lead not to millennium but to the return of history upon itself, as at the end of the final chorus of *Hellas*. His conscious beliefs about revolution were very similar to those of William Godwin, who opposed violent revolution on the ground that 'Revolution is engendered by an indignation against tyranny yet is itself ever more pregnant with tyranny'.[96] However, he also wrote in this same section:

Imperfect institutions, as has already been shown, cannot long support themselves when they are generally disapproved of, and their effects truly understood. There is a period at which they may be expected to decline and expire,

---

[93] G. M. Matthews, 'A Volcano's Voice in Shelley', in *Shelley: Modern Judgments*, ed. R. B. Woodings (London: Macmillan, 1968), p. 177.

[94] See n. 47 above.

[95] Gandhi's word meaning 'truth-firmness', as distinguished from mere passive resistance, seems appropriate here. See M. K. Gandhi's *Autobiography: The Story of my Experiments with Truth*, trans. Mahadev Desai (New York: Dover, 1983), p. 284. Gandhi once recited *The Mask of Anarchy* as an illustration of his own principles; see John Pollard Guinn, *Shelley's Political Thought* (The Hague: Mouton, 1969), p. 127.

[96] Godwin, *Political Justice*, 'Of Revolutions', IV. ii., p. 269.

almost without an effort. . . . Men feel their situation; and the restraints that shackled them before vanish like a deception. When such a crisis has arrived, not a sword will need to be drawn, not a finger to be lifted up in purposes of violence. The adversaries will be too few and too feeble to be able to entertain a serious thought of resistance against the universal sense of mankind.

(p. 274)

When Shelley learned 'the terrible and important news of Manchester',[97] both his hope and his fear came sharply to mind. 'The same day that your letter came', he wrote to his publisher Charles Ollier, 'came the news of the Manchester work, & the torrent of my indignation has not yet done boiling in my veins. I wait anxiously [to] hear how the Country will express its sense of this bloody murderous oppression of its destroyers. ' "Something must be done. . . . What yet I know not" '.[98] Had Shelley's hope and his fear not sometimes intermixed, he would indeed have been that angelic figure that he became for some later nineteenth-century readers. As it is, by quoting his own *Cenci*[99] he indulges a fantasy of violent revenge: Beatrice Cenci says the quoted words after being raped by her father, and what she does is to bring about his murder. The savage nature of the trope in line 151 (to be repeated in the last stanza of the poem) may image such retributive fantasies, in apparent conflict with Shelley's belief that violence would only bind its perpetrators into an ever more violent cycle of 'blood for blood—and wrong for wrong' (195), and that apocalypse would not then be followed by millennium. Such polarizations of pacifist tenors and violent vehicles in *The Mask* are one aspect of the dramatic reversals and striking, even shocking, contrasts that characterize the poem as a whole. This is yet another link with the Apocalypse of St John, in which the visions of the millennium and of the New Jerusalem are juxtaposed with evocations of terrible violence.

The organization of *The Mask of Anarchy* has so far seemed to be devoid of any sense of predetermined proportion. We have seen that after an introduction only four lines long come the Triumph and the Agon, asymmetrically divided into twenty- and twelve-stanza units. Then, after a three-stanza 'bridge', the Hortatory Address starts with two stanzas each beginning 'Men of England, heirs of Glory'. These are followed by a disquisition on the nature of freedom that occupies

---

[97] Letter to Thomas Love Peacock, 9 Sept. 1819; *Letters*, 2: 119.
[98] Letter of 6 Sept. 1819; *Letters*, 2: 117.
[99] III. i. 86–7, in *Shelley's Poetry and Prose*, p. 263.

the rest of the poem and that displays an almost geometrical architecture, one which is further reinforced by the rhetorical features of each of its sub-units. Such symmetry is appropriate to the millenarian vision that informs the Hortatory Address. If, as Woodring suggests, the poem leads from the triumph of the Dragon and Beast to 'the victory and marriage of the lamb', the latter demands a different kind of poetry to convey a sense of millennial peace emerging from the horrors that precede it.

In a paper entitled *Shelley's Socialism*, delivered to the Shelley Society in 1885, Edward Aveling and Eleanor Marx Aveling (Karl Marx's daughter) placed one of Shelley's most salient characteristics under the heading 'His Understanding of the Real Meaning of Words'.[100] Their first two examples are 'Anarchy' and 'Freedom'. The Hortatory Address is in the Avelings' sense an essay on the real meaning of words. It begins its answer to 'What is Freedom?' first by defining the present condition as slavery, then by showing what freedom really is. Each of these two sections, as Stuart Curran points out, is thirteen stanzas long.[101] The remainder of the poem moves to fill the mental space between these two divisions by showing how to get to freedom from slavery. This third part is precisely the sum of the preceding two plus one stanza, the additional stanza being the repetition of stanza 38, beginning 'Rise like Lions after slumber', at the very end. Each of these three subsections is, moreover, governed by a different type of predication, and each is bound together by a different, appropriate anaphoric structure.

The stanzas immediately following 'What is Freedom?' are characterized by predications of *being* followed by infinitives. ''Tis to' plus an infinitive occurs six times in the eight stanzas comprising lines 160–96, five of these at the beginning of a stanza. In stanza 48 these statements lead to 'Then it is to feel revenge'. 'What is? 'Tis to . . . Then it is' creates a feeling of inexorable cause and effect, of Shelleyan necessity. The end of stanza 47, 'Blood is on the grass like dew' (line 192), looks back to the figuration in lines 141–2, where it is as if Earth's face had been

---

[100] Aveling and Aveling, *Shelley's Socialism*, p. 33. This paper is the source of the statement by Karl Marx that 'those who understand them and love them rejoice that Byron died at thirty-six because if he had lived he would have become a reactionary bourgeois; they grieve that Shelley died at twenty-nine because he would always have been one of the advanced guard of socialism' (p. 16). For an additional testimony of Karl Marx's high view of Shelley as transmitted by his daughter, see Henry S. Salt, *Company I have Kept* (London: George Allen & Unwin, 1930), pp. 50–1.

[101] Currran, *Shelley's Annus Mirabilis*, pp. 192–3.

bedewed with blood. This effusion of blood on the grass bears two different kinds of association. One is like that of De Lisle's lines that Shelley had translated as 'And the rank gore of tyrants shall water your soil!' The second, which becomes the dominant meaning without ever entirely displacing the first, is reminiscent of Tertullian's declaration to the Roman officials that 'We become more numerous every time we are hewn down by you: the blood of Christians is seed'.[102] Shelley's evocation of self-sacrifice seems to precipitate the extended analogy of the Englishman and Christ in lines 197–204, after which the entire movement is concluded and summarized in a stanza that begins with another variant of the ''Tis to' anaphora: 'This is Slavery'.

'What art thou Freedom' at the beginning of stanza 52 is a marker leading us to expect a sequence of answers as in the section following 'What is Freedom?' thirteen stanzas before. The 'thou' in this question anticipates a new organizing anaphora. The twelve following stanzas feature 'thou art' seven times, 'thou art not' once, and 'art thou' once. Six of these begin stanzas. The change from 'it is' to 'thou art', with its transition from an inanimate to an intimately personal grammatical subject, prepares the way for the millennial transformation of the human universe.[103]

The last movement of the address, beginning with stanza 65, once more shifts into a new organizing anaphora with 'Let a great Assembly be / Of the fearless and the free' (lines 262–3).[104] As the subject changes from what Freedom is to how it can be actualized, predication moves from the declarative mode to the imperative. The construction 'Let' followed by a verb is found eleven times from line 262 on. Nine of these occurrences begin stanzas. Concomitantly we encounter other vital imperatives—'Be', 'Stand', 'Look', 'Shall'. Such monosyllabic initial predications also make the four-beat lines they introduce 'headless',[105]

---

[102] Tertullian, *Apology*, trans. Sister Emily Joseph Daly, in *Tertullian Apologetical Works* and *Minucius Felix Octavius* (New York: Fathers of the Church, 1950), p. 125. Of course, there are many variant versions, as for example Richard Price's: 'It is a very just observation that the blood of the martyrs has been the seed of the church' (*The Evidence for a Future Improvement in the State of Mankind* (London, 1787), p. 27). The tree of liberty watered by the blood of tyrants (cf. quotations from Jefferson and Barère in Ch. 2 n. 17) is of course a closely related image.

[103] This is close to a central argument of Harold Bloom's *Shelley's Mythmaking* (New Haven: Yale University Press, 1959), although *The Mask of Anarchy* is not discussed there.

[104] Ronald Tetrault interestingly distinguishes this type of 'optative' *let* from other let-constructions in this part of the poem. See *The Poetry of Life: Shelley and Literary Form* (Toronto: University of Toronto Press, 1987), pp. 205–7.

[105] See Curran, *Shelley's Annus Mirabilis*, p. 239 n. 13, on Shelley's 'acephalic tetrameter' and its association with the rhyming speeches of masques.

which both emphasizes the imperative nature of the verbs and calls our attention to the 'voice' speaking the lines. In this way a sense of increasing momentum is created, reinforced by a subsection in which the gathering of participants is rendered by the anaphoric 'From the' that begins stanzas 67, 68, and 69 and that also occurs in stanza 70. At line 295 the beginning of the third movement is virtually reiterated in 'Let a vast assembly be', and the poem plunges ahead to the confrontation between the people and their oppressors.

The military's attack is rendered in remarkably bloody imagery, while the people's weapon is, significantly, speech. This essential opposition is rendered in the simile 'Be your strong and simple words / Keen to wound as sharpened swords' (299–300). Once more, non-violent tenor and violent vehicle are polarized, with the image in the latter now ironically reflecting the literally envisioned 'fixed bayonets' and 'horsemen's scimitars' to come. And once more the people's weapon is a voice, associated as in stanza 36 with an effusion of blood:

> And that slaughter to the Nation
> Shall steam up like inspiration,
> Eloquent, oracular;
> A volcano heard afar.
>
> (360–3)

This is a powerful revolutionary image, one which is parallel to

> the realm
> Of Demogorgon, and the mighty portal,
> Like a volcano's meteor-breathing chasm,
> Whence the oracular vapour is hurled up.[106]

The voice that came over the sea to the poet, the voice of Hope, the voice of Earth, the voice that speaks the entire Hortatory Address, the voice of a bleeding people—all these concentre in a single metaphor, making it seem as if the repetition of stanza 38 at the conclusion were chanted in a great chorale:

> 'Rise like lions after slumber
> In unvanquishable number—
> Shake your chains to earth like dew
> Which in sleep had fallen on you—
> Ye are many—they are few.'

---

[106] *Prometheus Unbound*, II. iii. 1–4; *Shelley's Poetry and Prose*, p. 168.

Thus concludes the Hortatory Address, which contrasts as sharply with the Triumph and the Agon in structure as it does in tone. Up to line 134 *The Mask* speaks in a sardonic-macabre voice—Hunt's 'union of ludicrousness with terror'. Here the violent transformations of biblical and other texts stylistically parallel the plot's violent metamorphoses and are appropriate to its apocalyptic nature. There follow, as we have seen, three transitional stanzas (lines 135–46) that mime, in a series of rapid enjambments, the process they describe. 'Shuddering with a mother's throe', apocalypse gives birth to millennium. Consequently, the carefully plotted, deliberate rhetorical organization of the fifty-three stanzas from line 156 to the end projects a secularized version of Revelation 20: 4:

. . . I saw the souls of them that were beheaded for the witness of Jesus, and for the word of God, and which had not worshipped the beast, neither his image, neither had received his mark upon their foreheads, or in their hands; and they lived and reigned with Christ a thousand years.

If a sense of radical dislocation between the two main parts of the poem persists, that is perhaps an expression of the unsettled nature of the relationship between apocalypse and millennium in Shelley's vision of history itself.

To this far goal of Time

In the late summer of 1818,[107] a year or so before writing *The Mask of Anarchy*, Shelley had begun work on what would become his most ambitious and successfully realized long poem. By the end of April 1819 he considered a three-act version of *Prometheus Unbound* to be complete, but by September of that year he was working on a passage that would become part of a new Act, and he continued working on Act IV until it was finished in December 1819. This 'Lyrical Drama' develops the themes of apocalypse and millennium that had been prominent from Shelley's early work (especially *Queen Mab*) on, attempts to redefine the relationship between the two, and also provides the most extensive treatment of the millennium to be written during the Romantic period. As it also revises and extends these themes as they

---

[107] The summary of dating that follows is drawn from the indispensable research of Neil Freistat in *Bodleian Shelley Manuscripts*, vol. 9: *The Prometheus Unbound Notebooks* (New York and London: Garland, 1991), pp. lxi–lxxxiv.

were presented in Shelley's most ambitious preceding work, a few preliminary words must be said about *The Revolt of Islam*.[108]

At a crucial moment in *Prometheus Unbound*, Jupiter employs an image that Shelley expected his imagined reader to recognize:

> We two will sink in the wide waves of ruin
> Even as a vulture and a snake outspent
> Drop, twisted in inextricable fight
> Into a shoreless sea.[109]

(III. i. 71–4)

In picturing a joint suicide for himself and Demogorgon, Jupiter's words reflect back to Canto I of *The Revolt of Islam*, in which 'An Eagle and a Serpent wreathed in fight' (193) are featured. This canto that begins on an immediately apocalyptic note with its first line's reference to 'the last hope of trampled France' (127),[110] going back to Revelation 14: 19 and 19: 15, as Blake and as Byron had done and as Julia Ward Howe would do. The narrator, like Coleridge in 'France: An Ode', scales a promontory and looks over the sea. Then, in an echo of *The Rime of the Ancient Mariner* similar to that in *The Mask of Anarchy*, 'A speck, a cloud, a shape approaching grew, / Like a great ship in the sun's sinking sphere' (178–9). This turns out to comprise the intertwined figures of the two combatants. Typically for Shelley, the poet's sympathies are with the serpent and its beautiful 'mailed and many-coloured skin' (202), but the serpent loses the battle and falls into the sea. It is not dead, however; for on the shore, the narrator meets a beautiful woman who weeps for it, calls to it in its own language, and embraces it as it crawls from the sea. Together all three embark in a boat 'of rare device', in which the woman interprets the meaning of the events that the poet has witnessed.

As we saw in Chapter 1, the serpent was one of the traditional emblems of revolution, and as such was taken up by Blake in his works of the 1790s. Potentially, the snake can represent either regeneration or recurrence—a point to which we must return—but here it is only the positive aspect that Shelley chooses. Indeed, one of the nicknames by

---

[108] The original title was *Laon and Cythna; or the Revolution of the Golden City: A Vision of the Nineteenth Century*. This was published by C. and J. Ollier late in 1817 with a date of 1818 on the title-page, but it was then withdrawn by the publisher owing to objections to the incestuous love of the two main characters. Revised by Shelley, the poem was published as *The Revolt of Islam* by Ollier in 1818.

[109] References to *Prometheus Unbound* are to *Shelley's Poetry and Prose*, ed. Reiman and Powers.

[110] References to *The Revolt of Islam* are to *Complete Poetical Works*, ed. Hutchinson.

which the poet was known to his friends was 'Snake', and he adopted the cognomen in his poem 'The Serpent Is Shut Out from Paradise'.[111] Accounts of its origin differ,[112] but its meaning is clearly to be taken in the sense of Blake's 'Messiah or Satan or Tempter' in *The Marriage of Heaven and Hell*. Shelley's inner circle of readers would have had no difficulty in disentangling the serpent from the eagle, and the ensuing narrative makes their significance, Manichean in a sense that Byron's *Cain* is not, explicit to all others. Here there really have from the first been two powers, one originally manifest as 'a blood-red Comet', the other as the Luciferean 'Morning Star' (356). Their primordial conflict, like the one that the poet has just witnessed, was won by the Spirit of evil. By his power the Spirit of good was turned into a serpent, who continued to do battle against the Fiend. One manifestation of this elemental conflict was when, once more echoing Coleridge's Ode:

> great France sprang forth
> And seized, as if to break, the ponderous chains
> Which bind in woe the nations of the earth.

(470–2)

Although this too failed, the elemental conflict between serpent / Morning Star and eagle / Comet is perpetually renewed. The story is continued in a vast domed temple, an architectural fantasy worthy of the great domed conceptions of Etienne-Louis Bouillée or Claude-Nicolas Ledoux. Here we encounter 'two mighty Spirits' who will tell the 'tale of human power' that is the rest of *The Revolt of Islam*.

This very ambitious narrative has historical reference on three levels: the Ottoman Empire, the French Revolution and its aftermath, and England in 1817. Although John Taylor Coleridge professed to see no connection, his attack upon Shelley is too intelligent for such obtuseness, and one senses he could have answered his own question:

The laws and government on which Mr. Shelley's reasoning proceeds, are the Turkish, administered by a lawless despot; his religion is the Mahommedan,

---

[111] See *Shelley's Poetry and Prose*, pp. 447–8.

[112] According to E. J. Trelawny, Shelley, in translating *Faust* to Byron, read Mephistopheles' reference to 'My aunt, the renowned snake', and Byron remarked: 'Then you are her nephew' (*Records of Shelley, Byron, and the Author*, ed. David Wright (Harmondsworth: Penguin, 1973), p. 106). However, Reiman and Powers (*Shelley's Poetry and Prose*, p. 447 n. 2) see a pun on 'Bysshe Shelley' and Italian *bischelli* = a small snake. For further discussion, see Webb, *Shelley: A Voice Not Understood*, pp. 13 and 31 n. 28; John Buxton, *Byron and Shelley: The History of a Friendship* (London: Macmillan, 1968), p. 196; Charles E. Robinson, *Shelley and Byron: The Snake and Eagle Wreathed in Fight* (Baltimore: Johns Hopkins University Press, 1976), pp. 210–11.

maintained by servile hypocrites. . . . We are Englishmen, Christians, free, and independent; we ask Mr. Shelley how his case applies to *us*? or what *we* learn from it to the prejudice of our own institutions?[113]

Laon leads a revolution against the tyrant of the Golden City, a revolution that is one of Greeks against Turks at some unspecified future time, of France against its rulers in 1789, and as Shelley hoped, of England in 1817 or soon afterwards. Othman, the tyrant, is overthrown and would be killed by the populace did not Laon prevent this, as the Gironde (including Thomas Paine) would have spared the life of Louis XVI. Freedom is celebrated in a Festival of Nations, obviously echoing the first revolutionary Festival of the Federation (Canto V, stanzas 37–60).[114] But the tyrant returns with an army, like the Duke of Brunswick invading France in 1792, and carnage follows. The people defend themselves with 'rude pikes, the instrument / Of those who war but on their native ground / For natural rights' (2444–6). 'Natural rights' is a Painite, anti-Burkean idea, and, as Shelley must have known, in the State Trials of 1794, the Society for Constitutional Information was accused of amassing pikes.[115] At the last moment, Laon is rescued by an apocalyptic rider:

> A black Tartarian horse of giant frame
> Comes trampling over the dead, the living bleed
> Beneath the hoofs of that tremendous steed,
> On which, like to an Angel, robed in white,
> Sate one waving a sword.
>
> (2499–2503)

His rescuer, 'that Phantom swift and bright' (2505) is Cythna, and his deliverance is followed by a variation on the microcosm of millennium, with love-making in a domed ruin replacing domestic life in a

[113] See James E. Barcus, ed., *Shelley: The Critical Heritage* (London and Boston: Routledge and Kegan Paul, 1975), p. 129. Leigh Hunt replied in the *Examiner* [1819] with the analogy of *Gulliver's Travels* (*Critical Heritage*, p. 137), but much more could be said about Shelley's particular choice for displacement.

[114] 'A great deal of mummery follows', wrote John Taylor Coleridge, 'of national fêtes, reasonable rites, altars of federation, &c. borrowed from that store-house of cast-off mummeries and abominations, the French revolution' (ibid., p. 130). With greater sympathy, the Avelings remarked in 1888: 'The wild-eyed women thronging round the path of Cythna as she went through the great city were from the streets of Paris, and he (Shelley), more than any other of his time, knew the full strength and beauty of this wild mother of his and ours' (*Shelley's Socialism*, p. 16).

[115] See Manoah Sibley, *The Trial of Mr. Thomas Hardy for High Treason* (Dublin: P. Byrne, 1794), pp. 121, 128.

Cot.[116] Their happiness is not paralleled in the Golden City, where the populace is in Canto X ravaged by Famine and Plague. Laon goes there to offer his life for the people, and Cythna, once more on her black horse, joins him in immolation. After their deaths they are translated to another realm of being, where they travel in a 'divine canoe' down a river to the Temple of the Spirit.

In *Loan and Cythna / The Revolt of Islam*, the apocalyptic presents itself primarily in the Serpent of Canto I, in the figuratively angelic Cythna on her black horse, and in the plagues that ravage the Golden City under the tyranny of Othman. In Canto V the 'mighty brotherhood' (line 1840) temporarily achieved by the revolutionaries is millennial, as is Cythna's hymn of freedom at the Altar of Federation. The sculpture there of 'A Woman . . . feeding from one breast / A human babe and a young basilisk' (2161–3) transforms Isaiah's 'And the sucking child shall play on the hole of the asp' (11: 8). The millennial feast 'such as Earth, the general mother, / Pours from her fairest bosom' (2299–2300) may have occasioned John Taylor Coleridge's sardonically meant, but accurate, remark that 'According to him the earth is a boon garden needing little care or cultivation, but pouring forth spontaneously and inexhaustibly all innocent delights to her innumerable children'.[117] Furthermore, in addition to Laon and Cythna's love among the ruins, a displaced millennium may be seen in their haven in the Temple of the Spirit. Yet, despite this abundance of material, apocalypse and millennium are not brought into a definable relationship with each other; nor is it apparent that the first could ever lead to the second. The people of the Golden City enjoy only a short interval of peace, despite having done the right thing in sparing Othman, and the oppressors come in such furiously destructive hordes that it is hard to see how they could be resisted even with armaments more advanced than pikes. The only political view one could take from this would be one of despair. Had Shelley's intended meaning been that millennium is impossible, the outcome of *The Revolt of Islam* would not have been problematic, but as we know from *Queen Mab* and *The Mask of Anarchy*, he wished to affirm the opposite. Although *The Revolt of Islam* presented Shelley's most ambitious treatment of the revolutionary theme to date, Shelley must have felt that certain things about it needed to be corrected in *Prometheus Unbound*.

---

[116] On this scene and its antecedents, see David Duff, *Romance and Revolution: Shelley and the Politics of a Genre* (Cambridge: Cambridge University Press, 1994), pp. 180–92.

[117] *Shelley: The Critical Heritage*, p. 127.

The chained Prometheus at the beginning of Shelley's lyrical drama presents yet another instance of the extraordinary prominence of the chain as an image in Romantic poetry. It is important not only for its frequency but also at times for its psychological reference. 'The chains are', Blake wrote in *The Marriage of Heaven and Hell,* 'the cunning of weak and tame minds, which have power to resist energy' (E 40). In *Night the Fifth* of *Vala, or The Four Zoas,* Los and Enitharmon repent having chained Orc on a mountain, but when they come to release him, they find that the Chain of Jealousy has become part of Orc, 'a living Chain / Sustaind by the Demons life' (63: 3–4, E 342). Shelley uses a similar image in the preface to *The Revolt of Islam,* in explaining the fate of the French Revolution: 'If the Revolution had been in every respect prosperous, then misrule and superstition would lose half their claims to our abhorrence, as fetters which the captive can unlock with the slightest motion of his fingers, and which do not eat with poisonous rust into the soul'.[118] That the chained Titan could be in danger of becoming one with his chains is suggested by the striking resemblance of the Prometheus who cursed Jupiter to Jupiter himself,[119] but this ratio is completely transformed after Prometheus summons the Phantom of Jupiter from the anti-world to recall the curse. It could be said that the entire remainder of the drama takes place in the microsecond after Prometheus says 'I wish no living thing to suffer pain' (305), just as Blake's *Milton* takes place 'Within a Moment: a Pulsation of the Artery' (29: 3, E 127). William Keach has aptly observed how Shelley's remarkable control over the speed of his verse affects the reader's conception of what is going on in 'a series of remarkable images in which rapid motion converts itself into suspension and stillness'.[120] Shelley asserts in the Preface to *Prometheus Unbound:* 'The imagery which I have employed will be found in many instances to have been drawn from the operations of the human mind, or from those external actions by which they are expressed'.[121] This is certainly true of the compression and expansion of the sense of time that we experience in the language and imagery of the work.

Much of the early part of the first act builds toward apocalypse, with Earth recounting the early effects of Jupiter's reign and Prometheus

---

[118] *Poetical Works,* ed. Hutchinson, p. 33.
[119] As observed by Milton O. Wilson, *Shelley's Later Poetry: A Study of his Prophetic Imagination* (New York: Columbia University Press, 1959), p. 64.
[120] William Keach, *Shelley's Style* (New York and London: Methuen, 1984), p. 169. Keach's example here is i. 754–5: 'Twin nurslings of the all-sustaining air / On swift still wings glide down the atmosphere?' [121] *Shelley's Poetry and Prose,* p. 133.

describing the current situation. Earth's speech brings in the plagues that typically mark a situation in which apocalypse is near:

> When plague had fallen on man and beast and worm,
> And Famine, and black blight on herb and tree,
> And in the corn and vines and meadow grass
> Teemed ineradicable poisonous weeds.

> (172–5)

It is as if there were a finitude of images, here and elsewhere, to convey the apocalyptic, and in that very finitude lies the poet's confidence in establishing for the reader the meaning of events. Another way of marking the apocalyptic is through intertextuality, and later in Act I Prometheus's words have an interesting link with an earlier apocalyptic poem:

> . . . mighty realms
> Float by my feet like sea-uprooted isles
> Whose sons are kneaded down in common blood
> By the red light of their own burning homes.

> (612–15)

In Coleridge's 'Fire, Famine, and Slaughter', Fire says, 'By the light of his own blazing cot / Was many a naked Rebel shot' (56–7). Shelley had so admired Coleridge's poem that he composed an imitation of it, 'Falsehood and Vice: A Dialogue', in the Esdaile Notebook.[122] In writing the early part of *Prometheus Unbound*, Shelley reached out to Coleridge once more, having been engaged in reading and reciting 'Fire, Famine, and Slaughter' and 'France: An Ode' in the winter of 1815–16 (and probably later as well).[123] His echoing of Coleridge is not a matter of mere influence, but, as frequently with Shelley, a declaration of affinity.[124] This is also true of the presentation of the Furies, who in their grotesqueness and exultation in horror resemble the

---

[122] See *The Esdaile Notebook*, pp. 44–7. The poem was published by Shelley in the notes to *Queen Mab*, at the end of the note to iv. 178–9.

[123] Mary Godwin made a transcript of these poems, now in the Pforzheimer Collection: see Donald H. Reiman, 'Mary Godwin, Transcript of S. T. Coleridge's "France: An Ode" and "Fire, Famine, and Slaughter"', in *Shelley and his Circle*, 7: 1–11. From the numerous verbal differences between all printed versions and these transcripts, Reiman concludes that they derive not from any printed version, but from 'memorial reconstruction', having either been taken down from memory or from Percy Shelley's recitation.

[124] Shelley wrote to Thomas Love Peacock on 17 July 1816: 'Tell me of the political state of England—its literature, of which when I speak Coleridge is in my thoughts' (*Letters*, 1: 490).

female personifications in 'Fire, Famine, and Slaughter'. Of course Shelley's Furies have a deeper dimension. They are both within and without, tempting Prometheus (and Shelley) to despair. In so doing, they enact (line 539) a parodic apocalypse:

> A FURY
> Tear the veil!
>
> ANOTHER FURY
> It is torn!

They then present a fierce apocalyptic image for the outcome of the French Revolution:

> See how kindred murder kin!
> 'Tis the vintage-time for Death and Sin:
> Blood, like new wine, bubbles within
> Till Despair smothers
> The struggling World, which slaves and tyrants win.
>
> (573–7)

Having retracted the curse and being able to pity those whom the Furies' words torture not, Prometheus is proof against these words, and when the Chorus of Spirits comes with counterbalancing instances of human heroism, altruism, and love, they conclude by addressing Prometheus as a prophesied apocalyptic saviour:

> Though Ruin now Love's shadow be
> Following him destroyingly
> On Death's white and winged steed,
> Which the fleetest cannot flee—
> Trampling down both flower and weed,
> Man and beast and foul and fair,
> Like a tempest through the air;
> Thou shalt quell this Horseman grim,
> Woundless though in heart or limb.—
>
> (780–8)

At the end of Act I, however, the focus shifts to Prometheus's female counterpart, Asia, who 'waits in that far Indian vale' (826), and who will in Act II become the heroine of a quest romance, like Cythna in *The Revolt of Islam*.[125]

---

[125] On this aspect of Cythna, see Duff, *Romance and Revolution*, pp. 192–209.

The first mention of Asia, by Prometheus (I. 809–11), makes her seem very like a Blakean emanation:

> Asia! who when my being overflowed
> Wert like a golden chalice to bright wine
> Which else had sunk into the thirsty dust.

In a figure combining the erotic and the eucharistic, this chalice appears merely as a receptacle for Promethean fluids. Yet, unlike Blake's Jerusalem, Asia is not a passive figure. It is she who will initiate the descent to the Cave of Demogorgon after which Jupiter is overthrown. In preparation for this, her great lyrical speech to the approaching Panthea at the opening of the next Act establishes the millennial dawn:

> This is the season, this the day, the hour;
> At sunrise thou shouldst come, sweet sister mine,
> Too long desired, too long delaying, come!

> (II. i. 13–15)

Interestingly, the millennium dawns even though apocalypse has yet to occur or at least to be fully realized—but all the actions of the poem take place in the moment of Prometheus's renunciation of the curse. As so often in Shelley, the symbolic and the natural beautifully merge; 'and through yon clouds of cloudlike snow / The roseate sunlight quivers' (24–5) was written by a poet who had seen dawn in the Alps. At the same time, this dawn is the Spring (6), and as in Isaiah 35 water is about to come to 'The desart of our life' (11–12). Keach aptly calls this passage 'the poem's most intricate transition', in which 'mysterious precipitations of meaning take shape . . . through figurative sequences of dissolving, evaporating, and condensing'.[126] This fluidity of style in the opening out of Asia's thoughts is appropriate to the transformation of the world that is at hand.

Activated by Panthea's two dreams, one of a transfigured Prometheus, the other of the Spirits of the Hours yet to come, the sisters move in pursuit of the second dream to its refrain of 'Follow, follow!' In their quest they pass through a forest, a plane of being equivalent to Blake's Beulah, where all things may find temporary repose in the natural world. The two Fauns who inhabit it seem to have emerged from the great double sestina of Sidney's *Arcadia*, 'Ye goatherd gods,

---

[126] Keach, *Shelley's Style*, p. 133.

who haunt the grassy mountains', reminding us of to how great an extent Shelley was the heir of Elizabethan pastoral poetry. In their wonderfully sustained naïve discourse they uncomprehendingly relay Silenus's prophecy of the millennium that Prometheus will bring about, 'how he shall be loosed, and make the Earth / One brotherhood' (II. ii. 94–5). Indeed, millennium is in one respect an extension of the pastoral ideal, but apocalypse is beyond the limits of pastoral. In the next scene, we encounter it, or something very much like it, in the Cave of Demogorgon.

As the dominant movement of scene 1 was 'follow', that of scene 3 is expressed in the refrain of the Song of Spirits as 'Down, down!' Asia leads Panthea down into the chthonic plane of being, the nature of which was anticipated in scene 2 with 'from the breathing Earth behind / There steams a plume-uplifting wind' (II. ii. 52–3). In this role, Asia is, as Jerrold Hogle points out, 'a variation of Virgil's Cumaean Sibyl, who initiates Aeneas into Hades'.[127] The site that is revealed is conceived in terms of 'that deep romantic chasm' in Coleridge's 'Kubla Khan' (first published in 1816):

> the realm
> Of Demogorgon and the mighty portal,
> Like a volcano's meteor-breathing chasm,
> Whence the oracular vapour is hurled up.
>
> (II. iii. 1–4)

> And from this chasm, with ceaseless turmoil seething,
> As if this earth in fast thick pants were breathing,
> A mighty fountain momently was forced.
>
> ('Kubla Khan', 17–19)

Both Coleridge's poem and Shelley's passage culminate in images of inspired poets. Shelley's 'lonely men' who drink 'the oracular vapour', draining this 'maddening wine of life . . . To deep intoxication' (II. iii. 5–8) parallel the Coleridgean poet figure who 'on honey-dew hath fed, / And drunk the milk of Paradise' (53–4). However, Shelley has made an important change by substituting 'volcano' for 'fountain'. G. M. Matthews identifies the spot they have reached as 'the terminal

---

[127] Jerrold Hogle, *Shelley's Process: Radical Transference and the Development of his Major Works* (New York and Oxford: Oxford University Press, 1988), p. 185. Hogle also points out that Asia here is in one respect 'the prophetic figure of Liberty at a grand revolutionary ceremony', and compares Cythna in Canto V of *The Revolt of Islam*. Hogle's entire discussion of Asia, pp. 182–92, is of great interest.

core of a colossal volcano'[128] in an invaluable essay that explores the revolutionary implications of this image and links them with what Shelley would have known about the most recent eruption of Vesuvius, that of 1794. Both are aspects of 'Demogorgon's mighty law',[129] Necessity, which governs both nature and human events.

To encounter the apocalyptic, Asia and Panthea must literally cross a threshold, beneath 'the mighty portal' of Demogorgon, whose underground existence has been prefigured by two other beings in the poem. One of these is named in the fragment from Aeschylus's lost *Epigoni* that Shelley made the epigraph to *Prometheus Unbound*, after having copied it into a notebook under the title 'To the Ghost of Aeschylus': 'AUDISNE HÆC AMPHIARAE, SUB TERRAM ABDITE?'[130] Amphiarus was the only one of the Seven against Thebes who had foreknowledge that the expedition would fail. Fleeing afterwards, he was swallowed up by the earth. He thus becomes for Shelley's purpose an underground being whose purely textual existence is linked to the mention of Typhon (I. 212), the Titan who rebelled against Zeus, was struck by the sky-god's lightning bolt, and buried under the volcano Mount Aetna.[131] Both Amphiarus and Typhon prefigure the mighty chthonic figure of Demogorgon, whose name derives from a late Latin word with Greek roots meaning 'people' and 'grim, terrible'.[132] As is widely recognized, Shelley would have encountered Demogorgon in Boccaccio's *Genealogy of the Gods*, where he is among other things the origin of volcanic activity deep under the earth, as well as 'the dreaded name / Of Demogorgon' in Book II of *Paradise Lost*, 964–5. Among the various other possible Demogorgons—the *OED*'s examples include Statius, Ariosto, and Spenser—a further one should be suggested here, for it may indicate another instance of Shelley's incorporating in his own work the radicalism of the previous generation.

Demogorgon was a nickname employed for Thomas Paine by some of his British friends and acquaintances in the 1790s. Henry Fuseli, in a letter to his patron William Roscoe, wrote of the help he had received in moving a large painting of his into the house of William Sharp for engraving: 'We have contrived a roller for him from the design of

---

[128] Matthews, 'A Volcano's Voice in Shelley', in *Shelley: Modern Judgments*, p. 179.
[129] *Prometheus Unbound*, II. ii. 43.
[130] 'Do you not hear, Amphiarus, hidden under the Earth?' Earl K. Wasserman, *Shelley: A Critical Reading* (Baltimore and London: Johns Hopkins University Press, 1971), pp. 282–3, provides and discusses the context in Cicero from which Shelley took this quotation.
[131] See Wasserman's important discussion of Typhon in *Shelley*, 334–6.
[132] *OED*, s.v.

Mr. Paine who is a Mechanic as well as a Demogorgon, to enable him to place it, for it is 13 feet high by a width of 10'.[133] Evidently Paine also designed some kind of apparatus for another artist, George Romney (who painted his portrait in June 1792); for, some years later, William Hayley wrote to John Flaxman: 'It will please you to hear that, as a Tribute to the Genius of our poor Disabled Romney we have preserv'd, & I think improv'd, in a Copy of considerable size, the Miltonic design of our old Friend, that you remember on the Boards of Demogorgons Hall, as we us'd to call his painting apartment—[.]'[134] As we have seen, Blake compared Paine's overthrowing of the armies of Europe with a small pamphlet to one of Jesus's miracles, asserting that he saw the Holy Ghost in Paine striving with Christendom. Shelley, with his keen interest in the radicalism of the 1790s, could appreciate Paine's power. He was reading *Rights of Man* in December 1817, and on 3 November 1819 he wrote a long letter to the *Examiner* protesting against the prosecution of Richard Carlisle for republishing *The Age of Reason*.[135] Shelley's knowledge of Paine need not have been limited to printed sources, for, through Mary Godwin Shelley, he was in a position to benefit from whatever oral tradition had passed to her from Mary Wollstonecraft and William Godwin, both of whom had known Paine in the early 1790s. The point is not, of course, that the Demogorgon of *Prometheus Unbound* could be an allegorization of Paine, but rather that Paine as Demogorgon may have provided a further element to Shelley's richly syncretic conception.[136]

Scene 4 begins as a scene of instruction that at first appears to be an archetypal configuration of apocalypse:

PANTHEA
What veiled form sits on that ebon throne?

ASIA
The veil has fallen! . . .

(II. iv. 1–2)

---

[133] Letter dated 29 May 1792; G. E. Bentley, Jr., *Blake Records* (Oxford: Clarendon Press, 1969), p. 46. Paine's abilities as 'a Mechanic' extended to designing an iron bridge, the plans of which he brought with him to England for sale.

[134] Letter dated 16 July 1800; Bentley, *Blake Records*, p. 70.

[135] See *Letters*, 2: 136–48, 481. Hogle argues persuasively for the contribution of Paine's conception of Jesus as a revolutionary to Shelley's shaping of Prometheus. See *Shelley's Process*, pp. 174–5 and 371 n. 31.

[136] Wasserman (*Shelley*, pp. 332 n. and 362 n.) adds Lucan and Claudian as possible sources; Paul Foot points out the existence of a radical journal called the *Gorgon* in 1818–19 (*Red Shelley*, pp. 196–7).

However, what is seen behind the veil is scarcely seen at all. Panthea says:

> I see a mighty Darkness
> Filling the seat of power; and rays of gloom
> Dart round, as light from the meridian Sun,
> Ungazed upon and shapeless—neither limb
> Nor form—nor outline; yet we feel it is
> A living Spirit.

                                            (II. iv. 2–7)

This description, if that is what it can be called, recalls Death in *Paradise Lost*:

> The other shape—
> If shape it might be call'd that shape had none
> Distinguishable in member, joint, or limb,
> Or substance might be call'd that shadow seem'd,
> For each seem'd either; black it stood as Night[137]

In its consciously calling attention to indescribability, however, it is *Paradise Lost* as mediated by Edmund Burke, whose *Philosophical Enquiry* gives Milton's passage in support of the view that 'To make any thing very terrible, obscurity seems in general to be necessary'.[138] The Miltonic description, Burke says, is characterized by 'gloomy pomp' (cf. Demogorgon as a 'tremendous gloom' in I. 207), and he continues: 'In this description all is dark, uncertain, confused, terrible, and sublime to the last degree'.[139] Of course Demogorgon cannot be understood entirely in terms of the Burkean sublime—here, as in 'Mont Blanc', Shelley has transformed the earlier conception while maintaining a connection with it.

Asia's verbal exchange with Demogorgon takes the form of a catechism in which both parties know the answers to the questions, at least up to a point. As expected, Demogorgon says that God made the living world and the good things in it. However, when Asia gets to the crucial question of 'who made Terror, madness, crime, remorse' and other evils (II. iv. 19–28), the only response she can obtain from Demogorgon is: 'He reigns' (28, 31). This is curious in a way, because the answer is

---

[137] *Paradise Lost*, ii. 666–670, as noted by Reiman and Powers, *Shelley's Poetry and Prose*, p. 171 n. 8.

[138] Edmund Burke, *A Philosophical Enquiry into the Origin of Our Ideas of the Sublime and Beautiful*, ed. J. T. Boulton (Notre Dame, Ind., and London: University of Notre Dame Press, 1968), p. 58.   [139] Ibid., p. 59.

hardly a secret. The Earth gave it in her words to Prometheus early in Act I. It is as if Asia wants Demogorgon to participate in a magical act of naming Jupiter in order to destroy him. This Demogorgon declines to do, because 'a voice / Is wanting, the deep truth is imageless' (115–16). It may seem a strange thing for a poet to say or to have said on his behalf; yet it is entirely consistent with Shelley's deep philosophical scepticism.[140] In a sense, then, the revelation we so confidently expected at the beginning of this scene has been deflected, and one might suspect Shelley here of using a technique that Byron would employ in *Cain*, raising the expectation of apocalyptic knowledge only to deflate it. Yet in another sense the answer is immediately at hand in the world of action. To Asia's question of 'When shall the destined hour arise?' (128), meaning when shall Prometheus be freed and the millennium begin?, Demogorgon indicates with a 'Behold!' the two chariots of the Spirits who will destroy the old order and inaugurate the new one.

Jupiter, of course is unaware that the moment of transformation has come; or, rather, he has a false consciousness of the consolidation of his power that he believes is at hand. His speech at the beginning of Act III, out-Heroding Herod, brings together elements of various tyrants and ogre fathers as Shelley saw them, including both Milton's Satan and his God.

> Ye congregated Powers of Heaven who share
> The glory and the strength of him ye serve,
> Rejoice! Henceforth I am omnipotent.
>
> (III. i. 1–3)

The entire address is shot through with parodic elements. Returning to the original myth (which has been absent from *Prometheus Unbound* for some time), Shelley plays upon the idea that Thetis would have a son stronger than his father. 'Even now I have begotten a strange wonder' (line 18) echoes Psalm 2: 7—'the Lord hath said unto me, Thou art my Son; this day have I begotten thee'—and God's saying in *Paradise Lost*: 'This day I have begot whom I declare / My only Son' (v. 603–4).[141] Characteristically, Jupiter conceives of sexual intercourse in Sadean terms, as an act of phallic aggression that threatens to destroy its female object:

> Thetis, bright Image of Eternity!—
> When thou didst cry, 'Insufferable might!

---

[140] See C. E. Pulos, *The Deep Truth: A Study of Shelley's Skepticism* (Lincoln, Nebr.: University of Nebraska Press, 1954).

[141] As pointed out by Wasserman, *Shelley*, p. 297.

God! spare me! I sustain not the quick flames,
The penetrating presence.'

(36–9)

Shelley has transferred to Thetis the story of Semele, perhaps by way of Marlowe's 'flaming Jupiter / When he appeared to hapless Semele'.[142] Jupiter's telling how his sex object cried 'all my being . . . is dissolved' (39–41) during their intercourse contrasts with Asia's dream of a sexual exchange with the transfigured Prometheus in which 'My being was condensed' (II. i. 86). 'Dissolved' and 'condensed' may appear similar, but the world of difference here is between imagining sexuality as a mode of annihilation and as a transformative interchange. Unsurprisingly the result is not the heir apparent expected by Jupiter.

Jupiter imagines a ghastly parody of the Incarnation in the form of a spirit 'which unbodied now / Between us, floats, felt although unbeheld, / Waiting the incarnation, which ascends—' (45–7). The metaphor he chooses should tell him that something is amiss:

Feel'st thou not, O World,
The Earthquake of his chariot thundering up
Olympus?

(49–51)

Had Jupiter, like Shelley, been a student of the political discourse of the 1790s, he would have known that the earthquake of Revelation 11: 33 was (as mentioned in the Introduction) a figure for the overthrow of kings. However, Jupiter is not entirely wrong about Demogorgon. The 'Awful Shape' announces: 'I am thy child, as thou wert Saturn's child, / Mightier than thee' (50, 54–5). Jupiter deposed and castrated his father Saturn; now it will be done unto him. Yet, if that is so, Demogorgon can hardly be the incarnation of the process of Necessity that has been implied up to now. He can in this context only represent another turn of the wheel of history, leading not to a millennium but to a continuation of the cycle. His meaning oscillates further in what immediately follows:

JUPITER
                    Detested prodigy!
Even thus beneath the deep Titanian prisons
I trample thee! . . . Thou lingerest?
                              Mercy, mercy!

(61–4)

---

[142] Marlowe, *The Tragical History of the Life and Death of Doctor Faustus*, V. i. 113–14.

By 'prodigy' Jupiter appears to have in mind *OED* meaning 2, 'An amazing or marvellous thing; *esp.* something out of the ordinary course of nature; something abnormal or monstrous'; yet some association with 'progeny' lingers. He intends to relegate this abnormal son to the subterranean realm where he previously stowed Typhon and his fellow Titans. Yet what we witness is not so much a conflict of elemental forces as a shoving match. The situation is not in any way equal to the meaning it is supposed to bear. It's true that Shelley recovers poetically, first with Jupiter's unsuccessful wish to bring Demogorgon down with him, expressed in a trope that must be discussed further in a moment, then with a brilliant momentary view of Demogorgon from the perspective of the falling Jupiter—'like a cloud, mine enemy above / Darkens my fall with victory!' (82–3). However, the buckling of meaning we saw a few lines earlier was not a momentary failure of style, but a fault in conception. Clearly wishing to avoid the bloody encounters he had represented in *The Revolt of Islam*, Shelley appears at a loss as to how to convey the moment of apocalypse.

If we compare *Prometheus Unbound* at this point to *Queen Mab*, we see that Shelley's view can be characterized as millennialist or millenarian, depending on the point in time from which history is perceived. At the end of scene 3, the movement from apocalypse to millennium is marked by the reinstitution of the Lampadephoria[143] at 'this far goal of time' (174). The advent of the millennium is then described in the following scene by the Spirit of the Earth and the Spirit of the Hour, who, like two succeeding messengers in a Greek play, report on the result. The first tells of going through a great city and hearing a mysterious 'long long sound, as it would never end' (iv. 57). This must have been produced, as Webb points out, by the curved shell containing 'a voice to be accomplished' that Prometheus gave the Spirit of the Hour with the command:

> . . . as thy chariot cleaves the kindling air,
> Thou breathe into the many-folded Shell,
> Loosening its mighty music; it shall be
> As thunder mingled with clear echoes.[144]

The sound that Wordsworth dreamed he heard when he put the Shell to his ear in *The Prelude* foretold destruction to the children of the Earth, but this Shelleyan equivalent of the last trump has the effect of resurrecting the living:

---

[143] The torch race of youths in honour of Prometheus. See Edward B. Hungerford, *Shores of Darkness* (New York: Columbia University Press, 1941), pp. 197–8.
[144] III. iii. 67, 79–82; see Webb, *Shelley: A Voice Not Understood*, p. 181.

And all the inhabitants leapt suddenly
Out of their rest, and gathered in the streets,
Looking in wonder up to heaven.

(III. iv. 58–60)

The Spirit of the Hour follows with lines combining architectural and sculptural forms in a way characteristic of Shelley, whose imagination delighted in extending the text into the third dimension. Donald H. Reiman has shown that the architectural place described is partly based on the Vatican Museum's Sala della Biga (two-horse chariot), in which the horses are yoked by a sculpted snake with a head at either end.[145]

Yoked to it by an amphisbænic snake
The likeness of those winged steeds will mock
The flight from which they find repose.

(119–21)

The *amphisbæna* provides an alternative to the *ouroborous*. The latter, Blake's Orc serpent again, threatens to entrap humankind in cyclically repetitive history; the former can only go forward into the millennium. If it be objected that the two-headed snake is not found in nature, the Shelleyan reply might be that neither is the serpent with its tail in its mouth—both are constructions of the imagination taking as their point of departure the snake's metaphorically ambiguous casting off of its slough. In the world described in lines 126–204, the 'mighty change' is more internal than external. The disappearance of kings has made it possible for humans to associate in true fellowship. No longer do people engage in the demeaning, self-aggrandizing practices that made them hate themselves, and the inscription over the gate of Dante's Hell is therefore expunged. Shelley is characteristically brilliant at analysing the psychology of subjugation; he did so earlier in the portrait of the self-despising bureaucrat Mercury, and he does it again in the eloquent 'None talked that common, false, cold, hollow talk / Which makes the heart deny the *yes* it breathes' (149–50). The women of the world are concomitantly empowered, 'Speaking the wisdom once they could not think, / Looking emotions once they feared to feel' (157–8). Then, in a view of the present from the future, comes a gathering of the appurtenances of the old order, most of which were mentioned earlier in the

---

[145] See Donald H. Reiman, 'Roman Scenes in *Prometheus Unbound*', in *Romantic Texts and Contexts* (Columbia, Mo.: University of Missouri Press, 1987), pp. 279–83.

poem, now swept away. Jupiter was worshipped under many names—the long statement that begins on line 180 has as its grammatical subject 'shape', and the verb, 'frown', is delayed for a full ten lines. The veil and the mask, images of illusion, also return. The veil, combining aspects of the phenomenal world into deceptive 'colours' that provide but a distorted version of reality, has been 'torn aside', as the veil of the Temple was rent at the Crucifixion. The 'loathsome mask', or socially constructed false identity, has fallen to reveal the true human face. But despite the overthrow of external bonds and the consequent dissolution of some internal ones, the human condition remains even in the millennial world. There is still passion, pain, and guilt, because man 'made or suffered [allowed] them'. And, as Godwin had written, in a passage already quoted with reference to *Queen Mab*, perfectibility means 'that every perfection or excellence that human beings are competent to conceive, human beings, unless in cases that are palpably and unequivocally excluded by the structure of their frame, are competent to attain'. This was as true of Shelley's conception in 1819 as in 1811. Even in the millennial world, there is still chance, death, and mutability,

> The clogs of that which else might oversoar
> The loftiest star of unascended Heaven
> Pinnacled dim in the intense inane.
>
> (III. iv. 202–4)

So Shelley ended *Prometheus Unbound* at the beginning of September 1819. However, that very month he was writing lines that would become part of a new act, which he completed in early December 1819.[146] What he produced deserves much more than Byron's *Heaven and Earth* to be termed an oratorio. It comprises a structured series of lyrics and speeches, for the most part celebrating the millennial world—a world that is very much this world transformed and not another, to use Wordsworth's words,

> the world
> Of all of us, the place on which in the end
> We find our happiness, or not at all.[147]

Wordsworth, however, described a millennium only in the microcosm of *Home at Grasmere*, not in the larger world. Even Blake's *Jerusalem* devotes only the last four of its 100 plates of text and design to the

---

[146] Dates are once more from Freistat, *Prometheus Unbound Notebooks*, pp. lxi–lxxxiv.
[147] *The Prelude*, x. 725–7; see Ch. 3, p. 187.

millennium. Of the six poets discussed in this book, Shelley is the one in whose imagination the millennial played the greatest role. The two Spirits' speeches at the end of Act III total 158 lines, yet Shelley desired an expansion of the millennial theme into a fourth act. This, however, is only part of the reason. Shelley also wished to qualify the idea of the millennium in two substantial ways, and this could not have been done within the confines of Act III. These qualifications appear at two important points, while the body of the rest prevents them from eclipsing the millennial idea.

In the magnificent passages in which Panthea verbally recreates the Orb of the earth (IV. 237–68, 270–318) can be discerned elements that threaten to disrupt the millennial ballet going on in the cosmos. These begin seemingly innocuously with the image of the child that appears to parallel the white-haired winged Infant in the chariot of the moon described by Ione in the preceding lines (206–35).

> Within the Orb itself,
> Pillowed upon its alabaster arms
> Like to a child o'erwearied with sweet toil,
> On its own folded wings and wavy hair
> The Spirit of the Earth is laid asleep.
>
> (261–5)

Yet this child, unlike its innocent predecessor, turns out to be, as D. J. Hughes puts it in a penetrating essay, 'the Child of Apocalypse'.[148] 'Vast beams' shoot from its forehead, 'Filling the abyss with sunlike lightenings', and go on to 'Pierce the dark soil, and as they pierce and pass / Make bare the secrets of the Earth's deep heart' (270–9). Once back in the realm of the chthonic, what do we see? We begin with 'Infinite mine of adamant and gold, / Valueless stones and unimagined gems' (281–2), and then go on to past history:

> the beams flash on
> And make appear the melancholy ruins
> Of cancelled cycles; anchors, beaks of ships,
> Planks turned to marble, quivers, helms and spears
> And gorgon-headed targes, and the wheels
> Of scythed chariots, and the emblazonry
> Of trophies, standards, and armorial beasts

---

[148] D. J. Hughes, 'Potentiality in *Prometheus Unbound*', *Studies in Romanticism*, 2 (1963): 107–26; repr. in *Shelley's Poetry and Prose*, pp. 603–20; at p. 608.

> Round which Death laughed, sepulchred emblems
> Of dead Destruction, ruin within ruin!
>
> (287–95)

The list has a curious resemblance to one in Shakespeare's *Richard III*, in which Clarence recounts his dream of drowning:

> Methoughts I saw a thousand fearful wrecks,
> A thousand men that fishes gnaw'd upon,
> Wedges of gold, great anchors, heaps of pearl,
> Inestimable stones, unvalued jewels,
> All scatter'd in the bottom of the sea;
> Some lay in dead men's skulls, and in the holes,
> Where eyes did once inhabit there were crept,
> As 'twere in scorn of eyes, reflecting gems,
> That woo'd the slimy bottom of the deep
> And mock'd the dead bones that lay scatter'd by.
>
> (I. iv. 24–33)

The dream reflects Clarence's guilt for his past treachery and anticipates his murder in the Tower, and there may be an unconscious link in Shelley's recollection between this and the dead past. However, the 'cancelled cycles' refer back to a model of history that was supposedly abandoned with the downfall of Jupiter. Vincent De Luca has astutely pointed out the surprising force of this passage and what immediately follows, suggesting that 'the whole "cancelled cycles" passage is an instance of *anti*-millennial proclamation, as if there persisted beneath the balanced cosmos represented by the Magus Zoroaster "underneath the grave" (i. 197), a potent realm founded upon monstrosity, violence, and retrogression in time'.[149] Certainly the lines that follow would seem more at home in Byron's yet-unwritten *Cain* than in a celebration of the millennium:

> The wrecks beside of many a city vast,
> Whose population which the Earth grew over
> Was mortal but not human.
>
> (296–8)

The close of this passage would also seem at home in Byron:

---

[149] Vincent A. De Luca, 'The Style of Millennial Announcement in *Prometheus Unbound*', *Keats–Shelley Journal*, 28 (1979): 98. De Luca also calls attention to similar anti-millennial elements in the speeches of the Spirit of the Earth and the Spirit of the Hour that close Act III.

> . . . till the blue globe
> Wrapt Deluge round it like a cloak, and they
> Yelled, gaspt and were abolished; or some God
> Whose throne was in a Comet, past, and cried—
> 'Be not!' and they were no more.

$$(314-18)$$

These lines might well find a place in the undoing of the Creation in 'Darkness'. Despite this return of subject-matter that might have been thought left behind in the prehistory of Act I, the 'cancelled cycles' passage can be viewed, as it is by both Hughes and De Luca, as complicating, rather than undermining, the millennial component of *Prometheus Unbound*. It would be more difficult to take such a view of the new end of the poem.

In Act II a Song of Spirits anticipated that

> . . . the Eternal, the Immortal,
> Must unloose through life's portal
> The snake-like Doom coiled underneath his throne
> By that alone!

$$(iii. 95-8)$$

This serpent may be linked with Jupiter's simile and with Canto I of *The Revolt of Islam*, but at the end of Act IV the symbol returns in more ambiguous form. Demogorgon cautions that the millennium may yet turn out to be unstable, that the amphisbæna may turn out to be the ourobouros after all:

> . . . if, with infirm hand, Eternity,
> Mother of many acts and hours, should free
> The serpent that would clasp her with its length—

$$(IV. 565-7)$$

There is, as Timothy Webb observes, a suggestion here of the chaining of Satan in Revelation.[150] Indeed, Shelley had once begun a poem explicitly on the unloosing in Revelation of, 'that old serpent, which is the Devil, and Satan' (Rev. 20: 2), after his thousand years of imprisonment. It is an untitled fragment of fifteen lines transcribed by Richard Garnett and published in 1870 by William Michael Rossetti:

---

[150] See Webb, *Shelley: A Voice Not Understood*, p. 172.

> A golden-wingèd Angel stood
>   Before the Eternal Judgment-seat:
> His looks were wild, and Devils' blood
>   Stained his dainty hands and feet.
>   . . . The Father and the Son
> Knew that strife was now begun.
> They knew that Satan had broken his chain,
> And, with millions of demons in his train,
> Was ranging over the world again.
> Before the Angel had told his tale,
>   A sweet and a creeping sound
> Like the rushing of wings was heard around;
> And suddenly the lamps grew pale—
> The lamps, before the Archangels seven,
> That burn continually in heaven.[151]

Shelley may have dashed this off—it certainly does not appear to have been worked on thoroughly—after reading Coleridge's 'Ode on the Departing Year' in the *Sibylline Leaves* of 1817, with the passage alluding to the seven spirits of God in Revelation 4: 5 that Coleridge introduced to this version of his poem:

> Till wheeling round the Throne the LAMPADS seven
>   (The mystic Words of Heaven)
> Permissive signal make;[152]

Such explicitly Christian imagery was congenial to Coleridge, but Shelley probably did well not to attempt to develop it further. Demogorgon's figuration of the serpent is more characteristic of Shelley's imagination, though it presents problems of a different nature.

Although the whole process of tyranny and non-violent revolution might have to be lived over again, in Demogorgon's view hope would yet persist. The answer would be, as in *The Mask of Anarchy* (1819), non-violent resistance:

---

[151] *The Poetical Works of Percy Bysshe Shelley*, ed. William Michael Rossetti (2 vols., London: E. Moxon & Son, 1870), 2: 299. This poem was transcribed by Mary Shelley, and the transcription has been published in the *Bodleian Shelley Manuscript Series*, vol. 2: Bodleian MS. Shelley adds. d. 7, ed. Irving Massey (New York: Garland Press, 1987), p. 169. There are numerous incidental variants, but two important ones: in l. 3, 'weird' for 'wild', and in l. 11 'secret' for 'sweet', I am grateful to Neil Freistat for information on the MWS transcription.

[152] *Sibylline Leaves*, p. 54. See Paley, *Coleridge's Later Poetry* (Oxford: Clarendon Press, 1996), pp. 59–60.

> To suffer woes which Hope thinks infinite;
> To forgive wrongs darker than Death or Night,
> To defy Power which seems Omnipotent;
> To love, and bear; to hope, till Hope creates
> From its own wreck the thing it contemplates;
>
> (570–4)

Only by such means could the millennium be re-attained, for in Shelley's view violence would change the nature of even its righteous perpetrators. Yet one must take a very long view indeed to imagine such hope, and these lines, composed of a procession of parallel abstractions, make for a weak ending compared with the end of Act III. If the millennial ideal is not to be undermined by what precedes them, something different would be necessary, but what that could be is hard to imagine. There is also the disturbing possibility, whether or not Shelley intended it, that Demogorgon himself could be part of the cycle of history, as he had more or less declared in III. i. 54–5. This destabilization of millennium at the end of the poem complements, if that is the word, the inadequate representation of apocalypse earlier. These weaknesses do not, of course, obviate the poem's frequent power, beauty of conception and imagery, melodic richness, and moral perception. *Prometheus Unbound* remains the most ambitious and least unsuccessful Romantic attempt to unite apocalypse and millennium.

6

Keats

Why did Keats abandon his *Hyperion* poems? 'There were too many Miltonic inversions in it'.[1] This was of course said not of the first *Hyperion* but of the second, though most of us may think it much more applicable to the first. 'I w[as] ill at the time'.[2] But of course this statement, written into Keats's copy of his 1820 volume, refers to the insertion of the 'Advertisement' to the first *Hyperion*, not to Keats's giving up on the second. Indeed, if Charles Brown was correct in assigning 'The Jealousies' to the end of 1819, Keats was capable of writing a poem of almost 800 lines at a time when, again according to Brown, he was also 'remodelling' *Hyperion*.[3] Jerome McGann and, more recently, John Barnard have shown (with respect to the *Indicator* version of 'La Belle Dame Sans Merci') how we ought not to imagine Keats's periods of illness to fit our preconceptions about texts.[4] Whether or not Brown was correct about Keats's poetic activity in 1819, there was a reason for abandoning the *Hyperion* project in addition to Keats's all-too-real illness and his rejection of Miltonic influence, and that reason has to do with the subject of apocalypse and millennium. Before discussing this further, a few words are necessary about two interrelated subjects: Keats's interest in the political and in the apocalyptic.

In *The Use of Poetry and the Use of Criticism*, originally delivered as lectures to a Harvard audience, T. S. Eliot could say: 'Keats does not

---

[1] Letter to John Hamilton Reynolds, 21 Sept. 1819, in *The Letters of John Keats*, ed. H. E. Rollins (2 vols., Cambridge, Mass.: Harvard University Press, 1958), 2: 167; hereafter *Letters*.

[2] See *The Poems of John Keats*, ed. Jack Stillinger (Cambridge, Mass.: Harvard University Press, 1978), p. 737; hereafter *S*.

[3] See H. E. Rollins, ed., *The Keats Circle: Letters and Papers*, 2nd edn. (2 vols., Cambridge, Mass.: Harvard University Press, 1965), 2: 71–2.

[4] See Jerome J. McGann, *The Beauty of Inflections: Literary Investigations in Historical Method and Theory* (Oxford: Oxford University Press, 1985), pp. 16–65; John Barnard, 'Keats's Belle Dame and the Sexual Politics of Leigh Hunt's *Indicator*', *Romanticism*, 1 (1995): 34–49.

appear to have taken any absorbing interest in public affairs'.[5] Mr. Eliot had his own political agenda—this is the same lecture in which he declared that Percy Shelley, who unarguably did take an absorbing interest in public affairs, had the philosophy of a twelve-year-old. Nevertheless, one imagines that most of his audience and readers, except for those few perhaps who had read Clarence Thorpe's essay 'Keats's Interest in Politics and World Affairs',[6] agreed. This situation did not markedly alter until the publication of a forum on 'Keats and Politics' in *Studies in Romanticism*.[7] The essays in *Keats and History*, edited by Nicholas Roe, further expanded our understanding of this subject, and, more recently, Roe's *John Keats and the Culture of Dissent* has illuminated the effect of Keats's period as a student at the Dissenting Enfield Academy on his intelligence and imagination.[8] This rich body of work makes it unnecessary to argue at length that Keats was deeply engaged with the history and politics of his own time, and allows instead some selective observations about his socio-political interests.

In his earlier poetry Keats's political language is very much that of the contemporary liberal press, using 'liberal' in a deliberately fuzzy sense for the moment, a sense in which it was, indeed, employed at the time. To this discursive realm belong the 'sceptred tyrants' and 'chains burst' of 'On Peace' (?Apr. 1814; *S* 28), the use of 'patriot' as a term of opposition in 'Lines Written on 29 May, the Anniversary of Charles's Restoration, on Hearing the Bells Ringing' (1814 or 1815; *S* 28), and the libertarian iconography of 'To George Felton Mathew' (November 1815; *S* 43), which passes from the contemplation of Chatterton, Shakespeare, and Milton to Alfred, 'Helvetian Tell', and William Wallace, and then to Burns. The appeal to the Commonwealthmen Algernon Sydney, Lord William Russell, and Sir Henry Vane in 'To George Felton Mathew' is reminiscent of that made by Coleridge as a radical in his lectures two decades before. In the celebrated opening of Book III

[5] T. S. Eliot, *The Use of Poetry and the Use of Criticism* (London: Faber & Faber, 1933), p. 102.
[6] Clarence Thorpe, 'Keats's Interest in Politics and World Affairs', *PMLA* 46 (1931): 1228–45.
[7] 'Keats and Politics', *Studies in Romanticism*, 25 (1986): 171–229.
[8] Nicholas Roe, ed., *Keats and History* (Cambridge: Cambridge University Press, 1995); *idem, John Keats and the Culture of Dissent* (Oxford: Clarendon Press, 1997). I should also mention that, with respect to the *Hyperion* poems, I have especially benefited from essays by Kenneth Muir and by Jonathan Bate: Muir, 'The Meaning of "Hyperion"', *John Keats: A Reassessment*, ed. Kenneth Muir (Liverpool: University of Liverpool Press, 1969), pp. 103–23; Jonathan Bate, 'Keats's Two *Hyperions* and the Problem of Milton', in *Romantic Revisions*, ed. Keith Hanley and R. Brinkley (Cambridge: Cambridge University Press, 1992), pp. 321–38.

of *Endymion* (*S* 163–4), Keats adopts a strategy extensively employed by radicals of the 1790s by associating his own side with the fertility of 'Our gold and ripe-ear'd hopes' in contrast to the unproductive nature of those 'who lord it o'er their fellow-men / With most prevailing tinsel' (1–2), characterized by 'crowns, and turbans' (12). This passage culminates with a simile bordering on the apocalyptic: 'Like thunder clouds that spake to Babylon' (20), followed by the question 'Are then regalities all gilded masks?' This is answered by an evocation of *real* 'Powers' and more fertility imagery, beginning with 'our own Ceres' (38). As we know, Keats told Woodhouse that this passage showed 'what I think of the present Ministry';[9] but its rhetorical features, like those of other poems, go back at least to the language of what may loosely be called the left in the Burke–Paine debate, a language that was still current in extra-parliamentary oppositional circles.

Keats's most sustained radical statement in verse is of course the denunciation of the exploitative brothers in *Isabella; or, the Pot of Basil*, written from February to April of 1818,[10] material not in the Boccaccio source, as Keats acknowledges in lines 145–60. Of this passage Bernard Shaw remarked: 'Everything that the Bolshevik means and feels when he uses the fatal epithet "bourgeois", is expressed forcibly, completely, and beautifully in these three [*sic*] stanzas. . . . And so Keats is among the prophets with Shelley'.[11] Even more pertinent, because more distinctive of Keats, is what may be the last poem he ever wrote, originally written in a copy of Spenser (*S* 535). It shows the power of the people (the Giant) educated by the printing-press (the sage Typographus) to defeat the agents of their oppressors (Artegall and Talus) and establish a civil polity. The Byron–Shelley circle was typically less sympathetic to mass movements and their spokesmen. Whereas Byron and Percy and Mary Shelley expressed fear and abhorrence of figures like Henry Hunt, Keats gloried in Hunt's 'triumphal entry into London',[12] writing with enthusiasm: 'The whole distance from the Angel Islington to the Crown and anchor [Strand] was lined with Multitudes'. Mary Shelley,

---

[9] See *The Poems of John Keats*, ed. Miriam Allott (London: Longman, 1970), p. 206 n.; hereafter Allott.

[10] ll. 105–36, *S* 249–50.

[11] G. B. Shaw, 'Keats', in *The John Keats Memorial Volume*, ed. G. C. Williams (London and New York: John Lane, 1921), p. 175. I thank Matthias Zimmerman for drawing my attention to this essay.

[12] Journal-letter to George and Georgiana Keats, 17–27 Sept. 1819; *Letters*, 2: 194.

writing to Percy, likened William Cobbett to Marat;[13] Keats wished he could vote for Cobbett in the Coventry election;[14] and he exulted in the government's apparent fear of Richard Carlisle, who 'has been selling deistical pamphlets, republished Tom Payne and many other works held in superstitious horror'.[15] We see, then, that in his politics, especially in 1819, Keats differed from the Byron–Shelley and the Hunt circles in having strong sympathy for the populist side of radical reform and its spokesmen. Of one of these something more must be said, for it was William Hone who gave Keats an occasion to mix the political and the apocalyptic.

Writing to his brothers George and Tom in December 1817, Keats declared, with evident satisfaction, that '[Thomas Jonathan] Wooler & [William] Hone have done us an essential service'[16] after the two radical journalists were acquitted in a political prosecution. On 5 January 1818 he remarked with evident satisfaction that 'There are fine Subscriptions going on for Hone',[17] presumably to pay the cost of his defence. As Aileen Ward has brilliantly shown, it was Hone's acquittal of the charges of blasphemous and seditious libel at his trial—or, rather, three trials—in December 1817 that provided the impulse for Keats's untitled Petrarchan sonnet sometimes referred to as 'Nebuchadnezzar's Dream', a poem that draws on the one canonical Old Testament apocalypse. In this poem Keats conflates two episodes in the book of Daniel concerning the dreams of Nebuchadnezzar.[18] The first part refers to Nebuchadnezzar's second dream, also the subject of memorable prints by John Hamilton Mortimer and by William Blake, after which the Babylonian king is driven out among the beasts of the field to eat grass until he recovers his reason. Keats's conclusion—'Ye are that head of gold!'—refers to the first dream, that of the 'great image' with head of gold, breast and arms of silver, belly and thighs of brass, legs of iron, and feet of iron and clay (2: 32–3). This powerful conception elicited verbal and pictorial representations by, among others, Dante, Rembrandt, and Blake. As Keats says, 'any

[13] *The Letters of Mary Wollstonecraft Shelley*, ed. Betty T. Bennett (Baltimore: Johns Hopkins University Press, 1980), 1: 49.

[14] Letter to C. W. Dilke, 4 Mar. 1820; *Letters*, 2: 272.

[15] To George and Georgiana Keats, 17–27 Sept. 1819; *Letters* 2: 194.

[16] *Letters*, 1: 191.   [17] Ibid. 199.

[18] The importance of Daniel in the apocalyptic tradition is discussed in the Introduction above. On Keats's poem, see Aileen Ward, 'Keats's Sonnet, "Nebuchadnezzar's Dream" ', *Philological Quarterly*, 34 (1955): 177–88. On Hone's trials, see Olivia Smith, *The Politics of Language 1791–1819* (Oxford: Clarendon Press, 1984), pp. 177–190.

Daniel' can supply the meaning that Nebuchadnezzar could not make out for himself: that the destruction of the great image signifies the destruction of empires in historical succession, a theme especially prominent in radical discourse from the time of Volney's *Ruins*. The 'loggerheads and chapman' are the ministry; the 'naumachia for mice and rats' a reference to the mock sea-battle on the Serpentine staged as part of the celebrations of victory over Napoleon in 1814. The concluding 'Ye are that head of gold' can make 'their [the ministers'] lying lips turn pale of hue' in recognition of Daniel's irony: 'And wheresoever the children of men dwell, the beasts of the field and the fowls of the heaven hath he given into thine hand, and hath made thee ruler over them all. Thou art this head of gold' (2: 38). But the gold was destroyed with the rest, 'and became like the chaff of the summer threshingfloors; and the wind carried them away' (2: 35). In contrast is the millennial kingdom of 2: 44: 'And in the days of these kings shall the God of heaven set up a kingdom, which shall never be destroyed; and the kingdom shall not be left to other people, but it shall break in pieces and consume all these kingdoms, and it shall stand for ever.'

I am not, of course, suggesting that Keats was using the language and imagery of Daniel solemnly. The poem is more like political caricatures that used biblical texts and images for satirical ends; it borders on the apocalyptic grotesque, of Coleridge's 'Fire, Famine, and Slaughter'. It is likely that the sonnet was intended for publication in some anti-ministerial newspaper or magazine. The poem demonstrates, in addition, that although Keats is not usually thought of as an apocalyptic poet, he was familiar with apocalyptic material and could incorporate it into his own poetry. We also see this in the verses Keats sent to his brother Tom, where, in describing the rocks of Fingal's cave in Staffa, Keats found a comparison to the writing of the Book of Revelation appropriate:

> Not Aladdin magian
> Ever such a work began;
> Not the Wizard of the Dee
> Ever such a dream could see;
> Not St. John in Patmos' isle,
> In the passion of his toil,
> When he saw the churches seven,
> Golden ailed, built up in heaven,
> Gazed at such a rugged wonder.[19]

[19] *S* 277, from a letter to Tom Keats, 23, 26 July 1818.

The reference is to Revelation 1: 20—'The seven stars are the angels of the seven churches: and the seven candlesticks which thou sawest are the seven churches'. It is generally recognized that Keats's prose description of the cave is related to *Hyperion* (Allott 374), and it also seems pertinent that its architect, 'the great Oceanus' (l. 28), will be given a key speech in Book II of Keats's first epic fragment. Again, among the 'thousand things' that perplex Bertha in *The Eve of St. Mark* (*S* 319, ll. 33–4) are:

> Aaron's breastplate, and the seven
> Candlesticks John saw in heaven

As J. Livingston Lowes commented, 'The first chapter of *The Revelation of St. John the Divine* [*sic*] was actively stirring, at least for the moment, in Keats's mind.'[20] It has also been suggested that in *Lamia* (*S* 472, Part 2, ll. 231–4) the 'awful rainbow once in heaven' and the 'Angel's wings' allude to Revelation 10: 1, where 'I saw another mighty angel come down from heaven . . . and a rainbow was upon his head'.[21] There are also, as we shall see, explicit references to Revelation in both *Hyperion* poems; but there, it is important to stress, what is concerned is not limited to tropes or verbal echoes but involves conception itself. In the 'transcendental cosmopolitics', as Leigh Hunt termed it,[22] of the first *Hyperion*, Saturn bears with him remembrances of the classical golden age over which he presided before he was

> . . . smother'd up,
> And buried from all godlike exercise
> Of influence benign on planets pale,
> Of admonitions to the winds and seas,
> Of peaceful sway above man's harvesting,
> And all those acts which Deity supreme
> Doth ease its heart of love in.

> (1. 106–12, *S* 332)

Keats brought his knowledge of a golden age from his classical reading and, most of all, from (as Ian Jack has shown in *Keats and the Mirror of Art*[23]) the paintings of Poussin. In the latter the Arcadian is never depicted without some trace of inevitability about its loss, and the same

---

[20] J. Livingston Lowes, 'Moneta's Temple', *PMLA*, 51 (1936): 1107 n.

[21] See *Poems of Keats*, ed. Allott, p. 645 n.

[22] See G. M. Matthews, ed., *Keats: The Critical Heritage* (London: Routledge and Kegan Paul, 1971), p. 255.

[23] Ian Jack, *Keats and the Mirror of Art* (Oxford: Clarendon Press, 1967).

is true of Keats's presentation of the laments of the Titans. In his speech at the end of Book I, Coelus assumes the need for his son, Saturn, to reassume power, but says:

> My life is but the life of winds and tides,
> No more than winds and tides can I avail:—
>
> (341–2, *S* 340)

And when Oceanus tells Saturn, 'Thou art not the beginning nor the end' (190), an ironical contrast is being made with One who *is* the beginning and the end, and who asserts it in Revelation 1: 8: 'I am Alpha and Omega, the beginning and the end, saith the Lord'.

Not being master of time, Saturn must accept the evolutionary pattern that Keats sees at work in it, and that is the subject of Keats's now familiar remarks on modern history in his journal-letter to George and Georgiana of 17–27 September 1819: 'Three great changes have been in progress— First for the better, next for the worse, and a third for the better once more'.[24] The first is 'the gradual annihilation of the tyranny of the nobles, when kings found it in their interest to conciliate the common people, elevate them and be just to them'; the second is 'a long struggle of kings to destroy all popular privileges', resisted by the English in particular.

The example of England, and the liberal writers of france and england sowed the seed of opposition to this Tyranny—and it was swelling in the ground until it burst out in the french revolution—That has had an unlucky termination. It put a stop to the rapid progress of free sentiments in England; and gave our Court hopes of turning back to the despotism of the 16 century. . . . They spread a horrid superstition against all inovation and improvement—

However, Keats is now optimistic. 'The present struggle in England of the people is to destroy this superstition. What has rous'd them to do it is their distresses—Perpaps [*sic*] on this account the pres'nt distresses of this nation are a fortunate thing—tho so horrid in the[i]r experience. You will see I mean that the french Revolution put a temporary stop to this third change, the change for the better—Now it is in progress again and I thing [*sic*] in an effectual one.' Oceanus's long speech (2. 173–243, *S* 346–8) voices this literally progressive theme:

> We fall by course of Nature's law, not force
> Of thunder, or of Jove.
>
> (181–2)

---

[24] *Letters*, 2: 193–4.

The effect is to transfer the aesthetic to the realm of the political in a sort of epic parallel to the 'Ode on a Grecian Urn':

> So on our heels a fresh perfection treads,
> A power more strong in beauty, born of us
> And fated to excel us . . .
>
> . . . .
>
> . . . for 'tis the eternal law
> That first in beauty should be first in might.
>
> (212–14, 228–9)

It has been observed that there are self-undermining contradictions in Oceanus's speech, conflicts between 'evolution and eternal perfection'[25] and between 'a naturalistic emphasis on sustenance and growth and a language of usurpation and hierarchy'.[26] These contradictions, aesthetic and historical, are proleptic of the ultimately unresolved state of the first *Hyperion*, for it is evident that the speech is intended as a thematic statement. As Jonathan Bate has argued, '*Hyperion* is a progressive poem; it concerns a revolution, and Oceanus' lines make clear that the new regime is superior to the old'.[27] Furthermore, as Bate also points out, the contemporary reader could be expected to recognize *Hyperion* as 'a "progress poem" . . . concerned with the development of enlightened political institutions'. We might say that this is the converse of what Northrop Frye means by 'displacement':[28] through its figuration, the myth becomes a vehicle for political meaning without being allegorized. What went wrong is not hard to determine. After the brilliant opening of Book III with Apollo's dying into life, what could have happened? The epic machinery could have been mobilized for a flashback war in heaven, but in the post-Waterloo world this would have presented even greater problems than it had for Milton. Worse, a struggle between Hyperion and Apollo could have occurred in the mythical present. The shoving match between Demogorgon and Jupiter in *Prometheus Unbound* is at least mercifully

---

[25] See Nancy Moore Goslee, *Uriel's Eye: Miltonic Stationing and Statuary in Blake, Keats, and Shelley* (University, Ala.: University of Alabama Press, 1985), pp. 79–82.

[26] Carl Plasa, 'Revision and Repression in Keats's *Hyperion*: "Pure Creations of the Poet's Brain" ', *Keats–Shelley Journal*, 44 (1992): 131.

[27] Bate, 'Keats's Two *Hyperions* and the Problem of Milton', p. 335; see also Marilyn Butler, *Romantics, Rebels, and Reactionaries* (Oxford and New York: Oxford University Press, 1981), pp. 151–4.

[28] Northrop Frye, *Anatomy of Criticism* (Princeton: Princeton University Press, 1957), pp. 137–8.

short; Keats must have realized that a prolonged battle, whether past or present, would not do. Hyperion could have made a noble speech of renunciation after recognizing Apollo's superior beauty, but that would hardly have carried the poem even one Book further. So *Hyperion* eventually appeared as 'A Fragment', capitalizing on a Romantic mode given renewed appeal by the publication of Coleridge's 'Kubla Khan' in 1816; but this we know was not Keats's original intention. When he took up the subject again, he began *The Fall of Hyperion* before what had been Book I, expanding its scope magnificently, but at the same time introducing a problem of another nature.

When the narrator of *The Fall* describes what he sees in Moneta's temple, he draws upon imagery from the Old and New Testaments, beginning with a reference to Matthew 6: 19-20 in line 75—'Or in that place moth could not corrupt'. As Lowes shows, the furnishings of the temple and some of its architectural details are of biblical origin.[29] Some derive from Revelation, especially in the passage describing Moneta's ministering at the altar in l. 95-107 (*S* 480).

8: 3-4: 'And another angel came and stood at the altar . . . And the smoke of the incense . . . ascended up'

9: 13: 'and I heard a voice from the four horns of the golden altar'

15: 8, 16: 1: 'And the temple was filled with smoke . . . And I heard a great voice out of the temple'

The biblical references are not limited to Revelation, for there are also allusions to Exodus, Leviticus, and other books of the Old Testament, sometimes in the same phrases of Keats's text. Furthermore, the Temple's 'black gates / Were shut against the sunrise evermore' (85-6) because of God's command to Ezekiel in 44: 1-2: 'Then he brought me back the way of the gate of the outward sanctuary which looketh toward the east, and it was shut. Then said the Lord unto me; This gate shall be shut, it shall not be opened, and no man shall enter in by it; because the Lord, the God of Israel, hath entered in by it, therefore it shall be shut'. And in the 'mingled heap' of objects in lines 78-80— 'Robes, golden tongs, censer, and chafing dish, / Girdles, and chains, and holy jewelries'—Lowes shows that all but one originate in descriptions of the Tabernacle and its contents in Exodus 25: 38, 38: 4, 8, 13-14, and Numbers 4: 14. As Lowes argues, 'reminiscences of both Old and New Testaments, already merged in his [Keats's] memory,

---

[29] Lowes, 'Moneta's Temple', p. 1108.

blend again in the poem'.[30] They do not, however, blend haphazardly. Just as the Book of Revelation reconfigures images from parts of the Old Testament as the materials of apocalyptic vision—most importantly, those parts having to do with the structure and furnishings of the Temple,[31] Keats's echoes of the Old and New Testaments, sometimes simultaneous, in the passage under discussion, have to do with the Temple and Temple ritual. The description of the effect of the incense in line 105, for example ('And clouded all the altar with soft smoke'), recalls both Revelation 8: 4 as just cited, and Leviticus 16: 13, where the incense is to be put on the fire 'that the cloud of incense may cover the mercy seat'. Such recasting takes the method of Revelation further, by using its images, as well as those of the Old Testament, to create a context of apocalyptic expectation.

That expectation is fulfilled when the poet looks behind Moneta's veils, an act rich in significance. On one level it recalls familiar iconographic meanings, such as the unveiling of Isis or the pictorial subject of Time Unveiling Truth (as in Goya's great painting in the National Museum, Stockholm). Anne Mellor has called attention to the importance of what was then thought to be the weaving of the peplum in the Parthenon frieze, so important to Keats.[32] Once more, we may recall that the root of 'apocalypse' is the Greek *apokalupsis*, 'revelation', from *apokaluptein*, 'to uncover' (*apo* = 'away', *kaluptein* = 'to cover'). The uncovering of Moneta's face is literally and figuratively an apocalypse. The face 'deathwards progressing / To no death' (i. 260–1) may also echo a passage in a verse play by (ironically enough) a Scots reviewer, John Wilson's *City of the Plague* (Edinburgh, 1816), describing a victim of the plague of 1665:

> I saw something in her tearless eyes
> More than a mother's grief—the cold dull gleam
> Of mortal sickness hastening to decay.

(If the poet indeed had remembered these lines, it would reinforce Aileen Ward's contention that in Moneta's face Keats depicted the cathected image of his dead mother.[33] 'Progressing to no death',

---

[30] Lowes, 'Moneta's Temple', p. 1101.
[31] See Austin Farrer, *A Rebirth of Images: The Making of St. John's Apocalypse* (Westminster: Dacre Press, 1949).
[32] Anne K. Mellor, 'Keats's Face of Moneta', *Keats–Shelley Journal*, 25 (1976): 65–80.
[33] Aileen Ward, *John Keats: The Making of a Poet*, 2nd edn. (New York: Farrar, Strauss, and Giroux, 1986), p. 340.

however, extends mortality to an endless process like Wordsworth's 'woods decaying, never to be decayed' in a text Keats could not have seen (*Prelude*, vi. 557). In this context, 'progressing' ironizes the theme of progress in the first *Hyperion*, and this is continued a few lines later when the poet adjures Moneta 'by the golden age' that we know to be irrecoverable and calls her 'The pale Omega of a wither'd race' (288), inviting contrast once more with the God of Revelation 1: 8 who is *both* Alpha and Omega. Moneta is the vehicle of apocalypse, but it is now the poet who assumes the role of John of Patmos, describing the signs that appear to him in the light of Moneta's 'planetary eyes' (281). At this point it is the poet's voice that becomes oracular, uttering a 'conjuration' (291) that brings us to the point where the first *Hyperion* began.

Whatever the reason for the abandonment of the second *Hyperion*, it is appropriate that it should end—or discontinue—at the point that it does; for, in presenting Hyperion's palace, even the first *Hyperion* borders on the apocalyptic. Hyperion's 'diamond paved lustrous long arcades', which appear in both versions (*Hyperion*, i. 220; *Fall*, ii. 56), suggest the Jerusalem of Revelation 21: 19–21: 'And the foundations of the wall of the city were garnished with all manner of precious stones . . . And the twelve gates were twelve pearls.' There is, furthermore, the possibility of a link between the description of the palace, similar in both versions, and the apocalyptic paintings of John Martin:

> His palace bright,
> Bastion'd with pyramids of glowing gold,
> And touch'd with shade of bronzed obelisks,
> Glares a blood red through all the thousand courts,
> Arches, and domes, and fiery galleries:
> And all its curtains of Aurorian clouds
> Flush angerly . . .
>
> (24–30, *S* 490)

A parallel between Keats and Martin, though involving *Lamia*, not *Hyperion*, is drawn in an undated manuscript letter by G. M. Young tipped into the Victoria and Albert Museum's extra-annotated copy of *John Martin* by Thomas Balston.[34] Young compares the typical pillars of Martin's paintings with Keats's 'Mulciber's columns gleam in far piazzian line' (*Lamia*, 1. 212), and he sees connections going as far as the original designs for the Crystal Palace. 'It all points toward an idiom, a

---

[34] Thomas Balston, *John Martin* (London: Gerald Duckworth, 1947).

visual idiom, which was forming about that time, and which, but for the tremendous deflection of the Gothic revival, might really have created an industrial architecture. The only fragment that realized itself was the Doric portico at Euston through which, originally, the traveller was to see the steel rails shooting in endless perspective to the north.' Although Martin's most famous pictures were created too late to influence Keats, *Joshua Commanding the Sun to Stand Still Upon Gibeon* was exhibited at the Royal Academy in 1816. This painting (Freemasons' Hall, London) shows Joshua and his army assaulting a hill city with colonnaded palaces, pyramids, and round towers, with a fiercely apocalyptic sky in the background. More recently, the influence of Martin's *The Fall of Babylon* on the imagery of Hyperion's palace has been suggested.[35] (This would involve postulating that the passage was written out of sequence, as *Babylon* was first exhibited (at the British Institution) in early February 1819.) *Babylon* is an even more striking visual statement than *Joshua*, with its city of vast recessive colonnades shown at the very moment of its fall. Furthermore, the 'Fall' *topos* shared by Keats and Martin exemplifies the early nineteenth-century preoccupation with fixing on a moment of convulsive historical change. It is interesting, too, that Martin was also on what Keats called 'the liberal side of the question', a stubborn and courageous supporter of Reform.

When the narrative of *The Fall* breaks off with 'on he flared', we can no more see a suitable continuation for the second *Hyperion* than we could for the first. How is the 'progressive' theme of the earlier plot to be reconciled with the apocalyptic nature of *The Fall*? Apocalypse is by its very nature anti-historical, in that it envisions an end to history as we know it. However, in the model represented by the Book of Revelation and promulgated in early Christian doctrine, apocalypse is followed by a millennium within history. Such a model could be adapted in texts not specifically Christian: *Prometheus Unbound* is, as we have seen, the fullest example. Another option could be deflection by means of a frame story on the analogy of Last Man narratives, for although *The Fall of Hyperion* is not literally a Last Man narrative, it almost might be, for, like the speaker in Wordsworth's episode of the Stone and the Shell, the poet is the only human being in it. Such solutions are not available in *The Fall of Hyperion*, however, where the frame narrative itself is apocalyptic. The nature of the dilemma is generic, and we need not

[35] Ian Jack, *Keats and the Mirror of Art* (Oxford: Clarendon Press, 1967), p. 270.

imagine a change in Keats's political beliefs in order to explain it. The political-historical nature of the letters Keats wrote in 1819 accord with the themes of the first *Hyperion* but cannot be accommodated to (or be accommodated by) the vision of the second. As Keats may have recognized, in his decision not to continue the poem, *The Fall of Hyperion* does not succeed in connecting apocalypse and millennium.

Epilogue

Keats's decision not to try to effect a transition from apocalypse to millennium appears significant. As we have seen, even the most nearly successful works that make this endeavour betray weakness in passing from one to the other. Whether in recognition of this, or because of the possible abatement of the collective anxieties that had led to a wish for reassurance that millennium would follow apocalypse, the attempt was not repeated in later nineteenth-century English poetry. For the most part such subject-matter was relegated to utopian and dystopian prose narratives, and then to the science fiction. The conventions of such genres insulated readers from possibly disturbing effects, much as early nineteenth-century critics wanted to protect them from Byron's 'Darkness'. Poetry, potentially vatic and dangerous, was another matter. It is true that vestiges of the apocalyptic appear in a work like Eugenius Roche's long poem *London in a Thousand Years*,[1] not so much a Last Man narrative as a promenade among ruins, and that the millennial urge is expressed in Tennyson's longing for 'the thousand years of peace' in *In Memoriam*.[2] However, by the end of the Romantic period, the time for linking the two in a sequence that would secularize biblical paradigms was, as John of Patmos says of the millennium in Revelation 20: 5, 'finished'.

[1] London: Henry Colburn, 1830.
[2] *The Complete Poetical Works of Tennyson* (Boston: Houghton Mifflin, 1898), p. 190.

Select Bibliography

ABRAMS, M. H., *Natural Supernaturalism: Tradition and Revolution in Romantic Literature* (New York and London: Norton, 1973).

ADAMS, HAZARD, 'Synecdoche and Method', in *Critical Paths: Blake and the Argument of Method*, ed. Dan Miller, Mark Bracher, and Donald Ault (Durham, NC: Duke University Press, 1987), pp. 41–71.

ADLARD, JOHN, 'Blake and Electrical "Magic"', *Neophilologus*, 53 (1969): 422–3.

ALDISS, BRIAN, Introduction to *The Last Man* by Mary Shelley (London: Hogarth Press, 1985).

ALIGHIERI, DANTE, *The Paradiso of Dante Alighieri*, trans. P. H. Wicksteed (London: J. M. Dent, 1958).

ANON., 'Annals of the New Church', *New-Jerusalem Magazine*, 1 (1790): 175.

—— *Catalogue of the Valuable Library of the Late Robert Southey, Esq. L. L. D. Poet Laureate* (London: S. Leigh Sotheby & Co., 8–25 May 1844).

AVELING, EDWARD BIBBINS, and ELEANOR MARX AVELING, *Shelley's Socialism* (London and West Nyack, NY: Journeyman Press, 1979).

BAKER, CARLOS, *Shelley's Major Poetry: The Fabric of a Vision* (Princeton: Princeton University Press, 1948).

BALSTON, THOMAS, *John Martin* (London: Gerald Duckworth, 1947).

BARCUS, JAMES E., ed., *Shelley: The Critical Heritage* (London and Boston: Routledge and Kegan Paul, 1975).

BARLOW, JOEL, *The Works of Joel Barlow*, with an introduction by William K. Bottorff and Arthur L. Ford, 2 vols. (Gainesville, Fla.: Scholars' Facsimiles and Reprints, 1970).

BARNARD, JOHN, 'Keats's Belle Dame and the Sexual Politics of Leigh Hunt's *Indicator*', *Romanticism*, 1 (1995): 34–49.

BARRELL, JOHN, 'Imagining the King's Death: The Arrest of Richard Brothers', *History Workshop*, No. 37 (Spring 1994): 1–32.

BARRUEL, ABBÉ AUGUSTIN DE, *Memoirs Illustrating the History of Jacobinism* (4 vols., London, 1797–8).

BATE, JONATHAN, 'Keats's Two *Hyperions* and the Problem of Milton', in *Romantic Revisions*, ed. Keith Hanley and R. Brinkley (Cambridge: Cambridge University Press, 1992), pp. 321–38.

BAUDELAIRE, CHARLES, *Oeuvres complètes*, ed. Y.- G. Le Dantecrev and Claude Pichoise (Paris: Gallimard, 1961).

BEATY, FREDERICK L., *Byron the Satirist* (DeKalb, Ill.: Northern Illinois University Press, 1985).

BECKFORD, WILLIAM, *Vathek*, in *Three Gothic Novels*, ed. Peter Fairclough with an introduction by Mario Praz (Harmondsworth: Penguin, 1970).

BEDDOES, THOMAS LOVELL, *The Works of Thomas Lovell Beddoes*, ed. W. H. Donner (London: Oxford University Press, 1935).

BEER, JOHN, *Coleridge's Poetic Intelligence* (London: Macmillan, 1977).

—— *Blake's Visionary Universe* (Manchester: Manchester University Press, 1969).

BEHRENDT, STEPHEN C., '*Europe* 6: Plundering the Treasury', *Blake: An Illustrated Quarterly*, 21 (1987–8): 85–94.

—— *Shelley and his Audiences* (Lincoln, Nebr.: University of Nebraska Press, 1989).

BENTHAM, JEREMY, *The Works of Jeremy Bentham*, ed. John Bowring (11 vols., Edinburgh: W. Tait, 1843).

BENTLEY, G. E., Jr., *Blake Books* (Oxford: Clarendon Press, 1969).

—— *Blake Records* (Oxford: Clarendon Press, 1969).

—— *Blake Records Supplement* (Oxford: Clarendon Press, 1988).

BEWELL, ALAN, *Wordsworth and the Enlightenment* (New Haven and London: Yale University Press, 1989).

BICHENO, JAMES, *The Signs of the Times* (London, 1799).

BIDLAKE, STEVEN, 'Blake, the Sacred, and the French Revolution: 18th-Century Ideology and the Problem of Violence', *European Romantic Review*, 3 (1992): 1–20.

BINDMAN, DAVID, *Hogarth* (London: Thames and Hudson, 1981).

—— *The Shadow of the Guillotine: Britain and the French Revolution* (London: British Museum Publications, 1989).

—— 'William Blake and Popular Religious Imagery', *Burlington Magazine*, 128 (1986): 712–18.

—— *William Blake As an Artist* (Oxford: Phaidon, 1977).

BIRCH, THOMAS, *A Dressing for L***D T**R**W* (London, 1797).

—— *Essay on the Mechanical Application of Electricity* (London, 1802).

BISHOP, JONATHAN, 'Wordsworth and the Spots of Time', in *Wordsworth, 'The Prelude': A Casebook*, ed. W. J. Harvey and Richard Gravil (London: Macmillan, 1972), pp. 134–54.

BLAKE, WILLIAM, *Blake: The Complete Poems*, ed. W. H. Stevenson, 2nd edn. (London and New York: Longman, 1989).

—— *The Complete Poetry and Prose of William Blake*, ed. David V. Erdman, rev. edn. (Berkeley and Los Angeles: University of California Press, 1982).

—— *The Complete Writings of William Blake*, ed. Sir Geoffrey Keynes, rev. edn. (Oxford: Oxford University Press, 1966).

—— *The Continental Prophecies*, ed. Detlef W. Dörrbecker (London: Tate Gallery Publications for the William Blake Trust, 1995).

—— *The Early Illuminated Books*, ed. Morris Eaves, Robert N. Essick, and Joseph Viscomi (London: The Tate Gallery for the William Blake Trust, 1993).

292   SELECT BIBLIOGRAPHY

BLAKE, WILLIAM, Milton a Poem *and the Final Illuminated Works*: The Ghost of Abel /On Homers Poetry *[and]* On Virgil /Laocoön, ed. Robert N. Essick and Joseph Viscomi (London: William Blake Trust / The Tate Gallery, 1993).
—— *The Poetical Works of William Blake*, ed. John Sampson (London: Oxford University Press, 1925).
—— *William Blake's Writings*, ed. G. E. Bentley, Jr. (Oxford: Clarendon Press, 1978).
BLOOM, HAROLD, *Shelley's Mythmaking* (New Haven: Yale University Press, 1959).
BOGUE, DAVID, and JAMES BENNETT, *The History of Dissenters, from the Revolution in 1688, to the Year 1808* (4 vols., London: Printed for the Authors, 1810).
BOLTON, BETSY, ' "A Garment dipped in blood": Ololon and Problems of Gender in Blake's *Milton*', *Studies in Romanticism*, 36 (1997): 61–101.
BONNARD, C., 'The Invasion of Switzerland and English Public Opinion (January to April 1798): The Background to Samuel Taylor Coleridge's *France*', *English Studies*, 1 (1940): 1–26.
BOULTON, J. T., *The Language of Politics in the Age of Wilkes and Burke* (London: Routledge and Kegan Paul, 1963).
BRAILSFORD, H. N., *Shelley, Godwin, and their Circle* (London: Oxford University Press, 1951).
BRANTLEY, RICHARD E., *Locke, Wesley, and the Method of English Romanticism* (Gainesville, Fla.: University of Florida Press, 1984).
BRICAUD, JOANNY, *Les Illuminés d'Avignon: Étude sur Dom Pernety et son groupe* (Paris: Libraire Critique Émile Nourry, 1927).
BROTHERS, RICHARD, *A Revealed Knowledge of the Prophecies and Times* (2 vols., London, 1794–5).
BROWN, J. T., 'Bibliomania', *North British Review*, 40 (1864): 79–84.
LA BRUYÈRE, JEAN DE, *Les Caractères de Théophraste*, in *Œuvres complètes*, ed. Julian Benda (Paris: Pléiade, 1975).
BRYAN, WILLIAM, *A Testimony of the Spirit of Truth Concerning Richard Brothers* (London, 1795).
BULL, MALCOLM, ed., *Apocalypse Theory and the End of the World* (Oxford: Blackwell, 1995).
BURDON, CHRISTOPHER, *The Apocalypse in England: Revelation Unravelling, 1700–1834* (Basingstoke: Macmillan, 1997).
BURKE, EDMUND, *A Philosophical Enquiry into the Origin of Our Ideas of the Sublime and Beautiful*, ed. J. T. Boulton (Notre Dame, Ind., and London: University of Notre Dame Press, 1968).
—— *Reflections on the Revolution in France*, ed. Conor Cruise O'Brien (Harmondsworth: Penguin, 1984).
—— *The Writings and Speeches of Edmund Burke*, ed. Paul Langford (9 vols., Oxford: Clarendon Press, 1981–97).
BURNET, THOMAS, *The Theory of the Earth, Containing an Account of the Original of the*

Earth, and of the General Change which it hath already undergone, or is to undergo till the Consummation of all Things, 3rd edn. (2 vols., London, 1697).

BUTLIN, MARTIN, *The Paintings and Drawings of William Blake* (2 vols., New Haven and London: Yale University Press, 1981).

BUTTON, WILLIAM, *Prophetic Conjectures on the French Revolution and Other Recent and Shortly Expected Events* (London, 1793).

BUXTON, JOHN, *Byron and Shelley: The History of a Friendship* (London: Macmillan, 1968).

BYRON, LORD, *Byron*, ed. Jerome J. McGann (Oxford and New York: Oxford University Press, 1986).

—— *The Complete Poetical Works*, ed. Jerome J. McGann (7 vols., Oxford: Clarendon Press, 1980–93).

—— *Don Juan*, ed. Leslie Marchand (Cambridge, Mass.: Houghton Mifflin, 1958).

—— *Byron's Letters and Journals*, ed. Leslie A. Marchand (12 vols., Cambridge, Mass.: Belknap Press of Harvard University Press, 1973–82).

—— *Lord Byrons Werke in Kritischen Texte mit Einleitung und Anmerkungen*, ed. Eugen Kölbung (2 vols., Weimar, 1896).

—— *The Works of Lord Byron*, ed. E. H. Coleridge (13 vols., London: John Murray, 1898–1905).

CAMERON, KENNETH NEILL, *Shelley: The Golden Years* (Cambridge, Mass.: Harvard University Press, 1974).

—— *The Young Shelley: Genesis of a Radical* (New York: Collier, 1962 [1950]).

CAMPBELL, THOMAS, *The Poetical Works of Thomas Campbell*, ed. William Michael Rossetti (London: Moxon, 1871).

CHANDLER, DAVID, 'Blake's Man in the Iron Mask', *Notes and Queries*, NS 44 (1997): 321–2.

CHANDLER, JAMES, *Wordsworth's Second Nature: A Study of the Poetry and Politics* (Chicago and London: University of Chicago Press, 1984).

CHASTANIER, BENEDICT, *Emanuel Swedenborg's New-Years Gift to his Readers for MDCCXCI* (London, 1791).

CHRISTENSEN, JEROME, *Coleridge's Blessed Machine of Language* (Ithaca, NY: Cornell University Press, 1981).

CLARK, KENNETH, *The Romantic Rebellion* (New York: Harper and Row, 1973).

CLOWES, JOHN, *Letters to a Member of Parliament on the Character and Writings of Baron Swedenborg* (London: H. C. Hodgson, 1822).

COHN, NORMAN, *The Pursuit of the Millennium*, rev. edn. (London: Temple Smith, 1970).

COLERIDGE, SAMUEL TAYLOR: The most frequently cited works will be found in the List of Abbreviations, p. x.

—— *The Friend* (*CC* 4), ed. Barbara E. Rooke (2 vols., Princeton: Princeton University Press, 1969).

COLERIDGE, SAMUEL TAYLOR, *Lectures 1808–1819 on Literature* (*CC* 5), ed. R. A. Foakes (2 vols., Princeton: Princeton University Press, 1987).

—— *Letters*, ed. E. H. Coleridge (2 vols., London, 1895).

—— MS Notes to Samuel Noble, *Appeal in Behalf of the Views of the Eternal World and State* (London, 1826). British Library, Ashley 2885.

—— *On the Constitution of the Church and State* (*CC* 10), ed. John Colmer (Princeton: Princeton University Press, 1976).

—— *Poems*, ed. John Beer, 3rd edn. (London: J. M. Dent, 1993).

—— *Poems by S. T. Coleridge* (Bristol and London, 1797).

—— *The Poems of Samuel Taylor Coleridge*, ed. Derwent and Sara Coleridge (London: Moxon, 1854 [1852]).

—— *Poems on Various Subjects* (London, 1796).

—— *Shorter Works and Fragments* (*CC* 11), ed. H. J. and J. R. de Jackson, (Princeton: Princeton University Press, 1995).

—— *Sibylline Leaves: A Collection of Poems* (London: Rest Fenner, 1817).

COOPER, LANE, 'The Power of the Eye in Coleridge', in *Studies in Language and Literature in Celebration of the Seventieth Birthday of James Morgan Hart* (New York: H. Holt, 1910), pp. 78–121.

COWPER, WILLIAM, *The Poetical Works of William Cowper*, ed. H. S. Milford, 3rd edn. (London: Oxford University Press, 1926).

CRASHAW, RICHARD, *The Poems English Latin and Greek of Richard Crashaw*, ed. L. C. Martin, 2nd edn. (Oxford: Clarendon Press, 1957).

CRONIN, RICHARD, *Shelley's Poetic Thoughts* (London: Macmillan, 1981).

CURRAN, STUART, *Shelley's Annus Mirabilis* (San Marino, Calif.: Huntington Library, 1975).

CUVIER, BARON, *Essay on the Theory of the Earth*, trans. from the French of M. Cuvier . . . by Robert Kerr, introduction and notes by Professor Robert Jameson (Edinburgh, 1813).

DAMON, S. FOSTER, *A Blake Dictionary* (Providence, RI: Brown University Press, 1965).

—— *William Blake: His Philosophy and Symbols* (Boston: Houghton Mifflin, 1924).

DANILEWICZ, M. L., 'The King of the New Israel: Thaddeus Grabianka 1740–1807', *Oxford Slavonic Papers*, NS 1 (1968): 49–73.

DARLINGTON, BETH, 'Two Early Texts: *A Night-Piece* and *The Discharged Soldier*', in *Bicentennial Wordsworth Studies in Memory of John Alban Finch*, ed. Jonathan Wordsworth (Ithaca, NY, and London: Cornell University Press, 1970), pp. 425–48.

DARWIN, ERASMUS, *The Botanic Garden* (1791), Part I: *The Economy of Vegetation* (London: J. Johnson, 1791).

DAWSON, P. M. S., *The Unacknowledged Legislator* (Oxford: Clarendon Press, 1980).

DECHARMS, R., 'A Report on the Trine to the Central Committee and Other Documents for New-Church History', *New Churchman-Extra*, Nos. iv–xvi: 76–93.

DECK, RAYMOND HENRY, Jr., 'Blake and Swedenborg' (Ph.D. diss., Brandeis University, 1978).

—— 'New Light on C. A. Tulk, Blake's Nineteenth-Century Patron', *Studies in Romanticism*, 16 (1977): 217–36.

DE LUCA, VINCENT A., 'The Style of Millennial Announcement in *Prometheus Unbound*', *Keats–Shelley Journal*, 28 (1979): 78–101.

—— *Words of Eternity: Blake and the Poetics of the Sublime* (Princeton: Princeton University Press, 1991).

DINGLEY, R. J., '"I had a Dream . . .": Byron's "Darkness"', *Byron Journal*, 9 (1981): 20–33.

DRYDEN, JOHN, The *Works of John Dryden*, ed. William Frost and Vincent A. Dearing (Berkeley and Los Angeles: University of California Press, 1987), vol. 5: *The Works of Virgil in English*.

DUFF, DAVID, *Romance and Revolution: Shelley and the Politics of a Genre* (Cambridge: Cambridge University Press, 1994).

DYCK, IAN, ed., *Citizen of the World: Essays on Thomas Paine* (London: Christopher Helm, 1987).

DYER, GARY, 'Unwitnessed by Answering Deeds: "The Destiny of Nations" and Coleridge's *Sibylline Leaves*', *Wordsworth Circle*, 20 (1989): 148–55.

EDWARD, MALDWYN, *John Wesley and the Eighteenth Century* (London: Allen and Unwin, 1933).

EDWARDS, THOMAS R., *Imagination and Power: A Study of Poetry and Public Themes* (London: Oxford University Press, 1971).

ELIOT, T. S., *The Use of Poetry and the Use of Criticism* (London: Faber & Faber, 1933).

ENDY, MELVIN B., Jr., 'Just War, Holy War, and Millennialism in Revolutionary America', *William and Mary Quarterly*, 42 (1985): 3–25.

ERDMAN, DAVID V., '*America*: New Expanses', in *Blake's Visionary Forms Dramatic*, ed. David V. Erdman and John E. Grant (Princeton: Princeton University Press, 1970), pp. 92–114.

—— *Blake: Prophet against Empire: A Poet's Interpretation of the History of his own Times* (rev. edn., Princeton: Princeton University Press, 1969).

—— *The Illuminated Blake* (Garden City, NY: Anchor Press / Doubleday, 1974).

—— 'Unrecorded Coleridge Variants', *Studies in Bibliography*, 11 (1958): 144–53.

—— 'William Blake's Debt to Joel Barlow', *American Literature*, 26 (1954): 94–8.

—— ed., *Blake and his Bibles*, with an introduction by Mark Trevor Smith (West Cornwall, Conn.: Locust Hills Press, 1990).

ESSICK, ROBERT N., *William Blake and the Language of Adam* (Oxford: Clarendon Press, 1989).

—— *William Blake, Printmaker* (Princeton: Princeton University Press, 1980).

—— 'William Blake, Thomas Paine, and Biblical Revolution', *Studies in Romanticism*, 30 (1991): 189–212.

EVEREST, KELVIN, *Coleridge's Secret Ministry: The Context of the Conversation Poems* (Hassocks, Sussex: Harvester, 1979).

FARRER, AUSTEN, *A Rebirth of Images: The Making of St. John's Apocalypse* (Westminster: Dacre Press, 1949).

FERGUSON, FRANCES, *Wordsworth: Language as Counter-Spirit* (New Haven and London: Yale University Press, 1977).

FIXLER, MICHAEL, *Milton and the Kingdoms of God* (Evanston, Ill.: Northwestern University Press, 1964).

FLOYER, SIR JOHN, *The Sibylline Oracles, Translated from the Best Greek Copies, and Compar'd with the Sacred Prophesies, Especially with Daniel and the Revelations* (London, 1713).

FOOT, PAUL, *Red Shelley* (London: Sidgwick & Jackson, 1980).

FOX, SUSAN, *Poetic Form in Blake's Milton* (Princeton: Princeton University Press, 1976).

FRIEDMAN, BARTON R., *Fabricating History: English Writers on the French Revolution* (Princeton: Princeton University Press, 1988).

FRUCHTMAN, JACK, *The Apocalyptic Politics of Richard Price and Joseph Priestley: Transactions of the American Philosophical Society*, 73, part 4 (Philadelphia: American Philosophical Society, 1973).

—— 'The Revolutionary Millennialism of Thomas Paine', *Studies in Eighteenth-Century Culture*, 13 (1984): 65–77.

FRUMAN, NORMAN, *Coleridge: The Damaged Archangel* (New York: Braziller, 1971).

FRYE, NORTHROP, *Anatomy of Criticism* (Princeton: Princeton University Press, 1957).

—— *Fearful Symmetry: A Study of William Blake* (Princeton: Princeton University Press, 1947).

—— *The Great Code: The Bible and Literature* (London: Routledge and Kegan Paul, 1982).

—— 'Notes for a Commentary on Milton', in *The Divine Vision*, ed. V. de Sola Pinto (London: Victor Gollancz, 1957), pp. 97–137.

GARRETT, CLARKE, 'Joseph Priestley, the Millennium, and the French Revolution', *Journal of the History of Ideas*, 34 (1973): 51–66.

—— *Respectable Folly: Millenarianism and the French Revolution in France and England* (Baltimore: Johns Hopkins University Press, 1975).

—— 'Swedenborg and the Mystical Enlightenment in Late Eighteenth-Century England', *Journal of the History of Ideas*, 45 (1984): 67–81.

GEGENHEIMER, ALBERT FRANK, 'Artist in Exile: The Story of Thomas Spence Duché', *Pennsylvania Magazine of History and Biography*, 79 (1955): 3–26.

GERSHOY, LEO, *Bertrand Barère: A Reluctant Terrorist* (Princeton: Princeton University Press, 1962).

GIBBON, EDWARD, *The Decline and Fall of the Roman Empire*, ed. Oliphant Smeaton (3 vols., New York: Modern Library, n.d.).

GIBBS, WARREN E., 'An Unpublished Letter from John Thelwall to S. T. Coleridge', *Modern Language Review*, 25 (1930): 85–90.

GILCHRIST, ALEXANDER, *Life of William Blake*, ed. Ruthven Todd, rev. edn. (London: J. M. Dent, 1945).

GILL, STEPHEN, *William Wordsworth: A Life* (Oxford: Oxford University Press, 1989).

GODWIN, WILLIAM, *Enquiry Concerning Political Justice*, ed. Isaac Kramnick (Harmondsworth: Penguin, 1985).

GOODWIN, ALBERT, *The Friends of Liberty: The English Democratic Movement in the Age of the French Revolution* (Cambridge, Mass.: Harvard University Press, 1979).

GORDON, I. A., 'The Case-History of Coleridge's "Monody on the Death of Chatterton"', *RES* 18 (1942): 49–71.

GOSLEE, NANCY MOORE, *Uriel's Eye: Miltonic Stationing and Statuary in Blake, Keats, and Shelley* (University, Ala.: University of Alabama Press, 1985).

GOULD, STEPHEN JAY, *Time's Arrow, Time's Cycle: Myth and Metaphor in the Discovery of Geological Time* (Harmondsworth: Penguin, 1991).

GRABIANKA, COUNT THADDEUS, *et al.*, *Copy of a Letter from a Society in France, To the Society for promoting the Heavenly Doctrine of the New Jerusalem Church in London* (London, 1787).

GRAINVILLE, JEAN FRANÇOIS XAVIER, COUSIN DE, *Le dernier homme, ouvrage posthume; par M. Grainville, homme des lettres* (Paris, 1811 [1805]).

—— *The Last Man, or Omegarus and Syderia: A Romance in Futurity* [anonymous translation of *Le dernier homme*] (2 vols., London, 1806).

HAGSTRUM, JEAN H., ' "The Wrath of the Lamb": A Study of William Blake's Conversions', in *From Sensibility to Romanticism: Essays Presented to Frederic A. Pottle*, ed. Frederick W. Hilles and Harold Bloom (London and New York: Oxford University Press, 1965), pp. 311–30.

HALHED, NATHANIEL BRASSY, M.P., *A Calculation on the Commencement of the Millennium* (London, 1795).

HALLIBURTON, DAVID G., 'Blake's *French Revolution*: The *Figura* and Yesterday's News', *Studies in Romanticism*, 5 (1966): 158–68.

HALLORAN, WILLIAM F., '*The French Revolution*: Revelation's New Form', in *Blake's Visionary Forms Dramatic*, ed. David V. Erdman and John E. Grant (Princeton: Princeton University Press, 1970), pp. 30–56.

—— 'William Blake's *The French Revolution*: A Note on the Text and a Possible Emendation', *Bulletin of the New York Public Library*, 71 (1969): 3–18.

HAMILTON, WILLIAM, ed., *Parodies of the Works of English and American Authors* (6 vols., London: Reeves and Turner, 1886).

HARPER, G. M., 'The Divine Tetrad in Blake's *Jerusalem*', in *William Blake: Essays for S. Foster Damon*, ed. Alvin Rosenfeld (Providence, RI: Brown University Press, 1969), pp. 235–55.

HARRISON, J. F. C., *The Second Coming: Popular Millenarianism 1780–1850* (New Brunswick, NJ: Rutgers University Press, 1979).

HARRISON, J. F. C., 'Thomas Paine and Millenarian Radicalism', in *Citizen of the World: Essays on Thomas Paine*, ed. Ian Dyck (London: Christopher Helm, 1987), pp. 73–85.

HARTLEY, DAVID, *Observations on Man: His Frame, His Duty, and His Expectations*, ed. Rev. Herman Andrew Pistorius (3 vols., London: J. Johnson, 1791).

HARTMAN, GEOFFREY H., *Wordsworth's Poetry 1787–1814* (New Haven: Yale University Press, 1964).

HAVEN, R., J. HAVEN, and M. ADAMS, *Samuel Taylor Coleridge: An Annotated Bibliography* (Boston: G. K. Hall, 1976).

HAZLITT, WILLIAM, *The Complete Works of William Hazlitt*, ed. P. P. Howe (London and Toronto: J. M. Dent, 1932).

HENDRIX, RICHARD, 'The Necessity of Response: How Shelley's Radical Poetry Works', *Keats–Shelley Journal*, 27 (1978): 45–69.

HILL, CHRISTOPHER, *Milton and the Puritan Revolution* (Harmondsworth: Penguin, 1979).

HILTON, NELSON, *Literal Imagination: Blake's Vision of Words* (Berkeley: University of California Press, 1983).

HINDMARSH, ROBERT, *Rise and Progress of the New Jerusalem Church in England, America, and Other Parts*, ed. Edward Madeley (London: Hodson and Son, 1861).

HOGG, THOMAS JEFFERSON, *Life of Shelley*, in *The Life of Percy Bysshe Shelley*, ed. Humbert Wolf (2 vols., London: J. M. Dent, 1933).

HOLCROFT, THOMAS, *The Life of Thomas Holcroft*, ed. E. Colby (2 vols., London: Constable, 1925).

HOLMES, RICHARD, *Shelley: The Pursuit* (London: Quartet, 1976).

HOOD, THOMAS, *Poetical Works*, ed. Walter Jerrold (London: Oxford University Press, 1906).

—— *Selected Poems of Thomas Hood*, ed. John Clubbe (Cambridge, Mass.: Harvard University Press, 1970).

—— *Whims and Oddities* (London: Lupton, Rolfe, 1826).

HOUSE, HUMPHRY, *Coleridge* (London: Rupert Hart-Davis, 1953).

HUGHES, D. J., 'Potentiality in *Prometheus Unbound*', *Studies in Romanticism*, 2 (1963): 107–26; repr. in *Shelley's Poetry and Prose*, pp. 603–20.

HUNGERFORD, EDWARD B., *Shores of Darkness* (New York: Columbia University Press, 1941).

JACK, IAN, *Keats and the Mirror of Art* (Oxford: Clarendon Press, 1967).

JACKSON, J. R. DE J., ed., *Coleridge: The Critical Heritage* (London: Routledge and Kegan Paul, 1970).

JACOBUS, MARY, *Romanticism, Writing and Sexual Difference: Essays on* The Prelude (Oxford: Clarendon Press, 1989).

JAFFE, IRMA B., *John Trumbull: Patriot-Artist of the American Revolution* (Boston: New York Graphic Art Society, 1975).

JONES, STEVEN E., *Shelley's Satire: Violence, Exhortation, and Authority* (DeKalb, Ill.: Northern Illinois University Press, 1994).

KAYSER, WOLFGANG, *The Grotesque in Art and Literature*, trans. Ulrich Weisstein (New York: Columbia University Press, 1981 [1957]).

KEACH, WILLIAM, *Shelley's Style* (New York and London: Methuen, 1984).

KEATS, JOHN, *The Letters of John Keats*, ed. H. E. Rollins (2 vols., Cambridge, Mass.: Harvard University Press, 1958).

—— *The Poems of John Keats*, ed. Miriam Allott (London: Longman, 1970).

—— *The Poems of John Keats*, ed. Jack Stillinger (Cambridge, Mass.: Harvard University Press, 1978).

KELLEY, THERESA M., *Wordsworth's Revisionary Aesthetics* (Cambridge: Cambridge University Press, 1988).

KENNEDY, EMMET, *A Cultural History of the French Revolution* (New Haven and London: Yale University Press, 1989).

KEYNES, GEOFFREY, 'Blake, Tulk, and Garth Wilkinson', *Library*, 4th ser., 26 (1945): 190–2.

KING-HELE, DESMOND, *Erasmus Darwin and the Romantic Poets* (Basingstoke: Macmillan, 1986).

KITSON, PETER J., ' "The electric fluid of truth": The Ideology of the Commonwealthsmen in Coleridge's *The Plot Discovered*', *Prose Studies*, 13 (1990): 36–62.

KNAPP, STEVEN, *Personification and the Sublime: Milton to Coleridge* (Cambridge, Mass.: Harvard University Press, 1985).

KNIGHT, G. WILSON, *The Starlit Dome: Studies in the Poetry of Vision* (London: Methuen, 1964).

LAURENCE, RICHARD, trans., *The Book of Enoch the Prophet* (Oxford: Oxford University Press, 1821).

LEACH, EDMUND, 'Melchisedech and the Emperor: Icons of Subversion and Orthodoxy', *Proceedings of the Royal Anthropological Institute of Great Britain and Ireland*, 1972, pp. 5–14.

LEASK, NIGEL, *The Politics of Imagination in Coleridge's Political Thought* (Basingstoke: Macmillan, 1988).

LEVINSON, MARJORIE, *Wordsworth's Great Period Poems: Four Essays* (Cambridge: Cambridge University Press, 1986).

LINCOLN, ANDREW W. J., 'Blake's *Europe*: An Early Version?', *Notes and Queries*, 223, NS 25 (1978): 213.

LINEHAM, PETER JAMES, 'The English Swedenborgians 1770–1840: A Study in the Social Dimensions of Religious Sectarianism' (Ph.D. dissertation, University of Sussex, 1978).

LIPKING, LAWRENCE, *The Life of the Poet: Beginning and Ending Poetic Careers* (Chicago and London: University of Chicago Press, 1981).

The Literary Souvenir for 1830 (London: Rees, Orme, Brown and Green, 1829).

LIU, ALAN, *Wordsworth: The Sense of History* (Stanford, Calif.: Stanford University Press, 1989).

LOVELL, ERNEST J., JR., ed., *His Very Self and Voice* (New York: Macmillan, 1954).

—— ed., *Medwin's Conversations of Lord Byron* (Princeton: Princeton University Press, 1966).

LOWES, JOHN LIVINGSTON, 'Moneta's Temple', *PMLA* 51 (1936): 1098–1113.

—— *The Road to Xanadu: A Study in the Ways of the Imagination* (Princeton: Princeton University Press, 1986).

MCCALMAN, IAIN, 'New Jerusalems: Prophecy, Dissent and Radical Culture in England, 1786–1830', in *Enlightenment and Religion: Rational Dissent in Eighteenth-Century Britain*, ed. Knut Haakonssen (Cambridge: Cambridge University Press, 1996), pp. 312–35.

—— *Radical Underworld: Prophets, Revolutionaries, and Pornographers in London, 1795–1840* (Cambridge: Cambridge University Press, 1988).

MCCANN, PHILLIP, and FRANCIS A. YOUNG, *Samuel Wilderspin and the Infant School Movement* (London and Canberra: Croom Helm, 1982).

MCGANN, JEROME J., *The Beauty of Inflections: Literary Investigations in Historical Method and Theory* (Oxford: Oxford University Press, 1985).

—— 'The Idea of an Indeterminate Text: Blake's Bible of Hell and Dr. Alexander Geddes', *Studies in Romanticism*, 25 (1986): 303–24.

MACGILLIVRAY, J. R., 'The Pantisocracy Scheme and its Immediate Background', in *Studies in English by Members of University College Toronto*, collected by Principal Malcolm W. Wallace (Toronto: University of Toronto Press, 1931), pp. 131–69.

MACKINTOSH, ROBERT JAMES, *Memoirs of the Life of the Right Honourable Sir James Mackintosh* (2 vols., London: Moxon, 1835).

MCNIECE, GERALD, *Shelley and the Revolutionary Idea* (Cambridge, Mass.: Harvard University Press, 1969).

MAGNUSON, PAUL, 'The Politics of "Frost at Midnight"', *Wordsworth Circle*, 22 (1991): 3–11.

MALTHUS, THOMAS ROBERT, *Population: The First Essay*, with a foreword by Kenneth E. Boulding (Ann Arbor: University of Michigan Press, 1959).

MARGOLIOUTH, H. M., *William Blake* (London: Oxford University Press, 1951).

MARTIN, PHILIP W., *Byron: A Poet before his Public* (Cambridge: Cambridge University Press, 1982).

MATHER, RALPH, *An Impartial Representation of the Case of the Poor Cotton Spinners in Lancashire, &c.* (London, 1780).

MATTHEWS, G. M., 'A Volcano's Voice in Shelley', in *Shelley: Modern Judgements*, ed. R. B. Woodings (London: Macmillan, 1968), pp. 162–95.

MEE, JON, *Dangerous Enthusiasm: William Blake and the Culture of Radicalism in the 1790s* (Oxford: Clarendon Press, 1992).

—— 'Is there an Antinomian in the House? William Blake and the After-Life of a Heresy', in *Historicizing Blake*, ed. Steve Clark and David Worrall (London: St Martin's Press, 1994), pp. 43–58.

MEILLASSOUX-LE CERF, M., *Dom Pernety et les Illuminés d'Avignon* (Milan: Arché, 1992).

MELLOR, ANNE K., 'Keats's Face of Moneta', *Keats–Shelley Journal*, 25 (1976): 65–80.

MELVILLE, HERMAN, *Moby-Dick or, The Whale*, ed. Alfred Kazin (Boston: Houghton Mifflin, 1956).

MICHAELS, LEONARD, 'Byron's Cain', *PMLA* 84 (1969): 71–7.

MILLER, ARTHUR McA., 'The Last Man: A Study of the Eschatological Theme in English Poetry' (Ph.D. dissertation, Duke University, 1966).

MILLER, J. Hillis, 'The Stone and the Shell: The Problem of Poetic Form in Wordsworth's Dream of the Arab', in *Mouvements premiers: Études critiques offertes à Georges Poulet* (Paris: Corti, 1972), pp. 125–47.

MILLER, LILLIAN B., *et al.*, *'The Dye Is Now Cast': The Road to American Independence 1774–1776* (Washington: Smithsonian University Press for the National Portrait Gallery, 1975).

MILTON, JOHN, *Complete Poems and Major Prose*, ed. Merritt Y. Hughes (New York: Odyssey, 1957).

MORRISON, ANTHEA, 'Samuel Taylor Coleridge's Greek Prize Ode on the Slave Trade', in *An Infinite Complexity*, ed. J. R. Watson (Edinburgh: Edinburgh University Press, 1983), pp. 145–60.

MORTON, A. L., *The Everlasting Gospel* (London: Lawrence and Wishart, 1958).

MOSHEIM, JOHN LAWRENCE, *An Ecclesiastical History*, trans. Archibald Maclaine, M.A. (2 vols., London, 1765).

MUIR, KENNETH, 'The Meaning of "Hyperion"', in *John Keats: A Reassessment*, ed. Kenneth Muir (Liverpool: University of Liverpool Press, 1969), pp. 103–23.

NETHERCOT, ARTHUR M., *The Road to Tryermaine* (Chicago: University of Chicago Press, 1939).

NEWTON, SIR ISAAC, *Opera Quae Exstant Omnia*, ed. Samuel Horsley (5 vols., London, 1785).

NURMI, MARTIN K., *Blake's 'Marriage of Heaven and Hell': A Critical Study*, Kent State University Bulletin, Research Series, 3 (Kent, Oh., 1957).

O'BRIEN, CONOR CRUISE, *The Great Melody: A Thematic Biography and Commented Anthology of Edmund Burke* (Chicago: University of Chicago Press, 1992).

OLIVER, W. H., *Prophets and Millennialists: The Uses of Biblical Prophecy in England from the 1790s to the 1840s* (Auckland: Auckland University Press/Oxford University Press, 1978).

PAINE, THOMAS, *The Age of Reason* (London: Daniel Isaac Eaton, 1794).

—— *Rights of Man*, ed. Eric Foner (Harmondsworth: Penguin, 1985).

—— *The Thomas Paine Reader*, ed. Michael Foot and Isaac Kramnick (Harmondsworth: Penguin, 1987).

PALEY, MORTON D., *The Apocalyptic Sublime* (New Haven and London: Yale University Press, 1986).

PALEY, MORTON D., 'Blake and Thomas Burnet's *Sacred Theory of the Earth*', *Blake: An Illustrated Quarterly*, 2 (1991): 75–8.

—— *Coleridge's Later Poetry* (Oxford: Clarendon Press, 1996).

—— '*Le dernier homme*: The French Revolution as the Failure of Typology', *Mosaic: A Journal for the Interdisciplinary Study of Literature*, 24 (1991): 67–76.

—— *Energy and the Imagination: A Study of the Development of Blake's Thought* (Oxford: Clarendon Press, 1970).

—— 'The Fourth Face of Man: Blake and Architecture', in *Articulate Images: The Sister Arts from Hogarth to Tennyson*, ed. Richard Wendorf (Minneapolis: University of Minnesota Press, 1983), pp. 184–215.

—— '*The Last Man*: Apocalypse without Millennium', in *The Other Mary Shelley: Beyond Frankenstein*, ed. Audrey A. Fisch, Anne Mellor, and Esther H. Schor (New York and Oxford: Oxford University Press, 1993), pp. 107–23.

—— '"A New Heaven Has Begun": William Blake and Swedenborgianism', *Blake: An Illustrated Quarterly*, 13 (1979): 64–90.

—— 'William Blake, the Prince of the Hebrews, and the Woman Clothed with the Sun', in *William Blake: Essays in Honour of Sir Geoffrey Keynes* (Oxford: Clarendon Press, 1973), pp. 260–93.

—— '"Wonderful Originals": Blake and Ancient Sculpture', in *Blake in his Time*, ed. Robert N. Essick and Donald Pearce (Bloomington, Ind., and London: Indiana University Press, 1978), pp. 170–97.

PATRIDES, C. A., and JOSEPH WITTREICH, eds., *The Apocalypse in English Renaissance Thought and Literature: Patterns, Antecedents, and Repercussions* (Ithaca, NY: Cornell University Press, 1984).

PAUL, C. KEGAN, *William Godwin: His Friends and Contemporaries* (2 vols., London: Henry King, 1876).

PAULSON, RONALD, 'John Trumbull and the Representation of the American Revolution', *Studies in Romanticism*, 21 (1982): 341–56.

PEACOCK, THOMAS LOVE, *Headlong Hall* and *Gryll Grange*, ed. Michael Baron and Michael Slater (Oxford and New York: Oxford University Press, 1987).

—— *Nightmare Abbey* and *Crotchet Castle*, ed. with an introduction by Raymond Wright (Harmondsworth: Penguin, 1981).

PECK, WALTER EDWIN, 'Shelley and the Abbé Barruel', *PMLA* 36 (1921): 347–53.

PIPER, H. W., *The Active Universe* (London: University of London, Athlone Press, 1962).

PIRIE, ALEXANDER, *The French Revolution Exhibited, in the Light of the Sacred Oracles: or, a Series of Lectures on the Prophecies now Fulfilling* (Perth, 1797).

PLASA, CARL, 'Revision and Repression in Keats's *Hyperion*: "Pure Creations of the Poet's Brain"', *Keats–Shelley Journal*, 44 (1995): 117–46.

POE, EDGAR A., *The Complete Poems and Stories of Edgar Poe*, ed. Edward Hayes O'Neill (2 vols., New York: Knopf, 1946).

POLIDORI, JOHN WILLIAM, *The Diary of Dr. John William Polidori*, ed. William Michael Rossetti (London: Elkin Mathews, 1911).

POPHAM, A. E., 'Early Proofs of Blake's *Europe*', *British Museum Quarterly*, 11 (1937): 184–5.

PRICE, RICHARD, *A Discourse on the Love of Our Country* (London, 1789).

—— *The Evidence for a Future Period of Improvement in the State of Mankind* (London, 1787).

—— *Observations on the Importance of the American Revolution* (London, 1784).

PRIESTLEY, JOSEPH, *A Farewell Sermon: Letters to Members of the New Jerusalem Church 1791* and *The Present State of Europe Compared with Antient Prophecies 1794*, with an introduction by Jonathan Wordsworth (Oxford: Woodstock Books, 1989).

—— *Letters to the Right Honourable Edmund Burke* (London, 1791).

—— *The Theological and Miscellaneous Works of Joseph Priestley*, ed. John Towill Rutt (25 vols., New York: Kraus Reprint, 1972).

PULOS, C. E., *The Deep Truth: A Study of Shelley's Skepticism* (Lincoln, Nebr.: University of Nebraska Press, 1954).

REDDING, CYRUS, *Literary Reminiscences and Memoirs of Thomas Campbell* (2 vols., London: Charles J. Skeat, 1860).

REED, MARK, *Wordsworth: The Chronology of the Early Years, 1770–1799* (Cambridge, Mass.: Harvard University Press, 1967).

REEVES, MARJORIE, 'The Development of Apocalyptic Thought: Medieval Attitudes', in *The Apocalypse in English Renaissance Thought and Literature: Patterns, Antecedents, and Repercussions*, ed. C. A. Patrides and Joseph Wittreich (Ithaca, NY: Cornell University Press, 1984), pp. 40–72.

REEVES, MARJORIE, and WARWICK GOULD, *Joachim of Fiore and the Myth of the Eternal Evangel in the Nineteenth Century* (Oxford: Clarendon Press, 1987).

REID, WILLIAM HAMILTON, *The New Sanhedrin [Hebrew] and Causes and Consequences of the French Emperor's Conduct Toward the Jews* (London, 1807).

—— *The Rise and Dissolution of the Infidel Societies in this Metropolis* (London: J. Hatchard, 1800).

REIMAN, DONALD H., 'Mary Godwin, Transcript of S. T. Coleridge's "France: An Ode" and "Fire, Famine, and Slaughter"' in *Shelley and his Circle, 1773–1822*, ed. Donald H. Reiman (8 vols., Cambridge, Mass.: Harvard University Press, 1986), 7: 1–11.

—— *Romantic Texts and Contexts* (Columbia, Mo.: University of Missouri Press, 1987).

—— ed., *The Romantics Reviewed* (3 vols. in 9, New York and London: Garland, 1972).

RICHEY, WILLIAM, '*The French Revolution*: William Blake's Epic Dialogue with Edmund Burke', *ELH* 59 (1992): 817–37.

RIEDE, DAVID, 'Blake's *Milton*: On Membership in the Church Paul', in *Re-membering Milton: Essays on the Texts and Traditions*, ed. Mary Nyquist and

Margaret W. Ferguson (New York and London: Methuen, 1987), pp. 257–77.

RIEGER, JAMES, *The Mutiny Within: The Heresies of Percy Bysshe Shelley* (New York: George Braziller, 1967).

ROBERTS, FRÉDERIC, *La Marseillaise* (Paris: Imprimerie Nationale, 1989).

ROBERTS, J. M. *The Mythology of the Secret Societies* (New York: Charles Scribner's Sons, 1972).

ROBINSON, CHARLES E., *Shelley and Byron: The Snake and Eagle Wreathed in Fight* (Baltimore: Johns Hopkins University Press, 1976).

ROBINSON, THOMAS, *Remembrances of a Recorder* (Manchester and Boston, 1864).

ROBISON, JOHN, *Proofs of a Conspiracy against all the Religions and Governments of Europe, Carried on in the Secret Meetings of Free Masons, Illuminati, and Reading Societies* (London, 1797).

ROE, NICHOLAS, *John Keats and the Culture of Dissent* (Oxford: Clarendon Press, 1997).

—— *Wordsworth and Coleridge: The Radical Years* (Oxford: Clarendon Press, 1988).

—— ed., *Keats and History* (Cambridge: Cambridge University Press, 1995).

ROLLINS, H. E., ed., *The Keats Circle: Letters and Papers* (2 vols., Cambridge, Mass.: Harvard University Press, 2nd edn., 1965).

ROUSSEAU, JEAN-JACQUES, *The Social Contract*, trans. Gerard Hopkins, in *Social Contract*, ed. Sir Ernest Barker (New York: Oxford University Press, 1962).

RUDOLF, ANTHONY, *Byron's Darkness: Lost Summer and Nuclear Winter* (London: Menard Press, 1984).

RUTHERFORD, ANDREW, ed., *Byron: The Critical Heritage* (London: Routledge & Kegan Paul, 1970).

RYLESTONE, ANNE L., *Prophetic Memory in Wordsworth's* Ecclesiastical Sonnets (Carbondale and Edwardsville, Ill.: Southern Illinois University Press, 1991).

SALT, HENRY S., *Company I have Kept* (London: George Allen & Unwin, 1930).

SCHAMA, SIMON, *Citizens: A Chronicle of the French Revolution* (New York: Vintage, 1989), pp. 561–6.

SCHUCHARD, MARSHA KEITH, 'The Secret Masonic History of Blake's Swedenborg Society', *Blake: An Illustrated Quarterly*, 26 (1992): 40–51.

SCHWINNING, HEINRICH, 'Der Maskenzug der Anarchie', *Gulliver/Deutsche-englische Jahrbücher*, 1 (1976): 71–107.

SCOTT, SIR WALTER, *The Letters of Walter Scott*, ed. H. J. C. Grierson (12 vols., London: Constable, 1932–7).

SCRIVENER, MICHAEL, *Radical Shelley* (Princeton: Princeton University Press, 1982).

SHAFFER, ELINOR, *'Kubla Khan' and* The Fall of Jerusalem (Cambridge: Cambridge University Press, 1972).

—— '"Secular Apocalypse": Prophets and Apocalyptics at the End of the Eighteenth Century', in *Apocalypse Theory and the End of the World*, ed. Malcolm Bull (Oxford: Blackwell, 1995), pp. 137–58.

SHAKESPEARE, WILLIAM, *Troilus and Cressida*, New Variorum Edition, 26, ed. Harold N. Hillebrand (Philadelphia and London: Lippincott, 1953).

SHAW, GEORGE BERNARD, 'Keats', in *The John Keats Memorial Volume*, ed. G. C. Williams (London and New York: John Lane, 1921), pp. 173–6.

SHELLEY, BRYAN, *Shelley and Scripture: The Interpreting Angel* (Oxford: Clarendon Press, 1994).

SHELLEY, MARY W., *The Last Man*, ed. Morton D. Paley (Oxford and New York: Oxford University Press, 1994).

—— *The Letters of Mary Wollstonecraft Shelley*, ed. Betty T. Bennett (3 vols., Baltimore: Johns Hopkins University Press, 1980–8).

SHELLEY, PERCY BYSSHE, *Bodleian Shelley Manuscript Series*, vol. 2: *Bodleian MS. Shelley adds. d. 7*, ed. Irving Massey (New York: Garland, 1987).

—— *Bodleian Shelley Manuscripts*, vol. 9: *The Prometheus Unbound Notebooks*, ed. Neil Freistat (New York and London: Garland, 1991).

—— *The Complete Poetical Works of Percy Bysshe Shelley*, ed. Thomas Hutchinson (London: Oxford University Press, 1960 [1905]).

—— *The Esdaile Notebook: A Volume of Early Poems*, ed. Kenneth Neill Cameron (New York: Alfred A. Knopf, 1964).

—— *Letters of Percy Bysshe Shelley*, ed. F. L. Jones (2 vols., Oxford: Clarendon Press, 1964).

—— *The Manuscripts of the Younger Romantics*, Vol. 2: *Percy Bysshe Shelley: The Mask of Anarchy*, ed. Donald H. Reiman (New York and London: Garland, 1985).

—— *The Manuscripts of the Younger Romantics*, Vol. 4: *The Mask of Anarchy Draft Notebook*, ed. Mary A. Quinn (New York and London: Garland, 1990).

—— *Note-books of Percy Bysshe Shelley, from the Originals in the Library of W. K. Bixby, Deciphered, Transcribed, and Edited* by H. Buxton Forman (3 vols., Boston: Bibliophile Society, 1911).

—— *The Poems of Shelley*, ed. Geoffrey M. Matthews and Kelvin Everest, vol. 1 (London and New York: Longman, 1989).

—— *The Poetical Works of Percy Bysshe Shelley*, ed. William Michael Rossetti (2 vols., London: E. Moxon & Son, 1870).

—— *The Prose Works of Percy Bysshe Shelley*, vol. 1, ed. E. B. Murray (Oxford: Clarendon Press, 1993).

—— *Shelley: Selected Poems and Prose*, ed. G. M. Matthews (Oxford and New York: Oxford University Press, 1964).

—— *Shelley's Poetry and Prose*, ed. Donald H. Reiman and Sharon B. Powers (New York and London: Norton, 1977).

SIBLEY, MANOAH, *An Address to the Society of the New Church meeting in Friar Street, near Ludgate Hill* (London, 1834).

SIBLEY, MANOAH, *The Trial of Mr. Thomas Hardy for High Treason* (Dublin: P. Byrne, 1794).

SMITH, OLIVIA, *The Politics of Language 1791–1819* (Oxford: Clarendon Press, 1984).

SMYSER, JANE WORTHINGTON, 'Wordsworth's Dream of Poetry and Science: *The Prelude:* V', *PMLA* 71 (Mar. 1956): 269–75.

SOUTHEY, ROBERT, *Joan of Arc* (Bristol, 1796).

—— *Letters from England by Don Manuel Alvarez Espriella* (3 vols., London: Longman, Hurst, Rees, and Orme, 1808).

—— *The Life of Wesley and the Rise and Progress of Methodism*, 2nd edn. (London: Longman, Hurst, Rees, Orme, and Brown, 1820).

—— *New Letters of Robert Southey*, ed. Kenneth Curry (2 vols., New York and London: Columbia University Press, 1965).

—— *Poetical Works of Robert Southey* (10 vols., London: Longman, 1837–8).

SPEIRS, JAMES, ed., *Minutes of the First Seven Sessions of the New Jerusalem Church, Reprinted from the Original Editions* (London: James Speirs, 1885).

STEFFAN, TRUMAN GUY, *Lord Byron's Cain: Twelve Essays and a Text with Variants and Annotations* (Austin, Tex., and London: University of Texas Press, 1968).

STOMMEL, HENRY and ELIZABETH STOMMEL, 'The Year without a Summer', *Scientific American*, 240 (1979): 176–86.

STROTHERS, RICHARD B., 'The Great Tambora Eruption and its Aftermath', *Science*, 224 (1984): 1191–8.

STUART, DANIEL, 'Anecdotes of the Poet Coleridge', *Gentleman's Magazine*, NS 9 (1838): 485–92.

STUKELEY, WILLIAM, *Abury—A Temple of the British Druids* (London, 1743).

—— *Stonehenge: A Temple Restor'd to the British Druids* (London, 1740).

SWEARINGEN, JAMES E., 'Time and History in Blake's *Europe*', *Clio* 20 (1991): 110–21.

SWEDENBORG, EMANUEL, *Angelic Wisdom Concerning the Divine Providence* (London: R. Hindmarsh, 1790).

—— *Conjugial Love*, trans. John Clowes (London: R. Hindmarsh, 1794).

—— *The Doctrine of the New Jerusalem Concerning the Lord* (London: R. Hindmarsh, 1791).

—— *A Treatise Concerning the Last Judgment and the Destruction of Babylon* (London: R. Hindmarsh, 1788).

—— *True Christian Religion*, trans. John Clowes (London, 1781).

TERTULLIAN, *Apology*, in *Tertullian Apologetical Works and Minucius Felix Octavius* (New York: Fathers of the Church, 1950).

TETRAULT, RONALD, *The Poetry of Life: Shelley and Literary Form* (Toronto: University of Toronto Press, 1987).

THOMAS, D. O., *The Honest Mind: The Thought and Work of Richard Price* (Oxford: Clarendon Press, 1977).

THOMPSON, E. P., 'London', in *Interpreting Blake*, ed. Michael Phillips (Cambridge: Cambridge University Press, 1978), pp. 5–31.

—— *The Making of the English Working Class*, rev. edn. (Harmondsworth: Penguin, 1968).

—— *Witness against the Beast* (New York: New Press, 1993).

THORPE, CLARENCE, 'Keats and World Affairs', *PMLA* 46 (1931): 1228–45.

THRUPP, SYLVIA L., ed., *Millennial Dreams in Action: Essays in Comparative Study*, supplement 2 (The Hague: Mouton, 1962).

TOLLEY, MICHAEL J., '*Europe*: "to those ychain'd in sleep"', in *Blake's Visionary Forms Dramatic*, ed. David V. Erdman and John E. Grant (Princeton: Princeton University Press, 1970), pp. 115–45.

TRENEER, ANNE, 'Emily Trevenen's Album', *West Country Magazine*, 2 (1947): 171–8.

TULK, JOHN AUGUSTUS, *A Letter Containing a Few Plain Observations* (London, 1807).

TUVESON, ERNEST LEE, *Redeemer Nation: The Idea of America's Millennial Role* (Chicago and London: University of Chicago Press, 1968).

VAIL, JEFFREY, '"The bright sun was extinguish'd"', *Wordsworth Circle*, 28 (1997): 183–92.

VIATTE, AUGUSTE, *Les sources occultes du romantisme, illuminisme—théosophie, 1770–1820* (2 vols., Paris: H. Champion, 1928).

VISCOMI, JOSEPH, '*A Breach in the City the Morning After the Battle*: Lost or Found?', *Blake: An Illustrated Quarterly*, 28 (1994): 44–61.

—— 'The Evolution of *The Marriage of Heaven and Hell*', *Huntington Library Quarterly*, 58 (1997): 281–344.

—— 'Lessons of Swedenborg: or the Origin of Blake's *Marriage of Heaven and Hell*', in *Lessons of Romanticism*, ed. Robert Gleckner and Thomas Pfau (Durham, NC: Duke University Press, 1998), pp. 173–212.

VOLNEY, CONSTANTIN FRANÇOIS CHASSEBOEUF, COMTE DE, *A New Translation of Volney's* Ruins, with an introduction by Robert D. Richardson, Jr. (2 vols., New York and London: Garland, 1979).

WADSTRÖM, CARL BERNHARD, *Observations on the Slave Trade* (London, 1789).

WARD, AILEEN, *John Keats: The Making of a Poet*, 2nd edn. (New York: Farrar, Strauss, and Giroux, 1986).

—— 'Keats's Sonnet, "Nebuchadnezzar's Dream"', *Philological Quarterly*, 34 (1955): 177–88.

WARNER, JANET A., *Blake and the Language of Art* (Kingston and Montreal: McGill–Queen's University Press, 1984).

WASSERMAN, EARL K., *Shelley: A Critical Reading* (Baltimore and London: Johns Hopkins University Press, 1971).

WATSON, GEORGE, 'The Revolutionary Youth of Wordsworth and Coleridge', *Critical Quarterly*, 18 (1976): 49–66.

WATSON, ROBERT, M.D., *The Life of Lord George Gordon: with a Philosophical Review of his Political Conduct* (London, 1795).

WEBB, TIMOTHY, *Shelley: A Voice Not Understood* (Manchester: Manchester University Press, 1977).

WESLEY, JOHN, *John Wesley's Letters*, ed. John Telford (8 vols., London: Epworth Press, 1931).

—— *The Journal of the Rev. John Wesley, A.M.*, ed. Nehemiah Curnock (8 vols., London: R. Culley, 1909–16).

—— *Predestination Calmly Considered*, 5th edn. (London: R. Hawes, 1776).

WHALLEY, GEORGE, 'The Bristol Library Borrowings of Southey and Coleridge', *Library*, 5th ser., 4 (1949): 114–31.

—— *Coleridge and Sara Hutchinson* (Toronto: University of Toronto Press, 1955).

—— 'Coleridge, Southey, and "Joan of Arc" ', *Notes and Queries*, 199 (1954): 67–9.

WHITE, NEWMAN IVEY, *The Unextinguished Hearth: Shelley and his Contemporary Critics* (New York: Octagon Books, 1972 [1938]).

WHITEFIELD, GEORGE, *George Whitefield's Journals (1737–1741)*, a facsimile reproduction of the edition of William Wale in 1905 with an introduction by William V. Davis (Gainesville, Fla.: Scholars' Facsimiles and Reprints, 1969).

WILLIAMS, G. C., ed., *The John Keats Memorial Volume* (London and New York: John Lane, 1921).

WILSON, JOHN, *The City of the Plague and Other Poems* (Edinburgh: Constable, 1816).

WILSON, MILTON O., *Shelley's Later Poetry: A Study of his Prophetic Imagination* (New York: Columbia University Press, 1959).

WOODMAN, ROSS GREIG, *The Apocalyptic Vision in the Poetry of Shelley* (Toronto: University of Toronto Press, 1964).

WOODRING, CARL, *Politics in English Romantic Poetry* (Cambridge, Mass.: Harvard University Press, 1970).

—— *Politics in the Poetry of Coleridge* (Madison: University of Wisconsin Press, 1961).

WOOF, R. S., 'Coleridge and Thomasina Dennis', *University of Toronto Quarterly*, 32 (1962): 37–54.

WORDSWORTH, JONATHAN, *William Wordsworth: The Borders of Vision* (Oxford: Clarendon Press, 1982).

WORDSWORTH, WILLIAM, *The Borderers*, ed. Robert Osborn (Ithaca, NY, and London: Cornell University Press, 1982).

—— *Poems, in Two Volumes*, ed. Jared Curtis (Ithaca, NY: Cornell University Press, 1983).

—— *The Poetical Works of William Wordsworth*, ed. E. de Selincourt and Helen Darbishire (5 vols., Oxford: Clarendon Press, 1966–7).

—— *The Prelude*, ed. E. de Selincourt and Helen Darbishire (Oxford: Clarendon Press, 2nd edn., 1959).

—— *The Prelude*, ed. J. C. Maxwell, 2nd edn. (Harmondsworth: Penguin, 1972).

—— *The Prelude*, ed. Jonathan Wordsworth, M. H. Abrams, and Stephen Gill (New York and London: Norton, 1979).

—— *Prose Works*, ed. W. J. B. Owen and Jane Worthington Smyser (3 vols., Oxford: Oxford University Press, 1974).

—— *The Salisbury Plain Poems of William Wordsworth*, ed. Stephen Gill (Ithaca, NY: Cornell University Press, 1975).

—— *The Thirteen-Book Prelude*, ed. Mark L. Reed (2 vols., Ithaca, NY, and London: Cornell University Press, 1991).

WORRALL DAVID, 'The Immortal Tent', *Bulletin of Research in the Humanities*, 84 (1981): 273–95.

—— *Radical Culture: Discourse, Resistance, and Surveillance, 1790–1820* (Hemel Hempstead: Harvester Wheatsheaf, 1992).

—— 'William Blake and Erasmus Darwin's *Botanic Garden*', *Bulletin of the New York Public Library*, 78 (1975): 397–417.

WRIGHT, JOHN, *A Revealed Knowledge of Some Things That Will Speedily be Fulfilled in the World* (London, 1794).

WU, DUNCAN, *Wordsworth's Reading 1800–1815* (Cambridge: Cambridge University Press, 1995).

WYLIE, IAN, *Young Coleridge and the Philosophers of Nature* (Oxford: Clarendon Press (1989).

ZALL, PAUL M., 'The Cool World of Samuel Taylor Coleridge', *Wordsworth Circle*, 4 (1973): 25–30.

Index

COLEG POWYS
BRECON